THE ENGLISH MUSICAL RENAISSANCE

THE ENGLISH MUSICAL RENAISSANCE

⋙⋙⋙⋙⋙⋙⋙⋙⋙⋘⋘⋘⋘⋘⋘⋘⋘⋘⋘

Frank Howes

STEIN AND DAY / *Publishers* / New York

First published in the United States of America
by Stein and Day, 1966

Published in England by
Martin Secker and Warburg Limited

Copyright © 1966 by Frank Howes

Library of Congress Catalog Card No. 66-13763

Printed in Great Britain

Stein and Day/*Publishers*/7 East 48 Street, New York, N.Y. 10017

TO THE MEMORIES OF
BRUCE RICHMOND AND H. C. COLLES

CONTENTS

ILLUSTRATIONS

(Between pp. 192 *and* 193)

Acknowledgements

THE AUTHOR and publishers thank the Public Trustee and the Society of Authors for permission to quote from *Music in London 1890-94* by George Bernard Shaw, and Hutchinson & Co. (Publishers) Ltd. for permission to quote from *A Mingled Chime* by Sir Thomas Beecham.

The author and publishers thank the following publishers for their permission to quote musical illustrations: Boosey and Hawkes for excerpts from works by Britten and Warlock; J. Curwen and Sons for "Elsie Marley"; Novello and Co. for excerpts from the works of Elgar, Holst and Moeran, also for "The Seeds of Love"; the Oxford University Press for citations from the works of Vaughan Williams and Walton.

The author and publishers thank the following bodies for their co-operation in providing pictorial illustrations, for permission to reproduce pictures, for loan of prints and photographs or of blocks: Baron Studios, Bassano Studios, the Cheltenham Festival Company, the Dolmetsch Foundation, Elliott & Fry, E.M.I. Records Ltd., the English Folk Dance and Song Society, the National Portrait Gallery, the Oxford University Press, the Royal College of Music, *The Times*, Trinity College, Cambridge, the University of Birmingham. They also thank the following individuals for their similar co-operation: Miss Hilda Andrews (for R. R. Terry), Sir Thomas Armstrong (for Delius), Mrs. Joyce Finzi (for Gerald Finzi), Mrs. Vera Newman (for Ernest Newman), Mrs. Juliet Pannett (for John Ireland, Gordon Jacob and Alan Rawsthorne), Miss Joan Sharp (for Cecil Sharp), Mr. Cyril Townley (for Herbert Howells), Mrs. Antonia Tuck (for Sir Arthur Somervell), Mr. Guy Worsdell and Mr. A. F. C. Turner (for Michael Tippett). If they have inadvertently omitted to acknowledge an obligation they tender their apologies and thanks here and now.

Finally, the author and publishers thank Miss Margaret Dean-Smith for her invaluable service in preparing the index.

Introduction

THE SHAPE of this book needs some explanation, perhaps some justification. It has been a very long time in the writing, and the final revision has often needed a change of tense, occasionally a modification of view, and a wholesale remodelling of its original design, which was first sketched before the 1939 war.

Most histories, helped by Time's eliminations, speed over their early years and expand almost uncontrollably as they approach the present. Mine does the opposite: the pyramid stands on its base not its point. All histories imply some criticism, even if it is only the criticism of selection and exclusion, and critics, especially if they have been journalist critics, know that a rough-and-ready and by no means invalid criterion of quality is sheer quantity—length indicates value. Again this criterion does not apply to this book and is indeed sometimes stood on its head. Thus it will be observed that Parry is treated at greater length than Britten. This does *not* indicate that I judge Parry to be a better composer than Britten. In music it has often happened that a composer who is historically important, i.e. has had an influence on the future of the art, is not one of the great composers, who for their part may not have had much historical importance. J. S. Bach's historical importance lies chiefly in the fact that he determined equal temperament for keyboard instruments and showed that it was possible to write concertos for them. His son, Carl Philip Emanuel, who counts for less in artistic interest and merit, is much more important historically, for the part he played in determining the evolution of sonata form, one of the most fertile discoveries of the human mind, makes him historically one of the most important composers who have ever lived. Haydn alone probably among the great composers is as important historically as he is artistically.

It follows, therefore, that a historian will often need to deal at length with music that has every appearance to a later generation of being obsolete. Perhaps this is what Edward Dent meant when he made the challenging, mischievous remark that the history of music is written in bad music. I would not myself endorse this extreme statement, but I would say that much obsolete, disregarded, outworn music is of great historical importance, and I am not thinking of possible comebacks like that of J. S. Bach in the nineteenth century. I have examined quite seriously a good deal of music of the nineteenth century which critically I consider of no present or further artistic interest. But if one is to substantiate the argument that England, musically disregarded by the civilized world as unmusical save for the purpose of providing ready money for international executants, has in the course of the period in which it made and lost an empire restored itself to a place among the great powers of music, one must look at movements below the surface, at men who have laboured but left no conspicuous memorial, at composers who served their generation, with a historian's eye, and revalue their work in accordance not with its present esteem or even its intrinsic worth but with its more far-reaching consequences to the generations that succeeded it. This is my case for treating Parry as a catalyst of the future.

The plan, then, is to look at Victorian music, which I do in Book I, which I call Gestation, and compare it with the situation as it appears today, and as I have summarily surveyed it in Book III, which I call Growth. Book II is Birth, naissance or, in the perspective of our history from Dunstable onwards, renaissance. It involves a certain amount of duplication, more particularly in the cases of Vaughan Williams and the composers born in the present century (i.e. Chapters XII and XIV). In some cases I have given cross-references, in others I have let a repetition stand rather than send the reader flapping back to find an idea that is relevant to both contexts. The actual divisions have not always been logical —it is not logic but convenience that separates Stanford from Parry. And it has been the different point of view of Book II from that of Book III which has determined what works of what composers, such as Holst and Bliss, are discussed in which Book. The three Books indeed employ three different ways of writing history because the focus of each is different. Book I is straightforward historical writing based mainly on documents, leavened with a little first-hand experience and some criticism; Book II is almost wholly critical; Book III, consisting as it does of matter wholly within my own experience, is contemporary history and therefore approximates in method to journalism.

There is a further reason for the foreshortening of Book III. It has less need of an historian than the decades before the wars, for even those with memories that are still short have only to look about and maybe ask a question or two of their elders, to understand our situation of today. It is an unsatisfactory business writing contemporary history, and the reader is in as good a position as the writer for looking at the present harvest of the seeds sown by the Victorians in the last quarter of the nineteenth century. *Si historiam requiris, circumspice.* I have given you a summary of what you can see with your own eyes and hear with your own ears.

I have devoted some attention to scholars, and I would have liked to have devoted equal attention to the influence of such famous executants as Harry Plunket Greene and Hamilton Harty, Henry Wood and Thomas Beecham, who is perhaps the only international virtuoso of absolutely the first class that this country has produced since Dowland; to Fanny Davies whom I often heard and Leonard Borwick whom I never heard, to Kirkby Lunn and John Brownlee, even to Myra Hess and Clifford Curzon who in my own time have achieved international status among pianists; but the reputations of dead executants are too imponderable. All one can say is that since our conservatoires have realized the responsibilities which the renaissance imposed on them they have produced some artists of international standing, the most recent example being Miss Joan Sutherland. The interpreter's art quivers on the air for a moment and is gone, though it leaves memories and influences, again imponderables, behind. In future the gramophone may do something to make good this defect in the historian's apparatus. It does not, however, need much special pleading to declare that our home-grown (including Commonwealth) performers have done their share in making our country more musical in line with composers, orchestral players, critics, educationists and scholars.

My *terminus ad quem* may be taken as 1960. In some contexts a later work may be added to a composer's tally or a later event mentioned according to convenience, but no attempt has been made to be conscientiously complete after 1960. Thus Britten's

War Requiem written for the Coventry Festival of 1962 is mentioned and briefly described but belongs to the decade after the period under review.

I have called Parry the catalyst of the big change. I did so when I first thought about the book unquestioningly, because that was the truth handed down to me by my elders and betters. It may seem a little odd today when his name does not often crop up and most of his compositions have sunk below the horizon. It was his personality which provided the dynamic to effect our change, and personality, like personal charm, is difficult to bring back to life from the dead. Moreover, I never met him myself: I only remember seeing him once in the orchestral pit of the theatre at Oxford when he came to conduct his music to *The Frogs* of Aristophanes when it was performed by the O.U.D.S. in about 1909, but I felt the force of his personality at second hand—and I mean second not fifth hand. I remember my parents coming home from a rehearsal of the combined scratch choirs of our local competition festival at which *The Pied Piper* was being performed and exclaiming with astonished delight at the transformation he wrought in a few minutes. But much more seriously impressive was the attitude of two men not themselves easily given to hero worship, Hugh Allen and Harry Colles. Both had something like reverence for Parry in their regard for him, and they passed on to me a very strong impression of the inspiration that exuded from him. And so indeed with everyone else I ever encountered who knew him. I quote the implied tribute from Bernard Shaw, who did not admire his music, in Chapter XX.

November 1964   F. H.

BOOK ONE

≫≫≫≫≫≫≫≫≫≫≪≪≪≪≪≪≪≪≪≪

Gestation

1

The Thesis

FROM THE last decade of the nineteenth century onwards the word "renaissance" has been applied to changes which had come over English music about that time and its appropriateness has never since been seriously questioned, though a modern writer, Arthur Jacobs, dismisses the term as a "comic overstatement without any serious attempt at computation".* There is a general agreement that English music is better in quality and English musical life healthier than it was in Victorian times. It is held in greater esteem and occupies a more important place in public life. The general agreement is among ourselves and must not be accepted without scrutiny, since it may be due merely to the superficial view that old fashions are absurd and new ones always an improvement, or it may be due to an increase of national pride which likes to think that we cut a better figure, artistically speaking, in Europe today than we did a century ago. Certainly comparisons of the present century with Victorian England are perilous. For the first quarter of the twentieth century we were busy getting away from social customs derived from our Victorian grandparents that had grown stuffy and burdensome, and in our newly acquired elbow-room we were apt to decry everything Victorian. But reflection on the World wars and our frantic but ineffective efforts to cope with their legacies soon brought it home to us that on the whole they managed things better then than we do now.

We must beware therefore of fashion in opinion, either in its larger swings of reaction from one generation to the next or in its more obvious fluctuations from one decade to the next. Thus Lytton Strachey's studies in Victorian personality and history were regarded in the twenties of this century, apart from their literary merits, as shrewd estimates of a historical period;

* In Denis Stevens, *ed.*, *A History of Song* (Hutchinson, 1960), p. 155.

in the thirties his views were judged as dangerously incomplete and unbalanced. Later still they were held to be amusing in their arrogance and his laughs at the Victorians were turned against himself. For the pendulum has begun to swing again and with Mr. John Betjeman to lead the chorus of approval Victoriana are becoming fashionable, though not so far in music. It is difficult for an historian to allow for fashion and also for the tendency that each generation has to comment on the great improvements to be observed in its own time. This *does* apply to music—from Burney onwards every writer has thought he saw improvements in the English scene. But some evidence can be gleaned from the memoirs of Barnett, Cowen, Stanford and Mackenzie of the state of the musical profession, of standards of orchestral performance, of public taste, of musical education and of the relation of the art to the rest of culture. Thus Mackenzie, who was an able composer with a facile talent and held a prominent place in the musical life of London—he was conductor of the Philharmonic Society from 1893 to 1899—states without a sense of grievance, as though it was natural and normal procedure, that he never had a complete libretto handed to him in his life* and his texts were all by working journalists (though in the case of *Colomba* it was cobbled from Mérimée's work and *The Rose of Sharon* from the *Song of Songs*). This shows the lack of literary sensibility among the leaders of musical life and explains the rather startled reaction to Parry's choice of Shelley for his first important cantata, *Prometheus Unbound*, which thereby became an historic document.

It is next to impossible to compare standards of performance over three-quarters of a century, and individual recollection is unreliable—the gramophone arrived too late for this purpose, though connoisseurship of operatic singing may provide a few straws in the wind and conditions of orchestral rehearsal rather more than straws of information. Foreign opinion might provide a check on our own estimation of the improvement in composition in the past hundred years; though here it comes as something of a shock to discover that English operas, long forgotten, obtained a hearing in their day in continental opera houses—Balfe, H. H. Pierson, Wallace, Goring Thomas, Ethel

* *A Musician's Narrative* (Cassell, 1927), p. 122.

Smyth and Stanford all achieved this distinction. In the orchestral field the work of English composers has been even slower in getting into the international repertory, though it ought to be easier. Elgar's *Enigma Variations* have been known everywhere if they are not much played; the same composer's *Introduction and Allegro* and its companion piece for string orchestra, Vaughan Williams's *Tallis Fantasia*, have an international currency and are played the world over. Choral music interests the Continent less, but when the Germans acclaimed *The Dream of Gerontius* at the Lower Rhine Festival of 1902 this recognition of Elgar was regarded both at home and abroad as a symptom of this very renaissance whose validity we are seeking to establish. The opinions of some eminent musicians, notably Cortot, the pianist, and Hubermann, the violinist, expressed after the first war helped to kill the old jibe about *das Land ohne Musik*. The memoirs of international conductors, singers, instrumentalists, are generally enthusiastic about their reception, and imply, when they do not state in so many words, that British appreciation of music is keen and more discriminating than in countries with a better reputation for being musical than ours. But this again is not new, and the idea of England as a country with a big import trade in music is the very thing that over long periods of our history has stood between us and a reputation for being musical. It is on what we create that a claim for renaissance must be based.

In so far, however, as composers do not grow in a vacuum, but only in the right sort of soil, our whole musical life has some relevance to so individual a thing as composition. And not only our musical life. A perfectly serious and scholarly writer* declared that we have been sterilized by salt water: sea power and creative genius in a subjective art like music are incompatible. This may seem a rather extravagant application of a sound principle, the power of environment, to what is at once a social and a psychological problem, because in general politics and music do seem to have a mutual recalcitrance, but we have learned enough about *Zeitgeist*, Marxian determinism, international communications and heaven knows what besides to realize that some such remoter influences cannot be wholly excluded from the reckoning. They will therefore have to be considered.

* Cecil Forsyth, *Music and Nationalism* (Macmillan, 1911).

When did the change take place? The date given by a contemporary critic, J. A. Fuller-Maitland, is September 1880, when Parry's *Prometheus Unbound* was produced at a Three Choirs Festival. Maitland was an admirer of Parry and his testimony might not be accepted in some quarters, but so fiercely independent an authority as Ernest Walker, whose sympathies are by no means circumscribed, accepted this assignation and endorsed it in the remark: "If we seek a definite birthday for modern English music, September 7, 1880, when *Prometheus* saw the light at Gloucester and met with a distinctly mixed reception, has undoubtedly the best claim."* Stanford† supports the claim in that he regards *Prometheus* as marking "the first forward English step in the modern development of native choral music", against the opposition to its modernism by press critics, and rates it as an advance on anything of the sort created by an Englishman since Purcell. Hanslick, the Viennese critic, writing of his second visit to London in 1886—his first had been twenty-four years earlier— notes that "in the past few years England's national pride in respect of musical creativeness has experienced a re-awakening."‡ The only alternative is five years earlier, the date of *Trial by Jury* proposed by H. C. Colles,§ "a humbler event" but "more powerful in its effect on the public at large", though Stanford spoke of "the first fruits of the Renaissance of English music" as being S. S. Wesley and Sterndale Bennett.

Sullivan, on the strength of operas that bear every apparent sign of immortality in English-speaking countries, and further invigorated by the lapse of copyright in 1961, has strong claims to inclusion in the renaissance, since in the important sphere which has been the grave of more hopes for our native music than any other branch of the art, he has remained triumphantly alive through all passing fashions, has gone over the heads of the musical public to the great general public and established himself in their affections as no other English composer of any period has done. Surely, then, he has a greater claim even than Parry

---

* *A History of Music in England* (1907), p. 300. The revised edition of Walker by Westrup (1952) has a chapter headed "The English Renaissance".

† *Pages from an Unwritten Diary* (Arnold, 1914), pp. 207-8.

‡ *Music Criticisms 1846-99* (Penguin Books, 1963), p. 254.

§ *Voice and Verse in England* (1907), p. 300. (O.U.P., 1928), p. 143.

and Stanford, the architects of the renaissance, to belong to it, since his actual music is more alive now than theirs. To exclude him is to err in the opposite direction to Hadow, who acclaimed Parry as a great composer because he made English music that was tolerable to the educated classes as none of his predecessors or contemporaries (except Stanford) were doing. Sullivan would be elected to the new movement by the suffrages of the general public, Parry by the considered opinion of the cultivated few. Parry actually achieved substantially less in the field of composition than Hadow, without the advantage of our knowledge *ex post facto*, claimed.

Yet in this, as in all other matters, Sullivan's position is ambiguous and his reputation ambivalent. Too complaisant by disposition, too worldly by reason of success, he lacked critical standards. He left behind a lot of bad music that by its popularity did a deal of harm, and even in technical matters like the metrical setting of words he varied from genius in, for example, "'Tis a glorious thing I ween to be a regular royal queen" to the banality of "O gladsome light".

A further test of the validity of the renaissance is the number of singing birds in the nest, the quality of their song and their apparent ability to breed. By now the reborn art has come of age and there is more music made in England now at mid-century than at any time since Queen Elizabeth I was on the throne, more, better, more concentrated in quality and more diffused in popular currency.

"Made in England" was Walker's definition of English music, and it avoids difficulties raised by blood and birthplace. England in this case includes Britain, the lesser envelops the greater, for it is as uncouth to speak of British music as it would be of the British language. The tradition of serious musical composition, as of serious literary composition, is English: the link with Europe is through London; taste is formed and education centred in London and both are disseminated from the capital. There is the English language and there are the Celtic languages: English is spoken in England, Scotland, Ireland, Wales, Cornwall and the Isle of Man. Gaelic and the British languages (strictly so called), of which Welsh is the only fully alive example, with a living literature as well as spoken currency, are still heard in the

Celtic fringe of those countries. Music corresponds sufficiently closely to this geographical distribution of language, and, though it may be granted that Welsh, Irish, Highland and Lowland Scottish folk music show distinct traits, it is only an excess of local patriotism which will declare that the music of Mackenzie and Stanford, cast in the harmonic idiom of international Europe, is Scottish and Irish and not English music. A Scot and an Irishman had a hand in the English renaissance but the music they wrote was English music, though actually it was not English enough to break decisively with continental traditions. The next generation, of which the chief figures are Holst and Vaughan Williams, made the decisive break with continental training, returned to a study of our native idiom and re-established English music as an independent member of the European family and no longer a poor relation.

"Made in England" may seem unduly restrictive since songs are sung, organs are played and public concerts are given in Glasgow and in Dublin and Belfast, and the musical life of the Welsh people is concentrated into an Eisteddfod, which every year visits a different town of the Principality for a week. The musical life of a people, Welsh or English, consists of a number of distinct phenomena, some of which require assessment while others can be ignored. In Victorian times the music performed in church was an important determinant of taste, as it always has been; "church" included the great cathedrals, whose organ lofts were the centres of musical enlightenment through whole districts of provincial England, and the small nonconformist chapels where the hymns were mostly feeble or bad or both, but provided small communities with pretty well the only music they had. Today, when the general standard of church music has been much raised, it no longer exerts much influence; indeed the improvement of taste in hymns and anthems has come about by secular pressure. The changes in church music are therefore an effect rather than a contributory cause of our renaissance, evidence of the enlightenment that has taken place rather than themselves a movement for the rebirth of English music. Only in so far as the Anglican church, which has provided a centuries-old tradition of composition, continues to provide the stimulus and the occasion for the writing of new music will this permanent factor of our musical life need to be taken into the account. The music of the Presbyterian church of Scotland has never had the slightest influence on the creative side of the art, and though there has been the fairly common interchange of secular tunes borrowed for sacred words, sacred parodies from the time of the Wedderburns in the sixteenth century down to the latest psalter, the Presbyterian Church in Scotland and the Roman Catholic Church in Ireland can be omitted from the account.

But "made in England" is less comfortably applied to the domestic music made in those countries. Apart from folk-music proper there is a great store of song tunes accumulated by tradition which in the past two hundred years has been a force in the musical life of the separate kingdoms of the British Isles. Moore's *Irish Melodies* and the many eighteenth-century Scottish collections, from Allan Ramsay's *Tea Table Miscellany*, onwards through Burns and Scott to the fabrication of "The Skye Boat Song", have played a larger part in the national life than the comparable traditional songs of England. Church music and the music of sociability, which includes dance music and the now defunct salon music, play a small part in social history but no part in our recent musical history.

It is, however, rather with music pursued consciously as an art, enjoyed for its own sake and regarded as an independent sphere of activity of the human spirit, that we primarily have to deal. And into this reckoning performance as well as composition enters. Phenomena such as the competition festival movement, the brass band movement, the various enterprises for getting opera performed, the cult of Bach, the formation of libraries of gramophone records—such things have a place in the story. Artists of British birth who achieve an international reputation are neither new nor frequent, but they too come into the account. The main theme, however, must be the emergence of British composers writing English music.

The rise of the modern school has been in three stages. There was the original impulse to a sturdier kind of writing which is associated with the names of Mackenzie, Parry and Stanford. Their contemporaries, F. H. Cowen, Arthur Sullivan and Edward German (who have, however, a distinctive place in the theatrical tradition) belong to the old order, of which Sterndale Bennett

had been the leading figure in the previous generation. Even
Mackenzie's claim to be one of the pioneers is a little doubt-
ful—Dr. Walker on the whole classifies him with those Englishmen
whose musical outlook was wholly European (i.e. German and
Italian). Technically Parry and Stanford were nurtured on a
German training. But the change is associated with the three
names, Mackenzie, whose influence was exerted from the Royal
Academy of Music, and Parry and Stanford, who worked at the
younger rival establishment in South Kensington, the Royal
College of Music.

Holst and Vaughan Williams, both products of the Royal
College of Music, broke decisively with German methods. The
establishment of the Royal College of Music in 1883 at the
instance of the Prince of Wales had made available to progressively
minded English students an education comparable to that for
which Mackenzie, Sullivan and Stanford had gone to Germany.*
Even so Vaughan Williams found his inspiration limited and his
style fettered until he discovered for himself English folk-song,
the native English music which had continued in being since the
great days of Elizabeth I but had flowed on like an underground
stream all through the eighteenth century, to be completely over-
looked by nineteenth-century musicians until its rediscovery by
amateurs and enthusiasts at the end of the century. At the same
time as the folk-song revival the movement began for re-exploring
the Tudor madrigals and church music, which had not been
forgotten like the folk-song but had been overlaid by changes of
taste and the editorial itch to "improve" it. Holst, whose musical
affiliation is through Purcell to Weelkes, made a clean cut and to
the end of his life wrote uncompromising music that cannot be
called experimental, because his technique was too assured, but
which is spiritually and stylistically an unending adventure. Holst
and Vaughan Williams were therefore the revolutionaries who

---

* In his speech at St. James's Palace on February 28, 1882, at the meeting
convened to launch the project, the Prince said "It will be to England what
the Berlin Conservatoire is to Germany, what the Paris Conservatoire is to
France, or the Vienna Conservatoire is to Austria, the recognized centre and
head of the musical world." Because of the larger role in public life assigned
to it the Royal College undertook "the more extended function of a University", and its charter enables it to confer degrees as well as diplomas of
efficiency.

asserted English independence. Holst remained a somewhat solitary figure, but Vaughan Williams early embraced a nationalist creed and created a substantial corpus of new English music reared on the most substantial of foundations—folk-song and Tudor counterpoint (for he shared Holst's enthusiasm for the distinctively English polyphony of the sixteenth century).

So far Elgar (1857-1934) has not come into the picture. He was largely self-taught and whether on that account or because of his individual gifts, which had a comparatively brief period of efflorescence, he was late in making his appearance as a major factor in the English renaissance. But when he did he accomplished more than either of his elder contemporaries, Parry and Stanford, in putting England once more after several centuries upon the musical map of Europe. The recognition of *The Dream of Gerontius* at Düsseldorf was a spectacular revelation of the rising of a new star in the firmament, but what was ultimately decisive in asserting England's new contribution to the music of Europe was the fact that he was primarily, in spite of his successful oratorio, an instrumental composer. Richter's acceptance of the *Enigma Variations* in 1899 and the subsequent appearance of the two symphonies and the violin concerto proclaimed that at last England was refusing to allow her long vocal traditions to fetter her creative gifts.

Elgar had his share of experience of choirs and organs as a young man, but his bent, like Mackenzie's, was for the violin, and for some years he hoped to make a career as a concert artist. The fact that he attended no academy either English or foreign enabled him to form his own tastes, among which was at one time a liking for Meyerbeer, never a favourite among orthodox English musicians. It takes time and a great expenditure of effort to reach mastery without the help of the usual ropes, but when achieved, the self-made mind is in possession of a less compromised independence and individuality. Elgar, having paid the price of a late arrival, was able thereby to make a distinctive and decisive contribution to the new movement in English music.

Stanford offers a parallel example of the opposite case. By the good fortune of his thorough training he early acquired a consummate technical equipment, but to the end of his days his work was liable to lose its distinctive savour when inspiration was running at less than its full flood, because he knew only too well how the great Germans or the great Italians would have dealt with the problem in hand. One can point to his *Stabat Mater* and to his opera *The Travelling Companion*, both fine works, as instances of the handicap of early and easy mastery.

It is inevitable that Elgar and Stanford will jostle each other in this and later chapters. It is unfortunate because their personal relations were sometimes strained in rather a childish way, and the worst of this unfortunate but unimportant fact has been made by much unwise discussion. Both men are now beyond the reach of human words, both belong to history, both have rendered imperishable services to their country and their generation, and any element of partisanship is now meaninglessly irrelevant. Stanford certainly hoped to do what Elgar did, and more besides, in that opera was an abiding interest with him, but he failed to make for himself a European reputation as Elgar did. He died a disappointed man. Elgar, though successful, made himself miserable by an absurd touchiness which may at bottom have been an inferiority complex derived just precisely from the fact that he had not enjoyed Stanford's advantages. In one respect, however, Stanford accomplished more than Elgar in that he, more than any other single man, created the modern English school by his work as a teacher. Parry's contribution was social and cultural in that he raised the status of the art in English society, as well as standards of taste and scholarship among musicians. Stanford taught most of the composers of the next generation and in so far as one can speak of a school of English composition he was its maker. Elgar on the other hand left no followers, and though some of the younger men have shown that they have digested his scores—in Bliss and Walton one can occasionally catch the intonations of Elgar's voice—his influence as a direct force is small.

In assessing the value of the services rendered to the renaissance by these elder composers one has to take into account that they did other things besides composing, and that those other things, often dismissed as almost worthless, do in fact constitute a valuable contribution to the life of the times in which they lived. A man's first debt is to his own generation, not to his ancestors or to his posterity. And his workaday labours, which are usually undertaken for the mundane but honourable purpose of making a living, are not to be dismissed as so much waste of time. English composition did undoubtedly suffer some loss from the fact that Sterndale Bennett, Mackenzie and Parry put their main energies into education and administration, but the loss must not be regarded as a dead loss. The accumulation of masterpieces from the past is becoming a serious problem to twentieth-century music and there is more to be said in favour of local, temporary, *ad hoc* music, or at any rate music addressed to its own generation, than the romantic notion of writing nothing but immortal masterpieces allows. Eighteenth-century composers never contemplated anything more than current usage for their works and a good deal too much Bach, Haydn and Mozart has survived. Handel we have reduced to manageable dimensions, but we pay too much attention to the other three eighteenth-century giants. For this excessive preoccupation with the great dead we have probably to blame Beethoven. He extended the expressive and emotional range of music so widely by the explosive force of his concentrated nature that it took a century to comprehend his scope. Consequently everything he wrote came to be regarded as precious. As saturation point with Beethoven was approached, interest began to be transferred backwards to the eighteenth and then farther back to the seventeenth and sixteenth centuries, replacing the healthier concern with contemporary music which had been axiomatically accepted as normal in those earlier centuries whose products were now being scanned with so close and devoted a scrutiny. Hence began that search for unquestioned masterpieces of all periods which are now regarded as staple diet by the English musical public. It is indeed something of an irony that the drive by critics, educationists and other leaders of musical opinion to improve the standard of the music in ordinary use—surely a right and proper undertaking on their part—has had as a by-product an almost morbid insistence on nothing but the best in our concert programmes, with the result that much music, less than the greatest but distinctive and representative of its period, has fallen into premature neglect. There is some force in the contention that the international idiom of nineteenth-century romanticism had lost its savour, by the time Mackenzie used it, without infusion of national or other elements to freshen it. But the neglect of Parry and Stanford, whose music is infused with fresh elements, is deplorable.

On the other hand a social parasite like Wagner is worth more than all he cost his friends in money, women and exasperation, simply if he had done no more than write the *Meistersinger* overture. There are cases where the obtaining of a masterpiece is plainly worth the sacrifice of every other consideration, and we may be thankful that Elgar did not devote very much of his time to the socially valuable activity of conducting the asylum band at Worcester. Creation was better work for him than therapeutics. But in later Victorian England there was a great deal of work to be done in several directions at once if the general musical life of the country was to be stimulated to the point at which real composers could be produced and sustained. The greatest need was for a new education, whose influence would permeate the whole country from cathedral to chapel, from public school to board school, and from festival to small town concert. The sacrifices made by Mackenzie, Parry and Stanford have borne fruit, and to this Sullivan too contributed a small quota by his acceptance of the principalship of the National Training School and the policy he imposed upon this forerunner of the Royal College of Music.

It is no doubt a serious problem to the individual, and would be a cruel dilemma if it presented itself to him in the form which it assumes to the historian, whether to choose composition or administration as his life's work. After all we still have composers whose works we could comfortably do without and whose energies therefore would be better employed on more ephemeral tasks. No doubt a man thinks his work as a composer worth while at the time he is engaged on it, even if he changes his mind in later life. But he will not consciously choose between composition and an official appointment since he will be clear and confident that he can do both. Composition has in fact become a whole-time job, and unless a man devotes his whole mind to it his musical output will be less than fully—fully saturated, fully cooked—we have no word to describe the completion of the process of mental concentration to the highest degree. Some musicians fully competent to engage in composition do decide against making it their main business in life. S. P. Waddington won a Mendelssohn

scholarship and began a composer's career only to give it up for
active work as organist, conductor, and more especially teacher
at the Royal College of Music. Sir Hugh Allen, who divided
his energies between inspiring and instructing amateurs and
training professionals, put the claims of the younger generation
above the alternatives of composition and research. Sir Walford
Davies never gave up composition but his best work was done
by the time he reached middle life, and so the day-to-day work
of choir-mastering and subsequently of broadcasting made
the first claim on his energies, and he was content that it should
be so.

How much then are we to offset on the credit side of the account
from the loss that the three pioneers incurred from the diversion
of their energies to the great teaching institutions which they
served, to the performance as opposed to the composition of
music, and to that arch-consumer of time, committee work? The
place to recount the doings of the three men is in the sections
devoted to them. Here it is relevant to recall that without adequate
performance not only composers but general musical life
languishes. Mackenzie for twenty years conducted choral and
orchestral societies, including seven years' service as the conductor
of the Philharmonic Society, where he pursued a progressive
policy, and he undertook an important tour through Canada
which was pure missionary work. Stanford took an active part in
the musical life of Cambridge for a good many years both before
and after he became professor there, and the influence that
radiates from a university is incalculable. For the first decade of
the century he was conductor of the Leeds Festivals, another
position in which policy may have far-reaching effects.

All three men exerted a most powerful, long-sustained and
immensely effective influence on education for its immeasurable
good. The inadequacy of the Royal Academy of Music as a
British equivalent of the continental conservatoires had been so
apparent in mid-Victorian times that it had led to a project for
a new institution with a wider outlook, a more comprehensive
curriculum and higher standards, to open careers to talents and
to meet the needs of a public that was soon to have universal
education compulsorily provided for it. This new institution
ultimately emerged under the auspices of the Prince of Wales as

the Royal College of Music, founded first as the National Training School under Arthur Sullivan in 1876 and then reconstituted
as the Royal College of Music in 1883. Negotiations to take the
Royal Academy of Music (founded in 1822) into the new scheme
were undertaken as a measure of obvious prudence, but the Royal
Academy clung to its independence, probably because Sterndale
Bennett had been appointed in 1866 as part of a policy of reform
and his prestige was no doubt one of the factors in the decision
to have two conservatoires. The English love for a balanced
rivalry, observable in the coexistence side by side of Lancashire
and Yorkshire, of Oxford and Cambridge, of Eton and Winchester,
found another expression in this decision to have both a Royal
Academy of Music and a Royal College of Music, similar but
distinct, broadly alike but different in detail. Neither Sterndale
Bennett nor Macfarren who succeeded him were, however,
capable of making the Royal Academy other than a copy of
Mendelssohnian Leipzig. The Royal College started without this
handicap and with more liberal ideals* and it was left to
Mackenzie, appointed as Principal of the Academy in 1888, to
modernize the institution and bring it into line with the now
healthily growing College in South Kensington.

Parry and Stanford were both foundation members of the College
teaching staff. The long list of Stanford's pupils at the Royal
College of Music and the shorter list at Cambridge† is eloquent
testimony to the fact that he must have been one of the greatest
teachers of composition who ever lived, though to read the
accounts, supplied in after life by his pupils, of his methods
(of which more later) makes one marvel that he did in fact
succeed in founding a school of English composers, if not of
English composition, though he himself seems to have thought
that he had failed because the "school" showed no common
characteristics. Parry had among his pupils Hamish MacCunn,
Arthur Somervell, Percy Buck, Walford Davies and R. Vaughan
Williams, but when he became Director in succession to Sir

---

* All these ideals for the new institution, and one more besides, the career
open to talent by the provision of scholarships, were propounded by the
speakers at the inaugural meeting convened by the Prince of Wales at St.
James's Palace. See above, p. 24.

† See p. 151.

George Grove in 1895 his pupils became fewer in number while his disciples increased.* For Parry spread a vitalizing influence through the whole art. As an indication of the kind of influence he exerted, his book *The Art of Music* shows how he made music part of an educated man's general culture and how he brought general culture to the study of music. The world had just come through the upheaval of Darwinism and was acclimatizing itself to the enormously illuminating conception of evolution. What Huxley did in applying evolutionary ideas to ethics, Parry did in applying the doctrine of evolution to the history of music.

Enough has been said here—and much more will be said in assessing each man's individual career—to show how large a contribution was made to the rehabilitation of English music by the men who diverted time and energy from composition to the more urgent, equally necessary but in retrospect less heroic work of education, administration, musical politics and executive performance.

In this last matter of higher standards of performance, an effort was required similar to that undertaken on behalf of composition by Mackenzie, Parry and Stanford, whose common motto was "no compromise" (as compared with the more complacent standards of Sullivan, Cowen and Stainer). When this struggle was in fact begun, as it was for instance in the field of the recital by H. Plunket Greene and Leonard Borwick, it was precisely the influence of their seniors which inspired them. For Mackenzie and Stanford were themselves executants in the orchestral field and Stanford's exactions as teacher were terrifying to his pupils, while Parry's idealism was such that it is possible to hold that in the end it ran away with him. Good work, artistic integrity, the highest standards, intellectual foundations and the determination to bring the same meaning to the word first-rate in music as it bore in other fields of culture, were no mean benefit for these pioneers of revival to bring to their art.

* Tovey studied with Parry but not at the Royal College.

II

Victorian England

ACCEPTING THEN the renaissance as an historical fact, we can seek
its deeper causes in the Victorian scene. It occurred in three waves
and took a century to accomplish. Its fruits are still being gathered.
The motive power was generated in those movements around 1840
that looked backward to our own past, for our renaissance was
proved to be a form of nationalism, less self-conscious than the
similar movements in Europe at the same time, but none the less
a manifestation of the same spirit; the attempt to create a better
music and the attempt to create an English music eventually
became one, or at any rate two faces of the same coin. The
attempts of scholars to rescue the Elizabethans and to investigate
our folk-song were in effect a springboard to new creative effort,
an unconscious *recueillement pour mieux sauter*. The Bach revival
was similarly retrospective though not nationalist: so too the
tonic-sol-fa movement. The second wave was the conscious
effort of Parry and Stanford to reinvigorate the English tradition.
Like many pioneers they did not actually enter the promised land.
The achievement of their ideals was the work of Vaughan Williams,
and its international recognition was confirmed by Benjamin
Britten—the third wave.

What was English musical life like between 1830 and 1880? The
history, both factual and critical, has been well described by
Ernest Walker* and H. C. Colles.† Walker is not afraid of the
most pungent critical denunciations of the feeble, the sentimental
and the banal, and he finds plenty of occasions for castigating
the English music of the period. The inevitable comparison with
the continent is not unfair, but the Germans were at the time
producing such a prodigious quantity of first-rate music of all

---

* *A History of Music in England* (Clarendon Press, 1907).
  † *The Oxford History of Music*, Vol. VII (1940).

kinds that the nineteenth century must be accounted exceptional
even for them. Italian and French music can hardly stand up to
the German output in comparison, though with Verdi, Berlioz
and Franck they make a better showing in the international field
than we do between 1830 and 1880. It is one proof that we were
aware of the disparity that all the Victorian writers on music say
one after the other how we are improving. The testimony of these
witnesses is worth setting out.

Dr. William Crotch (1775-1847) was the outstanding musician
of his age both in ability and enlightenment. He was precocious
to a degree comparable with Mozart, a true infant prodigy, a
composer who served his own generation and an academic who
was one of the most eminent ever to occupy the Heather chair at
Oxford. The lectures he delivered at Oxford and for the Royal
Institution in London in the early years of the century were
published in 1831 and were accompanied by a book of "Specimens", i.e. musical illustrations. Their aim was, in his own words,
"the improvement of taste". Taste then carried some of the
meaning of what we now call appreciation, i.e. discrimination
fortified by knowledge.* This is how he justifies his endeavours:

"What, it may be asked, is the present state of the public taste
in this nation, that it should be thought necessary to interfere
with it by a work of this kind? Is there not already a sufficient
number of books on the subject? Have we not an abundance of
critics, connoisseurs and amateurs? Is not anyone possessed of a
musical ear capable of judging what is good or bad for himself?
Is it not for the public the composer writes? Whom else should
he endeavour to please? In answer to these questions I assert,
then, that the public taste still requires much cultivation, though
greatly improved since the commencement of the present century.
[In a later chapter he puts the last thirty years of the eighteenth
century as touching bottom: 'the lowest decline of taste in the
nation'.] Sound principles are more generally adopted as the
basis of critical observations [Hadow did not think so sixty years
later]; good music of all kinds is more frequently heard and duly
appreciated. Yet taste in perfection is neither universal nor
prevalent. It is found among the aged and experienced, it cannot
be expected in the young and untutored, to whom these Lectures

* *Cf.* pp. 291, 344.

B

are principally addressed; they must not be left to form their own taste. Small indeed are the advances which an unassisted individual can make in endeavouring to attain perfection in any of his powers. . . . The principles of just criticism must thus be acquired by the musical student. By criticism is not meant (what it is too often made to signify) the art of censuring in technical terms and in a learned manner, but that of separating excellence from defect; of admiring as well as finding fault; of discriminating and comparing the several styles and of appreciating [*sic*] their relative value on principles which are generally true as applied to all the fine arts."

From this he goes on to say that though a professed admirer of modern music (Beethoven and Schubert?) he would use the above principles to overturn "the absurd and mischievous opinion held by many writers that music is continually improving from every innovation and addition". This observation shows that critics then as now were either conservatives praising the past or progressives who found more to write about in *avant-gardisme*; also that before the doctrine of evolution was propounded (and applied to musical history by Parry) the fallacy that advance was always improvement was commonly accepted. It does, however, save Crotch from the charge that he is himself a victim of that fallacy when he speaks of the improvement shown by the music of the thirty years after 1800 upon the music of the thirty years before the turn of the century. At any rate Crotch thought there was still plenty of room for improvement.

Only a few years later George Hogarth, who was the father-in-law of Charles Dickens and wrote about music in *The Daily News*, published *Musical History, Biography and Criticism*, which quickly went into a second edition in 1838. It represents perhaps half a generation after Crotch, since the *Lectures* were a compilation made some years after their delivery. Hogarth's Preface begins:

"At a period when Music is more and more extensively cultivated as a branch of polite knowledge, as a powerful aid to the exercises of devotion, and as a rational and elegant recreation in social and domestic life a work like the present appears to be called for. Dr. Burney's *A General History of Music* from its magnitude is not calculated for general use and moreover does not embrace

the last half century [Burney's History was published in 1776]—
a most eventful and interesting period of the art." To be sure,
the period of Haydn, Mozart, Beethoven and Schubert.

He then makes a criticism that was prophetic in its anticipation
of the nationalism which from the middle of the nineteenth
century transformed European music.

"On one interesting topic he has not touched, further than in
the way of incidental remark. This is the *national* or *traditional*
music of different countries. But this, as yet, is more a matter of
enquiry and speculation than history. . . . Travellers are seldom
sufficiently versed in music to collect and note down accurately
the melodies or to describe distinctly the musical instruments and
the modes of vocal and instrumental performance of the countries
they visit. A historian of national music must not only spend
years in collecting and digesting the fragments of information
scattered through innumerable volumes, but like another Burney,
only on a much more extensive scale, must make a series of
'Musical Tours' through the remotest regions of the earth." The
first attempt to do precisely this was made by Carl Engel who
published *An Introduction to the Study of National Music* in 1866.
Hogarth then presents a short history which is very well done,
notably in its selection of topics—he mentions Quagliati, Byrd's
Reasons, Mace, North, Roseingrave on Scarlatti and Daines
Barrington on Wesley, and metrical psalmody, and devotes whole
chapters to Purcell, Handel, and Beethoven. Other chapters are
shared between Weber and Spohr, Paer, Spontini and Rossini;
his last is on the present position in England. In this he admits
some of our deficiencies:

"The composition of instrumental music either for a full
orchestra or in the form of concerted pieces for instruments, has
not yet been successfully cultivated in England. We have not
symphonies, quartets or quintets which can rival the works of the
German school." "England has produced few great performers
on the violin." He describes our institutions and notes the beginning of musical journalism—*Harmonicon*, *The Musical Library*
and *The Musical World*—and concludes—"the diffusion of a
taste for music and the increasing elevation of its character may
be regarded as a national blessing".

Other of his merits are his critical comments on the movements of taste and the revelation of his own taste. He observes that when Rossini's *Mosè in Egitto* was performed in England the leading character was changed "in conformity with the feelings entertained among us" to Peter the Hermit. Similarly he finds the secularity of the Masses of Haydn and Mozart regrettable as *seria mixta jocis*—this is an expression of his own opinion. He is inclined to be severe on Burney, though he probably made use of him. Thus he says "Burney lived and wrote when musical taste was at a low ebb in England" and "Burney was always disposed to go along with the public". So Burney got repaid for his misunderstanding of early English music through judging it by contemporary Italian canons. Hogarth wrote a history of opera, which he published in 1838 under the title *Memoirs of Music Drama*, which is a readable history of opera but not so designed because, as the author scrupulously observes, he has not treated the subject "with the degree of severity in regard to form and substance which 'the dignity of History' might have required".

Half a century later we again hear of the great progress made in the art from Francis Hueffer, who attributes it to the Queen herself, for that is the implication of his title *Half a Century of Music in England: 1837 to 1887* and of his words "a reign which among other important events has witnessed the revival of Music as a national art in England". He gives a grim picture of the musical scene of 1837: music was unknown to the majority of people as London concerts were few and limited to subscribing members. So too the Italian Opera. Lord Chesterfield's famous notion that fiddler and gentleman were incompatible terms persisted in so far that all public men disclaimed a knowledge of music—this as late as the seventies when they,[*] with Mr. Gladstone among them, attended the meeting to launch the scheme for a Royal College of Music. He castigates this attitude and quotes an anonymous writer of 1872 who said that the concert season of 1837 could be dismissed without the slightest reference and that equally dull and dreary was the operatic season. The Antient Concerts were attenuated, and to make up for their shortcomings the Sacred Harmonic Society had been founded in 1832. We can look with pity at our grandfathers' efforts in this direction, but with envy at their operatic experiences—just consider their

[*] See pp. 24, 30.

singers, Grisi, Labache, Pasta and Rubini's high notes. How familiar it all sounds!

He traces the changes during Victoria's reign and produces one or two oddly slanted views (as they now seem). The general decay of our music he attributes not to our Puritans but to the House of Hanover—yet Hueffer was a German born in Westphalia—who, he says, killed English music. Queen Victoria acted on the opposite principle and encouraged the art by such varied means as inviting Mendelssohn and Liszt to Buckingham Palace, by patronizing the opera, and by awarding knighthoods to musicians ("almost too lavishly"). He notes the disappearance one after the other of the Antient Concerts, the Sacred Harmonic Society and Exeter Hall, now "mute and inglorious", and welcomes in their place the establishment of the Crystal Palace concerts, Ella's Musical Union which served chamber music well from 1845 till it was killed by the Classical Monday Pops in 1859, the recent establishment of a London Symphony Orchestra by George Henschel, and the work with local orchestras of Hallé at Manchester, Stockley (a name to become historic in another connection) at Birmingham, and Riseley at Bristol. But it is significant that of his five chapters Hueffer devotes the middle three to Wagner, Liszt and Berlioz in England. He makes a sharp attack on the royalty ballad and he observes that there are people in England "who believe that our nation has no real taste for opera and that the oratorio takes its place as the real expression of our dramatic feeling in music". He then takes a look at the contemporary scene, applauds Carl Rosa's efforts, notes that Barnby is busy, thinks that Mackenzie has gone off a little since he wrote *Colomba* and the dream scene in *The Rose of Sharon*, declares Cowen's Welsh and Scandinavian Symphonies to be as good as any by a living master at home or abroad, deplores Sullivan's addiction to operetta though he rejoices that *The Mikado* was well received in Berlin and hopes that *The Golden Legend* will lead the composer along more serious paths. His conclusion is:

"If among this array of talent a genius in the proper sense of that much abused word has not yet made his appearance; if in secular music at least we have not a distinctively national type of art, we may take heart of grace from the thought that the race of great composers is, with one or two exceptions, extinct in other countries as well as ours." Nature had worn herself out by creating Schumann, Mendelssohn, Liszt, Wagner, Berlioz and Verdi. So she was resting. Not very plausible? But is there any better theory about the incalculable appearance of genius?

The life of the Rev. H. R. Haweis coincided exactly with Queen Victoria's reign. His famous book *Music and Morals* is not a systematic treatise either of aesthetics, psychology, biography, or organology, though it ranges over them all. It is in fact amateurish, "the studies of his leisure hours", but it is the product of an observant and thoughtful mind. Part IV is critical and deals with music in England. He is firmly of the opinion that the English are not musical. If they were, would they be so fond of ballads like "When other lips" and "Champagne Charley"? Still, he sees an immense advance in the discrimination of audiences, and "the present wave of musical progress" he dates from the advent of Mendelssohn. He speculates whether in the light of the improve- ment in orchestral music and the cultivation of chamber music "it may be that we are on the eve of a creative period in the history of English music".

Stanford, who to us seems to have been one of the principal architects of the renaissance, by his high standards, general culture, practical musicianship, and success both as a teacher of composition and as a composer of impeccable craftsmanship (to put it at its minimum), makes a number of allusions to the "new forward movement begun in the seventies", "Renaissance of Music in England during the last half-century". He attached a good deal of importance to general culture and pointed to the high level of all-round ability, wide reading and general education that was to be observed in all the world-famous executants as well as the greatest composers, pointing to Liszt, von Bülow, Joachim, as well as the romantic Germans and the emerging Russians like Borodin and Rimsky-Korsakov. He does not imply that musical genius is to be acquired by classical scholarship or distinction in mathematics and chem- istry, but he does hold that the general esteem in which the art is held depends on musicians being more than bohemian ignoramuses and narrow-minded artisans. In the context of his own matriculation at Cambridge in 1870 he says "in England this broad view of general culture for the musical profession had not yet taken hold, save in an isolated instance or two, such as Sterndale Bennett and Hugo Pierson (who left us and went off to Germany). After 1875 the atmosphere began to change." To Sterndale Bennett he attributes the credit of the renaissance, that is the awakening to a vigorous musical life, which a later generation has transferred to Parry and to him. He joined the name of S. S. Wesley with Bennett's as "the first fruits of the Renaissance of English music", i.e. as composers. Wesley's was the stronger personality but his influence was less because confined to the sphere of church music. Both were in fact the agents of the Bach revival in England, which was a fertilizer applied to the barren soil.

Bennett too was a pioneer for English music and some of his own has survived into the present century. *The May Queen*, which I remember hearing as a boy, must by now be dead, but his anthems are still in the service lists of collegiate choirs and his piano music, though not for public consumption, is agreeable to play. A little song like "May Dew" or "Gentle Zephyr" is excellent for a budding soprano. The verdict that all of it is mostly Mendelssohn without any infusion of the romantic spirit of the times is, however, correct and undeniable, but his career, which was sympathetically described by Stanford in an article commemorating the centenary of his birth, is enlightening on the deadening conditions of Victorian musical life. He is in fact the biggest figure of the mid-century. Costa dominated the scene at the time and there were a few men who contributed a song or two to the English tradition (Loder and J. L. Hatton, for instance), who sustained or stirred up academic life (Macfarren and Ouseley, for instance), or who played the organ (Goss and Smart, for instance), but Bennett's influence alone continues.

The story of his life is one of devastatingly hard work. Like Dr. Burney he travelled around in his own carriage teaching incessantly to earn a living. He began young as a chorister at King's College, Cambridge, but was sent at the instigation of the Vice-Provost to the Royal Academy of Music, where he had Dr. Crotch and Cipriani Potter as composition teachers. A piano concerto—he wrote four in all and played them himself—won him the friendship of Mendelssohn, whom he joined at Leipzig, where he found another friend in Schumann. Both these German composers thought highly of him: Schumann called him "eine poetische schöne Seele" and dedicated his *Etudes Symphoniques* to him, as well as devoting a New Year article to him in the *Neue Zeitschrift*, while Mendelssohn proclaimed him as "the most promising musician I know, not only in your country (Britain) but here also (Germany)". His piano concerto (No. 3 in C minor) and his overture *The Naiads*, which survived longest of all his major compositions, were both played at the Gewandhaus. He found the atmosphere of Germany very much more favourable to music and musicians than that prevailing at the time in England, though he could criticize adversely some of their choral and operatic performances. Altogether he paid three visits to Germany as a young man and later on repaid the friendship and recognition which he found there with hospitality to Spohr, Hiller and Clara Schumann. His songs had German texts or translations and so close was his intimacy with the musical life of Germany that centred on Leipzig that he was offered the conductorship of the Gewandhaus concerts in 1853. It is one of the ironies of history that Bennett's German involvement was the source and inspiration of his work for English music and English musical life and at the same time the partial cause of tying England still more tightly to the German chariot. The vitality of independence was not to be attained by schooling in German ways or accepting German ideals without question, though it is easy enough to see that Germany was the best and most natural model to copy. It was the copying that was fatal.

Bennett, however, was not merely a copy of Mendelssohn so much as a kindred spirit. One difference between them is thus described by Schumann:*

"The first thing that strikes everyone in the character of his compositions is their remarkable family resemblance to those of Mendelssohn . . . the same beauty of form . . . purity—but with a difference. This difference is still more observable in their playing than in their compositions. The Englishman's playing is perhaps more tender, more careful in detail; that of Mendelssohn is broader, more energetic. The former bestows fine shading on the lightest thing, the latter pours a novel force into the most

* *Music and Musicians*; tr. F. R. Ritter (Reeves, 1877).

powerful passages; one overpowers us with the transfigured expression of a single form, the other showers forth hundreds of angelic heads, as in a heaven of Raphael. Something of the same kind occurs in their compositions." Bennett was only twenty-one when this was written, but the delicacy noted by Schumann in his music corresponded to a fastidiousness in his character, good for his morals but not so good for his creative gift, which ultimately was extinguished by outward circumstances that it was not aggressive enough to defeat.

His career illuminates the conditions of the musical profession and musical life in Victorian England. There were very few salaried posts outside the organ loft—Cambridge appointed Bennett to its chair in music, but only discovered some years after he had held it that it carried no emoluments. A pianist had to earn a living by teaching: composition, before the days of performing rights, yielded too small a return for any English composer to depend upon it. Bennett therefore built up an arduous teaching practice and instituted some chamber concerts in his own home, concerts (subsequently transferred to the Hanover Square Rooms) which ran from 1842 to 1856. The Philharmonic Society produced his works regularly and he was a member of the Board of Directors. Years later in 1856 he became its regular conductor for a period of ten years following Costa. Although there is wide testimony to Bennett's charm and integrity, high principles and good temper, he fell foul of Costa, who still enjoys the reputation of being a ruthless martinet. The cause of the estrangement was trivial, namely the tempi of two overtures. In 1836 Bennett wrote from Leipzig "my new overture must not be played too fast";* in 1848 when Costa was conductor, another of Bennett's overtures was taken too slowly and Bennett passed a note to the cellist, Lucas, who handed it to Costa who read "Fast, fast, fast" as "Fuss, fuss, fuss" and was so offended that he refused to conduct it, and five years later, when Arabella Goddard was engaged to play Bennett's F minor concerto, he refused to conduct that too. It sounds like a clash of personalities similar to the cat-and-dog hackle-rising that bedevilled the personal

---

* This is in a letter to Davison in which he says that, if Costa conducted, the only advantage would be that "we might hear the whole of Beethoven's symphonies in one night and still have time for supper".

relations of Stanford and Elgar sixty years later. *Punch* described the whole episode in a poem called "The Embroglio at the Philharmonic":

> Sterndale Bennett was Indignant with Costa
> For not playing Bennett's Composition faster;
> Costa flew into excitement at Lucas
> For showing him Bennett's Order, or Ukase,
> Haughtily Resigned the Seat which he sat on,
> And Contemptuously told Lucas himself to Take the *bâton*.
> Moreover stipulated this Year with the Directors
> That Nobody was to read Him any more Lectures.
> Also he made it a Condition Strict,
> He was only to conduct what Pieces of Music he lik'd,
> Whereby this Year Costa doth Prevent
> Any performance of Music by Benn't;
> Likewise excluding the young and gifted Miss Goddard,
> Whom with Admiration all the Critical Squad heard:-
> All to be Deplored, and without Amalgamation,
> The Philharmonic will Tarnish its Hitherto Deservedly High
>   Reputation.

Arabella Goddard subsequently married J. W. Davison, the music critic of *The Times* (from whose memoirs the poem is taken), and there was a deal of trouble one way and another over Costa's stiff-necked attitude, and the subservience of the Philharmonic Directors which Davison attacked in *The Musical World* and in *The Times* "cut with irony".

Bennett broke his connection with the Philharmonic in 1848 and turned to the promotion of performances of Bach's choral music. This was a work which was to have consequences so far-reaching that they deserve separate consideration.* His next undertaking was the professorship at Cambridge to which he was elected in 1856 at the age of forty. He made a number of reforms in the regulations for and awards of degrees—Ouseley was similarly reforming Oxford at the same time. In 1866 he gave up the conductorship of the Philharmonic which he had held for ten years and was proposing to use his time in a more leisurely, less routine-ridden manner, for composition. But at that moment the

* See Chapter VI.

Royal Academy of Music, then on the point of dissolution, persuaded him to become its Principal. Things were so bad that he had also to become responsible for its management. He was successful in his endeavours and even contrived during these later years to write some music, notably the oratorio *The Woman of Samaria*, which was still being sung by nonconformist choirs of modest ability at the beginning of the present century. *The May Queen* had been written for the first Leeds Festival of 1858, of which he was conductor. There was thus no side of English musical life which he did not serve, except that of opera, where Costa reigned, and the devoted service so given was undoubtedly beneficial. It was recognized in 1871 by the bestowal of a knighthood. He died on February 1, 1875.

Costa's services were of a different order. He has left behind a miasma over his reputation and he helped to clamp foreign domination over English music, though he became a naturalized Englishman. We smile with a superior twist of the lip at his oratorios about Eli and Naaman, the fashion for Old Testament worthies having mercifully expired in Parry's hands and been buried by Elgar breaking new ground in Newman's poem. He does not seem to have been a lovable character, though there is testimony (from Stanford) that behind the formidable exterior there was geniality and kindness. At any rate after his lights and according to his very considerable skill he served English music as its principal conductor for forty years, first for the ballet at the King's Theatre, then at the Italian Opera at Covent Garden, then at the Philharmonic, where he reigned for eight years. It was he who put an end to the divided direction of the orchestra at the Philharmonic, the leader being displaced. The official history says that a better choice than Costa could not have been made to secure undivided responsibility, for "he was a splendid disciplinarian" and he stipulated that he would not accept the position on any other terms than sole control. He also said he would "only preside over *worthy* music". He was conductor of the Birmingham Festivals from 1849 till 1882. He also conducted the Leeds Festival of 1874 and from 1857 to 1880 he led the Sacred Harmonic Society through their Handelian rites. But he seems to have been more renowned for efficiency than art. Bennett complained of his speed, Stanford testifies to his love of loud noise and unbalance

—he had forty-eight strings. But Berlioz is the most eloquent witness to his obtuse lack of scruple. In articles to the *Journal des Débats* he describes Costa's additions of three trombones, an ophicleide, a piccolo, a big drum, and cymbals to Mozart's orchestra. "In Mozart's masterpiece during the supper scene, while Don Juan's private band is playing the naïve music of the *Cosa rara*, an incredible solo on the ophicleide has been introduced, which clashes in the most curious way with the occasion and style of the piece." In Rossini's *Barber* he introduced his trombones and ophicleide, "and to make the entry of the four instruments stand out more—the effect just there sounds like the chandelier falling into the stalls in a general lull—the violins are always made to play *pianissimo* up to this point and suppress the little accents of *rinforzando* marked by Rossini".

He was not a good symphonic conductor since his Neapolitan upbringing had conditioned him to opera. Yet Stanford testifies that for Mozart's G minor symphony he reduced his band to forty-five picked players. His generally haughty conduct and his rancour in his vendetta with Bennett can perhaps be attributed to his Spanish ancestry. His *Eli* is something of a curiosity, block harmony throughout and unadventurous at that. *The March of Israelites* from it is probably still played sometimes by organists in remote villages, but it would give an army flat feet. His career in this country, which began through the strange chance of being sent to supervise a performance at Birmingham of a cantata by Zingarelli and finding himself obliged instead to sing its tenor solos, is a fair epitome of the standards ruling in Victorian England.

He was succeeded by the generation that included Hans Richter at Birmingham, and at the Philharmonic Mackenzie and Cowen. After 1870 Stanford provides valuable evidence about the state of performance of orchestral music—how Richter put horn-playing on to the right lines for greater security and von Bülow for greater flexibility and expression. Manns at the Crystal Palace, with George Grove at his right hand, inaugurated a more symphonic attitude to symphonic music.

The Crystal Palace, as everyone knows, was built in Hyde Park to house the Great Exhibition of 1851. But the Exhibition itself took no interest in anything but the industrial side of music:

instrument makers submitted their wares to a jury consisting of Sir Henry Bishop (chairman), Sir George Smart, Sterndale Bennett, Sigismond Thalberg, Cipriani Potter and Hector Berlioz. Some organ recitals were given in the big glass house and the Hallelujah Chorus was sung at the formal opening. There was also a massed band concert at the Chelsea Hospital on June 15, 1851, and W. H. Callcott published on his own initiative a New Sacred Song for 1851, "The Desire of all Nations". But there was nothing of any special consequence. Berlioz has, however, left vivid accounts of what was going on during his stay here that summer which are appreciative, amusing, and in the case of what he heard at the opera, critical. His first article was about our musical institutions. He notes the Sacred Harmonic Society, whose performance of *Elijah* at Exeter Hall he heard, the Musical Union of John Ella, which dispensed chamber music, a Beethoven Quartet Society, founded by Thomas Alsager of *The Times* (on the financial not the musical side), the Philharmonic Society, too well known to be described, and the similar societies of Liverpool and Manchester which he knew only by repute from impartial judges, who found the northern voices better than those of the Londoners. Berlioz, like Haydn before him, found English choral singing to be unlike anything they heard elsewhere, and the service for the Charity Children at St. Paul's sent him into ecstasies, out of which he made a complete article for his newspaper. "All people that on earth do dwell" haunted him for days. His account of the Beethoven Quartet Society contains two points of interest beyond his appraisal of the playing and the players. He relates that each programme contained three quartets, usually one from each period, and then adds: "it is always the last, that of the third period (the period of Beethoven's compositions alleged to be incomprehensible) which excites the greatest enthusiasm". The other point is an early appearance of the miniature score: "You see these English people following the fanciful flight of the composer's imagination in little pocket scores printed in London for this purpose; which might mean that several of them can read the score after a fashion." But he has his doubts about that, for he records that "he looked over the shoulders of one of them and caught him with his eyes fixed on page 4 while the performers were at page 6". The analytical programme, afterwards to be set

by Grove on the path that led to Tovey, he also found in use at
Ella's concerts.* Ella sent them in advance to his subscribers. The
analyses, Berlioz says, were good, "appealing to the eye as well
as the mind, by adding to the critical text musical extracts, the
theme of each piece, the most important musical figure or the most
striking harmonies or modulations". He adds "One could not do
more" and compares this enlightenment with the state of affairs
at the Opera, to which the audience comes stuffed only with
truffles and champagne—he is no doubt thinking of the Paris
Opera. He makes no mention of Jullien's Promenade Concerts,
so probably regarded them as not a serious English Institution.
They were, however, the direct ancestor of Henry Wood's Proms.

Adam Carse† has written a biography of this picturesque
Frenchman who was prominent in London music from 1840 to
1860, when bankruptcy overtook him and brought tragedy in its
wake. The history of all London Promenade Concerts he traces
on the one hand to the London pleasure gardens, Vauxhall and
Ranelagh and others, which dispensed musical entertainment for
nearly a century from 1735 onwards, and on the other to Musard's
promenade concerts in Paris, which were aimed at the same sort
of people who came to dance to the strains of Johann Strauss and
Lanner in the same ballrooms: let them come sometimes not to
dance but to listen. Jullien copied this type of programme with
an overture thrown in. *The Musical World*'s announcement of
January 5, 1838, said that "the success of Musard's concerts in
Paris and the increasing taste for music in England had induced
Mr. Pilati to undertake the establishment of a series of instrumental concerts for the performance of overtures, quadrilles,
waltzes and galops, so arranged as to offer a promenade between
the acts." Others besides Pilati promoted such concerts during the
next two years. Jullien began his series at Drury Lane in 1840 and
continued sometimes with summer, sometimes with winter seasons
till December 1858, when he decided to give up in favour of a
world tour to civilize all peoples. The strain of megalomania,
which made him such a successful showman and such a teller of
tall tales as make up "A Sketch of the Life of Jullien", published

* Professor John Thomson had provided analytical notes at the first Reid
Concert in Edinburgh in 1841.
† *The Life of Jullien* (Cambridge, Heffer, 1951).

anonymously in *The Musical World*, may have got out of hand, for by the spring of 1860 he had suffered imprisonment in Paris, had a mental breakdown and died a few days after admission to an asylum.

The story of his life as told by Carse is most entertaining. Its significance a hundred years later is that he began the process of educating the slightly musical by giving them light music and slipping in symphonies among it, a policy adopted by Henry Wood in 1895 and extended to introduce to the ordinary listener, the *homme moyen sensuel*, the worthy citizen, the man on the Clapham bus, the average man who appears in all these guises as a representative of the British public, novelties by living composers as an admixture to his diet, once quadrilles, now piano concertos. Jullien also conducted dance music like Strauss and opera like Costa; he toured the provinces and went to America; he launched all sorts of spectacular schemes, gave masked balls and benefit concerts. "Sensational" was the word to describe him before the word had depreciated by newspaper poster use. At first he was naturally regarded as a vulgarian outside the musical pale of the Philharmonic and critical attention. But J. W. Davison of *The Times* and *The Musical World* became his friend, and though *Punch* laughed at him it recognized what he had done for English musical life in an Ode it published during his last season. He was a force for good in spite of, and indeed with the help of, his exhibitionism, and began to leaven the lump of Victorian taste.

The Crystal Palace concerts did the same thing at a higher level, embracing more cultured audiences, though they were started with the same idea of using music as an adornment to public entertainment. In 1854 a brass band was installed, but according to Davison it was really bad. Other accounts, however, say that it was as good as visiting foreigners and regimental bands. In any case the idea of giving concerts at Sydenham had taken root— perhaps because George Grove had been appointed secretary to the Crystal Palace Company—and in the summer of 1855 operatic concerts under Costa showed there was an audience for something a little more ambitious. By 1856 August Manns had been appointed band-master and began to enlarge his forces with strings and to introduce symphonic music, notably the symphonies of Mendelssohn, Schumann and Schubert. In due course Brahms and the lesser romantics like Raff, Goetz and Rubinstein had their symphonies played for the first time in London. English composers were also given their airing—Sullivan (*Tempest* music), Parry (piano concerto), Mackenzie (*Scottish Rhapsody*)—and festivals devoted to Handel were organized, which lasted with some intermissions till 1926. Under Grove's influence the programmes included not only much music that was then new, but curiosities such as Beethoven's second *Leonora* overture, his arrangement of his violin concerto for the piano, and Mozart's alternative slow movement for his *Paris Symphony*. This scholarly infusion seems likely to have been prompted by the work Grove did in writing analytical programme notes for the concerts.* Grove was in fact being caught up by the head waters of the infant stream of musicology—a term not known till three-quarters of a century later—which led to the great *Dictionary of Music and Musicians*. There is testimony to the value and standards of the Crystal Palace concerts, which were conducted by Manns for forty-five years, from men who lived well into the twentieth century, for example Bernard Shaw, Stanford, Ernest Walker and Fuller-Maitland. Indeed it would seem as though the regularity of these orchestral concerts, like Hallé's in Manchester, spread the knowledge of and fostered a taste for orchestral music to provide a foundation on which the renaissance could lever itself out of the uncertainties of Victorian music.

George Grove is thus the pioneer who led the way forward on all fronts. An eminent Victorian if ever there was one, for music was only one of his many activities, and not his profession, he was trained as a civil engineer and in that capacity superintended the erection of a lighthouse in Jamaica and took part in the erection of the Menai railway bridge. He sent an account of the latter to *The Spectator* and thus appeared in print for the first time. After the railway slump of 1846 he had to look for other work and in 1848 was appointed secretary to the Society of Arts, whence he removed to the secretaryship of the Crystal Palace, as already recorded. About 1854 he met Dean Stanley who fired him with the project for a dictionary of the Bible, which in turn sent him off to Palestine to investigate its topography and at a

* See Charles L. Graves, *The Life and Letters of Sir George Grove*, C.B. (Macmillan, 1903), pp. 53-4, for forerunners.

later date to Oberammergau, when he sent to *The Times* the first newspaper account of the Passion Play to appear in an English newspaper. He paid a second visit to Palestine in 1861 and continued to make numerous contributions to Smith's *Dictionary of the Bible*. Music he zealously cultivated all his life and he took up the young Arthur Sullivan, with whom he went off to Vienna in 1867 in the same spirit of exploration as had sent him to Palestine, the object in this case being Schubert in general and *Rosamunde* in particular, which he unearthed in a cupboard—the story is told in his own words in C. L. Graves's biography. Grove had almost as much enthusiasm for poetry as for music and he knew all the literary lights of the time; he even published a number of papers on Tennyson. His literary bent and his wide range of interests led him to the editorship of *Macmillan's Magazine*, for which he secured contributions from everyone of eminence from Samuel Butler to Andrew Lang, from R. L. Stevenson to Walter Pater and even Mr. Gladstone. C. L. Graves does not say whether the idea of a *Dictionary of Music and Musicians* originated with Macmillans, who have always been its publishers, or in the fertile mind of Grove himself, but in 1873 he resigned from his post at the Crystal Palace to devote himself to this new project. In 1876 the National Training School for Music was opened with Grove's protegé Sullivan as Principal. Six years later, when the National Training School was transformed into the Royal College of Music, Grove was offered and accepted the post of Director, and to that institution he devoted his energies, which were no longer so widely diffused, until his resignation in 1894. He died in 1900 at the age of eighty, having served music as administrator, scholar, educationist and evangelist. The gospel he preached and practised was broadly based on wide reading and a wide experience of life, and the tradition of music as one of the humaner letters, which was to be preached by Parry, began in him. He was a characteristic product of the Victorian age at its best: high ideals, unwearied effort, broad culture, ingratiating personality and public spirit were the ingredients of this remarkable man's influence upon his own and the next two generations.

III

Sullivan, Mackenzie, Cowen and Smyth

BORN IN the middle of the nineteenth century, Arthur Seymour
Sullivan (1842-1901), Alexander Campbell Mackenzie (1847-
1935) and Frederick Hymen Cowen (1857-1935) represent the
achievements of Victorian music at their highest. They wrote the
sort of music which, in so far as the renaissance was a crusade
against anything, the new men were concerned to improve out of
existence. Not that the renaissance *was* a crusade—the polemics
were mostly left, as they should be, to the critics, with Hadow
and Fuller-Maitland to call for higher standards. But their
attempts to build an English music on the basis of a German
training, amid the prevailing Mendelssohnian fashions, axioms
and assumptions, have demonstrated by their very failure that
talent of the highest order (such as they all three possessed) was
not enough either to produce a national school of composition,
or a characteristic expression of Britain in music anywhere comparable to its literary, political or even scientific manifestations,
or to raise the status of the art to its proper place in English
culture. For the first of these purposes the German training was
fatal; in the second they were fairly successful in the opinion of
their contemporaries but have left no lasting mark on Europe as
their contemporaries Dvořák, Fauré and Tchaikovsky have done;
for the third a university education would have been necessary,
as was shown by the success of Parry and Stanford in this particular respect.

Every thesis in the above argument as well as many of its
premises is disputable and calls for substantiation. In the first
place claims have been made to include both Sullivan and
Mackenzie in the revival, while for Cowen, who has since his
death rather dropped out of the reckoning, it may be urged that
he was an exact contemporary of Elgar—why then these dis-

tinctions which savour of snobbery? Not snobbery but criticism. Criticism has to consider not only achievements, but artistic aims and ideals in appraising the total effects of a revivalist movement.

Sullivan's achievements are curiously ambivalent. He has left a lot of really bad music behind, and, what is worse, popular bad music that resists death. His great achievements, the comic operas with Gilbert, whose claims to permanence and excellence cannot be lightly dismissed, are still oddly streaked—somehow the church organist and the Anglican anthem play curious games of hide-and-seek with an incongruous quasi-Gallic frivolity. Furthermore, though no musician will deny their merits, their appeal is far more to the unmusical than to regular music lovers. Opera connoisseurs, for instance, of the widest sympathies have difficulty in raising any enthusiasm for the Savoy operas, which, whatever may be said against them, are very distinctive works. The actual achievements of the composer are affected by the outlook and ideals of the man, and on that score Walker is not overstating the truth when he says that "anything like steadiness of artistic purpose was never one of his endowments". One of Sullivan's biographers goes farther and says that his judgment was so easily swayed by popularity and success that he was "market-minded". On the other hand his views about musical education were enlightened, and he helped to formulate the liberal policy which was the animating ideal of the Royal College of Music founded in 1883 after a preliminary and experimental venture, the National Training School, of which Sullivan was Principal, and in an address delivered to students at Birmingham in 1888 he speaks of the improvements in English music during a half-century which make it possible for it once more to appear among the leaders of Europe.

Mackenzie's claims to be one of those chiefly responsible for the regeneration of English music during the last years of the nineteenth century are differently calculated but come to much the same result. He was so closely identified with Parry and Stanford alike in musical education and in the musical leadership of the country that his name is often coupled with theirs. But he belonged to the older type of professional musician with less general culture, less literary taste—which is important for its bearing on vocal music with which the revival was chiefly concerned in its early years—and his music unlike Sullivan's has failed to keep any place for itself in the repertory. This may be due to a too harsh judgment by a generation which was forced to a policy of the clean cut. In other words the continental training which stood him in such good stead in his lifetime and in fact constituted the strength of his position has been fatal to his works since the emancipation effected by Holst and Vaughan Williams. His aim was more consistent than Sullivan's but not so high as that of the reformers.

Cowen is chiefly remembered as the composer of "The Better Land", a shop ballad of considerable demerit, and his more substantial compositions are all forgotten. But he served his generation not only as a conductor who was something more than capable—he directed the Handel Festival at the Crystal Palace as late as 1923—but as a purveyor of very agreeable orchestral music of light weight and small calibre. He was your all-round musician of great professional eminence but undistinguished mind, like so many English musicians of the nineteenth century. He has in fact no claims to be a part of a movement of regeneration, whatever his services, which were many, to our national music.

Sullivan, born in Lambeth, the son of a humble Irish musician who became band-master to the Royal Military College, was something of a prodigy who showed his natural talent by the time he was eight years old, when he composed an anthem. He became a chorister of the Chapel Royal and won the Mendelssohn scholarship to the Royal Academy of Music, which was extended to take him to Leipzig in 1858, where he studied piano, conducting and composition. Just before he left Leipzig he composed some music for Shakespeare's *The Tempest*, which on his return to London got a performance at the Crystal Palace in 1862. This was a success and launched him into London music, giving him contacts with Grove, Costa and Chorley. With Grove he went on the famous expedition to Vienna in search of Schubert (1867). The other two men served to introduce him to the theatre and festivals: for Costa he wrote a ballet, and with Chorley as librettist he began an opera and furnished Birmingham with a cantata. For a living he played the organ for six years until he found he could do better by composing anthems, part-songs and drawing-room ballads. He met Burnand of *Punch* in 1866 and *Cox and Box* was the outcome. Gilbert he met in 1870 and *Thespis* was the first product of the collaboration, which lasted for twenty-five years and produced another dozen operas. In 1876 he was persuaded to become Principal of the National Training School. In 1880 he became conductor of the Leeds Festival and conducted the next six festivals, only resigning for reasons of health in 1899. He had been conductor of the Philharmonic Society for the seasons 1885 to 1887. When to these activities is added the composition not only of the operas but of incidental music and festival commissions it will be seen that he filled his 57 years pretty full of music. He led a busy social life too in spite of poor health, so that whatever posterity thinks about his music he certainly served his generation.

Outside the Savoy operas little enough of Sullivan has survived except some hymn-tunes and the pretty and sparkling *Overture di Ballo*, so that it is perhaps flogging a dead horse to submit to adverse criticism the *In Memoriam* overture, *Ivanhoe* and *The Golden Legend*. Yet a post-mortem is a valuable form of inquest not only to ascertain the cause of death but also to discover why Sullivan's music as a whole had not in it the seeds of the revival that was on the very verge of taking place. The lack of sustained effort, that is artistic effort proved by vigorous self-criticism, is responsible for the impression of weakness, the streaks of poor stuff among the better metal, and the consequent general ambiguity that is left by his music. His contemporaries deprecated his addiction to high life, the turf and an outward lack of seriousness. Without adopting the simplified morality of the women's magazines it is possible to urge that his contemporaries were really right, in that such addiction implied a fundamental lack of seriousness towards his art in spite of his own protestations that it had been his "incessant occupation, a second nature and his mistress in every sense of the word". The success of the Savoy operas, whose permanence in the light of their ephemeral intention and topical allusiveness could not be foreseen, was regarded as the obstacle to Sullivan's realizing the position which both he and his critics felt should have been his destiny, to lift English music out of its stuffy fifth-rate state. Actually the trouble went deeper, to the roots of his character and to Victorian obtuseness.

For the canker was the same that affected English church music, inability to perceive the smugness, the sentimentality and the banality of the Mendelssohnian detritus which all English composers of the nineteenth century set themselves assiduously to augment. The root of Sullivan's trouble was the infection of his music by his church training. Even in the theatre the organist with his evensong preludizing was not far away; and on the concert platform, though he did not wear his surplice, he had on his Sunday organ-playing suit. And the church music of that day was at a lower ebb than at any time in the history of the Anglican communion. Of Sullivan's own church music the reverse complaint is made, that he was insufficiently interested to stir himself to effort worthy of the cause, and was content to let his facility turn out pretty part-songs of the type of "O Hush thee my baby" or the Evening Hymn in *The Golden Legend* in the form of anthems. It is this failure to perceive what is appropriate, to observe the tawdriness in what is pretty, to remain content with the flattest and most obvious rhythms, this yielding to a fatal facility, that excludes Sullivan from the ranks of the good composers.

The *In Memoriam* overture starts with a *religioso* theme that has justly been pilloried.*

Ex 1 Andante Religioso

Sullivan seems to have had a partiality for repeated notes, a sign

* By Walker, who quotes the opening on p. 294 of *History of Music in England*. Westrup's revision omits the quotation but retains the verbal criticism. However, Stanley Marchant told me that when the overture is played in St. Paul's Cathedral sufficiently slowly for the acoustics of the building the banality of the theme disappears into spacious grandeur.

of melodic weakness visible from Friar Tuck to the weary organist of "The Lost Chord", though in a hymn like "Onward Christian Soldiers" they have as it were a functional justification to establish march rhythm.

The Golden Legend, which alone of the oratorio-cantatas preserved for a while any semblance of life, shows just how far his firm stride upon the high road of good serious music is let down by weakness at the knees. The book extracted from Longfellow by Joseph Bennett of *The Daily Telegraph* is not free from bathos, but it suffers from a worse defect in that most of the scenes are laid at eventide and woke almost at once Sullivan's evensong manner. He includes beside "O gladsome light", a psalm with organ accompaniment, some plainchant and a *religioso* part-song "O pure in heart"; Ursula's music is a cross between the usual fussy operatic contralto's attentions to the heroine and a meek Victorian hymn-singer. But the Prologue is stronger meat, Lucifer has traces of characterization, and the duet between Prince Henry and Elsie has positive qualities of impulse and lyrical expression. But this eloquence of Victorian vespers cannot be taken seriously today, and we are left asking ourselves how it is that such robust and accomplished people as the Victorians sank into anaemic complacency when their softer, and especially their religious, emotions were touched. Colles[*] compares Lucifer's Prologue to its detriment, "flaccid and nerveless", with Parry's *Prometheus*.

Ivanhoe had some success when it first appeared—it ran for 160 performances, a record such as no recent opera has surpassed, unless it be *The Immortal Hour* in its several revivals. The book is well constructed to provide dramatic situations and the Wardour Street convention is not out of place with a chivalric subject; there are some good songs in it, some of which, notably Friar Tuck's "Ho Jolly Jenkin", have survived; the action and dialogue move on easy-running, conventional music, light in texture, apt enough though liable to drop into the compound time which was Sullivan's bane; there are some effective ensemble and choral numbers; but the fatal touch of the organ and the part-song instead of something symphonic when strength is needed have laid the opera aside without hope of revival. And if we would

[*] *The Oxford History of Music*, Vol. VII (1940), p. 469.

question the justice of this neglect the answer can be found in a comparison with *Lohengrin*, written forty years earlier.

The rest of Sullivan's serious music is also dead, except some of the songs. He had no literary discrimination, either to take the measure of the good by exerting a comparable musical effort or to eschew the bad which he set with complete naïvety. The poems of "The Lost Chord", "Thou'rt passing hence, my brother" and "The Sailor's Grave", all of them prettifications of the death motif, are so bad as to be almost funny. And to Victorian credit "The Lost Chord" was seen to be so and parodied heartily—to Sullivan's distress. But art that is bad from banality has the quality of simplicity, and the settings that Sullivan made in all seriousness of these cheap ballads—the honourable name "ballad" acquired a new pejorative meaning in these decades—won an enormous popularity. The art in them is the lowest common denominator of artistic creation. They are bad enough to be a disgrace to the composer, but they have in them skill and just a flicker of the fire enough to keep them alive and still pull off a cheap effect.

But Sullivan could write a good song, though outside of the operas the only one that now testifies unequivocally to that ability is his early "Orpheus with his lute". Even here his treatment of "killing care" shows his usual lack of poetic appreciation, but the song has a fresh purity that makes it one of the standard settings of that immortal lyric. Put it against the others that have survived and we can see how Sullivan's abuse of his genius amounted to a betrayal of a trust. No wonder his friends of Sir George Grove's circle were aware that something was the matter. If they regretted the time and effort spent on the comic operas they were barking up the wrong tree, as time has shown. But their barks were justified, for Sullivan did less than nothing for a revival of English music.

The Savoy operas are another matter. They are curious in that they make little appeal to musicians and amateurs of taste, who are yet bound to recognize that they have besides many lapses some unique virtues. They present a lucky accident in the collaboration of two complementary minds. Gilbert was salt, Sullivan sweet. Gilbert was critical and exacting, Sullivan yielding and desirous of pleasing. Gilbert was satirical and forbidding, Sullivan spontaneous and charming. Gilbert was the male,

Sullivan the female partner in an extraordinary marriage, for which the history of art has no exact parallel, not even that of Strauss and von Hofmannsthal. For neither artist was successful without the other, neither could stand on his own feet, whereas together they conquered whole worlds. What was undertaken as the normal work of providing entertainment in the contemporary theatre, what was essentially topical in its choice of target, what each partner regarded as something a little derogatory to his true intentions and functions, this collection of ephemera has survived for three quarters of a century without any abatement in the strength and immediacy of the appeal which brought them their original success. They are an astounding phenomenon. Neither partner can be regarded as better or more important than the other, but Gilbert provided the element of strength that was lacking in Sullivan. Without Gilbert, Sullivan produced nothing with the sap of permanence in it, *Cox and Box* excepted. The Savoy operas are the product not of a single genius but of this strange marriage of two unusual minds, each the perfect complement of the other. They have had no successors; they have had no continental currency, only some sporadic performances, but they are liked in the United States; they are not to everybody's taste; they are a biological sport, an isolated phenomenon. As such they are interesting and important, but except in the single matter of word-setting they lie outside the renaissance.

With Mackenzie we come to the turning point in the century-old movement of revival. He was himself of the older type of professional musician but he had a better brain and a more positive personality than his fellows—the Scot in him gave him grit. He was German-trained and had no university education. His music is even more out of fashion than Parry's and Stanford's, since it is rare for anything of his to be heard since the *Britannia* overture and the *Scottish Concerto* disappeared from the Proms. Besides his compositions his services to English music were two: he served his own generation as a performer, first as a violinist and later as a conductor, and he served several successive generations by helping to educate them. And in both he was concerned to raise existing standards.

His career can best be related from his own book of reminiscences published in 1927 when he was eighty years old. *A*

Musician's Narrative, though far from being a profound book, gives in spite of its anecdotal and episodic character a clear impression of its author's steadfastness of purpose. Its criticism is not very penetrating and will not compare with either Parry's or Stanford's, but its vigour (compare it in this respect with the flatfooted narrative of his contemporary J. F. Barnett) shows that in the prime of his life the writer was quite capable of lecturing acceptably for the Royal Institution and presiding over an international society for musical scholarship (1905-1911). Mackenzie's music shows a similar integrity and strength of purpose even if its aims are not so high by critical standards. Certainly it does not suffer from the lapses of taste that disfigure all the other 'professional' music of late Victorian times, Sullivan's, Cowen's, Barnby's, Stainer's. It had, too, the bonhomie which was characteristic of the man and this gives to all his work a less exclusive appeal than that which emanated from the universities. Parry and Stanford achieved what they did for English music precisely because they were university men. A man like Hadow, to whom music was merely one of several intellectual interests, could feel at home with the trained minds of Parry and Stanford, but was ill at ease with the rank and file of English musicians and indeed was frankly contemptuous of the pretentions of a critic like Joseph Bennett to enlighten the public. The fact that music could now take its place beside literature, including the ancient classical literature of Greece and Rome, was pure gain to the art in this country. But this recognition, this rise in intellectual society, may well have led Hadow to rate the men who made the advance possible too high, judged by musical standards alone. Certainly there were plenty of people, Bernard Shaw among them, who did not see that this general culture made any actual improvement in the music turned out by minds so trained. To those outside university circles the music of Mackenzie seemed every bit as good as the new products of the university school and had the advantage of being free from any prejudice engendered by a superior general culture. Foreign executants like Richter and Joachim were of international stature and therefore overtopped the ordinary English professional, who consequently felt at a disadvantage with regard to visiting musicians and European composers.

Mackenzie describes the battles which he and all his contemporaries, of whatever persuasion, waged on behalf of English music and musicians. The fact that he had a continental training and was a pure professional was an advantage in the actual day-to-day conditions of the struggle for the right of English music to be heard. His personal connections with the giants of Europe, Liszt, Anton Rubienstein and Hans von Bülow, secured a measure of recognition for English music abroad. The continental training in fact showed both profits and losses in the struggle for the emergence of English music at home and recognition abroad. It was the final cause of the battle for English music, in which Mackenzie, Sullivan and Cowen no less than Parry and Stanford consciously and strenuously engaged, not being won, since the strategy was fundamentally unsound, but it was at the time the only possible tactic to try to transplant a European growth to English soil. Mackenzie himself was half aware of this and thought that an infusion of Scottish nationalism could provide the vitamin without which our native music would not grow. Nationalism was proving elsewhere in the music of Dvořák and Tchaikovsky that new shoots could grow on the old European stem. But here for some deeply obscure reason it was doomed to failure. Something more than melodic idiom is involved. Orthodox sonata form as employed by Brahms is not any too happily employed by Tchaikovsky—on the other hand Dvořák's quite extraordinary powers of assimilation were able to swallow negro melody and German thought processes in one gulp and show no sign of indigestion—but when used with unquestioning fidelity by Parry (in the *English Symphony*, for instance) the result is a hybrid and barren. Some of Mackenzie's best works, however, are "in the Doric" (his own description), and profit from his use of Scottish idioms just as Stanford's do from that of Irish.

Alexander Campbell Mackenzie (1847-1935) was the son of an Edinburgh musician of good repute, leader of the band at the Theatre Royal and himself the son and grandson of musicians. He was thus "born into two professions" and so took more naturally to opera than most British musicians. He went for training to Sondershausen in Germany at the age of ten. In 1862, at the age of fifteen, he returned to London and took engagements as an orchestral player and piano accompanist at the same time as he competed for and won a scholarship at the Royal Academy of

Music, to which twenty-six years later he was to return as Principal. When his training was completed he returned to Edinburgh and became a busy teacher, performer and organizer of the city's musical life, where he began to make contacts with the big international figures of music who came there on tour. Overstrain led him after a few years to make a complete break and go to live in Florence, which was his home for ten years until increasing calls for his services as a conductor in London brought him back to England. Most of his best work as a composer was done in this Florentine period, since from 1888 onwards his duties as Principal of the R.A.M. and his many activities as a conductor and a leading light in all the affairs of English music precluded him from whole-hearted absorption in the creation of music, as similar distractions had precluded Sterndale Bennett before him and were to preclude Parry at the Royal College a few years later. He was conductor of the Philharmonic Society from 1892 to 1899 and was in demand at the Crystal Palace, the Albert Hall and provincial festivals. His lectures and his chairmanship of the *Internationale Musik-Gesellschaft* have already been mentioned and testify to his versatility, to his busy professional life and to his importance in the musical life of his own generation. In 1922 the R.A.M. celebrated its centenary and two years later Mackenzie, now seventy-seven years old, made way for a younger man to deal with the new conditions, not to mention the revolutionary new music, brought about not merely by the passage of time but by the convulsions of a major war. Three features of his work at the R.A.M. require comment: he modernized the curriculum and improved the teaching, he saw the institution into a new and worthier habitation, and by a stroke of statesmanship he regularized relations with the new rival in South Kensington by proposing the joint examining body which came to be known as the Associated Board of the Royal Schools of Music, which had for its objects the raising of the standard of music teaching throughout the country and the diplomatic co-operation of the two bodies.

Of his compositions only the earlier works call for discussion, and on them it is impossible to disagree with Walker's verdict pronounced as long ago as 1907 which speaks of "highly modernized Mendelssohnianism", musicianly standards of workmanship but "lack of any particularly distinctive qualities of any kind". He is the representative of the transitional school who "recognizes the unworthiness of anything short of the highest ideal without, save sporadically, being able to make any notable personal contribution towards its attainment".

His violin concerto may be cited as an instance to which all these judgments may be applied. It was naturally welcomed in its day and was played by Sarasate to whom it is dedicated. It is good that every generation should cater for itself and not rely wholly on a diet of classics, but this concerto is not for posterity, it follows a tradition (of Mendelssohn) but leads to no envisaged goal of future development. A little more may be claimed for the *Scottish Concerto* for piano, though performances are not more frequent. But it was a right instinct on his part to look to nationalism to give his work distinction, and it was wisdom, justified in the event, to avoid the composition of symphonies and instead to write orchestral rhapsodies. The piano concerto bears the title Scottish and justifies it by the pervasive occurrence of the Scotch snap in all the chief themes of all movements and still more by the cut and feeling of the melody of the slow movement and the suggestion of pentatonism in the main theme of the finale. These are not mere external features of national melody any more than is the hint of a bagpipe's drone in the finale. The slow movement in particular is redolent of the tender Lowland melodies which fired Burns to the same kind of expression in his lyric poems. The first movement is somewhat conventional but is none the less quite effective and provides a basis for two following movements which are quite distinctive. The *Scottish Concerto* in fact is a work that should not have been allowed to die here at home.* The merits which found for it an executant in Paderewski and a publisher in Germany are sufficient to invest it with more than a period interest —the date was 1877, and it is one of the few things composed by Mackenzie after he had immersed himself in official routine that has the freshness of his earlier work.

Pibroch, a suite for violin and orchestra, written in the first year of Mackenzie's duties at the R.A.M., was taken round the world by Sarasate. As its title indicates it, too, has a nationalist flavour, but it is diluted in the virtuoso writing required by an

* It was played at the Promenade Concert of April 21, 1943.

international celebrity and is colourless compared with the piano concerto.

He wrote no symphony, as Cowen, Parry and Stanford all did, possibly because he sensed the inherent difficulty of reconciling nationalist elements with symphonic procedures. The way out of the dilemma presented by the fact that folk-tune into symphony won't go was to write rhapsodies, in which self-subsistent tunes are not subjected to intensive development to which they are recalcitrant, but strung together according to the original meaning of the Greek word "rhapsody", which is to stitch songs. Mackenzie wrote three *Scottish Rhapsodies* and used Scottish tunes in them. In the second Rhapsody, which he entitled *Burns*, he prefixes each section with the words of the songs he is going to employ. No. 3 is called *Tam o' Shanter*, and there are a number of other smaller orchestral works with a Scottish flavour and titles. But he had not sufficient intimacy of feeling for the tunes: he was indeed a nationalist manqué, since his idiom acquired abroad was cosmopolitan.

Beside his orchestral work Mackenzie's cantatas and operas, of which he wrote six, were important in their day, as indeed was a good deal of the incidental music to plays which he was particularly well qualified by the circumstances of his upbringing to provide. The doom of both classes of big vocal works is pronounced in a parenthesis of the composer's own penning—"I never had a complete libretto handed to me in my life". This indifference to literary requirements differentiated him from Parry and Stanford. This was in fact the point on which they took their stand. Many of Parry's libretti are not above criticism and his inability to write poetry that would match either his ideals or concomitant extracts from Scripture or the poets spoiled much of his later choral writing, but he broke away from hackwork once and for all; and Stanford went to Tennyson and Browning and the immortals for his texts. Mackenzie put up with journalism turned out as journalism is turned out by journalists, Hueffer of *The Times* and Bennett of *The Daily Telegraph*. Journalism, whatever its merits, is not suitable for musical setting, and in the case of *The Rose of Sharon*, Mackenzie's most successful oratorio, a cure had to be found in cuts, which as every journalist knows usually improve the "copy". In its revised form it is fairly compact, and its libretto, though put together by Bennett, is taken from the *Song of Songs* and other passages of Scripture to fill out a quasi-dramatic scheme (it is called a dramatic oratorio), in which the love of King Solomon and the Sulamite is set forth in oriental imagery. Mackenzie's music has great charm; it is sensuous but more chaste than the words; it flows easily with picturesque modulations and orchestral decorations. But its literary scheme does not provide it with backbone enough to survive the feeble convention of libretto writing in 1884, the date of its production at a Norwich Festival. The picturesque, as noted by Colles, is not enough. Much the same may be said of the operas as of the oratorios. *Colomba* (1883), which had a libretto by Hueffer based on Mérimée's novel, attempted a second span of life in a revised version twenty years later. Hueffer was responsible also for his second opera, *The Troubadour*, which was described by Hanslick as "one of the dullest and most disagreeable affairs I have ever encountered in the form of music in costume."* *The Cricket on the Hearth* (1902), never reached public performance. His last opera, *The Eve of St. John*, composed in 1919 and produced at Liverpool in 1924 by the British National Opera Company, was very thin gruel indeed.†

A better though less conscious nationalist than Mackenzie, yet still a nationalist manqué, was Hamish MacCunn (1868-1916) who attracted attention at the early age of 19 by a romantic overture, *Land of the Mountain and the Flood*, which for many years kept a place in the repertory. His opera *Jeanie Deans*,‡ founded on Sir Walter Scott's *The Heart of Midlothian*, is a romantic affair relying in a general way on Verdi as a model but lacking Verdi's force. Its melodies are only redeemed from the commonplace by a freshness which may ultimately have been derived from Scottish folk-song, for which there is some evidence in the form of dance tunes, suggestions of the bagpipe and an imitation ballad in the last act in which the flattened seventh is conspicuous.

* *Music Criticisms 1846-99* (Penguin Books, 1963), p. 258.

† I wrote *The Times* notice of it as one of my early assignments and treated it more brusquely than I should have done with more experience and regard for my seniors.

‡ Revived in Glasgow during the Festival of Britain in 1951 and also noticed by me. See *Musical Britain: 1951* (*The Times* and the Oxford University Press).

As the date was 1894 it had no connection with the discovery of neo-modalism by English composers—Scotland had discovered its folk-songs 150 years before—but it is a straw in the wind of incipient nationalism. It is hardly a folk opera like *The Bartered Bride* because it belongs to the grand tradition, but its Scottish theme, in which the bad and the good side of Knox's Calvinism are in conflict, brings in some reference to Scottish Psalmody and to the Border balladry already mentioned.

MacCunn was one of the Carl Rosa Opera Company's conductors and the opera's weaknesses are largely due to the fact that much of it is conductor's music. It did not lead to a Scottish national opera nor indeed to a Scottish national music because, as a later nationalist Scot, writing in *Grove*,* has said, he was "born out of time when Scotland could not sustain a native talent such as his" since "all his influences were basically Germanic".

Cowen was born in Jamaica, brought to England at the age of four, and soon showed signs of the musical prodigy both as a pianist and as a composer. He had his early training from English masters but in due course proceeded to Leipzig and Berlin. Returned to England he devoted a long life to varied professional activity, composing operas, oratorios, symphonies, concertos and a great many songs. His German training never completely overlaid his talent for the lighter, prettier things that were possible in the romantic idiom of his time, but his elegance is of the suburban kind. Even his songs, which avoided pretentiousness, have lapsed into oblivion. Not even the B.B.C. light music department uses his amiable orchestral pieces, which have a certain sweet poignancy, a deftness that light music must have and a daintiness that emerges at the smallest excuse even in a "grand" historical opera like *Harold*. Indeed this score shows almost at a glance how music that is essentially commonplace is commonplace and nothing more in the heavier passages of drama, but becomes distinctive as soon as the touch is lightened for the female characters to become lyrical. What he aimed at was to please, and in his symphonies, of which he wrote six, he reverts to a Haydnesque view of the symphony's function. The *Welsh Symphony*, for instance, is light in the hand, without Victorian seriousness and with a jolly scherzo, conventionally written but intended and able to carry a little

* 5th ed. (1954).

more weight than the entr'actes and things like *The Butterfly's Ball*. His music has this personal quality but no national character. It is no more Germanized than Sullivan's, yet it is even less English. The songs are English in that they mostly belong to the category of the drawing-room ballad, which had an enormous hold on the English public because they were easy to perform by amateurs and had a frankly sentimental appeal to audiences. Before 1880 distinctively English music, in church, theatre, home and hall, meant rather bad music. When it was not bad it was not distinctive nor distinguished.

This may be the place to say something about Ethel Smyth, although she set her sights higher and owing to the particular battle she fought and her survival into the middle of the next century she seems to belong to the next generation. What her career shows even more decisively than the men's is the effects of dependence on German training. It was only by insisting on going abroad that she was able to take up music seriously at all. Coming of a military family, where it was unheard of for a girl to adopt a profession, she had to fight for her emancipation. Thereafter she remained a fighter, to secure recognition as a woman composer, a composer, moreover, not of salon music like Mme. Chaminade, but of full-scale operas, cantatas and chamber music, to get her works performed, and to further the cause of women's suffrage. She generally got her way.

She went to the Leipzig Conservatorium in 1877 and was admitted to the Brahms circle through Elisabeth von Herzogenburg, with whom she lived and whose friendship forms the theme of the first of the autobiographical books by which she acquired literary in addition to musical fame, *Impressions that Remained*, that came out in two volumes in 1919. She had shown musical talent early enough to make her decide on a musical career at the age of twelve. Her first instruction was from the composer of the hymn-tune "Jerusalem the Golden", a Lt.-Colonel Ewing, whose wife laid the foundations of her literary prowess. By 1884 she had had a string quartet performed in Leipzig and was writing a good deal of chamber music in the idiom of German romanticism. A serenade for orchestra in four movements was played at the Crystal Palace in 1890. But chief of the first-fruits of her determination was her *Mass in D*, an oratorio setting on the most

C

ambitious scale, which, when it was revived thirty years after its first performance by the Royal Choral Society under Barnby, did not seem unduly derivative and demonstrated her command of large structure, masterly counterpoint and rich orchestration —nothing feminine about it, virile enough in all conscience. But the chamber music, revived after a longer interval, while revealing the promise it had shown at the time of its composition, struck a less individual note and exposed the friability of thematic material cut on the German pattern. Many years later when she was seventy-three she wrote another ambitious oratorio, *The Prison*, on a philosophical text by H. B. Brewster, who figures largely in her memoirs, which only served to show that intellectual and imaginative sincerity are not the same thing. The work no doubt expressed her creed but it carried no imaginative conviction. Furthermore it enforced a general point that political and literary distractions, however much they enrich an artist's life, are not conducive to fully saturated artistic creation.

Her greatest achievement was undoubtedly in opera, in itself a remarkable fact. The earlier operas she wrote to German libretti, mostly of her own composition. There are six altogether: the first, *Fantasio*, was produced at Weimar in 1898, the last, *Entente Cordiale*, to her own English text at Bristol (Napier Miles season) in 1925. This farce was preceded by *Fête Galante* (1923), a very different story, a tragi-comedy in which the composer exercises a delicacy of touch rare in her work; she calls it a dance-dream and has written a score that is capable of, and indeed demands, exquisite interpretation, such as it never had in English operatic conditions of the day. Her greatest achievement was the three-act *The Wreckers*, with a Cornish plot though given in German at Leipzig and Prague in 1906, subsequently revived by Beecham in 1909, at Covent Garden in 1910 and 1931 and at Sadler's Wells in 1939. Her one-act *Der Wald* had been produced at Dresden in 1901, Covent Garden in 1902 and 1903, and at the Metropolitan in New York in 1903. These facts speak for themselves and so remarkable an achievement would naturally at the time make any nationalist ideas look parochial. If on the other hand it struck an English musician as odd that these operas should have German titles and productions he might think the later ones, beginning with *The Boatswain's Mate* in 1916, when the wind had shifted away from the coasts of Germany, might well contribute to a national English opera. *The Boatswain's Mate*, however, though it is certainly viable as a good English comic opera, is marred by a mixture of styles. The first act is ballad opera with spoken dialogue and it even quotes folk-songs (though "Lord Rendal" is a solecism in its context), whereas the second act becomes more symphonic in the German manner, with continuous music. *Entente Cordiale* is not to be taken seriously, being little more than a charade.

She wrote as many songs with German as with English words. Her chief symphonic work was a double concerto for horn and violin. Among her vocal pieces was a *March of the Women* composed for militant suffragettes, which she herself once conducted with her toothbrush from the window of her cell in Holloway Prison. The criticism to be made in retrospect of this considerable output and achievement is, apart from insidious and unsuspected consequences of the German entanglement, that it needed concentration. Composition is really a whole-time job and fighting battles is a distraction. It is the distraction rather than the dissipation of energy which interferes with artistic creation, for Dame Ethel Smyth had abundant energy. Indeed the tale of her life-work is rounded off with a whole series of books, mostly autobiographical but quite first-rate in raciness, wit and pungency.

She thus stands to one side of the renaissance, or was perhaps one of its heralds, a portent of the more serious and more strenuous attitude to the art than the Victorians were willing to accord it. She was a real composer, and unlike Mackenzie's and Cowen's hers is a very curious and complex case-history. For she was not only a musician but one of the race of English eccentrics. In her eighty-six years she enriched English musical life when- and wherever she impinged on it, even tying Beecham to her chariot, and if as a composer she was born a generation too soon, as an artist she made history in bridging the centuries.

IV

The Folk Music Revival

THE TWO influences which directed the revival of English music into channels comparable to the various nationalist movements in Europe, the recovery of English folk-song and renewed interest in Tudor counterpoint, were roughly contemporary in origin, *circa* 1840; they converged at the beginning of the twentieth century to make the break with German and Italian supremacy decisive. To us looking back on these two nationalistic movements it seems obvious that no healthy native growth could be expected on the lines along which the elder generation of English musicians was working. Parry and Stanford with their German training hoped to grow an English tree by planting German cuttings in English soil. An older generation still, Sterndale Bennett, Macfarren and Balfe, had hardly thought in terms of nationality at all. Theirs was indeed an international outlook. Modern music to them was all one, and it was like Mendelssohn—the full force of Wagner's impact on European music was still a few years ahead. The only recognizable distinctions along national lines were the bias of Italy towards opera, of Germany towards instrumental sonata, of England by long-established tradition towards choral music. English composers were content to follow foreign models when they wrote anything but cantatas. Mendelssohn even provided them with a pattern for oratorios. He was their example in all forms of instrumental music from salon music to orchestral overtures. In opera the Italian models, heard at the Royal Italian Opera, Her Majesty's Theatre or Drury Lane and chronicled by H. F. Chorley, upheld the ideals of tunefulness which Signor Verdi's "violence" did not seriously alter. In the late eighteen-fifties Bellini and Donizetti were still regularly heard, and their general texture and temper is not unlike Mendelssohn's. Sullivan has a French streak in his melodies but his harmony is blamelessly cosmopolitan even if it is sometimes culpably banal.

On the continent of Europe itself, however, the various nationalist movements, which are sometimes regarded as an offshoot of the general romantic movement that swept the continent at the beginning of the nineteenth century, but which more probably have a political origin, were stirring in all the countries of the fringe. Germany, Italy and France culturally hang together in spite of the wide stylistic and temperamental differences between them. But their tyranny in music, a tyranny of melodic and harmonic language based on key and a tyranny of structure and design as evolved in sonata form, was provoking revolt in Russia, in Scandinavia, in Hungary, in Bohemia, in Spain and finally in England. The fact that the tyranny was beneficial—for surely no more fruitful principle than that of sonata form has ever been discovered by the human mind—may have delayed rebellion, as it did in Russia, where Glinka's music, which raised the standard of revolt, still sounds extraordinarily Italianate. It certainly did in England where Parry and Stanford consciously adopted German models as the best available, and Elgar, for all his greater eclecticism, remained as far as vocabulary and ideals were concerned cosmopolitan rather than national, at any rate as musician though certainly not as man, where the exact opposite is nearer the truth.

Dvořák and Tchaikovsky represent a somewhat similar compromise between nationalist sentiment, native language and German modes of thought. They wrote symphonies with thematic material that could never have come out of a German head, but they treated it in the symphonic manner evolved by the Viennese school. For all the Italian elements in symphonic style as evolved from Emanuel and Christian Bach through Haydn, Mozart, Beethoven and Brahms, elements that are accounted for geographically by the position of Vienna as the great cross-roads of Europe, the sonata and the symphony are essentially German (or Austrian) modes of thought, German in their method, and German in their logic. This is not to deny the universal validity of the great aesthetic principles involved in tripartite structure, the cardinal importance of key, or the general utility of the technique of "development", but it is to say that there are more ways than one of handling musical material and pursuing lines of musical thought, though owing to the enormous success of sonata form and its resultant prestige it took some little time for the small powers of Europe's music to realize the need to reduce their dependence on the great supra-national block based on Rome, Vienna and Paris.

The most obvious, as it was the most powerful, weapon in the struggle for independence was each country's rediscovery of its own native music, especially the folk-music with its almost biological appeal. Politics might lend urgency to this blood-appeal, as it certainly did in the case of Bohemia, where political discontent with Austrian dominance raised a battle over language, which includes a newspaper press in the vernacular, over education which means control of the schools, and over the theatre, which provides an outlet and expression for the imagination of a people. Smetana who led this nationalist movement did not imagine that the quotation and the imitation of folk-tunes was in itself a sufficient basis for the establishment of a new and independent musical culture, but he did see that in culture as in politics the old overriding unity of Christendom had yielded to the need for developing the latent differences between European peoples, differences that depended on blood, climate, language, tradition and social organization. For good and evil, consciousness of nationality became the dominant factor in European public life in the nineteenth century, and music was not to escape its influence.

With the possible exception of the economic machine, nationalism—which may be defined as awareness of nationality, a certain self-consciousness and an unwillingness to take one's nationality for granted—was the greatest single force in public life until it was superseded by ideology. In our recent experience during the present century it has been largely responsible for the colossal evils of two great wars, for a morbid condition of social life as in Germany, and for all sorts of minor follies such as are brought home to one every time one crosses a frontier in a trans-continental train. It is in fact nowadays predominantly a disruptive force. But it is not necessarily so. The ancient Greeks, for instance, would have preserved their civilization for a longer period if their national consciousness had been more highly developed. They had national feeling, since they differentiated themselves as "Hellenes" from all "barbarians", and they combined to fight the Persians from Asia, but the common bond was not sufficiently powerful in their minds to prevent them flying at each others' throats in petty factious warfare and ruining the loose federation that was their equivalent for a nation state. Furthermore, nationalism is not all evil, even in fostering a narrow patriotism, if that patriotism conserves national traditions, for it enriches the European body politic with variety. "It is better for us all to be different and friendly than all alike and at rivalry and enmity", as someone has well said. Even in the troubled years between the wars one only needed to have attended some of the international festivals of the arts to see how rich is European culture in the variety of its traditions. The International Folk Dance Festival held in London in 1935 showed the dazzling variety not only of dances, but of music, of costume, of rites, of sense of colour and, *pace* Sir Julian Huxley and the late Professor Haddon,* of racial type.

In an exchange of commodities both parties to a commercial deal may profit to the extent that each will get something he ardently wants by giving away something which he wants less. But in the things of the mind an exchange can be made which enriches all parties to it without cost of any impoverishment, for what you give away you also keep. In exchanging cultures all Europe is enriched. The corollary of nationalism is international-ism, its antithesis is cosmopolitanism. European music has been vastly enriched by the fissiparous growth of national traditions. From every quarter of Europe the nations have come bringing their distinctive songs, their melodic idioms, their individual ways of thinking in music, their national, and indeed their racial rhythms, and so have enlarged that already great central pool of Western music.

Non-European music is another story, for the break-up of the European language of music into dialects has not weakened its consanguinity as compared with Oriental and outlandish musics. Cosmopolitanism within the European tradition, once so fruitful, is now barren. There are a few outstanding figures, of which Liszt is the chief, whose music may be judged to be more European than national—and Liszt resumed his nationalism in the *Hungarian Rhapsodies*—but in the main exile from his native land dries up

* In *We Europeans* (Cape, 1935).

the inspiration of a composer—he has no roots, and without roots he produces sapless stuff.

Stravinsky was for some years a victim of deracination, but Busoni is perhaps an even better example. Busoni had one of the greatest musical minds that ever was, but it was sterilized by a cosmopolitan way of life; always a wanderer in exile, mostly in trains and hotels, uncertain whether he was Italian or German, he led a life whose triumphs constituted a tragedy, as can be read between the lines of Edward Dent's sympathetic biography. His music has every quality—interest, skill, euphony—but vitality, and it has not vitality because its creator grew no roots. Consider also the poverty of the mannered, tasteless music that was written in Paris, mostly by *émigrés*, in the nineteen-twenties and compare it with the abundance of the nationalist music of the preceding generation: the Russian Big Five, the Bohemian Smetana, the Spanish Albeniz, Granados and Falla, and in France Debussy and Ravel who broke away from the cosmopolitan style of Franck and Saint-Saëns. Nationalism is at any rate justified of her musical children in productivity and in vitality.

In England, however, there was no political motive to drive musicians on to nationalist courses. Here, indeed, faith in the great central tradition of European music was not questioned in the early days of the national resurgence of our music; conscious nationalism did not raise its head until Vaughan Williams wrote his celebrated article in 1912, "Who wants the English composer?"*

Stanford deliberately wrote an Irish-flavoured opera in *Shamus O'Brien* as long before that as 1897, and wrote Irish Rhapsodies like other continental composers who made these concessions to the claims of local dialects; he wrote Anglo-Irish songs;† like Bernard Shaw he was born in Dublin and retained through life many Irish traits of mind. But he was not concerned to found an Irish school of musical composition. On the contrary he did hope to be the fountain-head of an English school. Possibly the raging politics of the "Irish Question" played some part, if a negative

---

* *R.C.M. Magazine*, Vol. IX, No. 1. Reprinted in *Ralph Vaughan Williams* by Hubert Foss (Harrap, 1950).

† i.e. songs in the English not the Gaelic language by Irish-born poets and reflecting Irish scenes or characters.

one, in that so far from being a Nationalist he was an Orange-man.

The paradox of an Irish patriotism that cherished its own folk-music, its own brogue and Irish use of the English language but yet aspired to enrich the English heritage of music, as Shaw did of letters, is one that was not found on the continent. There alien domination was the motive power of nationalist art. In Russia the domination was not political but cultural, chiefly Italian and French; in Bohemia it was political; in Spain it was the dead weight of inertia induced by three centuries of political coma. In each case the reaction was a strong uprising of nationalist feeling and the use of folk-art as a national rallying point for it.

In England the new interest in folk-song was of long incubation, only mildly tinged with nationalism. On the whole it was probably a part of the wider movement for a more intense and worthier musical life. The imitation of Mendelssohn-cum-Handel was an inferior counterpart to the energies in other spheres of a vigorous and wealthy people. The wealth was probably partly responsible for the weakness. England's Free Trade principles encouraged the purchase and import from abroad of the very best, whether it was wine, Paris models or music, and this quite healthy practice, which gradually made London a great clearing-house for the world's music, only had morbid results because it was not accompanied then, as it is now, by vigorous native creation. Official and wealthy musical England was aware of Purcell and even of Byrd, though Burney's views still interposed a screen between their real value and their Victorian estimation, but it was totally ignorant of its great stream of popular melody, still flowing by several traditions and still alive. Its rediscovery coincides with the renaissance of which it was a part. Parry and Stanford were both interested in it and Stanford took an active part in the folk-song movement by his editing of Petrie's collection of Irish airs. But neither were collectors, field-workers as it were, and neither formed his style on the newly recovered national music. That was left for the next generation. The renaissance was accompanied by a revival of folk-music and it was consolidated in its independence by the results of the revival, but it did not owe its start, as in continental countries, to the music of the people.

Folk-music is the music created by the common people, and in

practice this means by peasants not by townsmen. Popular music
is music addressed to the people and this generally is a town
product addressed to urban people. There is thus a wide difference
between them; folk-music grows, popular music is composed.
But the history of the carol shows that the two kinds of plebeian
music are in contact with each other. Carols were written mainly
in the late Middle Ages by clerical authors who wanted to preach
the Glad Tidings to the common people, such as knew no more
Latin than a few tags like *Gloria in excelsis*. To ensure popular
adoption they included elements drawn from common speech,
common experience, and common knowledge. Individual and
communal authorship were thus mingled. Such a carol as the now
universally known "The Holly and the Ivy", a true folk carol, still
shows half a dozen different strains. Its doctrinal teaching is
plainly clerical in origin, its refrain of jumbled images:

> The rising of the sun,
> The running of the deer,
> The playing of the merry organ,
> Sweet singing in the choir.

is witness to its origin in the round dance (a carol is by definition
a dance-song); its tune has been handed down not only in print,
but by an independent oral tradition which was picked up by
Cecil Sharp in Gloucestershire nearly two hundred years after it
was printed on a broadside.

But though the traditions are mixed—the professionals have
had a hand in many a traditional ballad—the distinction is quite
clear, and can be even more clearly discerned in the tunes than in
the poems of traditional songs and ballads. After all the scholarly
warfare of the last century on the origins of this traditional and
anonymous art—fought mainly by literary men and philologists
—it has become clear that folk-song owes its distinctive character
to its communal and not to its individual element. It is no longer
claimed that "das Volk dichtet". Committees cannot write letters,
still less could they compose lyrical ballads. "First of all one man
sings a song, and then others sing it after him, changing what they
do not like" (or do not remember, which comes to much the same
thing). This was the formula for explaining the origin of folk-
song which Cecil Sharp, with his immense first-hand experience

of the material, took over from Böhme and adopted as the explanation of the problem of origins, and he adds: "The solution of the mystery of the origin of the folk-song is not to be found by seeking an original—that is a vain quest—but by examining the method by which it has been preserved and handed down from one generation to another. In other words, the method of oral transmission is not merely one by which the folk-song lives; it is a process by which it grows and by which it is created."

This does not contain the whole of the matter, since carols, as already indicated, show how a more professional element is often gathered up in the communal process, and the folk-songs of the Celtic peoples in this country show a similar professional influence of bards and harpers; experience of American negroes also shows that something not far from spontaneous communal composition is possible, given the currency of certain stock phrases and a certain emotional temperature to provide the flash point at which the diverse elements will fuse into a new folk-song. But Sharp's theory is basically sound and contains the root of the matter in it. The distinctive character of folk-song, which is so marked that those who deal in it soon learn to recognize the genuine article almost by the smell, arises from its continuous evolution by oral tradition as it passes from the lips of one singer to the ear of another and so on to his lips and thence down the generations without ever a note of it or a line of verse being put to paper. The song, then, is actually fashioned by its oral transmission ; by passage through many minds whatever of individuality it once had is transformed into a communal product. And it is this representative quality, so acquired, winning the assent of unnumbered singers, who may each reject it in whole or in part or in detail but who in fact love it enough to transmit it, that gives to the folk-song its national character. And because no song has a chance of survival which does not bear repetition by generations of singers and which does not conform in the last resort to national taste and character, the folk-singer is in the happy position of being able to declare that his best is also his most typical. It was, however, the quality of the tunes, not their national character, which first caught the attention of the early collectors in England. It is worth observing that Scotland and Ireland had both found collectors of their traditional music a round century before England began in earnest to preserve what it was in danger of losing through the spread of industrial civilization, a soil in which for some reason the plant seems not to thrive.* England's delay was in the event more gain than loss, since the ethics of collecting, editing, and preserving were not realized all at once and some considerable outrages were perpetrated by Scottish and Irish editors.

In the early part of the eighteenth century polite society in Edinburgh began to take an interest in Scottish vernacular poetry, both lyrics and ballads. Perhaps there was some politcal impetus behind the fashion, since nationalist feeling was banking up behind the exile of the House of Stuart. The movement was primarily a literary one, just as the interest in the great ballads from Bishop Percy to Professor Child was literary, so that it is only in the present century that it has been possible to impress upon editors not only that the tune is as important as the words but also that the two are integrally united, even if they occasionally become unstuck. All the early battles over the question of origins were fought out with purely literary weapons and without the information that folk-music could have contributed to the issue. It was common form to print the texts without the tunes—it is still done sometimes in America, though the general principle that it is unscholarly to divorce words and music is in a fair way to acceptance. Scottish editors and collectors, however, erred in the other direction and their ordinary procedure was to keep the tunes but to write new verses to them. Burns wrote many of his short poems to pre-existing tunes.

The history of the collection of Irish folk-tunes follows similar lines and editorial scrupulousness was not achieved till the experience of English collectors had been thoroughly assimilated. Even Stanford's treatment of the Petrie collection was criticized as not altogether blameless, but Herbert Hughes who, unlike Stanford, was a collector, at last brought modern standards of editorial ethics to bear on Irish folk song. Thomas Moore, whose

* There was an urban upsurge of interest in the nineteen-fifties which was stimulated by the skiffle craze, in which new songs on topical subjects were made up in the folk style and these folk-songs were sung by parties of young people in public houses, at social and political gatherings. Skiffle was an attempt to make music in the simplest possible way by and for people with the most rudimentary skill.

Irish Melodies popularized the Irish songs throughout the British Isles, was shameless about what he called "very admissible liberties" and, unlike Burns, he disregarded the character of the original verses which he replaced with more sentimental ones of his own. He shared the general delusion that there were no English folk-songs, for he wrote in his introduction to *A Selection of Popular National Airs* (1818): "It is Cicero, I believe, who says *natura ad modos ducimur* (we are led to harmony by nature), and the abundance of wild, indigenous airs, which almost every country except England possesses, sufficiently proves the truth of his assertion."

The classical statement of this belief was made by Carl Engel only to question it. He was a German who had settled in South Kensington and was interested in antiquities, notably instruments, from which the step to folk-lore was direct. Writing in 1866 in *The Study of National Music* and finding himself thwarted in his comparative studies by the lack of English national tunes, he said:

"Although the rural population of England appear to sing less than those of most other European countries, it may nevertheless be supposed that they also, especially in districts somewhat remote from any large towns, must still preserve songs and dance tunes of their own, inherited from their forefathers."*

In point of fact the search had already begun. In 1843 the Rev. John Broadwood (1798-1864), squire of Lyne in Sussex, published privately a small collection of sixteen songs sung traditionally at Harvest Homes and other rural festivals by the villagers near his home in Surrey and Sussex. The title page is explicit that the "Airs are set to music exactly as they are now sung" and it is related in the Broadwood family that he had an accurate ear, and when a local organist disputed some of the inflexions, he insisted on preserving the fluctuating thirds and sevenths, reinforcing his argument by blasts on a flute which he played. "Musically it may be wrong," he said to the Worthing organist who harmonized them, "but I will have it exactly as my singers sang it." Here, then, emerges the true scientific approach of folk-song for which the Scottish and Irish collectors of the previous century had no respect.

* p. 173.

From him his niece Lucy took up the task, republishing his little book with some additions in 1889 and combining with J. A. Fuller-Maitland to bring out in 1893, just fifty years after her uncle's book, their *English County Songs*, which is a landmark in the folk-song revival. Another pioneer was Sabine Baring-Gould (1834-1924), another parson-squire, of Lew Trenchard in Devonshire, who is more widely known as a hymnologist, author and composer of "Now the day is over" and author of "Onward Christian soldiers". He was induced by a chance remark at a dinner table to start collecting the folk-songs of Devon and Cornwall. In his collection appeared "The Evening Prayer" or "The White Paternoster". The modal flavour (Phrygian in this instance) was the feature in the rediscovered folk-song that most strongly impressed the collectors and the musicians to whom they showed them.

In the north of England there had been an independent movement towards the preservation of folk-music. Thus in Newcastle as long ago as 1805 a firm of publishers brought out a volume of tunes used by the players of the Northumbrian small-pipe, a form of bagpipe blown by an under-arm bellows with three drones and a chanter. Fifty years later the Society of Antiquaries of Newcastle upon Tyne undertook the collection of the ancient melodies of Northumberland, and in 1882 after thirty years' delay a book containing ballad airs as well as pipe tunes was published under the editorship of John Stokoe. W. G. Whittaker's modern edition of *North Countrie Ballads, Songs and Pipe Tunes* (1921) was based mainly on Stokoe. The importance of this collection, which is sometimes forgotten because characteristically the northerners worked independently of the movement in the south, is that here there is a true regional music. English folk-song is much less regional than the early collectors thought—the grouping of the songs by separate counties in *English County Songs* has no real scientific or musical significance—and most songs have a general currency, spreading across the border and across the Irish sea. The Northumbrian collection contains ballads which are also found over the border, e.g. "The Twa Sisters o' Binnorie" and such a universal English song as "The Oak and the Ash", but many of its songs are quite distinct, and the pipe tunes naturally preserve a traditional melody that is not found elsewhere because the small-pipes are not found elsewhere either in England or Scotland. The two categories can be illustrated in a single song. "Elsie Marley" is obviously a pipe tune in origin—Mixolydian with no sixth—but it has been turned into a song with a characteristic Northumbrian turn of dialect and sentiment.

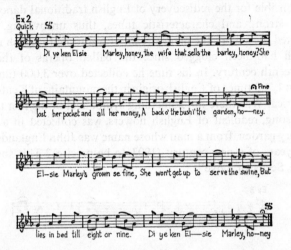

Ex 2
Quick

Di ye ken Elsie Marley, honey, the wife that sells the barley, honey? She lost her pocket and all her money, A back o' the bush i' the garden, ho—ney. Elsie Marley's grown se fine, She won't get up to serve the swine, But lies in bed till eight or nine. Di ye ken El—sie Marley, ho—ney.

And so then at the end of the century it was at last discovered that England after all had its folk-songs. The work of individual pioneers in the field of collection became ripe during the nineties for co-ordination, and in 1898 the Folk Song Society was founded in London with "the collection and preservation of folk-songs, ballads and tunes, and the publication of such of these as may be deemed advisable" as its primary object. Official English music set the seal of its approval upon the work from the beginning: Stainer, Stanford, Mackenzie and Parry became vice-presidents and took an active part in the society's early meetings. Among the first members it is interesting to note the names of the singers, David Bispham, Plunket Greene and Helen Trust; the working musicians Frederick Corder, Spencer Curwen and Percy Pitt; the newspaper critics Alfred Kalisch, J. A. Fuller-Maitland and F. Gilbert Webb; the literary men W. H. Hadow and A. P. Graves; and the composer Edward Elgar. Lucy Broadwood and Frank Kidson, the Leeds antiquary, were also among the original one hundred and ten members. In 1904 Vaughan Williams and Cecil Sharp joined the committee and pressed a more active missionary policy upon what was essentially a learned society.

Sharp was not the first nor the last nor the only collector of folk-songs, but his name has been identified in the mind of the general public with folk-song and its revival, and rightly. He also was responsible for the rediscovery of English traditional dances with their strong and characteristic tunes, thus uncovering by his devoted life's work the main stream of traditional English melody which had been clogged since the ballad operas of the early eighteenth century. In his time he collected over 3,000 tunes and about 1,700 tunes of English origin in the mountains of Kentucky in America. Was there not something symbolical in the fact that his first song, redolent of English flowers, was collected in a village rectory garden, from a man whose name was John England, in the first years of a new century (1903 to be precise)? This song was "The Seeds of Love".

Ex 3

I sowed the seeds of love, I sowed them in the spring, I gathered them up in the morning so soon, while small birds did sweetly sing, While small birds did sweetly sing.

Among the other collectors were Anne Gilchrist of Lancaster, H. E. D. Hammond in Dorset, G. B. Gardiner in Hampshire, George Butterworth, who began collecting in Sussex and developed as a composer on nationalist lines, Clive Carey, a singer, E. J. Moeran, specializing in East Anglia, and Maud Karpeles, Sharp's literary executor. Vaughan Williams stands out historically, because when in 1903 he went to East Anglia, he found there not only a small treasure of folk-songs but also the musical idiom which he had sought as the foundation for his personal style at the Royal College of Music, at Cambridge and in Berlin, but in vain. *In the Fen Country* and three

Norfolk Rhapsodies were the immediate outcome of his field work.

One other name remains to be mentioned, William Chappell (1809-1888), who bridged this mysterious gulf between the folk-song of the Elizabethan period, which we know from Shakespeare, from Ravenscroft and from *The Fitzwilliam Virginal Book*, and the modern rediscovery. He did not believe in the oral tradition—regarding it as corrupt and unreliable—and he approached the task of gathering together "the popular music of the olden time" in an antiquarian frame of mind. But he systematically ransacked the libraries, collected literary allusions to music and gleaned from the great collections of broadside ballads. He published his *National English Airs* in 1840 and the bigger collection *Popular Music of the Olden Time* in 1859. He was a contemporary of John Broadwood, was possessed of the same spirit of search for authentic English melody and so helps to fix the beginning of the folk-song revival in the forties of the last century.

There was another revival of traditional melody proceeding simultaneously and producing the unmathematical phenomenon of two parallel lines which met. This was of the carol, which was fostered by the Oxford Movement and ultimately joined the folk-song revival, in that folk-carols were discovered and were presented to the world by Vaughan Williams in his *Fantasia on Christmas Carols* (1912). The carol is by definition a seasonal song with a burden which was derived from the dance. It flourished in the late middle ages along with the mystery play—the Coventry Carol is representative of the way in which an originally pagan and secular song was christianized and attached to the Nativity. The Christmas carol therefore had a clerical element in its origin and was transmitted in manuscript and print as well as by oral tradition. Early in the nineteenth century it was in decline or tending to go underground as the folk-songs did, and conscious attempts to preserve it were made by two antiquarians, Davies Gilbert and William Sandys, who published in 1822 and 1833 respectively two small collections containing those carols best known in Victorian times, such as "God rest you merry", "The First Nowell" and "The Cherry Tree Carol". But the Christmas spirit as revealed in Dickens's short novel, *A Christmas Carol*, consisted of heavy eating and general benevolence—the only actual carol mentioned being "God rest you merry" piped through Scrooge's keyhole. The next collection to be published marked the change of attitude which gradually brought back the more religious aspect of the festival, its mysticism and the tenderness of the mediaeval lullabies. This was *Carols for Christmastide*, published in 1853 by the Rev. T. Helmore and the Rev. J. M. Neale, both high-churchmen. They had been given a copy of *Piae Cantiones*, printed in Finland in 1582, which had been brought from Stockholm by Her Majesty's Envoy to that capital and from which the tunes of "Good King Wenceslas" and "Good Christian men rejoice" (*In dulci jubilo*) were taken. The Oxford Movement encouraged the practice of singing carols in church rather than leaving them to street performance, and to meet the growing taste for this ancient music Bramley and Stainer published their famous collection, *Christmas Carols, New and Old*, in 1865, which restored to currency a number of traditional carols. In 1900 *The Cowley Carol Book* proceeded farther in the same direction and added still more carols from abroad. Other tributaries that swelled the now vigorous carol tradition were the discovery by the folk-song collectors of ballads of the Nativity and mummers' carols (e.g. "O mortal man remember well"), pagan wassail songs and a true folk-carol like "The Holly and the Ivy".* The macaronic carol, in which Latin and the vernacular alternate (e.g. *In dulci jubilo*), French noëls (e.g. *Quittez pasteurs*), Christmas hymns (e.g. *Adeste fideles*), German lullabies (e.g. *Joseph lieber, Joseph mein*) were further additions to carol literature, for which a largely agnostic twentieth century has shown an insatiable appetite. Musically the carol, now largely confined to Christmas, has united scholars, ecclesiastics, musicians and the great public, including the unmusical, into a fellowship unparalleled in the realm of music. By 1930 the new liturgy of Nine Lessons and Nine Carols, devised by Archbishop Benson after ancient precedent when he was Bishop of Truro as far back as 1880, and adopted by King's College, Cambridge, for Christmas Eve, had become a national institution, to which millions attend through its broadcast by radio.

Though terminologically carols should more properly be called

* See p. 74.

popular than folk, both folk-song and carols can rightly be called traditional and their revivals have coalesced.

What then has this revival of traditional melody achieved? Apart from the corpus of folk-song itself, which provides us with constant delight, it has had two important consequences. Whether its direct influence on composition has been as great as was originally expected in view of the comparable experience of nationalism in Europe may be debated. But certainly it has produced one great composer in Vaughan Williams, although the youngest generation does not pay much heed to folk-song. In one respect it has brought forth good fruit: the best English songs written since the beginning of the century, including Stanford's but excluding Parry's, have come from those who have at one time or another nourished themselves on folk-song. Holst, though less indebted than Vaughan Williams to folk-song, was in direct contact with it. Patrick Hadley and Gerald Finzi, whose settings of Hardy and the metaphysical poets are achievements of the highest distinction, both found a valuable part of their education in folk-song. Rubbra and Moeran, who have written symphonic works out of musical experience which included the assimilation of folk-song (though still more perhaps of Elizabethan music) are both good song writers. John Ireland, who was certainly a song writer, was not directly influenced by folk-song, but the modal quality of his writing, both melodic and harmonic, is the outcome of the folk-song and Tudor revivals. Elgar, Walton and Lambert, who followed a more cosmopolitan tradition, are not natural song writers. In opera we have an English *Bartered Bride* in *Hugh the Drover*, but Britten's flirtations with folk-song—they are not more than flirtations—can hardly be said to have influenced *Peter Grimes* or *Lucretia*, and only a very little more perhaps *Let's Make an Opera*. Direct accessions to the orchestral repertory have not been large. Stanford wrote Irish Rhapsodies; Vaughan Williams's several fantasias and such smaller works as *The Running Set* and *Five Variants on Dives and Lazarus* use folk-tunes and folk idioms. Delius's *Brigg Fair* owes nothing to folk-song but the tune, but Butterworth's *A Shropshire Lad Rhapsody* and *The Banks of Green Willow* are among the first fruits of the nationalist movement based on folk-song. Moeran is probably the most considerable of our nationalist composers after Vaughan

Williams, and folk-song is all-pervasive in his output from the string trio to the *Sinfonietta* and the cello concerto. But what has not happened, which might have been expected to happen in the light of continental experience, has been the formation of a national school. It would seem as though the assertion of national independence from too strong continental influences was so successfully made by Vaughan Williams and Holst that there was no further need for conscious nationalism—and nationalism as a political force is in decline in the twentieth century. When Walton and Rawsthorne began to write after the First World War the independence of English music could be taken for granted and needed no brandishing of folk-song or reliance on a diet of English history to give it confidence.

This brings us to the second consequence which is less immediate and more pervasive than the enlargement of our repertory with nationally tinged compositions, but is of considerable importance. This is the technical development aptly called by Sir George Dyson neo-modality, which has emancipated English music not only from Germany but also from the nineteenth century and the over-ripe romanticism which persisted in some parts of Europe up to the Second World War. The significance and possibilities of neo-modality can be summarily envisaged in Vaughan Williams's *G Minor Mass*. It has been pervasive in post-war English music.

V

The Tudor Revival

LIKE THE folk-song revival the re-awakening of interest in the
English music of the Tudor and early Stuart periods began a
century and a quarter ago. In 1840 the Musical Antiquarian
Society was founded and during the course of its seven years of
useful life it published nineteen volumes.

Publication is the test of renewed life in the music of the past,
since the more obvious test of performance is in the last resort
dependent on the accessibility of a reliable text. An apparent
exception to publication as the criterion of true revival is offered
by Arnold Dolmetsch and the tradition which he founded. His
practice was to build the old instruments, teach their use and then
provide in manuscript the music for them to play. This is indeed
revival and proves that a pioneer does not need the printing press.
But it remains a fact that the movement for performing old music
in the old way cannot spread far nor exert much influence on the
general musical life of the country unless players and singers can
get easy access to their repertory. The popularity of the song
"Have you seen but a white lily grow?", which Dolmetsch made
generally known by including it in his little book of *Selected
English Songs and Dialogues of the XVI and XVII Centuries*,
proves the rule and tests the exception—for publication of
virginal music, viol music and music for recorders has been gradually following in the wake of the revival of performance to which
he devoted his life. The validity of the publication test is confirmed
by the experience of E. H. Fellowes, who did more than any other
single person to revivify Tudor music, for his main work was to
provide texts of the music and get them published, to which his
books, valuable as they are, and his other activities subsequently
to be described, were but subsidiary parerga.

Publication by itself will not ensure performance and without performance the music is as dead between a modern pair of covers as between an ancient pair. The case of Purcell is sometimes cited as an example of a failure to regain currency among musicians and their public in spite of the publishing activities of the Purcell Society, which only issued a library edition and gave up all plans to organize performances quite early in its career. Purcell, however, has in fact had a very considerable revival—largely instigated from Cambridge—and there is no dearth of cheap performing editions. Publication should therefore be of two sorts—library editions generally issued by subscription or subvention, and performing editions to attract a wide sale at a cheap price. The Musical Antiquarian Society's nineteen volumes, like the later publications of the Purcell Society, were large folios printed for the members of the Society who subscribed a pound a year and obtained the music at cost price. Sixteen corresponding volumes in compressed score edited by Sir George Macfarren were not official publications of the Society but were undertaken by the publisher, William Chappell, on his own responsibility in order to try to increase the subscription list. Both types of edition are in fact necessary to any complete revival.

William Chappell, whom we have already* encountered as an early pioneer of folk and popular music, was the moving spirit behind the Musical Antiquarian Society. This remarkable man has had less than his due from our historians. His name does not occur in the indices of the *Oxford History* or of Dr. Walker's *A History of Music in England*.† He was not a composer and his work was done, as we can now see, largely below ground—at the foundations of the revival that was to come. But when Wooldridge issued his revision of Chappell's *Old English Popular Music* he ought to have included a biographical note about him.

He was the eldest son of the founder of the firm of Chappell and Co., publishers, concert agents and promoters, and piano manufacturers. He was born in 1809 and died in 1888. He was your true antiquarian, assiduous in the search for dates and facts, a respecter of documentary evidence and an enthusiast for things past because they were past, though not altogether without

---

* See p. 81.

† Nor in the edition revised by Westrup, who refers to his *Popular Music of the Olden Time* as Wooldridge's, who revised it in 1893.

critical appreciation. His interests extended beyond music to ballad literature and he acted both as treasurer and editor for the Ballad Society, for which he edited three volumes of the *Roxburghe Ballads*. He was also a member of the Camden Society and a Fellow of the Society of Antiquaries. He was an original member of the Musical Association and one of its early Vice-Presidents. To it he read a paper on music as a science of numbers and discoursed on "Sumer is icumen in", to which he had devoted considerable first-hand study. He is enthusiastic about the song's artistic merits but is apologetic about its nonconformity with the accepted rules of counterpoint and of his own day. This kind of limitation of vision invalidated (to our later minds) much of the work done by the Musical Antiquarian Society, and in the editing of the madrigals their characteristic features of rhythm and part-writing were ironed out to conform more nearly with the Mendelssohnian ideals then prevailing. For Chappell's fidelity to his text, which in itself prevented him from adopting what is now regarded as the correct attitude towards orally transmitted folk-song, did not suffice to reproduce the lute part of the songs of Dowland which he edited for the Musical Antiquarian Society—he was content to print the four-part vocal version without reference to the lute tablature to which in the original edition the lower voice parts are always an *ad libitum* addition. He regarded unwritten songs as "corrupt versions of printed copies", as indeed they sometimes are, though it was disregard of this view which uncovered the wealth of English folk-song whose existence was denied.

Chappell, then, according to his lights assisted at the birth of these two quite different movements, and if his interest in traditional melody was more from the national than the folkloristic angle it may be accounted for by a piece of fortuitous prejudice, just as his enthusiasm for the Tudor masters was kindled by his antipathy for Burney. Burney had committed what was in his eyes the greatest of all the sins of scholarship—he had neglected to verify his references and made matters worse by misquotation. "There is nothing of the kind in the books Dr. Burney pretends to quote" he says of one misrepresentation. For Burney's opinion therefore he entertained no respect; he saw in him a readable author with a lively style who had only one enthusiasm, Italian music, especially Italian opera, and he did not err in rejecting Burney's estimate of Elizabethan music. What was bad enough for Burney's disparagement was good enough for Chappell to take up and the Musical Antiquarian Society to publish. There were backsliders, however, among these nineteenth-century Antiquarians. Horsley, a decent musician who took a prominent part in English music in early Victorian days, found things in Byrd which shocked him, and he explains his surprise in the Preface to the *Cantiones Sacrae*, which he edited for the Musical Antiquarian Society, that masters who had been admired for a couple of centuries and been applauded by poets and historians could transgress the rules of composition, even though as he admits they must not be judged by modern ideas. "The examples it furnishes" he writes "are of a school long since passed away and like other music of the time it contains principles of composition no longer received."

What chiefly worried both the eighteenth and the nineteenth centuries was the use of false relations and semi-tonal clashes contrapuntally produced in disregard of harmonic progression. Chappell himself had been distressed at the consecutive fifths and octaves made by the ground bass parts or the burden of "Sumer is icumen in" with the upper parts, which he says "will produce a very indifferent effect on a modern ear". And then he adds a delicious footnote: "We ought perhaps to except the lover of Scotch Reels."

This is not quite so innocent and inconsequential as it sounds superficially. Chappell had been goaded by a shopman in the employment of his firm who had proclaimed his Scottish birth by boasting of Scottish traditional music and sneering at England's lack of such a national art. His taunts drove Chappell to a study of English balladry and folk-music with the result that he published his first collection of old English tunes in 1838. This was *A Collection of National English Airs*—245 in number—which formed the basis of the much enlarged *Popular Music of the Olden Time*, issued with the change of name twenty years later. English musicians of the twentieth century owe much to the exasperation of this amiable scholar and his two prejudices against Scottish nationalism and Burney's Italianate tastes. His chief musical interest seems to have lain in tunes, since he did not harmonize the songs in his own collection of national airs but got Macfarren to do it for him, and he undertook nothing but the Dowland volume for the Musical Antiquarian Society and in this solved the problem of transcribing the accompaniments by simply running away from it and sticking only to the alternative voice parts of the airs.

Chappell's is not the only name common to the two revivals of folk and Tudor music. J. A. Fuller-Maitland (1856-1936), who was one of the pioneers who collected and published folk-song, was also the moving spirit in the publication of *The Fitzwilliam Virginal Book* which he edited in association with his brother-in-law, William Barclay Squire. Richard Runciman Terry (1865-1938), to whom the revival of interest in the church music of the Elizabethan composers owes the initial impulse of performance while he was choir-master at Westminster Cathedral, was also an authority on, and collector of, sailor shanties.

As one after another these names of musicians have cropped up in this preliminary glance at the field of old English music they have been specially associated with particular branches of music—virginals, viols, recorders and other instruments in various degrees of desuetude, and music for vocal ensemble of various kinds, sacred and secular, as well as solo songs to the lute. During its brief career the Musical Antiquarian Society published specimens of each kind of music that had survived from the sixteenth and seventeenth centuries. They began with Byrd's five-part Mass which was edited by Dr. E. F. Rimbault (1816-1876), a pupil of Samuel Wesley who was a considerable historian besides being a practical musician who played the organ and composed in a small way. Rimbault shared Chappell's tastes and took part in the formation of the Percy Society, which had the same kind of aim as the Musical Antiquarian Society, namely the publication of old ballads and "garlands", and he was the honorary secretary of the Musical Antiquarian Society throughout its life. He was responsible for editing eight of the nineteen volumes including a volume of Morley's ballets, Gibbons's fantasies for viols, Este's Psalms, a volume of anthems, Bateson's first set of madrigals, a reprint of *Parthenia*, and an edition of Purcell's *Ode on St. Cecilia's Day*. Purcell was included among the antiquities and had four volumes devoted to him, among them *Dido and Aeneas* and *King Arthur*.

The Musical Antiquarian Society's activities are indeed a land-mark, but they did not succeed in what they set out to do. Seven years was a short life, and nineteen volumes only represented samples of the music that was available for use if it had com-mended itself to the romantic tastes of the eighteen-fifties as it did to the more austere classicism that began to emerge in the early nineteen-hundreds. Some of this Elizabethan music had never been forgotten or suffered the eclipse which shrouded the bulk of it. Byrd's "short" service in D minor had never been wholly banished from the cathedral service lists and had been retained by Boyce in the collection he made in the eighteenth century; Gib-bons's madrigal "The Silver Swan" had similarly retained its popularity among all generations of singers long after the original fashion for madrigal singing which produced it had been super-seded by changes of taste. A publication of 1837 calling itself *The Musical Library* leads off its first volume with the four-part version of Dowland's "Awake Sweet Love" (republished with an editorial anacrusis to the first bar), and includes madrigals by Weelkes and Wilbye among the glees of Samuel Webbe and Dr. Callcott, "canzonets" and "cavatinas" of Haydn and the modern works of Meyerbeer and Mendelssohn.

Purcell, whose case is not quite parallel with that of the Eliza-bethans, since he has never needed restoration to the same extent but equally has never succeeded in gaining an equivalent amount of favour, must be included among the older composers who have influenced the modern renaissance. He likewise has always enjoyed representation in every generation and by a more generous selection of his works. Grove's *Dictionary* even says "By way of exception to the usual course of composers' reputations, there has always been a tradition of Purcell's greatness and a more or less continuous stream of editions of his works. Even the vogue of Handel was not enough to obliterate all trace of Purcell's fame." Certain of his songs turned up in the most varied anthologies of the eighteenth and nineteenth centuries, notably "Mad Bess". *Dido and Aeneas*, it is true, seems to have had no stage perform-ance between 1699 and 1895, but a concert edition was prepared during the eighteenth century and it was subsequently given as a cantata. The score of *The Fairy Queen* disappeared for a like period and only turned up (in the R.A.M. Library) in 1901. But certain of the anthems had a permanent place in the cathedral repertory, and even before the Musical Antiquarian Society began operations a Purcell Club was founded to promote performances of both sacred and secular works. This club lasted from 1836 to 1863 and during its existence helped to celebrate the bicentenary of Purcell's birth. The Purcell Society came later and was founded in 1876 "for the purpose of doing justice to the memory of Henry Purcell, firstly by the publication of his works, most of which exist only in MS, and secondly by meeting for the study and performance of his various compositions". As happened with the Folk Song Society, meetings for performance soon dropped out of the scheme and publication remained its only, but most important, work.

The Purcell tradition, then, was stronger and more continuous than the Tudor. During the second half of the nineteenth century there was a certain amount of madrigal singing and two choirs in London, Henry Leslie's (1855-1887) and the Magpie Madrigal Society (conductor: Lionel Benson), which followed a somewhat similar career from 1885 to 1911, created a demand for editions of the madrigals which were undertaken by their conductors. Sir Frederick Bridge (1844-1924), organist of Westminster Abbey, who was of an antiquarian turn of mind, found time among his many activities for a certain amount of work on the music of the past and was responsible for those editions of the Elizabethans and Purcell which were only superseded by the work of the next generation of scholars. Godfrey Arkwright (1864-1944) was another editor, who between 1889 and 1902 issued twenty-five volumes of old English music and subsequently was responsible for editions of Purcell.

The Bristol Madrigal Society (founded in 1837), like the much older Madrigal Society of London (founded in 1741), kept the practice of madrigal singing alive along with the glees and part-songs which were the eighteenth- and nineteenth-century equivalents of the madrigal, and this society, still alive and flourishing after a hundred years, was destined to play its part in the twentieth-century revival in as much as it numbered E. H. Fellowes among its members and so was one factor in turning his mind to the madrigal. R. L. Pearsall (1795-1856), the only composer to write easily and without conscious archaism in the old madrigalian style, was one of its original members and had many of his madrigals, glees and part-songs performed at its meetings. He was indeed a "sport" born out of time in his appreciation of the Elizabethans, comparable perhaps to Warlock and Moeran in producing new and distinctive works deliberately founded in the past. "Great God of Love", "When Allanadale went a-hunting", "Why do the roses", "Sing we and chaunt it" are still sung and his setting of *In dulci jubilo* is unexcelled even by Bach himself.

If the Bristol Madrigal Society can claim the credit of stimulating compositions of such sterling merit it also has a more ambiguous title to share in the glory of the present revival, since dissatisfaction with its performances led E. H. Fellowes to turn his attention to the authenticity of the texts then in current use. Fellowes's work of restoration of the madrigal is the central fact of the Tudor revival. With him higher standards of editorial accuracy were set up and were applied not only to the madrigals but to the church music and the solo songs. The second wave of the revival was sponsored by his scholarship and Terry's taste.

Edmund Horace Fellowes (1870-1951) did a good deal more for modern English music than provide a reliable text for the whole body of madrigalian literature produced in that wonderful efflorescence which began with Byrd in 1588 and finished with Tomkins in 1622. But it is his standard edition, scrupulously edited in two forms, one for the library and the other for performance, which is his greatest personal achievement and his main contribution to a movement whose force is still unspent.

Like Fuller-Maitland his taste and musicianship were grounded in the German classics. As a boy he was taken to the Saturday and Monday Pops at St. James's Hall and sat at the feet of Joachim. As a violinist he ardently engaged in chamber music during Oxford days and, though an amateur, often took part in performances with professionals. He entered the church and was appointed precentor of Bristol Cathedral in 1897. Here he renewed acquaintance with the madrigals that had first been brought to his attention by John Toye, housemaster at Winchester and father of two musical sons, Francis and Geoffrey, who were both to attain honourable rank in music. In the days before there was a director of music in the modern manner at the public schools Toye ran a musical society for the boys, at whose concerts its was customary to include some madrigals. In retrospect three facts have emerged from this far off and comparatively obscure circumstance: one, that the repertory was small and confined to the most famous of the madrigals, which were at that time the only ones readily available in print; two, that they were sung slowly and ponderously regardless of the character of the words; and three, that in style they were treated like part-songs with little regard to the internal rhythms of the several parts. When Fellowes went to Bristol he found the famous Madrigal Society proceeding on much the same sort of lines, which he soon felt must be wrong. The society had lost the tradition of performance, if it had ever possessed it, and indeed at that time no longer put madrigals into the forefront of its operations. Fellowes observed in church the same indifference to the rhythmic independence of parts, the same metrical rough-riding over subtleties of verbal accentuation as he found in the treatment of the secular music of the period. He had not, however, realized at this time by how much the narrow repertory could be increased nor had he examined this branch of music historically. He had, however, already tried his hand at scoring a few madrigals from the original part-books, encouraged to do so with a quite different end in view by J. H. Mee and Stainer at Oxford. So personal and irrelevant an event as a lawn tennis tournament provided the missing link in the chain of circumstance which was to lead to the huge enterprise of publishing *The English Madrigal School* in 36 volumes. He realized that the Elizabethans issued their madrigals not singly like the modern composers but in whole sets. He spent the leisure of several years in transcribing every set of every composer that had survived, and by 1913 was ready to publish. Owing to the incidence of war he had for a number of years to carry with the aid of private subscriptions the financial responsibility of the enterprise. Ultimately the business side of the undertaking was shouldered by Stainer and Bell, who completed the issue in 1924.

The moment was propitious, and the war, which must at the time have seemed like a disaster to the project, actually brought about such a change in taste as to engender a new wave of enthusiasm for all this Tudor music and a resumption of its performance. On the one hand the competition festival movement (see Chapter VI) put classes for madrigal singing into the syllabuses and on the other the English Singers, newly founded by Steuart Wilson and Cuthbert Kelly, set an example and a standard of concert performance which was a revelation of the grace, the fire, the vitality, the poetic subtlety, the sheer beauty of songs that had previously been treated as dirges and were therefore thought to be as dreary as they sounded.

The English Singers, who soon adopted the quasi-Elizabethan practice of sitting round a table as the most musically convenient method of presenting their songs to an audience, carried the gospel of English music all round the world. Their singing of the old music struck the American public as something fresh and new. At home other sextets followed their example and madrigal groups were formed to explore the unknown riches that Fellowes had brought within their reach. In Germany, whenever English choirs toured that country with English music, the difference between this native tradition and the work of later composers, which inevitably owed something to the great central stream of European music, was immediately noticed. Parry and Stanford, for instance, might speak with an English accent but their language was European, whereas Byrd, Morley, Weelkes and Gibbons talked in a way the Germans had never heard before. When the British Council began its work of attempting to familiarize a curiously misinformed continent with all things English they wisely seized on the madrigal as a vehicle for educating the foreigner. From Scandinavia to the Balkans this revelation of the English character, this artistic heritage of a reputedly unmusical people, was carried by expeditionary forces of choristers. King's College, Cambridge, T. B. Lawrence's Fleet Street Choir, a London Madrigal Group and Cuthbert Bates's Tudor Singers followed in the wake of an earlier expedition by W. G. Whittaker with his Newcastle choir and other occasional missions.

Parallel with the new enthusiasm for madrigal singing was the reappearance in cathedral service lists of the church music composed by the same men as wrote the madrigals. Nor is the revival confined to church choirs. The Latin motets of Byrd and the more serious madrigals of Byrd, Gibbons and Tomkins, are in general use by choirs and choral societies that do not confine themselves to madrigal singing but sing Bach and moderns at will. Tudor anthems take their place with the music of every other period in the Anglican church.

The prime motive power in this department of the revival, however, was not Anglican but Roman Catholic. Richard Runciman Terry (1865-1938) began his musical career as an academic clerk first at Magdalen College, Oxford, and then at King's College, Cambridge. He was converted to Catholicism during a period spent in the West Indies. In 1896 he returned to England and was appointed organist and choirmaster of Downside Abbey, and it was here that he began to revive the old liturgical music of the Elizabethan composers. He edited and issued a series of *Downside Motets*, as well as masses by Tallis and Byrd. The work he did at Downside in improving the standard of performance marked him out as the first director of music at the new metropolitan cathedral of Westminster, to which he was appointed in 1901. At Westminster, where he remained till 1924, he set his face against the more meretricious, Gounodesque type of music, which was then customary in the Roman communion. He complemented the traditional plainsong of the Church with the polyphonic music of the sixteenth century, English as well as Italian and Flemish, thus restoring to the liturgical use for which they had been designed many of the works of Palestrina as well as the masses of Byrd and motets of all the continental schools. The policy which he pursued was endorsed by a papal decree, the *Motu proprio* of Pope Pius X issued two years after he had begun at Westminster the practice of using the polyphonic music which it commended. The Westminster service list for Holy Week and Easter gradually drew large congregations to hear all this music of the past, now by his exertions restored to active service in the Church and to a vigorous musical life of its own. For interest spread from the Latin to the English music and in 1916 the Carnegie Trust of the United Kingdom resolved to publish an authoritative library edition of what had now been revealed as a large corpus of liturgical music by English composers. They placed the editing in Terry's hands. "Dr. Terry later on finding the work beyond the scope of one editor, gathered round him an editorial committee, with whose aid he collected the great bulk of the material and planned the whole edition."* His collaborators were E. H. Fellowes, Percy Buck, the Rev. A. Ramsbotham and Miss Sylvia Townsend Warner (the novelist), and to them ultimately

* Preface to *Tudor Church Music*.

Terry had to leave the completion of the job owing to breakdown from overwork. The first series of ten volumes of *Tudor Church Music* was completed in 1929. They contained: 1. Taverner (masses), 2. Byrd (English services, etc.), 3. Taverner (motets), 4. Gibbons (services and anthems), 5. Robert Whyte, 6. Tallis (Latin music), 7. Byrd (the Gradualia), 8. Tomkins (services, etc.), 9. Byrd (masses, etc.), 10. Marbecke, Aston and Parsley (Latin and English). The Carnegie publication scheme also provided for a cheap octavo performing edition of a selection from the larger volumes. The value of Terry's work in thus restoring to currency the great English music of the past was publicly recognized by a knighthood conferred in 1922.

The essentials of performance of this polyphonic music as discovered by Terry and Fellowes and embodied by them in their editions have now become widely understood. It is in fact in these technical features that nineteenth-century practice has been revolutionized. Even when bar-lines are inserted for convenience of reading to modern singers they are understood to carry no accentual significance and the rhythmic independence of the several voice parts is equally well understood.

Concurrently with the revival of interest in the vocal music of the sixteenth and seventeenth centuries was the exploration of the instrumental music of the period. Two oddly assorted names, J. A. Fuller-Maitland and Arnold Dolmetsch, emerge in the context of this part of the Tudor revival.

Fuller-Maitland, whose part in the folk-song revival has already been mentioned,* managed to leave behind him when he retired from *The Times* the impression that he was crusty and prejudiced. He did not like the way music was developing and he speaks of 1900 as the close of an epoch: ideals of beauty which informed the German classics (including those of the Romantic composers) were being thrown overboard, a revolution was in progress and, as he frankly says in his autobiography,† he began to feel that he had better leave to others the task of expounding and discriminating a music that he disliked. He calls the new music a "welter" or "the mess that the young people seemed to be making of what had been the fairest of the arts". He is referring to what he heard day by day in London concert halls and is not therefore referring

* *See* pp. 78-9.   † *A Doorkeeper of Music* (Murray, 1929), p. 227.

particularly to English music but to all the new tendencies in Europe, especially the cult of dissonance. For him the new music that mattered was the work of Parry and Stanford who had brought about a revolution, using that word in a laudatory sense —odd how twenty years of middle life change the value and the emotional tone of the word "revolution" in almost all of us. And it was Fuller-Maitland who first recognized that the new impetus given to music in this country by three pioneers of the eighties amounted to a Renaissance. That word was his choice and its justice has been generally accepted.

But if Fuller-Maitland did not like the "new music" of the early twentieth century he was wise enough to perceive that the movement of taste towards older pre-classical music was complementary to the restless search by modern composers after novelty —both were a reaction against the dominance of the classics. No doubt the stirrings of nationalism played a contributory part in the movement, but as they appeared to him the two tendencies were not so much historical or political as revolts against the axiomatically accepted supremacy of the classics, the German classics in instrumental music, the Italian tradition in opera. He says "Up to the time when I left Cambridge [i.e. 1878] the only good or original [note that 'original'] music to be found was either classical in its origin or based, consciously or unconsciously, on the patterns of that great and all-important period. If it were not in one of the accepted classical formulae it seemed incoherent to a good many of us." Debussy was the first of these stumbling blocks to be surmounted.

If his own ears were never wholly acclimatized to the music of the twentieth century—though his autobiography contains some admissions in his last years of things which he would previously have shut out—he was among the first to see the value of the old music, to appreciate its differences in kind from the classical music that had caused its supersession, and to labour for its restoration. Because he was so closely associated with what has been called the South Kensington point of view, which meant not only the influences radiating from the Royal College of Music but the German ideals of Joachim and the public concerts of the old St. James's Hall, justice has not been done to the real breadth of his mind or to the astonishing liberalism which in a single embrace

D

could take in the issues of scholarly antiquarianism and the living art of the old music, and reconcile it with his strong faith in the continental classics.

Apart from folk-song Fuller-Maitland's efforts to revive old English music were mainly directed at the rehabilitation of the Elizabethan keyboard music. He began playing it in public on the piano even before he acquired a harpsichord; he shared with his brother-in-law, W. Barclay Squire, the editorship of *The Fitz-william Virginal Book* which was brought out in 1899 by Breitkopf and Härtel (in default of a sufficiently enterprising English publisher) and followed it up with cheaper editions of pieces from the other Elizabethan collections and from Purcell. His interest, however, was not limited to the instrumental music, for he brought out with W. S. Rockstro a volume of *English Carols of the Fifteenth Century* from a manuscript in the library of Trinity College, Cambridge. He edited the *Ode on St. Cecilia's Day* and the catches for the Purcell Society (as well as the Sonatas of Three Parts). The madrigals and Elizabethan church music only concerned him incidentally though he knew something about the technique of scoring them. Barclay Squire on the other hand edited a series of madrigals for Breitkopf and Härtel, in which he included English among continental specimens, and brought out new editions of Byrd's masses. He also wrote biographical and other historical articles on the period.

Fuller-Maitland and Squire seem to have had their interest aroused in this (at that time) forgotten music of the past by a request from Sir George Grove, then preparing the first edition of his *Dictionary*, for an account of the music in the Fitzwilliam Museum at Cambridge. Fuller-Maitland catalogued it in 1879 and this work called his attention to the existence of pre-classical music. The next stage in his awakening came, according to himself, from some concerts given in connection with a Music and Inventions Exhibition at South Kensington in 1885. Here a party of Dutch singers sang the polyphonic music of the Flemish masters and revealed their peculiar beauty to him. Acquaintance with Rockstro (1825-1895), who gave him lessons in piano playing, deepened his knowledge, for Rockstro was one of the few people with a knowledge of the modes. Another older musician who helped to stimulate Fuller-Maitland's archaeological tastes and researches was A. J. Hipkins (1826-1903), an expert on instruments who worked all his life with the firm of Broadwood (he had regularly tuned Chopin's pianos on his English tours) and is still remembered for his book *Musical Instruments, Historic Rare and Unique* (1888). Rockstro is as warmly praised by Fuller-Maitland for his general scholarship as he is summarily rebuked by R. O. Morris for the "dishonesty" of his textbooks. He may have known a great deal about modal counterpoint, but Morris reluctantly but mercilessly indicts him for teaching pure academic textbook counterpoint and pretending that it embodies the practice of the sixteenth-century masters—he at least should have known better.

These conflicting estimates are typical of the history of all these movements which revitalized our music. The first generation is absorbed with its discoveries, with their advocacy, with primary research. Its successors of the next generation are shocked with its lax editorial standards or the blind spots in its artistic conscience. In folk-song Chappell mistrusted the oral tradition; Sharp reversed the attitude and defended the sanctity of wrong notes orally transmitted. In Tudor music the editions of the Musical Antiquarian Society were rendered not only obsolete but erroneous by the work of E. H. Fellowes. In composition Fuller-Maitland accepted Parry and Stanford as evangelists of a new gospel of English music and did not come to appreciate their successors, Holst and Vaughan Williams, until he had given up criticism, while the conservatives of 1950 are inclined to undervalue the Parry and Stanford school as mere pioneer work of little intrinsic interest. Revival comes in two waves.

The gains from the restoration of all this keyboard music were manifold. The pianist's repertory was enriched with something that, apart from its intrinsic interest, provided a contrast to every other sort of music that the most catholic recitalist could lay hands on. As *hors d'œuvre* to a recital or as part of an English group they had a distinctive flavour to contribute. And with the growing vogue of the harpsichord as a recital instrument in its own right, that could even claim modern additions to its literature (e.g. by Delius and Falla), an English contribution to an international corpus of music was valued by the recitalist. But the public concert is not the chief beneficiary. Rather the amateur (if he practises the florid passage work), the student and the domestic pianist reap the harvest of the publication of *The Fitzwilliam Virginal Book*, of *Parthenia* (the first printed music for virginals and often reprinted since 1611), of *Ladye Nevells Booke* (containing forty-two pieces by Byrd and first published in 1926 in an edition by Hilda Andrews that is as scrupulous as it is handsome), of *Benjamin Cosyn's Book*, and other manuscripts. Composers, too, have been stimulated by the early morning freshness of the music, and a certain amount of pleasing music "after" Bull, Byrd, Farnaby and company has been written. Of this neo-antique music for keyboard Herbert Howells's *Lambert's Clavichord* is the most considerable. Here is a collection of twelve short pieces named in the Elizabethan manner after prominent personalities in the musical world of 1927 designed in the first instance to be played on the clavichord of Herbert Lambert, who in his other personality of Elliott and Fry had made photographic portraits of the new English school of composers.* Not one of the pieces could conceivably have been written by an Elizabethan, yet their texture, the contrapuntal disposition of their lines, the embodiment of little mannerisms, the quasi-quotation of an Elizabethan cadence, and above all the sober gaiety of their mood, are the signs of a thinking back on the composer's part into a bygone age but taking with him three centuries of harmonic development. The use of old idioms, notably false relation, the working into the decorative finger-work of *gruppetti* hinting at the primitive delight in newly found agility, total avoidance of tonic and dominant such as would have been a worse anachronism than the frank modernism of a key signature containing one sharp and one flat or of a time signature consisting of the words "Variable time" written perpendicularly across the stave—these stylistic elements are delightful as learned allusions and are essential features of new music for an old instrument. Robin Milford has also written piano music in an English idiom derived ultimately from the virginalists, and the influence may be detected in Vaughan Williams's orchestral suite of the ballet *Job*. The transcriber, ever on the look-out for old music that can be translated into the alluring medium of the modern orchestra, has also cast his eyes upon it. Gordon Jacob compiled a suite of Byrd's

* A second set was issued in 1961.

virginal music transcribed both for orchestra and military band.

No one is likely to question the claims of the reigns of Queen Elizabeth I and King James I to have been a period of wonderful efflorescence of English music, but there were heroes before Agamemnon and great composers before Byrd—Dunstable is the most conspicuous case of an Englishman with a continental reputation. Early church music, plainsong and mediaeval polyphony attracted attention as far back as 1888—like the carol revival as a by-product of the Oxford Movement—and a society was formed with four objects in view, of which publishing, as in similar revivalist movements, has been in the event the most important. But the founders of the Plainsong and Mediaeval Music Society envisaged also its use as a centre for collecting information and communication with similar bodies abroad, as a means of cataloguing the plainsong of the English use and the early polyphonic music of the Church up to the middle of the sixteenth century, and as a body for practical study of plainsong and mediaeval music by actually forming a choir for singing it and demonstrating how this remote music should sound.

Its earliest publications were a facsimile of the Sarum Gradual with an Introduction and a Sarum Antiphonary, a book on notation, *Piae Cantiones*, on which the carol revival drew for several carols which have since become popular favourites, the anonymous Mass, *O quam suavis*, and, very important, the Old Hall Manuscript, which is an early-fifteenth-century choir book of the Chapel Royal, now at St. Edmund's College, Ware, in Hertfordshire. The Society continues its work though its publications are intermittent. Its history has been written by Dom Anselm Hughes in his semi-autobiographical *Septuagesima* (1959).

The revival of interest in instrumental music of Tudor and Stuart times was stimulated by the work of another man of very different outlook working upon different lines from those of our native musicians. Eugene Arnold Dolmetsch (1858-1940) was not so much interested in English music as in old music. Old music included old English music and it therefore came into his sphere of operations. One branch of it was virtually a rediscovery, the concerted chamber music for viols. But he researched into every kind of music written not later than the introduction of the pianoforte and into the instruments for which it was written. He played them all himself. He was craftsman as well as scholar: having discovered the design, the dimensions, the way of working of the old instruments (all of them except the violin family obsolete), he restored old specimens and constructed new ones. He even improved the mechanism of the harpsichord, and some wag said that if he went any farther along those lines he would reinvent the piano. Had he done so he would have taken it to his heart and loudly proclaimed its unique merits! For he was no detached critic, as up to a point Fuller-Maitland certainly was, but a fanatic. He was not a restrained Englishman, product of an older university, but a Swiss, born in France and only in later life naturalized. He was as confident in his enthusiasms and as outspoken in his own praise as Bernard Shaw. He loathed professionalism, believing that it had ruined home-made music: the domestic music of the home, which had created the environment out of which the great Tudor music had come, gave him his ideal and his creed. His own performances were not conspicuous for artistic feeling though they were competent and workmanlike. He was more craftsman than artist, though to say this is to do less than justice to his playing of the clavichord, an art which had never died out in his father's family. He was also a scholar for he investigated the instruction books as well as the music of bygone centuries and his *Interpretation of the Music of the Seventeenth and Eighteenth Centuries* (1915), with its elucidation of the ornaments of those periods, is an authoritative classic.

Dolmetsch learned the crafts of instrument making and tuning in his parents' workshops and in patriarchal fashion he brought up his own family to the bench as well as to the music desk. His father was a piano maker and his maternal grandfather an organ builder. But his own early proficiency on the violin took him to the Brussels Conservatoire and afterwards to the Royal College of Music in its early days. In London in 1889 he discovered the collections of old instruments and the collections of manuscript music in the British Museum written for them. Thereafter he gave up conventional music teaching at Dulwich College, or so he himself said, though it is difficult to believe that it ever was conventional, and devoted his life to the old music of every European country within reach; he unearthed it from museums and libraries, studied its manner of performance, obtained the proper instrument for its execution, brought it to performance, advocated it by exhortation, example and the tyranny of his flashing eye, making claims for it that seemed exaggerated in the light of a not too well polished interpretation, yet ultimately convincing a heedless musical public that his doctrines were sound and the music of the first order in its kind. So that no less balanced a judge than Sir Henry Hadow said of his work that it has opened the door to a forgotten treasurehouse of beauty; it has been a true renaissance, comparable in its measure to that which restored to Western Europe the masterpieces of classical literature.

Dolmetsch formulated his principles in these words: "This music is of absolute and not antiquarian importance; it must be played as the composer intended and on the instruments for which it was written with their correct technique; and through it personal music-making can be restored to the home, from which two centuries of professionalism have divorced it." In the last sentence the faddist speaks, though the steady advance in technical standards of execution that began with Beethoven and went on through the nineteenth century has in effect shut off the amateur of today from the music of his own times. Dolmetsch, although he himself gave concerts, always assumed that public concerts executed with professional standards of virtuosity had no artistic value—an extreme position that could only be defended by a fanatic. Dolmetsch during the last part of his life had no interest in modern music, though not long before his death he gave a concert of his own early compositions, and indeed went farther and farther back into the past for music which he could revive at his London concerts in Bloomsbury and at his summer festivals at Haslemere—his last discovery was claimed as the bardic music of Wales in the Dark Ages. All his geese were swans for him, but not all of his revivals will fulfil his own condition that they must have more than antiquarian interest. The most debatable case of this kind is the English music for viols.

Dolmetsch revived and performed enough of the consort music of the early seventeenth century, and in particular the fantasies for viols of John Jenkins (1592-1678), to establish his case that here is music of a very high order. Jenkins was called "the mirrour and wonder of his age" by his contemporaries, but with the obsolescence of the instrument for which he wrote he himself fell into an almost complete oblivion. Will it then ever be possible to revive his music as the madrigals of the generation preceding his have been revived? The viol music of Byrd—such as the four six-part fantasies, "The leaves be green", and the various compositions called "In Nomine"—have found a certain amount of favour when transferred from viols to violins either for chamber ensembles or for small string band. The modern vogue of the string orchestra every now and again brings to light one of these buried treasures by the great Elizabethans—Gibbons for instance. But so far the fantasies of Jenkins have only been played on viols, and this is in accordance with Dolmetsch orthodoxy. The revival of the viol, however, even to the extent of revival to which the harpsichord and the recorder have attained, is improbable. It seems likely that its extinction during the seventeenth century at the hands of the "scoulding" violin, which cannot compare with it for sweetness of tone, was due to its comparative lack of power, of decisive phrasing and of emotional expression resulting from its peculiar method of bowing. The violin bow wielded by pressure of the wrist has enormous flexibility, range and subtlety of gradation both of tonal power and of line drawing. Compared with it the bowing of the viol held between the knees and played with an underhand stroke of the bow yields a short and abruptly tapered phrase-length, a limited dynamic range of loud and soft and a somewhat wooden articulation. The actual music shows few phrase marks until the time of Matthew Locke and Jenkins, who make occasional use of the slur. Thereafter instructions to the player in the shape of graces, phrase marks, "relishes", "slurs" and "slides", are increasingly used, and the instruction books indicate that a good deal of thought might be given to the rendering. Yet to our ears, acclimatized by two centuries' development of the violin's powers of expressive phrasing, the gait of the viols sounds flat-footed. It will not compare, for instance, with the shapeliness of madrigals. Yet the madrigals were marked by their composers "apt for voices or viols" and words impose some sort of flexible phrasing on any melodic line. Must we conclude that the domestic music parties of the late sixteenth century were content with a more pedestrian performance of the madrigals they had just sung when they transferred them to a consort of viols? The answer, I think, is that we must, on the ground that an instrument with so enchanting a tone as the viol would not have been ousted by the violin after almost two centuries of concurrent existence with it, if its executive powers either in the matter of power or of phrasing had not gradually been found to be inadequate. And of the two factors, power and phrasing, phrasing is the most important. It is therefore unlikely that the viol will be revived beyond the stage of antiquarian curiosity. If, then, Jenkins is to have a resurrection it must be brought about through the violin family.*

The new interest in the harpsichord has been more powerfully aided by the music of the eighteenth century than by that of the earlier periods. Dolmetsch's contribution to the restoration of the harpsichord was his manufacture of new instruments of more powerful tone than the worn-out specimens by Ruckers or Kirkman, that had survived more than a century of use. His manufacture of clavichords for the domestic performance of Bach was extremely valuable but a luxury of limited influence.

The case of the recorder was the exact opposite. Here he has put into service a new popular instrument. Of ancient lineage but like the viol put out of business by a more progressive rival, the recorder or English flute, the straight as opposed to the transverse or German flute, never went farther than the Brandenburg concertos into orchestral music, but it has a consort of its own. A quartet of recorders can conduct a musical argument in a soft-spoken unexciting discourse that beguiles the listener and fully occupies the player. This is the real old Elizabethan consort restored to bodily life: it has equal validity as archaeology or as contemporary art of a homely order. Arnold Dolmetsch's son Carl has specialized in the study, practice and manufacture of the instrument since boyhood and has carried it into the world's concert halls as a solo instrument capable of sustaining a recital. He has developed execution upon it to the pitch of virtuosity and has caused new music to be composed for it. Unlike viol, lute and virginal no corpus of music specially composed for it is in existence. Then, as now, its genius was to join in whatever was going

* Roger North, who saw the displacement happening and regretted it, was alive to the potentialities of the violin. See John Wilson's *Roger North on Music* (Novello, 1959), p. 222.

on that conformed to its nature. Its significance is as a popular instrument, a vastly superior and slightly more expensive penny whistle, easily portable, capable of playing a folk-tune out of doors for the player's own pleasure without disturbing a neighbour or for accompanying a dance. The movement for making and playing bamboo pipes is an adjunct to recorder playing and the good piper can matriculate into the ranks of recorder players and ultimately graduate as a member of a consort. Dolmetsch did not take up the recorder till 1924. The subsequent growth of the practice of recorder playing has been astonishing.

The first efforts to revive the lute called attention to the defects which had sent it out of fashion during the seventeenth century, the frail tone and the apparent imbalance of voice and plucked string. But an unexpected revival of interest in the guitar outside the Iberian peninsula gradually accustomed ears that had been weaned from plucked string tone by two centuries of louder and lusher keyboards and orchestras, to the characteristic evanescence of lute, mandolin and guitar. Guitarists like Mr. Julian Bream, following in the steps of the great Spaniard Segovia, were accepted as string virtuosi with as much title to artistic respectability as violinists, and they not only explored the forgotten repertory of the lute but learned to play the instrument. So that once more the lutenist ayres of Campion and Dowland were heard in authentic performances. The intimacy of voice and instrument was revealed as compensation for the lack of volume, which was felt as an obstacle to appreciation only because of the increased size of modern auditoriums and the change in conditions of performance since Jacobean times. It was, however, Frederick Keel's anthology of *Elizabethan Love Songs* (published in 1909), though frowned on by purists, that was the real pioneer in restoring Dowland, Bartlet, Campion and the others to current use. Fellowes and Warlock, who were more scrupulous about the text and rhythm of these ayres and represent the second wave in the revival, were not able to dispense with the piano as the medium for their accompaniment, and mere faithful transcription of the lute tablature was found to make an unsatisfactory piano accompaniment, because characteristic lute figures depending on the fingering of the plucked string sound lame or fussy on the piano, and the kind of part-writing that sparkles on the lute is so unpianistic as to sound clumsy. Thus in Dowland's "Now o now I needs must part" a passage such as:

Ex 4

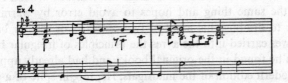

is really more satisfactory, though more colourless, if cleared of its figural part-writing. Keel boldly does this:

Ex 5

His version is spoiled by the fact that it does not adhere to the harmonic progression of the original. The last minim beat of the first bar of Ex. 4 shows how part-writing that is smooth and logical on the lute acquires a hobble when transferred to the piano: treble and alto lead into a gap and the harmonic resolution when it comes gives the effect of syncopation, which is precisely wrong in music in which the bar-line has no accentual significance.

When Keel's interest was aroused in these lutenists' songs by the publication of Bullen's anthologies of their poems he determined to see if their music was as good as the poetry, and, finding that it certainly was, he prepared a performer's edition which was meant to interest singers and give them something which they could offer to their audiences. He therefore wrote a few bars of piano intro-duction and clarified the figuration (both justifiable procedures), but was too cavalier with the bass and the harmonic progressions of his accompaniments so that to a fastidious ear the period flavour of the songs is impaired. His solution of the problem of the rhythmic declamation of the words was to insert time-signatures and bar-lines in the modern manner. He was careful to preserve the original time values, but the process of putting it into modern notation has been criticized as likely to mislead the un-instructed singer who will be apt to produce a syncopated effect from a perfectly simple sustaining of the note over the bar-line because the bar-line has come to denote an accent in modern musical notation. Even Warlock (in the Warlock-Wilson edition) does the same thing and hopes to avoid error by warning the singer to disabuse his mind of two centuries of regular barring. Fellowes carried into the ayres the principles of irregular barring which he found in the original books and had already applied to his modern edition of the madrigals. He, too, in spite of a prefer- ence for literal accuracy, modified the lute parts for piano. But he printed also an exact transcription of the lute part and claimed that his piano versions were so close to the original that they might be regarded as truly representing it. The claim may cer- tainly be allowed: they represent the original better than the literal transcription, but it is possible that an even greater liberty might have been on the whole better still—better, that is, in conveying to modern ears through modern instruments the atmosphere of the original. In these matters there is never any finality. Keel's edition certainly succeeded in opening this new- old world to singers, amateurs and audiences, but his licences are now frowned upon. On the other hand Fellowes's scholarly transcriptions are a little forbidding to the newcomer, though more austere tastes will prefer them.

The general rehabilitation of the old instruments, and in par- ticular the renewed interest in the harpsichord, which crowned with success Dolmetsch's life-long work for their revival, made possible a more scholarly performance of the operas and oratorios of the seventeenth and eighteenth centuries in which the *basso continuo* is an essential feature. The performance of *Messiah* by enormous choirs had made Handel's original accompaniments impracticable—and the more nearly it approached festival scale the farther from the composer's idea it emerged. Furthermore Mozart's "additional accompaniments" had early in their career indicated a practical way round that problem. The practice of transforming eighteenth-century orchestral accompaniments into nineteenth-century, post-Wagnerian orchestration, became com- mon form. The harpsichord had lingered on in many opera houses into the nineteenth century for use in Mozart's and even Rossini's operas long after it had disappeared from concert platforms. But as the old instruments grew older their tone became feebler and the problems of tonal balance when used with forces on the modern scale, still a difficulty that admits of no automatic solution, became insuperable. And so re-orchestration or extreme recourse to the organ became the common practice in performances of Bach, Handel and Mozart. The general sharpening of editorial consciences in later Victorian times, however, began to question the justice of this practice and to cause experiments to be made in the restitution of the harpsichord to the orchestral pit of the theatre, to occasional participation in early symphonic music and above all to its use in the accompaniment of recitatives in Bach.

Bernard Shaw, writing in *The World* under the date November 26, 1890, records an attempt at restitution of a harpsichord and in characteristic Shavian fashion states the objection which is still to be heard even from those who would prefer, other things being equal, to take the scholarly line:

"During the performance of an old overture composed by one of the minor Bachs I was annoyed by what I took to be the jingling of a bell-wire somewhere; but it turned out to be Dr. Parry playing the cembalo part on a decrepit harpsichord. As, though the overture is a hundred years old, it was not written for a harpsichord of that age, Dr. Parry might almost as well have played the Emperor concerto on a Broadwood dated 1809."

Complaints about the jingling of the old-fashioned bell-pull are still occasionally heard from the uninitiated and it is possible for the least enthusiastic admirer of the piano to see why it so completely superseded the harpsichord. Plucked string tone had steadily declined in favour through the centuries until its sole modern representative, the harp, was relegated to a subservient position near the back door of the modern orchestra. On the other hand the jangle of the harpsichord is compensated for by a wonderful diapason-like sonority in its bass and tenor registers and when combined with strings it imparts flecks of golden tone to the ensemble at the top in an effect quite unobtainable by any modern instruments. The silks and satins of chords and arpeggios "realized" with a flourish from a figured bass are unmistakably in the style of the period and therefore "right" in a way that no modern substitute, however euphonious, can be. Its tenuous tone may be inadequate in a large public hall with an orchestra of modern dimensions—electrical amplification is not wholly satisfactory either—so that a conductor often has to balance the claims of correct style against direct musical effect. But the outcome of every attempt to perform music as the composer intended it— whether it be giving long works like Wagner's *Ring* and Bach's *St. Matthew Passion* in their entirety without cuts or by restoring the ancient instrumentation of early scores—has been to show the rightness of his judgment, with the partial exception of the lute. The use of a sonorous modern harpsichord to accompany solo singers in Bach and Handel has similarly justified itself and is no longer debated. When a small auditorium and an intimate style of performance is possible, as it was in Playfair's long run of *The Beggar's Opera* at Hammersmith in the nineteen-twenties, it proved beyond question to be the best and indeed the only right course. It was therefore astonishing to find that at Glyndebourne, where no trouble was spared to get superlative performances of Mozart's operas, the harpsichord was deliberately rejected by a musical director who no doubt knew better but put his own taste above the claims of stylistic scholarship. In general, however, the harpsichord between the wars resumed its place in modern performances of early works unless practical or countervailing musical reasons made it impracticable. After the war Glynde-bourne conformed.

The Bach Revival
and Other Movements

AMONG THE factors contributing to the renaissance of our English music are a number of miscellaneous movements which in various ways prepared the soil for a more abundant growth of truly indigenous music. Social and economic conditions are other factors, no doubt, but their bearing on the production of great composers is hard to estimate and somewhat dubious when done. One can point to J. S. Bach as the product of a system of municipal and church offices filled generation after generation by musicians, and he can be regarded from another angle as the ultimate outcome of a religious outlook moulded by the Thirty Years War; his musical genius is not to be accounted for either by psychology or politics; but it is not fanciful to account for the appearance of him and his sons and Handel and the long line of German composers by the broad fact that music was important in the life of Germany, was actively pursued and seriously regarded. The soil at any rate was right for any chance seed of genius falling upon it to strike root and bear fruit.

The refertilization of the English soil was brought about by three popular movements and three more professional movements. All are just over a hundred years old and originated before 1850. The popular movements which gained their momentum from the zeal of amateurs were the tonic-sol-fa system of notation for singers, the formation of brass bands and the establishment of competitive festivals. The three professional movements were the Bach revival, the folk-song revival and the Tudor revival. The last two are so important that they have each had a chapter to itself. The Bach revival may conveniently be considered here.

The first stirrings in this country were the work of Samuel Wesley, who took Burney to task for the lack of perception shown in his *A General History of Music* in 1782, i.e. thirty years after Bach's death when his reputation was in the trough of disfavour brought about by the change to the *galant* style. *The Well Tempered Clavier*, though circulating only in manuscript, was even then fairly widely known—it finally got into print in 1801. Wesley had received a copy as a gift from Karl Friedrich Horn (father of "Cherry Ripe" Horn and himself a Saxon musician who was in Queen Charlotte's employment), and with him subsequently (1810-1813) published an edition with Birchall of New Bond Street. Wesley began to preach the gospel according to Saint Sebastian, as he called him, and the first of the letters he wrote to Benjamin Jacob (dated September 17, 1808) describes how he tackled Burney on the subject:

"I am grieved to witness in my valuable Friend Doctor Burney's Critique (for he is a man whom I equally respect and love), so slight an acquaintance with the great and matchless Genius whom he professes to analyze: and I have however much satisfaction in being able to assure you, *from my own personal experience*, that his present judgment of our Demi-God is of a very different Nature from that at the Time he imprudently, incautiously, and we may add, *ignorantly* pronounced so rash and false a verdict (although a false Verdict is a contradiction in Terms) as that which I this Day read for the first Time upon 'the greatest Master of Harmony in any Age or Country'." Burney, though now an octogenarian, kept his mind open and eager to the end, and can be said to have died in the new faith.*

Professor Blume† traces the survival of pockets of interest in Bach in Germany and Austria during the time of his eclipse. The best-known adherent of the cult was Baron van Swieten at whose house in Vienna Mozart became acquainted with Bach's fugal writings. It was as a contrapuntist that Bach's name survived and as a composer of fugues that the early revivalists advocated his cultivation. The choral works came later and Mendelssohn's performance of the *St. Matthew Passion* in 1829 is by common

* Burney's conversion is described in full by Percy Scholes in *The Great Doctor Burney*, Vol. II (O.U.P., 1948).
† *Two Centuries of Bach* (O.U.P., 1950).

consent the turning point in the appreciation of the complete Bach. Forkel, however, by his biography published in 1802 (and dedicated to van Swieten) was the first to show that Bach was not "an unintelligible musical arithmetician" but a composer who believed that music was a language for the poetic expression of feeling. Wesley soon became aware that there was another Bach besides that of the fugues, as in the last of the Jacob letters (dated February 15, 1816) he says "how mistaken and false was the Report of those who have Impudently pretended to prove that the great Sebastian Bach could not Compose truly Vocal Music".

It is difficult to discover how Wesley made his acquaintance with Bach. *Grove** only gives the date, which was that of his recovery from the mental derangement he suffered in consequence of his fall in 1787, namely seven years later, but one possible source is quoted by Scholes from Wesley's manuscript auto-biography. This was a young violinist called George Frederick Pinto (1786-1806), who may therefore have acquainted him with the violin sonatas—but this only pushes the problem one notch farther back. Johann Christian had done nothing to make his father's music known since he regarded it as out of date and nicknamed Sebastian "Old Wig". Wesley adopted the nickname but pronounced it with a different expression. He set to work to study the organ works and the *Well Tempered Clavier* and with Jacob organized concerts at the Surrey Chapel (of which Jacob was organist) in 1808 and 1809, at one of which *Jesu meine Freude* was sung for the first time in England and was so probably the first of the vocal works to be sung here. The letters between the two organists are, however, mostly concerned with instrumental works, including the first book of the *Forty-Eight*, the violin sonatas and the "stupendous trios for organ". They mention Wesley's lectures to the Royal Institution, a copy of the *Chorale Vorspiele* and the loan of Bach's Lutheran Hymns (presumably Carl Philip Emanuel's collection). In letter XXI he touches on the choral works in the sentence: "I can't fix Thursday positively till the day of our grand vocal rehearsal be settled, and this depends on Mrs. Vaughan and the rest of the Lungs to be exerted in the Proof of Sebastian being *no mere Organist*." The proof in question was no doubt *Jesu meine Freude*. The tone of the letters is jocular

* 5th ed. (1954).

in the rather facetious manner of the correspondence between Elgar and Ivor Atkins a century later.

Wesley's zeal likewise worked upon Crotch, who is reported to have given the first performance of the *St. Anne Fugue* on the piano in 1816. Organ performance had to wait another eleven years, when it was played by Gauntlett and S. S. Wesley. The organ works made slow progress until the compass of English organs was changed from G as the lowest note to CC with pedal board to match, which was not effected till the middle of the century and was brought about largely by the desire to give adequate performances of Bach and Mendelssohn. Thus the influences of Bach and of organ design were mutual in operation.

The influence of Mendelssohn was decisive as time went on. His famous performance of the *St. Matthew Passion* in Berlin on March 11, 1829, came about through his having received for a Christmas present when he was fourteen years old a manuscript score which had been in the possession of his teacher, Carl Zelter, who was also director of the Singakademie. Zelter was prevailed upon by the actor Edward Devrient to let Mendelssohn direct the performance with the Singakademie choir, so that it was "an actor and a young Jew" who were responsible for the first performance outside Leipzig.* This performance, though of the first historical importance, was neither complete nor in accordance with modern ideas of authenticity. Nine arias, six chorales and sixteen verses of the scripted narration were omitted,† and Devrient explained that it was not to their purpose to give the whole of a work "which was influenced in many points by the taste of the period" (i.e. Bach's). William Sterndale Bennett when he prepared the work for its first English performances between 1854 and 1858 did so according to the version adopted by Mendelssohn, but omitted still more of the narrative—fifty verses were cut but one less each of aria and chorale than by Mendelssohn, thereby "rendering it more acceptable to the English public, without in the slightest degree affecting the musical importance". Length was no doubt the principal objection. These performances

---

* Schweitzer, *J. S. Bach*, Vol. I (1911), p. 242, gives an account of it.

† This was shown by the book of words, of which a copy was in the possession of Mr. R. Sterndale Bennett.

by Sterndale Bennett were the beginning of the Bach revival in England, which gathered momentum for three-quarters of a century until devotion to Bach was an axiom of English music and his music a standby of English choral societies. He mooted the idea of founding a society for active propaganda in the cause to his pupil and subsequent colleague at the Royal Academy of Music, Charles Steggal, and together they got the Bach Society founded on October 27, 1849. The work which this society set before itself, and successfully accomplished until its dissolution in 1870, was in the first instance to collect copies of Bach's music either in manuscript or print and to practise the vocal works in private but subsequently to publish and give public performances. Their first effort was the private performance of *Sei Lob und Preis mit Ehren* (which actually is not Bach's work). They next prepared six motets for publication with English words under Steggal's editorship which Ewer issued in June 1851. Meantime a zealous member, Miss Helen Johnston, was at work preparing an English text of the *St. Matthew Passion*, which was finally brought to performance on April 6, 1854, at the Hanover Square Rooms under Bennett after three years' work. It was repeated in November but was not given in public till 1858 when the Prince Consort graced its performance with his presence. Meantime the *B minor Mass* was put into rehearsal and Bennett declares that in consequence boys could be heard whistling the *Sanctus* in Long Acre. Publication and private performance went on side by side. In 1863 Bennett prepared a *Chorale Book for England* with Otto Goldschmidt, who was to be the founder of the Bach Choir and thus now comes into the picture. Important dates in the Bach Society's career may be tabulated:

June 21, 1859.	Miscellaneous programmes, including the C minor concerto for two pianos, and the Chaconne for violin, played by Joachim.
January 24, 1860.	Eleven movements of the *B minor Mass*.
June 13, 1861.	Parts I and II of the *Christmas Oratorio* conducted by Bennett.
March, 1862.	An English edition of the *St. Matthew Passion* published.
May 24, 1862.	Fourth performance of *St. Matthew Passion*.

Bennett had similarly inaugurated a Bach movement at Cambridge as soon as he became professor there in 1856. Here he built on ground already prepared by the enthusiasm for Bach of Walmisley, who prophesied truly enough a future for the choral works. He repeated his London procedure and collected singers, undergraduates and choristers to practise regularly in Trinity.

The early performances of the *St. Matthew Passion* were none of them complete. Even the notion of authenticity took time to permeate the minds of the pioneers. By 1885, however, when on March 21 Goldschmidt conducted a special performance with augmented choir in the Albert Hall, he had secured oboi d'amore specially made in Paris and the trumpet invented (and played on this occasion) by Julius Kosleck for playing Bach's high parts (of the post-horn type, called misleadingly the Bach trumpet, used for about forty years and now discarded). The performance of the work complete seems to have been uncommon, at any rate outside performances in St. Thomas's Church at Leipzig. Stanford, in a letter about the Leeds Festival of 1910, says that he has conducted it in full twice. The probability is that he did so during his conductorship of the Bach Choir (1885-1902) on occasions referred to in the pamphlet reprinted from *The Christian Science Monitor* and privately circulated in 1920, which, referring to "one or two specially interesting occasions that call for mention", says: "These were the three-days festival held in the Queen's Hall, London, in April 1895 and another, on a still larger scale, two years later. On this occasion the *St. Matthew Passion* occupied the first day." The work performed complete takes three and a half hours—Straube's Leipzig performance in 1929, which was interrupted by a dinner interval, took two hours fifty minutes without repeating every aria in full but in some cases making the opening ritornello suffice for repeat. But after the First World War the problem of complete performance was seriously tackled with various dispositions of the interval between the two parts—by Sir Hugh Allen at Oxford in 1925, by Sir Henry Wood with the students of the Royal Academy of Music in 1926, by C. Kennedy Scott with the Bach Cantata Club in London in 1929. Most notable, however, because they have established a tradition, were the annual performances by the Bach Choir on Passion Sunday, which were begun by Sir Adrian Boult in 1930 and have been continued by Reginald Jacques and David Willcocks. At some of these performances a harpsichord has been used for accompanying the recitative, as well as viola da gamba, oboi d'amore and oboi da caccia for their respective obbligati, so that the interpretation has been more and more a reconstruction of Bach's own performances, with a movement after the second war towards employing smaller forces nearer to Bach's own.

Sir Joseph Barnby also played a part in the establishment of the Passions in English musical life. He conducted the *St. Matthew Passion* in Westminster Abbey in 1871, the same year as he was appointed organist at St. Anne's, Soho, where he established annual performances of the *St. John Passion*, which continued for sixty years.

The history of the *B minor Mass* in England goes back to a performance of parts of it at the Antient Concerts in 1838. The Sacred Harmonic Society put it into rehearsal in 1840 but did not perform it. Bach continued all through the Handel domination of Victorian times to be regarded as unvocal, and Bennett had experienced great difficulty in getting chorus and solo parts learned. The "unvocal" view found explicit statement in professional criticism. Thus *The Times* in its notice of the Bach Choir's performance of the *Christmas Oratorio* in 1878 complimented the soloists on getting through their parts, "for truth to tell Bach's arias and duets are not only difficult but terribly wearisome, uninteresting and ineffective. The connection of words and music is, strictly speaking, no connection at all; and the singer does little more than use his voice as one instrument among several engaged in the display of ingenious polyphonic exercises . . .". At any rate it was left to the next generation of amateurs after Bennett's to attempt an adequate performance of the *B minor Mass*. Arthur Duke Coleridge, grandson of the poet, an amateur musician, collected a choir in 1875, five years, that is, after the dissolution of the Bach Society, to study the *B minor Mass* under Otto Goldschmidt (Jenny Lind's husband). The work was duly performed at St. James's Hall on April 26, 1876, and repeated a month later. The success was such that the temporary choir decided to become a permanent association for performing the works of Bach and also choral works of other schools—a wise liberality of aim, but it called itself the Bach Choir. Soon after this celebration Gold-schmidt resigned the conductorship after the celebration of the bicentenary of Bach's birth and was succeeded by Stanford and he in turn by Walford Davies (1902-1907). Hugh Allen (the most ardent Bach evangelist of the twentieth century in this country and founder of the Oxford Bach Choir) was conductor from 1907 to 1920. His successors have been R. Vaughan Williams (1920-1926), Adrian Boult (1926-1932), Reginald Jacques (1933-1960) and David Willcocks. During its career the Bach Choir has been responsible for the introduction of a dozen of the church cantatas. To complete the process of exploring the whole of Bach's two hundred church cantatas the Bach Cantata Club was founded in 1926 by Hubert J. Foss and continued under the musical direction of C. Kennedy Scott until the outbreak of war in 1939 to give performances of the church cantatas interspersed with other of his music, including secular cantatas and instrumental works, with forces comparable in size and balance to Bach's own. The B.B.C. went farther and at one period worked steadily through the whole series, a procedure which probably defeated its own aim since it induced satiety in the listeners by its uncritical acceptance of all the cantatas written by Bach as occasional pieces for next Sunday's service as equally capable of appeal to posterity. The best of the cantatas have become standard fare for choral societies of all sizes.

The rest of the tale can be more briefly told. By the time of the 1914 war Bach had won acceptance at the universities, where Allen's influence was strong, in the public schools (represented by some famous performances of the *B minor Mass* at Sanderson's Oundle), at all the big festivals (such as Leeds), with all the major choral societies. The Brandenburg Concertos and the orchestral suites were put into Bach evenings at the Proms by Henry Wood. The keyboard works were played in series of recitals lasting a week at a time by Harold Samuel, and singers, for whom Dorothy Silk stands as a representative name, and violinists put together programmes of arias and chamber music.

The next stage was a move towards greater authenticity of performance, which was facilitated by the revival of the harpsi-chord. Dolmetsch had published a book on the interpretation of the ornaments. Sanford Terry wrote a biography which was accepted in Germany till later research made it out of date. Terry also provided useful studies of Bach's cantata texts and his orchestra. By the thirties something called a baroque organ began to be discussed and the registration of the organ music to be demonstrated, the Austrian Susi Hock (Lady Jeans) being a pioneer in Britain on this point which led to lively, fruitful and prolonged controversy. A similar attempt was made in the field of string music to reconstruct a violin bow slack enough to enable the quadruple stops of the Chaconne to be sounded like chords instead of snatched arpeggios. Schweitzer's great book was established as a Bach bible in Ernest Newman's translation and was not seriously challenged for thirty years. Bach had won parity of esteem with Beethoven at nearly all levels of English musical society. It was not till after 1945 that further researches conducted into Bach's life and times in the record offices and muniment rooms of Germany began, not to provoke any reaction, but to modify some of the attitudes that had hardened in the process of establishing Bach alongside Handel as the Englishman's musical messiah.

If the analogy of Italy and Germany holds good, or even of our own Tudor times, the higher manifestations of the art of music are only possible in societies which cultivate it seriously and at all levels according to the available leisure and ability. Late Georgian and early Victorian England did not cultivate music seriously. They imported it as a luxury like wine and cigars or, as Vaughan Williams put it, the best brands of cigars and champagne. The various retrospective movements that began to give a forward push to our native music in Queen Victoria's reign have already been discussed, but some further impetus stirred at the lower levels of society in the new industrial working class. The Bach revival was the work of academics and the educated middle classes; folk-song had belonged to the peasantry, as long as there was a peasantry; but the tonic-sol-fa and brass band movements, especially the latter, were proletarian movements; the competition festival movement united the classes and the masses in town and country.

The tonic-sol-fa movement promoted a system of teaching sight-singing to the unlearned, though not unlettered. It borrowed the apparatus of Guido d'Arezzo, who had exactly the same object in view eight centuries earlier. Guido devised a system of hexachords with typically devious mediaeval ingenuity to avoid some difficulties in the Greek system of tetrachords, using an acrostic from a Latin hymn to John the Baptist for his vocables:

> *Ut* queant laxis
> *Re*sonare fibris
> *Mi*ra gestorum
> *Fa*muli tuorum
> *Sol*ve polluti
> *La*bii reatum
> *Sancte Ioannes.*

This hymn is quoted in most histories, with various translations of the difficult *laxis fibris*. It may be rendered, literally:

> That thy servants may be able to sound forth, with their bonds (of sin?) undone, the wonders of thy deeds, free them, Saint John, from the guilt of a polluted lip.

Or *laxis fibris* may mean, not "with their bonds undone", but "with cleared (or open) vocal chords", which may be paraphrased as "freely", or better still (in Imogen Holst's version) "with easy voice". *Ut, re, mi, fa, sol, la* were then arranged on the great stave or gamut, to which, when the hexachord scale gave way to the octave scale, *si* (*Sancte Ioannes*) was added for the seventh degree.

Ex 6

Ut re mi fa sol la.   Ut re mi fa sol la,   Ut re mi fa sol la.

In this hexachordal scale the order of tones and semitones is identical in all three hexachords and identical with the modern major scale. The syllables thus became identified with their alphabetical equivalents—so that to this day *Ut* is found in French scores for C, *Re* for D, etc., and a semi-tone is called a mi-fa—but equally and contrariwise they could be associated with transpositions to other pitches. The hexachord system lasted for five centuries (so that for instance there are pieces in *The Fitzwilliam Virginal Book* based on it), and its name even longer in the curriculum of continental conservatoires, *Solfège*. In America a primitive notation of notes of different shapes (hence "shape-note" hymns) in revivalist hymn-books was called Fasola, and is used to this day.*

It was not therefore a revolutionary step for the socially minded philanthropist of the nineteenth century to take up again the acrostic syllables for teaching singing at sight, for plainly Guido's notion of associating syllable with pitch-sound was psychologically well founded. In 1841 the Rev. John Curwen, a Congregational minister, was prompted by a conference of Sunday-school leaders to investigate the methods† of teaching people to sing most suitable for nonconformist bodies. He lighted on one used by a Miss Glover, who kept a girls' school in Norwich. Curwen was not particularly musical—his chief motives in encouraging popular singing were moral, religious and social. The idea must have been in the air, for contemporary with him in his endeavours was John Hullah (1812-1884), who was a professional musician, a composer of light operas and songs —his "Three Fishers" was still being sung in the first two decades of this century—an organist and a professor. He was fired with the same idea, gave it practical expression at a higher level in the educational field and obtained official recognition for it. There were similar movements on the Continent.

Sectarian controversy broke out over the comparative merits of the systems variously employed. The crux was the "movable Doh" (Doh had been substituted for Ut). Hullah wanted to associate the syllables with fixed pitches. Glover and Curwen saw that all the difficulties of pitching intervals correctly could be avoided in a manner impossible with the staff notation (which does not without accidentals differentiate between tones and semi-tones) if having the tonic stated at the beginning, e.g. Doh = A, the singer had his syllables, ultimately enlarged to include the chromatic semi-tones, in front of him.

In the event Curwen's system prevailed and he founded a publishing firm (still in existence) to print music in tonic-sol-fa (as the system was called from its emphasis on a tonic rather than on

---

* Or at any rate until 1933, when George Pullen Jackson published his *White Spirituals in the Southern Uplands.*

† See R. Nettel, *The Englishman Makes Music* (Dobson, 1952), Chapter VI, where a "fasola" Psalter of 1750 is mentioned.

a fixed note) for the singing classes which sprang up all over the country. Chapel choirs welcomed it, so that as a remote consequence a complex modern score like Howells's *Hymnus Paradisi* prescribed for the Welsh Eisteddfod is put into tonic-sol-fa notation. A good many of the competing choirs in North Country tournaments still sing from tonic-sol-fa, which has of course had to develop appropriate rhythmic signs. *Ut* was changed to *Doh* and *Si* to *Te* in order to have the series of syllables conform to the pattern of consonant, vowel, with a different initial for each degree of the scale. To a musician brought up on the staff the gain in simplicity seems small and the loss in coverage great, since an orchestral score in tonic-sol-fa is inconceivable. But in practice the association of a syllable with a sound was able to provide a security of intonation that was normally found only among musicians with absolute pitch. It did mean therefore that the industrial workers without musical education could soon be singing *Messiah*, learn easily enough to master test-pieces set for competition festivals, and read an unknown hymn-tune confidently and correctly.

Henry Coward (1849-1944) educated himself on tonic-sol-fa, and ultimately took a doctorate of music at Oxford and became the leading choral conductor of the north of England for more than a generation. The Tonic-Sol-Fa College still exists in London and though possibly the proportion of choralists now using tonic-sol-fa to staff notation is less than formerly there can be no doubt that in its career of over a century tonic-sol-fa has done much to make the country musical.

The brass band movement has a similar history, alike in motive, chronology, independence of professional music, industrial associations and linkage with competition. It too was a fertilizer applied to the rather thin soil of Victorian music. It is still very much alive and apart from local manifestations it keeps itself in the public eye with its annual festival in London, which is at once competition and concert demonstration of the extraordinary skill achieved by amateurs in handling a somewhat clumsy medium.

Wind bands are universal and have a long history—all armies have had them for centuries. In the military band are found wood-wind as well as brass and percussion: clarinets are the equivalent of the violins of the orchestra in the military band, cornets in the brass band. The all-brass ensemble was evolved under pressure of social rather than musical circumstance and for a century competition has been the main incentive to the cultivation of the medium. Even earlier, however, cavalry regiments found brass easier to play on horseback than wood-wind. Technical improvements in instruments, which made uniformity of fingering possible, induced such amateur bands—the Stalybridge Old Band, which was founded in 1814, is the earliest known formation—to adopt brass instruments, which were in any case easier to manage for horny hands. Industrial conditions turned the attention of both employers and workmen in the north of England to the social and educational values of music-making. Chapels, the temperance movement, the philanthropic impulses that led to the foundation of Mechanics' Institutes, and later on the Salvation Army, all encouraged the formation of bands from the eighteen-thirties onwards.

The famous and still extant Besses o' th' Barn is older, and organized local contests in 1821 and 1838, but did not become an all-brass ensemble till 1853. Indeed the brass-band movement as a movement dates from that year, in which the Belle Vue contest at Manchester was established. Seventeen years later a contest was promoted at the Crystal Palace in London and the movement spread to the south; Luton and St. Albans in the nineties developed a rivalry like that of Besses o' th' Barn and Black Dyke Mills, in the north, and ultimately the brass band contest reached Cornwall. But in 1897 one of the magazines of the movement, *The British Bandsman*, remarked that "London will never do as a contending ground."

The prophecy was soon falsified, however, as in 1900 a National Brass Band Festival was organized by J. Henry Iles, who had first promoted a concert at the Albert Hall in aid of War Charities, at which Sullivan was induced to conduct a massed performance by eleven bands of his Boer War marching song, "The Absent-Minded Beggar". Sullivan used his influence with the Crystal Palace authorities to establish the festival there with a trophy. Twenty-nine bands competed in three grades, and the test-piece in the chief section was a pot-pourri of Sullivan's operas. Thereafter the contest was held annually until the destruction of the Crystal Palace by fire in 1936, after which it removed to the Alexandra

Palace and then after the Second World War to the Albert Hall.

A brass band has three main constituents (and some subsidiary ones, such as uniforms and a place to rehearse in): players, instruments and compositions to play. The players came from the industrial working classes; money for instruments and facilities for rehearsal were often provided by employers, and individual firms have given their names to famous bands, e.g. Foden's Motor Works Band and Fairey Aviation Works Band, which thus have more than a merely local loyalty to their town. The constitution of the bands was evolved during the second half of the nineteenth century. The music played was almost all of it borrowed from vocal music, since there was nothing in existence suitably scored for the various shapes and sizes of bands. The use of vocal music affected the style of playing both for good and ill. For good in that it made for legato playing: it has been noticeable during the past generation, in which the old brass band style has been modified, that trombones trained in wind bands have a better legato than most orchestral players of the instruments, and what cornets can do in rendering violin passages is a source of continual astonishment. For ill in that it has led to four-square phrasing and flatfooted rhythm. The medium is of course by nature elephantine, but that it can tread nimbly and phrase significantly was demonstrated suddenly when Sir Adrian Boult at a special war-time Brass Band Concert of 1942 conducted a potted version of Beethoven's fifth symphony. He treated the massed bands, which included "Besses", Black Dyke and Foden's, as though they were his own B.B.C. Symphony Orchestra—they responded, almost naturally, by playing symphonically—the music flowed instead of being soberly pumped.* Thereafter conductors from the orchestral world were called in to supplement the experts like J. H. Iles and Harry Mortimer. The new flexibility pervaded the brass band world.

Another factor in emancipating the band from the part-song style of playing was the commissioning of special works, usually as test pieces for competition, from established composers outside the movement, so that alternatives to arrangements became available.

* I wrote of it at the time: "The effect was a magnified projection of the music which had moments of real magnificence."

At the first competition, at Hull in 1853, competitors played, as pieces of their own choice, the "Hallelujah Chorus", "The Heavens are telling" from Haydn's *The Creation*, a cavatina from a Bellini opera, a cavatina from a Rossini opera and a selection from Donizetti's *Anna Bolena*. Two competitors, however, offered overtures. Military marches were of course available and waltzes, otherwise selections from operas or even from Mozart's Twelfth Mass were the standby. It was at the suggestion of J. H. Iles, who had incidentally taken the Besses o' th' Barn on a tour around the world in 1906-1907 and was for a long time the moving spirit in improving the status and standards of the brass bands, that composers were invited to write works specially as test pieces for the festivals. Percy Fletcher was the first in 1913, Bantock followed; Cyril Jenkins, Hubert Bath, H. Geehl and Denis Wright provided test pieces in the twenties and in 1930 Elgar wrote his *Severn Suite*. Holst (1928), Ireland (1932), Howells (1934), Bliss (1936) and Vaughan Williams (1957) have all provided something worthy of the bandsmen's skill but better than mere competition fodder. So that a repertory proper to the medium has been gradually built up.

Contests in music are as old as Apollo and Marsyas or at any rate as the Olympic Games of classical Greece. A certain incompatibility of aim in combining an art which exists for nothing beyond itself and a competition which aims at honour and glory and financial reward has naturally been exposed from time to time in the nineteenth-century movements for harnessing a spirit of emulation to the pursuit of musical ideals. The brass band movement was not exempt from scandals, such as abuse of the judges by losers, tampering with instruments of rivals, hostile demonstrations by the audience. Right up to recent times adjudicators have been made prisoners while the competitions are on in order to ensure that they have no contact whatever with competitors, to avoid corruption or molestation. However, in general the sporting spirit has prevailed and the movement has adopted in effect a slogan coined by Walford Davies for the similar competitive movement in choral singing: "To pace one another on the road to excellence." It is a sign of health in the musical body politic that in 1950 there were estimated to be some three thousand brass bands active in Britain comprising probably 60,000 players of cornets, flugel horns, euphoniums, trombones and basses—the trumpet belongs to the military, not the brass band.

The movement for choral competitions started, as a movement, about thirty years later than the brass band movement, but there had been numerous sporadic competitions* for solo singing, vocal quartets and choirs, both in the north and in London, from 1855 at least. The Welsh Eisteddfod in its present national form dates from about the same time or a little earlier in the century, but it has a long history behind it and contains other elements than musical competitions. Nevertheless, local eisteddfodau and some attempts in the eighteenth century to foster Welsh culture gave the present form to the national Eisteddfod and served as an example to English choral enthusiasts. John Spencer Curwen, for instance, who founded a festival at Stratford in East London, which is usually regarded as the starting point of the modern nationwide movement, had been one of the adjudicators at the Welsh Eisteddfod and acknowledged his indebtedness for the idea to Wales. The idea of turning a competition into a festival by means of a culminating concert in which the competitors combined in a joint performance of some of the test pieces and for a specially designated work of larger scale emanated from Miss Mary Wakefield, who organized vocal competitions in connection with the local flower show at Kendal in 1885. By 1887 she was able to present a cantata, Mendelssohn's *Lauda Sion*, and followed it in succeeding years with Bach's *O Light Everlasting*, Gounod's *Gallia*, Bach's *God's Time is the Best*—the leaven of the revival was obviously at work—Schubert's *Song of Miriam* and Parry's *Ode on St. Cecilia's Day*. In 1905 she suggested an Association of Competition Festivals, which in 1921 was incorporated as the British Federation of Musical Competition Festivals. 1905 was also the year in which the Leith Hill Festival was founded at Dorking with which Vaughan Williams was associated as conductor for forty-eight years. This festival through the personality of its musical director developed a number of unusual features, notably regular performances of Bach's *St. Matthew Passion*, and did not join the Federation, but it was founded on the Kendal model, which had been copied at some thirty-six centres in various parts

* Percy Scholes (*The Oxford Companion to Music*, 9th ed., O.U.P., 1955), gives instances from the eighteenth century onwards.

of the country, including a notable one at Petersfield, which was supplied with its orchestra from Oxford by Hugh Allen. By 1921 the picture of the festival movement is complete; moreover it has spread overseas.

Festivals fall into different categories. Some are exclusively vocal, some even exclusively choral; some include classes not only for vocal but for instrumental soloists, for chamber music, for folk-dancing even. Some are exclusively tournaments—the big festivals in the north, Blackpool, Morecambe and Newcastle are of this type; some make the competition subsidiary to the joint performance at a concert; some even eliminate the competitive idea and make themselves more like the song-swapping ceilidhs of the Celtic countries but retain combined performance. These slight differences in character result from the advocacy of slightly different ideals. The value of combined performance by all competitors under the adjudicator (if he happens to be a conductor) or an adept at pulling choirs together in a single rehearsal as Sir Adrian Boult has been, is denied by the crack choirs of the north, who dislike seeing their finesse steam-rollered into a greatest common factor. Nevertheless festivals to which small choirs come, often from rural communities in which the conductor is a local farmer, schoolmaster, or vicar's wife, and perform prodigies with the inspiration generated by singing together, with an orchestra, in the great masterpieces, or even cantatas that are not masterpieces but ornaments of the repertory from its byways—such festivals have a spirit, as I can personally testify, that sweeps technical difficulties on one side and produces artistically exhilarating performances. Another debated issue is the relative importance of the sight-reading test. Still another, whether public criticism may not undermine the candidates' confidence in conductor or teacher. This has gone so far, especially in the case of classes for school competitors, as to lead to the formation of non-competitive festivals in which the criticism is made privately. In any case adjudicators have to learn to combine tact and good humour with truthfulness, but it may seem to go too far to forgo the stimulus of competition and the educational value of criticism, on the spot and by an expert, of what has just been heard. The competitions which admit solo classes have sometimes thrown up candidates of such exceptional ability that the adjudicators have been moved to recommend a professional career—a conspicuous case was that of Kathleen Ferrier.

The social value of the competitions needs no emphasis; from the point of view of music the movement has spread the practice of the art through all sections of the community, has improved sight reading and musicianship and implanted a love of the art in many unlikely quarters. It has helped to fortify the national tradition of choral singing. It has even produced a certain amount of music from sympathetic composers: Elgar, Bantock, Armstrong Gibbs and George Dyson are some who have written with the competition festival in mind.

These three popular movements, tonic-sol-fa, brass bands and competitions, originating, like the folk-song and Tudor revivals, somewhere round 1850, have enriched English musical life, and so prepared the atmosphere, if not the soil, for the wide extension of the love of music brought about in the present century by broadcasting, and can hardly fail to have helped the renaissance in native composition. At any rate it has made the country more musical, more appreciative, more aware than it was a hundred years ago.

VII

Parry the Instigator

To Hubert Parry must go the chief credit for the awakening of
English music from the complacent lethargy that had been growing on it for the best part of two centuries. He more than anyone,
except Stanford, pulled it out of the rut of sentimentality, easy-
going standards, and disregard of literary values in vocal music;
he raised the intellectual status of the musical profession and with
that its place in public regard; he infused new life into musical
education, set up higher standards and established worthier
ideals; he gave to the art as practised in Britain an integrity,
moral, social and aesthetic, that it had not possessed since the time
of Byrd and Gibbons.

This summary balance sheet conceals a very curious and complex profit-and-loss account. It is instructive to put it against a
similarly abridged reckoning-up of Elgar's contribution to our
national heritage and to the modern renaissance. Parry and Elgar
are unlike in almost every respect. Parry was a voluminous composer; Elgar's productive life is hardly longer than twenty years.
Parry never achieved the highest results; Elgar sailed into the
front rank of composers with two unquestionable masterpieces,
the *Enigma Variations* and *The Dream of Gerontius*. Parry exercised an enormous influence both on his own generation and on
every serious musician who has practised his art in this country
ever since; Elgar had practically no influence either on his contemporaries or his successors. The only thing the two composers
had in common was a West Country origin.

Influence and achievement were their several contributions to
their generation. In an estimate of his achievements a composer's
character is a secondary concern of the critic. Elgar's personality
is not without psychological interest, but no estimate of Parry can
be complete without close scrutiny of his whole make-up. His

E

success and failure as a musician is directly explicable by other than musical factors in his life—his heredity, his education, his zestful nature, his diversity of gifts, the width of his interests, the quantity of work he accomplished and above all the strain of Puritan earnestness which developed greater strength the older he grew. By the paradox of puritanism, a kind of inversion of the hedonistic paradox, Parry's earnestness and zeal are responsible for careless work and a lack of self-criticism which was hardly noticed at the time, though Shaw's estimate of his music in the early nineties agrees astonishingly with what a more sympathetic critic finds fifty or sixty years later. He was a big man; he has left a few things that belong to the imperishable heritage of English vocal music; he was the best scholar that England has ever produced to use a pen equally for writing music and for writing about music. Composer, executant, scholar, administrator, he transformed all the values current in the musical life of Victorian England. A curious idea that he was stuffy, conventional and "academic", which was the reverse of the truth, grew up after his death.

He was born in 1848 at Bournemouth (where his mother died of consumption twelve days later), of stock that included merchants among the Parrys, admirals among the Gambiers whence he derived a strain of French blood and perhaps his impetuosity, and landed gentry among the Fynes Clintons whose tastes were scholarly. Artistic ability Hubert Parry used to trace to his paternal grandmother's family, the Oakeses. He followed the family tradition and went to Eton, where he distinguished himself by taking his Oxford Mus. Bac. degree at the age of 17. His talent for music was thus early made apparent and its quality can still be savoured in the charming song "Why does azure deck the sky?", which will stand up to the sophistication of Wigmore Hall today without the slightest need to apologize for its simplicity. At Eton he was a vigorous games player, a voracious reader, a moderate classic and a sociable schoolboy. He got valuable instruction in music all through the middle years of the nineteenth century from Sir George Elvey, organist of St. George's Chapel, Windsor, who worked over his compositions and performed his first anthem (went farther, indeed, and got it published by Novello from whom its substantial folio can still be obtained). S. S. Wesley, then organist of Gloucester Cathedral, was another influence in his musical development while he was at Highnam, the family home near Gloucester. From Eton he went to Exeter College, Oxford, where he took an arts degree in the old Law and History school. In his first summer vacation he went abroad with Henry Hugo Pierson, Oxford-born, German-trained, for further study in music including orchestration. Later on he had lessons in counterpoint from Macfarren but the only other training he had was from the teacher who made him, Edward Dannreuther (1844-1906), and to whom he owed a triple debt as his "instructor, critic and champion".

Dannreuther, to whom Parry went in 1873, after Oxford and marriage, was the right man for him. He was a cosmopolitan of German training, a good pianist, a good enough writer and scholar to be entrusted with a volume of *The Oxford History of Music* and a progressive who championed the cause of Wagner. His mind therefore marched with Parry's and it was under his guidance that Parry's first serious compositions, a piano concerto produced at the Crystal Palace, chamber music at Dannreuther's own concerts, and the epoch-marking *Prometheus Unbound* at the Gloucester Festival of 1880, were brought to completion and performance. Dannreuther was Wagner's great apologist in England in the seventies and through him Parry met Wagner personally after absorbing a good deal of his style.

Parry's business at Lloyds gave him up after a year or two and he only launched himself upon a musical career by degrees. While he was pursuing his studies with Dannreuther he was asked by Sir George Grove to contribute to, and act as assistant editor of, the *Dictionary of Music and Musicians* then in preparation. From writing he proceeded to lecturing and when the Royal College of Music was opened in 1883 he joined its staff, a small step large with destiny. He was given an honorary doctorate at Cambridge in that year and began to examine for degrees there, another step along the academic path he was to follow. In 1890 he lectured at Oxford and for the Royal Institution. In 1900 he succeeded Stainer as professor at Oxford. In the meantime, however, he had succeeded Grove as Director of the Royal College of Music (1894). To all this fury of activity Parry added a full social life and incessant composition. No festival was complete without a new work from his pen—indeed it is devastating to read the processions of cantatas and oratorios from Hereford to Birmingham, Gloucester to Leeds and Worcester to Norwich. His health was erratic since he strained a naturally robust constitution by the terrific demands he made upon his energies. Any man's energies are limited, however well endowed he may be with vital force, quick mind and enough of the world's goods to make rough paths smooth. One does not therefore have to look very far for at any rate one explanation of Parry's enormous influence and his failure, in spite of his great natural talent, to reach high rank as a composer.

But unless he had been a good composer, a better composer than his Victorian predecessors, a more serious and, where there is common ground for comparison, a better composer than his senior contemporary, Arthur Sullivan, he could not have accomplished the regeneration of English choral music nor contributed what he did to the general revival. The German bias of his mind encouraged by the German sources of his musical training, his admiration for German seriousness, thorough methods and respect for scholarship, complemented by his mistrust of the seemingly meretricious quality of much French music—the reader of Graves's official biography will find many passages of his diary quoted in which he comments adversely on French music, and his published criticism deliberately sets forth the same judgments, supported by critical argument rather than outbursts of personal preference—these Teutonic predispositions sufficed to prevent the realization in him of a thoroughbred English music. He was born just too soon to assimilate the influence of the folk-song and Tudor revivals. By following an alien tradition he partly neutralized the native Englishness of his blood and the thorough impregnation of his mind with English literature.

There he was, however, an Englishman of character and of abundant natural talent, writing music that was far from the pale shadows of Mendelssohn that passed for English music in the names of Sterndale Bennett (far the best of this kind of stuff), Macfarren or J. F. Barnett. He began writing at 14—there is a little piece extant dated from early Eton days—and he continued till 1916 when in the midst of the troubles of ill health and war he produced those noble national songs, "England" and "Jerusalem" and the equally great but more recondite motets, the *Songs of Farewell*. If any of Parry's cantatas is compared with *The May Queen* (Bennett), *May Day* (Macfarren) or *The Ancient Mariner* (Barnett), the difference that becomes immediately apparent is one of sheer strength. *The May Queen* is graceful and fluent—excellent qualities in which Parry was lacking—but commonplace and bloodless. *The Ancient Mariner* is melodious but its ding-dong metre is a travesty of the poem's rhythms. It is arguable that the emptiness of mid-Victorian music was due to the lack of general culture in the chief musicians. Sheer genius like Mozart's and even that saturated musicality that is to be found in masters of lower rank like Rachmaninov need no general culture and make do without much greatness of character. But the mid-Victorian musicians, though they lived in a great age of progress, were themselves static in mind. It never occurred to them to question their own conventions, let alone religious orthodoxy. Their competence in music was sound but there was nothing much else in their minds on which they could exercise it. This is no doubt too harsh a judgment of Sterndale Bennett, who certainly did a good deal for the R.A.M. by saving it from extinction and who was the prime mover in the Bach revival (already considered), but Ernest Walker's verdict on him as a composer is that he is "the great instance in music of a man who might have reached real greatness being slowly but very effectively killed by his environment".

Barnett (1837-1916) has left a volume of reminiscences which reveal a mind typical of the professional musician at the top of the tree before the new spirit stirred in English music. He writes a flat English prose such as his equivalent today would scorn to publish, and though there is no doubt about his musicianship or his amiability his mind seems to be unable to rise to anything higher or of wider range than anecdote. Imagine then the effect of Parry's eager, well-read, intellectually curious mind upon a society which allowed continentals but not Englishmen to be bohemian, a society which expected no more from its musicians than unadventurous orthodoxy in art and life. That he did not immediately disturb the profession was due to the fact that he was not of it at the time of his first coming before the public as a composer—he was an amateur and an aristocrat. When he died the professional musician was accepted as a gentleman of some pretensions to culture, and the changed attitude of the public towards its musicians—reflected perhaps as clearly as anywhere in the status of music in the universities then and now—was Parry's doing.

His influence was far-reaching because it touched the art at many points; as Director of the Royal College he was the unofficial head of the profession and its diplomatic contact with the larger world of public affairs. But had he not been a composer he could not have wielded the authority he did. His compositions therefore have some historical importance, even when their artistic value, whatever it may have been at the time of their first appearance, has subsequently depreciated.

As a composer Parry stands or falls by his vocal works, the cantatas, the solo songs of the twelve sets of English lyrics, some part-songs and a handful of unison songs, though he has left a number of instrumental compositions that claim a niche in the repertory of the string orchestra such as *The Lady Radnor* and the *English Suites*, and of the organist, notably the late sets of *Chorale Preludes* on English hymn tunes and the *Wanderer Fugue*. The chamber music is forgotten and the symphonies though surviving precariously a little longer were rarely performed after his death.

Of the cantatas, the first, *Prometheus Unbound*, is of historical interest and is even worth occasional revival since it is a good deal fresher than the later works, in which Parry's idioms had hardened into mannerisms. It was last given at Cambridge in 1927. *Blest Pair of Sirens* (1887) has won a special place of its own in the hearts of choral singers and festival audiences of all sorts, since it gives explicit utterance to what English people feel in their heart of hearts about music; *Job* (1892), in which philosophy has not run away with the music but has stated those universal truths that mid-Victorian oratorio had abandoned for the brute facts of ancient history, is a work that can withstand the hostile criticism brought against it as others of Parry's cantatas cannot; though to be sure its orchestration is drab; *The Pied Piper of Hamelin* (1905), a comedy cantata that gives the happiest possible opportunity for the composer's large humour, never quite lost the favour it won at a Norwich festival.

In the second rank are four cantatas which merit for various reasons more frequent performance than they have received since Parry's death: *The Glories of our Blood and State, L'Allegro ed il Pensieroso, De Profundis* and the *Ode on the Nativity. The Lotus Eaters* (1892), which belongs to the same period as the first three of these, is a fair counterpart to Tennyson's words, shows Parry in the unusual mood of languor and seduction, and is indeed relatively well scored; it has served a turn at competition festivals. What is surprising is that *The Glories of our Blood and State* was not requisitioned for Armistice celebrations between the two world wars, for it is a setting of Shirley's funeral ode which evokes a mood of lofty resignation, rather like that of Brahms's *Requiem*, and looks forward, at any rate in the revision to which it was subjected in 1914, to the *Songs of Farewell* that were soon to follow it. The merits of *L'Allegro ed il Pensieroso* (1890) arise out of the affinity between Milton's and Parry's minds. *De Profundis* (1891) to the Latin text is laid out in twelve parts so as to permit of choral writing in Parry's most spacious and vigorous writing. The *Ode on the Nativity* (1912) is the best of all the late cantatas, tender, warm-hearted, and free from the mechanical progressions of harmony, fussy passage-work and automatic sequences that disfigure so many of Parry's cantatas from the *St. Cecilia Ode* (1889) onwards. The difference in inspiration between these two odes is irrespective of date and may be attributed to the poets; the Nativity ode is a setting of Dunbar's not Milton's words; Pope even in hymning St. Cecilia was not the poet to fire Parry's aspiring mind.

The third class contains the later cantatas which have no chance of revival. In them aspiration has become almost wholly ethical and yet has elicited pedestrian verse and perfunctory music from a preacher who was once an artist. This is the paradox of Parry's mind and personality.

Since *Prometheus Unbound* is a historical landmark it may be well to scrutinize it. Colles in the seventh volume of *The Oxford History of Music* calls attention to the "sense of forceful declamation which English music had not known since Purcell" and quotes the opening monologue. An earlier critic of *The Times* may be quoted in full, since his criticism is good and will serve as a text for a discussion on criticism in a later chapter.* The writer was probably Francis Hueffer. He puts his finger at once on the salient

* See Chapter XX.

features of Parry's style—his attitude to words, the "Wagernian" character of his mixture—if this seems curious now we need only compare Parry's declamation with what had gone before to see the truth of it—and the expansiveness of his choral writing. Here is the notice to the extent of half of the column devoted to the Three Choirs Festival's first day, Tuesday, September 7, 1880. It is worth observing that the same issue of *The Times* contained a column-and-a-half review of Schliemann's book on Troy, indicating the importance attached by that newspaper, then as now, to other than political issues.

The Times, Wednesday, September 8
"This evening's concert [i.e. September 7] given at the Shire Hall and well attended, introduced the first, and what may safely be called the more important of the two English novelties of the present festival. Mr. Hubert Parry, known to the London public chiefly by a piano concerto recently performed at the Crystal Palace and Richter concerts, has selected the words of his cantata (if this it can be called) from Shelley's *Prometheus*, and his choice cannot be sufficiently commended. English composers are too frequently forgetful of the fact that bad poetry rarely inspires good music, and English poets have sometimes returned the compliment by writing some of their weakest stanzas 'for music'. At the same time there are in our literature untold treasures of lyrical impulse which only await the hand of genius to sound forth in musical beauties. Among such treasures the choral portions of Shelley's classical drama must no doubt be counted, and the capability of musical treatment will be accepted without hesitation. Mr. Parry would indeed have done better in confining himself exclusively to these lyrical episodes, treating them as independent rhapsodies. Instead of this, he has given us detached bits of monologue, equally tantalizing to those who are and those who are not acquainted with Shelley's poem and moreover somewhat beyond the young composer's power. Mr. Parry is unmistakably a disciple of Wagner's school, and the declamatory style adopted, for example, in Prometheus's first monologue is therefore sufficiently familiar to him. He indeed treats the words with laudable attention to their poetic as well as their metrical significance. But this is not all that is necessary. The declamatory type of music, paradoxically though the statement may sound, requires an

infinitely greater fount of melody than the ordinary hum-drum
style of Italian opera. This melody, though it only at intervals
develops into a distinct rhythmical phrase, is always potentially
present, being heard now in the orchestra, now in the voice parts.
Without it the declamation is dry and void of interest. It is in this
'endless melody', as it has not inappropriately been called, that
Mr. Parry seems somewhat deficient. Not that he is an un-
melodious composer. There are charming melodious phrases, for
example, in the female chorus 'From unremembered ages', and in
the solo quartet to which the beautiful lines 'Life of life thy life
enkindle' have been set. But the latter is essentially strophic in
treatment and is perhaps of all the numbers the one least representative of Mr. Parry's peculiar gift. On the other hand there
is a decided want of coherence in the first monologue of Prometheus. Again the address of Jupiter is more noisy than powerful,
and the kind of brindisi with which it winds up to the words 'Pour
forth Heaven's wine, Idean Ganymede' is scarcely in accord with
the moderate amount of dignity which even Shelley must leave to
the God. The piece, by the way, was most admirably rendered by
Mr. Edward Lloyd, a singer of whom it may justly be said that he
touches nothing without adorning it. This is scarcely the place to
enter upon the detailed analysis of a work which should be heard
more than once to be fully appreciated, and it must suffice to dwell
on one or two features which at once suggest themselves to the
attentive listener. One of these is the close connection of Mr.
Parry's music with the words it tends to illustrate. It may be said
of him that in more than one instance he has succeeded in giving
additional force to Shelley's lines. There is a case in point in the
female chorus alluded to, where the import of the words 'As
the thoughts of man's own mind' is admirably emphasized by the
high G of the first soprani. Equally impressive is the entry of the
trombone to 'We laugh thee to scorn' in the chorus of the Furies.
The finale of Mr. Parry's work based on the fourth act of the
drama is a choral piece of considerable expansion, rising to a
climax of almost dithyrambic enthusiasm. It contains excellent
contrapuntal writing, also some *cantabile* passage of great sweetness. Here, as elsewhere, Mr. Parry's music, as all vocal music
should do, grows from and is inseparably wedded to the words.
The orchestral prelude which introduces the cantata shows

Wagnerian influence, perhaps more even than the vocal portions
of the work. Without containing any distinct reminiscence it
resembles structurally the marvellous prelude to 'Tristan and
Isolde' with which it also shares the oneness of sentiment. Its
motto might be 'Ah me, alas, pain, pain ever, for ever', and the
feeling of despairing grief is sustained throughout. There is on
the other hand a total absence of the demonstrative defiance,
which is so prominent a feature in Shelley's picture. The hero who,
it may be presumed, is depicted in Mr. Parry's prelude, may well
be a Prometheus; he is certainly not Shelley's Prometheus. The
reception of Mr. Parry's work on the part of a crowded audience
was most favourable. The chorus of Furies and the solo of Miss
Williams and Mr. Lloyd being especially rewarded by well
deserved applause. Madame Patey also did excellent service. Mr.
Francis, the representative of Prometheus, was less satisfactory.
He had evidently studied his part carefully, but his voice is harsh
and his method very imperfect. The performance generally,
although conducted by the composer, betrayed the want of
sufficient rehearsing, the choral singing being occasionally anything but refined. It must, however, be borne in mind that the
music is very difficult and complicated. Mr. Parry's work was
preceded and followed by a miscellaneous selection which does
not call for detailed notice."

This is good criticism, and even in detail much of it can be
endorsed after eighty years. Hueffer picks out the female chorus
"From unremembered ages" for its sheer melodic charm, and in
the light of Parry's subsequent asceticism one may appreciate the
sensuous beauty to be found not only here but elsewhere in this
early work. Jupiter's address, he says, is more noisy than powerful.
We know more about noise and power than Hueffer did, but the
critic is at any rate shrewd enough to have hit on one of Parry's
rather arid and tiresome idioms, the square dotted-note figures
pursued persistently and sequentially till one is battered and out
of breath with them.

Ex 7

On the other hand the complaint that the fine broad diatonic tune, forerunner of many such, to the words "Pour forth heaven's wine" lacks dignity shows the Victorian confusion of that manly quality with starched primness. One may also disagree about the "demonstrative defiance" of Shelley's Prometheus and concur that Parry's dignified characterization in the overture has some sort of irrelevant resemblance to the Prelude to *Tristan*. On the main issue posterity has agreed with the implied judgment that here a new voice was sounding in English music. This bold, energetic and aspiring music makes the usual festival cantata of the time look anaemic, and indeed almost brainless.

Parry stuck to the poets and eschewed the Bible for his cantata texts for some years. The setting of Milton's *Ode on a Solemn Music* owes its success, both immediately at its first performance by the Bach Choir in 1887 and subsequently at innumerable festivals, to the fact that in it the "sphere-born harmonious sisters, Voice and Verse" do unquestionably "wed their divine sounds and mixed power employ". There is a deep personal affinity between poet and composer; both were artistic puritans (or rather puritan artists), and both imparted to their "noble numbers" a certain massive gait that is the mark of English dignity. Parry's setting of *L'Allegro ed Il Pensieroso* shows a similar congruity of Voice and Verse, sufficiently happy to disarm a critic so confessedly biased against Parry and all his works as Bernard Shaw. He says of *L'Allegro ed il Pensieroso** that "it did much to soften the feelings with which I have regarded the composer for some time past. Dr. Parry is so genuine an enthusiast, so thorough a workman at his craft, so engaging an essayist, and in short so unexceptionable a musical fellow creature that *Judith* was a hard blow to bear from him. Perhaps he was right—as a doctor of music—to dissemble his artistic feeling: but why did he write an oratorio? I have hardly alluded to him with common civility since; but now that his genius, released from an unnatural and venal alliance, has flown back to the noble poetry that was its first love, let the hatchet be buried—and *Judith* with it as soon as possible. This new cantata of his is happy, ingenious, as full of contrapuntal liveliness as *Judith* was full of contrapuntal deadliness, and genuine in feeling throughout."

* Cf. pp. 349-50.

This notice of 1890 not only shows Shaw's musical perspicacity but points to the difficulty in which Parry found himself by reason of the success of *Blest Pair of Sirens*. Festival committees pestered him for new works instead of repeating those he had already written, and he still continued to find poetical texts. He had set Shirley's *Glories of our Blood and State* after *Prometheus* in 1883, Pope's *St. Cecilia Ode* in 1889 and Milton's *L'Allegro*, as we have seen, in 1890, but between 1888 and 1894 come three biblical oratorios. Parry was aware that sclerosis had afflicted the form—had he not pointedly avoided it himself with *Prometheus* in 1880? But he thought that if some more profound and contemplative element, whether of faith and dogma as in Bach or of a more philosophical attitude to the mysteries of human life, such as is found in Brahms's *Requiem*, were restored to the merely dramatic interest on which composers, bemused by the success of *Elijah*, had been content to rely, oratorio could live again. In theory this is sound doctrine, for true oratorio is not history but reflections upon the great events of history. In a preface to *Judith* he says that it was the universal aspect of events, not the fates of individuals, that attracted him to historical episodes. But the universal element hardly emerges and the oratorio remains, at any rate until a point near the end, at the level of historical, not of poetic, truth.

Job, the second of the biblical oratorios, performed at the Gloucester Festival of 1892, was likewise castigated by Shaw. But it is really quite a different matter. In it metaphysics do fertilize music, as they do in Wagner, where Shaw had no difficulty in recognizing the process, and indeed was at this very time expounding it in *The Perfect Wagnerite*. The theme of *Job* is of permanent significance to humanity, and it fully engaged Parry's philosophical mind. The philosophical qualities of the work recommended it to Herbert Spencer if not to G.B.S. He has successfully employed a quasi-dramatic form and representative themes to make a concise and challenging cantata that would be twice as vivid and compelling if only it had been reasonably well scored. Such of the text as is not biblical is his own. The outstanding features are the *scena*, Job's Lamentation, and the similarly large and powerful piece of declamation which follows from the chorus, who personify the voice of God—"Who is this

that darkeneth counsel?", culminating in half a dozen bars of
the unaccompanied choral writing in which Parry excelled.

The part of Job was created by Harry Plunket Greene, who in
testifying (in *Interpretation in Song*) to Parry's power of writing
for the voice cites this great solo as an instance of perfect
declamation which is easier to sing from a technical point of view
than "Drink to me only with thine eyes".

Of *King Saul* (Birmingham: 1894) even so faithful an admirer
as Fuller-Maitland can find nothing good to say except for the
literary skill of the libretto, for which the composer was responsible.

Then came the period when the "ethical twist" began seriously
to cramp Parry's natural gift for writing choral music. Except for
the lucid moment in 1905 when *The Pied Piper* saw the light of a
festival day, the later cantatas, culminating in *Vision of Life*,
written in 1907 for a Cardiff festival and revised in 1914, are
increasingly weighed down by ethical sentiment. The composer is
to a considerable extent his own librettist in these works and
there is no doubt that what he was trying to do was an artistic
task of the first magnitude. It was nothing less than to think out
with the rigour of a philosopher the vision of a prophet and present
the result with all the art of the musician to create an agnostic
oratorio. He failed. Which is not surprising. R. O. Morris,
writing candidly but still under the influence of Parry's own
inspiring personality, calls them "noble failures". And so, of
course they are, if to aim high constitutes nobility. But half a
century later it is of no use attempting to disguise the fact—and
it would be of no service to Parry's memory—that they are not
only as dreary as festival audiences found them at the time but,

speaking critically and using the word without offence, half-baked. Parry was too busy, too quick, too inexperienced in rigorous philosophical thinking, to have got life's major issues either focused into philosophical sharpness or made incandescent in poetry. He was so keen on the ideas and had so much of the evangelist in him that he was content to throw the ideas into pedestrian verse which could inspire no one to musical utterance, not even the poet himself. He was too facile and too uncritical in musical technique to struggle through to the intense and concentrated music that lofty themes have a right to exact. Brutally put, this ethical idealism is superficial and the music into which it was translated perfunctory.

It is the same with a book to which Parry devoted much labour in his last years, *Instinct and Character*. His publishers and executors wisely and rightly refused to publish it. Here he tried to think out the conclusions which a life rich in experience suggested to him. Parry was a wise man, and his wisdom and personal goodness were a source of inspiration to his disciples. The book contains much wisdom and is indeed remarkable as the hard-won conclusions of a mind working towards its own solution of problems that face us all. Musicians who are capable of sustained ratiocination based on cool, almost scientific observation are rare: Parry was naturally respected by his contemporaries for his ability to speak a philosophical language, but he had no philosophical training nor did he ever have the opportunity for concentrated philosophical thought until he started to work it out in this book. The result is that it presents an argument and conclusions, often quite sound in philosophy and psychology, but elementary and jejune. It is a melancholy conclusion that all this valuable effort to do what a man ought to do, namely think for himself, was so much waste of time.

Very few of Parry's numerous instrumental works have survived. Time's sifting process has probably not greatly erred in deciding that his choral music is of greater worth and more lasting appeal. And it is noteworthy that in his catalogue of 225 works those for instruments cluster fairly thickly in the early part of his career and get increasingly rare in the later, though his small distinctive contribution to organ literature comes at the end and he continued to write for the piano all through right up to the very last number on the list which is a suite of five miniatures for piano.

He made his first impression on the musical public with his piano concerto in F sharp which was played at the Crystal Palace (with Dannreuther as soloist) in 1880—the year of *Prometheus Unbound*. Previously he had written mostly small pieces, church music and some chamber music including several piano trios, a combination of instruments to which he seems to have been partial. 1880 marks the beginning of his middle and most flourishing period as a composer, before his duties at the R.C.M., and the change of mental attitude which seems to have accompanied them, turned him towards his more ethical and introspective productions. In the eighties he produced four of his six major works for orchestra. The chamber music belongs to the same period. To the early nineties belong an overture, *Lady Radnor's Suite* for string orchestra and the *Symphonic Variations*, his best orchestral work. After the turn of the century his symphonic and his choral writing approximate and one finds oratorios called "sinfonia sacra".

Of the four symphonies No. 3 in C has more character than its two predecessors and its successor. Indeed it established itself at once as "The English". Why English? What makes music English? The question of national style was fully argued during the last half of the nineteenth century. The use of folk-song as a basis for thematic material was the first and most ready answer to the question and is satisfactory as far as it goes but is not exhaustive. Parry's style was too set to be influenced by the rediscovery of English folk-song, to which he gave his interest and support. But it is not for that reason *non*-English.

Tovey says (apropos of the *Symphonic Variations*): "Parry never pretended to found or foster a 'distinctively English' style of music—as if it were a smaller thing to be English than to be a musician. He could no more help writing an English style than he could help being a musician." Which is all very well for Tovey, who shared this view of nationalism himself, but it is actually the reverse of the truth. The trouble with Parry's symphonic music, as with Tovey's music, is that these two composers accepted without question, and indeed without it ever occurring to them that there might be a question, what is essentially a German way of thinking musical thoughts. Those English composers who took Tovey's view, that English music is just music that happens to be written by composers born in the British Isles, are those who failed in spite of great gifts to write a music of sufficient distinction to hold its own against the competition of the classics. Stanford, Tovey himself, Parry, F. S. Kelly, Hamilton Harty—and to some extent Bantock and the Frankfurt group, though they achieved greater distinction—all tried to grow an English (or Irish) music on a continental stem. Parry most nearly succeeded in doing this in his *English Symphony* and in his *Symphonic Variations*, where the problem is less acute than in the sonata forms, since variation is universal.

The *Symphonic Variations* of 1897 Parry seems not himself to have esteemed very highly—at any rate he records that they sounded to him rather tiresome. They were, however, played abroad, and had many performances in England and continued to crop up occasionally after his other orchestral works were forgotten. An analysis is to be found in Tovey. Their theme is distinctive (of six bars' length) and their over-all design "symphonic" and original. The work is long enough for substance and not too long for the material, and there is felicity of detail in the general bonhomie. Here was the most promising attempt—saving *Enigma*—of the last decades of the nineteenth century to create an English orchestral music. The next generation discovered that the method was wrong and began digging and planting direct into English soil. How narrow a margin of time divides the two schools may be seen by comparing Kelly and Butterworth, who were both killed in 1916 and were separated at the university by exactly one generation of four years. Kelly missed and Butterworth caught the new breeze (of nationalism) blowing through English music just before the 1914 war.

All his life long Parry wrote songs. The series of *English Lyrics* in twelve volumes by no means embodies them all, for he composed bigger things, scenas with orchestra, and smaller things, school songs for various places and people. But the seventy-three songs of the *English Lyrics* are more than enough to show his emotional range, his literary taste, his melodic invention and the aptitude of his accompaniments. Harry Plunket Greene (in an essay contributed to Graves's biography) has said all that needs to be said about Parry's ear for declamation, and if anyone urges the over-riding claims of singable melody he will find them met in the great unison songs "England" and "Jerusalem" which testify in no un-certain measure to his command of strong self-supporting melody. His taste in second-rate verse was not perhaps so certain as his taste in first-rate poetry, and some of the lyrics he set, those by Julia Chatterton for instance in the last posthumous volume of *English Lyrics*, are touched with late Victorian sentimentality. A similar flaw in the harmony of some of his opening bars dates some of the songs, so that one cannot now hear them without catching the echoes of much inferior shop ballads of the time which talked the same harmonic language. Yet he could make a big thing out of the most conventional progressions as in "When the Sun's great orb" of Volume 12 of *English Lyrics* which has the stride of the big Schubert songs like "Prometheus" or "Die Allmacht". It is, however, in general the smaller things which show that perfect reconciliation of all the elements which constitutes the art of song writing. "The Lover's Garland" to A. P. Graves's trans-lation of the song to Heliodora in the Greek Anthology is utterly happy. "There is a lady" and "To Althea from Prison" have a similar lyricism and warmth of feeling.

Parry's contributions to scholarship were three: his *The Art of Music* published in 1893, in which he applied to musical history the concept of evolution in much the same sort of way as Sidgwick had applied it to ethics—evolution was probably the greatest single concept thrown up by the nineteenth century, comparable in value to Bacon's empiricism in the seventeenth—Volume III of *The Oxford History of Music*, which was devoted to the seventeenth century (1902); and *Johann Sebastian Bach, the Study of a Great Personality* (1909). Their intellectual solidity won over the educated classes to a belated recognition of the art of music as a part of general culture. In these and his other writings, notably *Style in Musical Art* (1911) which was based on the lectures which he was statutorily required to deliver as Professor of Music at Oxford, Parry urged the view, in which he was supported by W. H. Hadow, that music could properly be regarded as one of the humaner letters. These literary works must be registered in any account of his total contribution to English musical life.

BOOK TWO

Birth

VIII

Stanford and the Academic Tradition

THE NAME of Charles Villiers Stanford (1852-1924) is regularly and rightly coupled with that of Parry as joint architect with him of the movement for giving new vitality and higher standards to native English music, which we call our renaissance. A writer who published a book on Stanford in the form of an annotated catalogue of his works in 1921* begins his first essay by assigning Stanford to the "Parry Group". In it he includes Mackenzie and Cowen, and Mackenzie was certainly associated with Parry and Stanford in what they all consciously accepted as a missionary enterprise for the betterment of English music, as Bernard Shaw's witty caricature of them as a mutual admiration society testifies.† But Mackenzie was not, like them, a man of university education; he belonged to the older tradition of the working musician, and it was the working musicans who had kept English music stuffy— Sterndale Bennett's attempt to break through the stifling complacency ended in failure. Mackenzie in his turn, though not in the least stuffy in personality, had his talent quenched by his academic duties.

The university connections of Parry and Stanford are important, because an infusion of general culture was necessary, even with a genius like Elgar appearing from nowhere and causing a tidal wave, and because the deeper roots of the art needed irrigation, the status of the profession needed to be raised if the educated classes were to be weaned from their acceptance of music as part of the import trade and the business of foreigners. This atmosphere of condescension bred the inferiority it postulated. The conquest of

* John F. Porte (Kegan Paul).
† *Music in London 1890-94* (Constable, 1932), Vol. 1, p. 260. See p. 350.

the universities by music—a process only completed after the 1939-1945 war—was a necessary step for the self-respect of the art. It was essential if the aims of a higher standard of literary scrupulousness on the part of composers, which had not obtained since Purcell, who had worked on terms of equality with a great poet like Dryden, were to be realized, if a more fastidious taste in performance and a keener appreciation of quality, which had been lacking in English music since Mendelssohn had involuntarily debilitated composition, criticism and popular appreciation alike, were to be generated. The universities were the organ through which this more exacting music was injected into the national blood stream, since their influence permeated the whole educational system.

Stanford was given a sound classical education at his school in Dublin and in 1870 went up to Cambridge where he held a classical and an organ scholarship at Queens' College. At the age of twenty he was appointed conductor of the Cambridge University Musical Society and was offered the organistship of Trinity College in 1873. In the following year he graduated in classics, but he had already become a musician, and during the next two years spent part of his time studying composition in Germany. He retained a life-long connection with Cambridge, but his relations with the university were chequered, as all his relations with everybody were. Though his portrait hangs in the hall of Trinity, he was never made a fellow—to his chagrin—and the reasons must have been personal, since he was a man of the utmost distinction and brilliance. It is true that Oxford and Cambridge were not in the habit of making their musicians fellows, but there is abundant testimony to Stanford's brilliance as a young man, and his academic standards were of the highest—indeed he was so exacting that all through his professorship (to which he was elected in 1887) few doctorates were awarded and those who wanted them mostly took them at Oxford or Durham. However, both he and Parry, who similarly but later became Professor at Oxford, did most of their academic work not at the universities but in London at the newly founded (1883) Royal College of Music. The two men were thus thrown together by birth—Stanford was four years Parry's junior—by education, by identity of ideals and their long academic association. They were therefore able between them to accomplish a great deal for the better estate of English music and of music in England for a period of half a century.

All this is without regard to their work as composers, though it was the prestige of their compositions that provided the basis of their enormous influence and authority. If half a century later those compositions enjoy neither the currency nor the esteem of which they then seemed worthy, they are still of historical importance. Stanford furthermore was not only a composer but a performer and a great teacher, one of the greatest in fact who has ever produced a galaxy of pupils: Plunket Greene in his biography lists some fifty names, among which are found those of Vaughan Williams, John Ireland, George Dyson, Herbert Howells, Gustav Holst and Eugene Goossens. Conducting was a life-long occupation from his undergraduate days at Cambridge in the seventies, when he introduced a number of works, including the first symphony fresh from Brahms's pen, to his last years in charge of the College orchestra in London in the twenties of the next century. He had an acute ear, invincible musicianship and a forceful personality, and his operations in charge of the Leeds Festivals, of which he conducted four (1901-1910), of the Bach Choir (1885-1902), and of the College opera (at that time given annually in a London theatre) were magisterial in the days before the vogue of the virtuoso conductor—of whom the first to light upon the English scene was Nikisch (who was one of Stanford's successors, along with Elgar and Allen, at the Leeds Festival of 1913).

No doubt Stanford wrote too much. His technical mastery was such that he could, like Haydn, sit down to a daily stint of composition and never a bar of shoddy work in it. But his facility was not all good. It meant that he found the solutions to all problems too easily. It was observed that the least characteristic scene in his unusual and striking opera, *The Travelling Companion*, was that of the wizard and his goblins, because he knew only too well how that sort of stuff was written, whereas Elgar in *Gerontius* found a new expression for demonology and Holst in *The Perfect Fool* a strange and disturbing wizardry. This knowledge, the double knowledge of what had been done and how to do it, also won him the reproach of being academic. The word ought not to carry a reproach, for it implies both erudition and skill, an approach to the things of the mind that regards them as intrinsically worthwhile for their own sake without ulterior purpose. Stanford caustically dismissed it as "the latest catchword for the works of all men who learn their business before they practise it." But in critical usage it does carry the imputation that, though all composers need some intellectual skill to support structures in which inspiration cannot be at full flood all the time, the proportion between skill and inspiration, intellect and intuition, is wrong: there is too much conscious contrivance in proportion to the originality of the upsurge from the subconscious (which is what inspiration is). The great composers are usually very fertile and even their output usually contains a good deal that is more skilful than inspired. Stanford's output was enormous in every branch of music: he composed nine operas, seven symphonies, ten concertos, six *Irish Rhapsodies* for orchestra, four masses, about twenty anthems and services for the Anglican church, twenty-two secular cantatas, eight string quartets as well as six duet sonatas and other chamber music, six organ sonatas, a large number of songs and part-songs, and incidental music to plays. But it is noticeable that his most distinctive, which is to say his most vital, which is to say his best, work is in the smaller forms, in which the skill to sustain large structures, which he had in plenty, is not required and the danger of inflation is avoided.

Large works like the *Stabat Mater* and the *Requiem*, in which all the resources of nineteenth-century harmony, orchestration and vocal part-writing are used, are saved from over-ripe sentiment and sensuousness by his most characteristic aesthetic virtue of economy; sometimes they stand up in performance, and sometimes they fall down because ultimately they seem to be copies of Verdi. In this respect the *Requiem*, written for Lord Leighton in 1896, is the stronger work, since it prompts fewer unwanted memories. Thus the *Dies Irae* begins with a murmur, not with a crash, and its constituent figure

Ex 9   Allegro moderato ma energico

is maintained throughout with short intermissions (where it would not suit the text) and with several transformations—this for instance for *Judex ergo cum sedebit*:

which builds up to a formidable threat. The effect is not only one of symphonic unity but of a pictorial stroke of imagination of a power that has to be heard to be believed. In general too his conception seems not to have been *Dona eis requiem*—Verdi's prayer has been described as for the peace of the churchyard— or a plea for light, *lux luceat eis*, but Death where is thy sting? For the *Agnus Dei*, though in the form of a *marcia funebre*, sounds more like a paean. The early (1891) oratorio *Eden* (to a book by Robert Bridges and dedicated to Parry) has long been dead, and Shaw alas! proved right when he said of it "I caught not a single definite purpose or idea at all commensurate with the huge pretensions of the musical design. That pretension is the ruin of *Eden*." This criticism puts its finger on a spot which more sympathetic critics have conceded: Stanford accepted the classical forms and sought to fill them by orthodox procedures. Dunhill says it of the chamber music,* Howells of the large-scale choral and orchestral works.† Vaughan Williams, a devoted pupil and admirer, said the same without naming him in his famous article "Who wants the English composer?"‡ When this last appeared Stanford fitted the cap on his own head and there was a domestic row about it. Content determines form not *vice versa* in musical composition.

The symphonies are usually written off as Brahmsian, and so no doubt they are in the same sort of way as the *Stabat Mater* is Verdian, the result probably, as other composer-conductors have found, of too much conducting of other men's music. Even No. 5., which is based on "L'Allegro" and "Il Penseroso", is a misfit of an English programme into Teutonic habits which Stanford liked to wear but which did not suit him. But one must be careful. The

* H. P. Greene, *Charles Villiers Stanford* (Arnold, 1935), pp. 224-8.

† *Proceedings of the Royal Musical Association*, LXXIX, 1952-1953.

‡ *R.C.M. Magazine*, Vol. LX, No. 1, 1912.

resemblance of the opening strain of the Lament movement in
Stanford's third symphony in F minor, the "Irish",

Ex 11

to that of the slow movement of Brahms's fourth was easily
spotted,* but Stanford took it from a Lament in the Petrie collection of Irish folk-songs† and according to his account the
symphonies were being composed simultaneously.‡ This symphony contained two other quotations, the tunes "Molly
McAlpin" and "Let Erin remember" in the finale, and it has a
hop jig for scherzo. If the first movement shows the inadequacy
of competent workmanship going through the correct motions,
the general Irish atmosphere of the rest justifies the nickname,
though the total effect is like leaving and returning to Ireland for
a holiday in Germany.

Actually this Irish element is fundamental in Stanford, though
it is not always in evidence—not for instance in the church music
nor in most of the big choral and orchestral works. He was an
Irishman of the Orange persuasion, who had a love-hate relationship with his native city of Dublin. He had the Irishman's strange
belief that pugnacity is a virtue and his conduct accorded with his
creed. He loved Irish tunes even before he undertook the editing
of the Petrie collection (published in 1902-1905) and his best songs
are settings of Irish (though not Gaelic, of which he had none)
texts. So here was a contradiction—one of many in his make-up:
the Irishman goes into voluntary exile, like many other Irish
artists from Sheridan to Shaw, to England, whose traditions he
accepts, and then he becomes continental in musical outlook as a
result of training in Germany. He thus combated the nationalism
that pervaded Europe in the last part of the nineteenth century
instead of embracing it, as Dvořák and Grieg did in like case. It

* For Bülow's sporting action before the Berlin performance see Stanford's
Pages from an Unwritten Diary (Arnold, 1914), p. 262.

† "The Lament of the Sons of Usnach." Stanford only uses the opening
phrase, which he repeats over and over as an accompaniment figure.

‡ But the history books do not confirm this. Brahms's fourth symphony
was composed and had its first performance in 1885. Stanford's symphony
was a product of 1887. I once heard it stated at a performance of the "Irish"
that it was earlier than Brahms's by four years, which is plainly not the case.

follows that his rhapsodies are better than his symphonies and may even yet have life in them. For the rhapsody was the accepted way of overcoming the recalcitrance of self-subsistent national tunes to the third-degree processes of symphonic development. There are six such *Irish Rhapsodies* in which some of Ireland's best tunes appear; two of them are quasi-concertos with solo parts for cello (No. 3) and violin (No. 6). No. 4, known as the "Ulster" and bearing the sub-title "The Fisherman of Lough Neagh and what he saw", is judged by T. F. Dunhill* as his most beautiful orchestral composition, "full of wild natural poetry and the scoring more inspired than that of the symphonies, more full of light and shadow, of colour and glamour". Of the chamber music even Dunhill, who greatly admired it, has to admit that it lacks thematic distinction. Again classical procedures are not enough.

When, however, the Irish strain is dominant and the continental strain of polished technique is secondary the best of Stanford appears, as in the song "The Fairy Lough" from the *Irish Idyll* cycle and in at least three of *A Sheaf of Songs from Leinster*, in the effective and affecting cantata *Phaudrig Crohoore*, and in the opera *Shamus O'Brien*, which enjoyed a world success—it was produced in America and Australia and in Berlin as well as London. Oddly enough there is another department of Stanford's output in which he achieved not only permanent success but a distinction of utterance that is his alone, in his Anglican church music, where there is no trace of Irish melody nor influences from abroad. The service in B flat (1879)—note the date†—inaugurated a new era in which the sentimental chromaticism of the Victorians, such as Dykes and Barnby, was eliminated in favour of a classical purity of idiom and a scrupulous sense of fitness for its liturgical purpose. The similar but later (1910) set of canticles for all three services in C major shows how without repetition of words the verbal declamation can proceed with dignity and plenty of musical interest, especially the harmonic interest of clean modulation and juxtaposition of keys. The G major *Magnificat* with its feminine suggestion of a spinning wheel is described by Howells‡ as "ecstasy without crisis" and the anthem "The Lord is my

* In Plunket Greene's biography.
† In current use nearly a century later.
‡ *Proceedings of the Royal Musical Association*, LXXIX, 1952-1953.

Shepherd" as "one of the supremely lovely anthems of all our history". Their virtue is that they sound right, exactly right without qualification. There are also three motets *Justorum animae, Coelos ascendit* with a glorious Alleluia cadence, and *Beati quorum vita*, masterly examples of spacious writing with unerring recognition of the capabilities and the limitations of unaccompanied voices, and because functionally they do not require an intensity of personal expression they stand out as sheer splendid compositions.

Another sphere in which neither German nor Irish proclivities make or mar his personal style is part-songs and some other short pieces. "The Blue Bird" and "Heraclitus" are examples of perfection achieved in their small compass. *The Songs of the Sea* and *The Songs of the Fleet* for baritone chorus and orchestra achieve the same rightness on a larger but still not very large scale. In fact the small things have the individuality that the larger works lack and call all the more strongly for the impeccable craftsmanship which he possessed so abundantly.

The operas, of which there were seven that came to production, were dogged by persistent ill-fortune. Even *Shamus O'Brien*, which like *Phaudrig Crohoore* was set in the context of the '98 Rebellion, had at one time to be withdrawn by the composer during later Irish troubles for fear of exacerbating the situation. It exists in two versions; the first was with spoken dialogue, which goes better with Irish actor-singers, the second was a version with recitative which was performed at La Scala, but is regarded by Greene, who heard both, as inferior to the comic opera version which goes more nimbly. Of the first *The Veiled Prophet*, produced at Hanover in 1881 and at Covent Garden in Italian, if you please, in 1893, only the splendid song, "The Bower of Roses" survives. *Savonarola* (1884), also produced in Germany at Hamburg, failed in London. *The Canterbury Pilgrims* got a good start from Carl Rosa in London at Drury Lane and, being described as an English *Meistersinger*, might have been expected to keep afloat but mysteriously sank without trace along with *Savonarola* of the same year. *Much Ado about Nothing* (1901) has twice been revived* after a miserable couple of performances at Covent Garden in 1901.

---

* Royal College of Music, 1935; Oxford University Opera Club, 1949, both of which productions I saw.

As with all operatic settings of Shakespeare sub-plot and quick dialogue are something of an embarrassment but this setting of a libretto reduced from the play is very light. It starts, and finishes, with a captivating setting of "Sigh no more, ladies", it contains a sarabande and a serenade with guitar that have the enchantment of a summer night, and an impressive church scene. The whole thing is delicious. *The Critic* is satirical, full of esoteric allusions and therefore not likely to win a wide popularity. *The Travelling Companion* on the other hand did run successfully at Sadler's Wells in 1935. From the death of Purcell to the arrival of Britten, English opera has had a chequered career with only *Maritana* and *The Bohemian Girl* to conquer a reluctant public and go abroad. Stanford's efforts seemed to suffer the usual fate of native operas. Mackenzie also wrote seven operas with much the same sort of reward. Parry disliked opera and Elgar only contemplated the idea of operatic composition half-heartedly near the end of his life. Stanford was therefore a champion in an unpromising cause. But unless and until the British public accepted opera as a legitimate art form and not an import from Italy for connoisseurs of singing, there could hardly be said to be a healthy musical life in Britain; no renaissance could be complete without opera. Historically therefore Stanford undertook a necessary task in writing operas. His academic work made an immediate and lasting contribution to the awakening of our music to a new vigour. And among his huge output there are some fine things, many of them small like the part-songs already mentioned, which are perfect in art and craft and proportion and feeling and verbal illumination. One is almost tempted to sum him up by saying that he might have been a great composer if he had not been so superlatively good a musician.

Another Irishman and English academic working in some though not all of Stanford's fields and altogether less prolific was Charles Wood (1866-1926), of whom similar qualities are to be predicated—a restrained and fastidious taste, an impeccable technique, harmony that is euphonious and very clean on the ear, and every now and then an emergent splendour of imagination in one of the smaller forms, as in the fine Whitmanesque song, "Ethiopia saluting the Colours." Wood was actually a pupil of Stanford at the Royal College from 1883 to 1887, and became his colleague both there and at Cambridge, where he eventually (1924) succeeded him as Professor. Among his private pupils he had Thomas Beecham for a couple of years. Academic duties filled most of his life but he wrote much church music in which two slightly unusual influences for an Anglican composer influenced his style, plainsong on the one hand and Genevan psalmody on the other. He made himself acquainted with the use of ecclesiastical modes and this knowledge coloured the settings he made of the tunes in *The Cowley Carol Book*, which had been drawn from mediaeval and foreign sources by the Rev. G. R. Woodward. Following the same ideal of a church music at once purged and enriched he wrote a *St. Mark Passion* requiring less elaborate resources than Bach but avoiding the banality and sentimentality of Stainer's *The Crucifixion*, which had been written with the needs of small church choirs in mind. Wood's *Passion* is dignified, austere even, and uses plainsong and psalm-tunes instead of hymns and chorales. In his motets, such as "O thou, the central orb", he writes a richer, more modern harmony, more like what he uses in his secular part-songs, of which he wrote a great number with and without piano.

His posthumously published string quartets, of which there are seven, were little played either in his lifetime or since, but they combine a melodious quality derived directly from Irish folk-song with his great contrapuntal ability "by which he never failed to show that ingenuity was a valuable servant of beauty" (E. J. Dent). He made a number of settings of Irish folk-songs and wrote a set of variations for string quartet on one. Wood was a retiring man, with, however, an Irish wit, who spent all his adult life in Cambridge. From there and the Royal College he exercised a far-reaching influence, second only to Stanford's, on a whole generation of pupils, from Vaughan Williams to Armstrong Gibbs, who won distinction.

Of the same generation as Wood, likewise a Cambridge man and a pupil of Stanford, Arthur Somervell (1863-1937; knighted for services to education in 1929) also produced a Passion oratorio, which is a superior *Crucifixion* but simpler than Wood's. He was a product of Uppingham School, which was the first of the public schools to treat music as an essential instead of an extra. Its great headmaster, Edward Thring, brought over a

German, Paul David, to devise a place for it in the curriculum, and was a pioneer in an educational movement that took a couple of generations to spread. It certainly contributed to making the country take music seriously and so to the renaissance. Somervell had some study in Berlin and some teaching from Parry. The result is that his music is German in its axioms but not in its accents. Just as Parry's "English" symphony sounded an English note in spite of its complete German orthodoxy, so all Somervell's music, and all the more in that he was a considerable song writer, had an English flavour but no other token of nationalism. His affiliation was more with Mendelssohn than with Brahms; he has the fluency, but a sweeter fragrance and a little more weight. Nor is there anything harmonically later than Sterndale Bennett in what he wrote, but it is not derivative. His taste, like Wood's and Stanford's, was fastidious, and he did nothing to add adventitious excitement to what was quite capable of standing on its own feet in its own style. Somervell was interested in folk-song and made a number of excellent settings—"The Twa Sisters o' Binnorie" is a finely cumulative version of the traditional ballad—but his compositions contain no conscious national influence. His instrumental works, the *Normandy Variations* for piano and orchestra, a symphony *Thalassa*, a *Concertstück* and a concerto for violin and orchestra, did not long survive their early performances and the changes of taste brought about by the war. It is otherwise with his song-cycles, of which he wrote five. His *Maud* (Tennyson) became a classic and has with some justice been called a minor masterpiece.* Equally good for sheer felicity of vocal line and imaginative figuration in the accompaniments is *A Shropshire Lad*, ten Housman settings, with the last turning an unusual metre into 15/8 time, dating from 1904. *Love in Springtime* is a smaller set, more anthology than cycle, but contains one or two delicate settings of poems by Christina Rossetti. Besides these he wrote two Browning sequences.

Composition, however, receded, though it was never abandoned, after he became an Inspector of Schools for the Board of Education. Here he did work of great value on the grass roots of education right down to the primary schools. He also interested himself, though in composition no progressive, in all the

* J. A. Westrup in Walker's *A History of Music in England* (1952).

progressive movements of the time, the folk-song movement, the newly founded Church Music Society and the competition festival movement.

The academic line among English composers established by these three late Victorians has continued, and in George Dyson, Herbert Howells, Alan Bush, Gordon Jacob, Edmund Rubbra, Howard Ferguson, to name no more, has produced much music of sterling worth, high quality and often distinction.

Slightly younger than Wood and Somervell was Frank Bridge (1879-1941), who can fairly be assigned to the school of Stanford, whose pupil he was, though less certainly to the academic tradition. The common reproach of British amateurism could not conceivably be applied to Bridge, for he was the complete professional and versatile at that. Indeed it is possible that he suffered in his reputation from the plenitude of his talents. Also he suffered from being awkwardly placed by the Time Spirit. Born in 1879, he was one of the first generation to benefit from the influence of Parry and Stanford, which meant that he grew up at the end of the romantic period and spoke its harmonic language naturally, but lived on into the reaction against it after the First World War and became aware of finding himself being shelved at the height of his career. To meet this galling situation he did what Bax, who was an even more conspicuous victim of the *Zeitgeist*, refused to do: he began to uglify his music to keep it up to date. In more polite terms this could be phrased as willingness to experiment with greater harmonic freedom, but the results sounded unnatural and unconvincing. The change began in the nineteen-twenties.

As a composer he certainly served his generation, notably in his chamber music, but it may be that he compromised his future by his practical services to his generation as string player and conductor. He began his professional life as a violinist in the Grimson Quartet and was sufficiently good to deputize in the Joachim Quartet, which in those days brought him immense prestige. He continued as a quartet player for nearly ten years in the English String Quartet. Chamber music was thus his chosen field as performer and composer. But he was a sufficiently good orchestral conductor to deputize for any star at short notice, though the only orchestra he ever regularly conducted was largely amateur, the Audrey Chapman Orchestra. The best of his orchestral compositions was the suite, *The Sea*.

This all-round musicianship ensured that he had complete technical mastery of everything he touched. Indeed Dr. Howells in writing of the crisis of his attempt to change his style spoke of "This composer-without-a-problem" who had "somehow run full tilt into an enigmatic development". Critics could hardly fail to comment that his works, chamber or orchestral, were "well written for strings". Unfortunately this just observation came to carry the implication that there was more skill than imagination to them. Which was unfair though not untrue. The imagination is most patent in one or two songs that achieved popularity and, as far as one can judge, permanence, which is to say a place in the long tradition of English song: such were "Love went a riding" (to a text by Mary Coleridge, from whom he took two other poems) and "Go not happy day" (Tennyson) and "Isobel".

But it was mainly in the field of chamber music that he won distinction in his lifetime. There are five string quartets, two piano trios, a sonata apiece for violin and cello, and many rather delightful short pieces not only for solo strings, but for string quartet in settings of "Sally in our alley", "Cherry ripe" and "Sir Roger de Coverley". Three of the works in this list were Phantasies in the Cobbett sense.* One of these is a piano quartet, which it is natural to compare with Brahms, though the general effect is lighter. The piano writing though intricate is also light and the form being concise is suited to the material. The piano trios are separated by twenty years. The first from 1907—a Phantasy—is also Brahmsian in flavour but with the lean athletic rather than the plump *Schwärmerei* side uppermost. In the second (1929) the search for modernism had begun but not got out of hand: the harmony has a tart flavour and there are some unusual sound effects. The texture in the piano is elaborate but the copious material is held together by internal logic and the romantic idiom is animated by classical ideals. The string quartets represent the rake's progress of a romantic gone wrong. The first two, a Phantasy of 1905 and No. 1 in E minor, were prize-winning works. No. 2 was described as one of those eager forward-looking works of the early years of the century which

* See pp. 335-6.

F

promised more than they actually accomplished, while No. 4 of 1937 was roundly condemned (at any rate by me in *The Times*) as straining after something so unnatural as to be not even well written for strings. Similarly the cello sonata (1917) is more acceptable than the violin sonata written in 1934, in which apart from the scherzo there seemed to be no interplay between the partners in making their way through a tortuous attempt at modernism. There is something lamentable in those pages of English musical history where the lives, careers and works of good composers like Bridge and Bax are set out, when their considerable achievements are seen within a generation to count for so little. This is not to deny that Bridge served his generation well, and indeed the next by his perceptive handling of the young Benjamin Britten, who was at a crucial time his pupil, so that he did not live in vain; but in the field of artistic creation, for which he seemed so well equipped, there is not a great deal that has kept its significance outside the songs, the early phantasies and maybe an instrumental piece or two which meets the needs of competitors, examinees and amateurs.

IX

Elgar

ELGAR WAS the first composer of full stature to be thrown up by English music since Purcell. He was not a direct product of the renaissance movement initiated by Parry, nor like Vaughan Williams had he dug in English soil to thrust his roots to the life-giving waters of nationalism. He is a curious figure, enigmatic from whatever aspect he is regarded, and his place in European music is still the subject of debate. The Continent has never wholly accepted him as a front-rank composer—it likens him to Strauss but holds him in lighter esteem. Yet it was the Continent—Germany in fact in the person of Richard Strauss—who hailed him as a "Master" after the famous performance of *The Dream of Gerontius* at Düsseldorf in 1902, which was the chief factor in reversing English judgment of the work upon its disastrous first performance at Birmingham in 1900. Such a toast* as Strauss gave on that occasion was certainly unusual, but the performance of English works abroad was not. Stanford had had operas performed on German stages—so had Ethel Smyth. Elgar, however, went farther than any previous English composer since the Elizabethans in penetrating the European mainland, by writing one of the few really great violin concertos and getting it played first by the Austrian, Kreisler. Menuhin in more recent times has carried it round the world, and the violoncello concerto has also engaged the interest of international artists like Feuermann and

* Strauss's toast of Elgar on this famous occasion was in these terms:

"I raise my glass to the welfare and success of the first English progressivist (Vorwärtsmann), Master Edward Elgar of the young progressive school of English composers."

Strauss recognized in Elgar a kindred spirit, striving for a larger expressiveness against the then hardening arteries of the German romanticism which had dominated European music for three quarters of a century.

Casals, Fournier and Tortelier. The *Enigma Variations* has a world-wide vogue as far as Japan and the *Introduction and Allegro for Strings* has found a place in the repertory of the great continental (including Russian) and American orchestras. Five works, and those his greatest, have, then, won a place in the international repertory, and foreign opinion may therefore be said to endorse the highest claims made for Elgar by his compatriots, though the two symphonies have so far failed to convince foreign opinion that they are music of the same calibre and importance.

We are not, however, bound to defer to foreign opinion and should have the courage of our own judgment. But here at home opinion, or rather perhaps taste, is quite sharply divided. Professor Dent raised a hornets' nest about his ears when in a contribution in 1931 to Adler's *Handbuch der Musikgeschichte* he enumerated, with the bluntness required by the compression of a handbook, four features of Elgar's style which give offence to a section of English opinion (which incidentally Dent described by implication as the academic and conservative): "too emotional", "not quite free from vulgarity", "pompous", and "too deliberately noble in expression". This criticism offers a parallel to the literary criticism of Kipling, his contemporary who similarly reflects the Edwardian age of English social life. Indeed it is tempting to regard Elgar's music as representative not so much of his country as of his period, and it is significant that European music critics, invited to London in 1935 by the British Council, sooner or later fell back on the name of Richard Strauss to describe to their readers the kind of music Elgar's was (independently of the judgment they may have passed upon it). Elgar reflects the last blaze of opulence, expansiveness and full-blooded life, before they perished in the twentieth century, qualities which take one somewhere near to that abundance of vitality which we call vulgarity. We may well envy the Edwardians the liberty, wealth and well-being which was to be swept away by world-wide wars, but we need not be deterred thereby from saying that it was after all just a little vulgar.

Contemporary opinion was also somewhat confused by a long series of works, especially early works, which could not be absolved of the charge of triviality, sentimentality and café music style. The explanation of such lollipops as "Salut d'amour", "Rosemary", "Chanson de matin" and "Chanson de nuit", coexisting embarrassingly alongside the great works, is the same as that of the conventionality of the early cantatas—they were the product of time and place, the work of a provincial musician of the Midlands in the nineties.

Elgar grew up outside the influence of the universities or London, which were the training grounds of Parry and Stanford. The process of self-criticism was thus not sharpened by his work having to satisfy the canons of metropolitan and, through the capital, of cosmopolitan taste. He was a working musician who provided music for the Asylum band at Worcester, which he himself directed, for Mr. Stockley's orchestra in Birmingham, or for his friend Dr. Swinnerton Heap's many enterprises in the shires of Worcester, Warwick and Stafford. He played the violin both for Stockley and for Heap, and in due time, viz. 1896, Heap secured *King Olaf* for first performance at the North Staffordshire Festival. North Staffordshire appears to have taken him to themselves as one of themselves. The association was fruitful and coincided with the supremacy of North Staffordshire in choral music. Even after the supremacy had passed to Yorkshire and Elgar had passed on to symphonic composition, North Stafford retained its love for the early cantatas when they had begun to seem old-fashioned in other parts of the country. As late as 1932 Elgar returned to Hanley to conduct a performance of *King Olaf*.* It was natural for Elgar to take to the form of quasi-dramatic cantata and he had not the literary discrimination to secure adequate texts at a time when English vocal music was becoming more exigent about poetic quality in words for music.

But self-education is not all loss. It may delay a man's arrival but it ensures that when he does arrive he is himself and his music shows fewer of the influences indicated by labels of foreign cities on his baggage. Elgar's own taste was eclectic—he liked for instance Meyerbeer, who is an abomination to academic England. No doubt that love of glittering effect, the pomps and shows of

---

* Mr. Reginald Nettel in *Music in the Five Towns* (1944) traces the evolution of choral music in industrial districts and shows how Elgar's development as writer of cantatas fitted in with this evolution. Elgar, he says, was the last to accept the working-class choral tradition which proceeded from part-song through cantata to oratorio, and *King Olaf* stands in the line of the common man's development at the period when it was written.

things, were elements that drew him to Meyerbeer, as to Liszt, of whom he had not the horror of the conventionally educated Englishman. His growth in the working-class tradition helped him to make his way in the years before 1900 and it gave him the common touch, which finds its happiest expression in the *Pomp and Circumstance* marches. It gave him humanity and saved him from having that humanity submerged, as it was ultimately submerged in the music of the academics, Parry and Stanford.

The early part-songs and cantatas are the culmination of nineteenth-century choral music along Victorian lines, of both working-class and polite choralism. Parry and Stanford had already tried by means of better literary texts to lead into something new and better. Elgar burst into the twentieth century with *The Dream of Gerontius*. *Caractacus* (1898) was the last of the elaborate quasi-dramatic constructions upon texts furbished from Longfellow or other narrative poets by literary friends of a composer in search of a libretto. *The Music Makers* (1912), though a cantata of similar dimensions, is not dramatic: it is in form an ode to music and to that extent is not prejudiced by a bad libretto.

There are four of these secular cantatas, all of them to chivalric texts and all belonging to the period before 1900. The *Froissart Overture*, Elgar's first contribution to a Three Choirs Festival (1890), testifies similarly to the appeal of romantic chivalry at this stage of its development to a mind that swung between wistful dreaming and splendid pageantry.* *The Black Knight* came first in 1892 and does not suffer from the elaboration of dialogue and dramatic business which weighs down longer secular cantatas. It is a choral ballad to a respectable but uninspired text by Longfellow in four compact and contrasted scenes. Elgar never had the certainty of touch with words possessed by his contemporaries and he permits himself repetition of lines to suit the choral development of the music, which he conceived as a symphony for voices and orchestra rather than as a secular oratorio. But apart from this the music, fresh though it is, proclaims nothing new. The cantata went the rounds, introduced a new name to concert programmes and so far encouraged the composer to proceed.

* Elgar and Ivor Atkins called one another by mediaeval nicknames. See Wulstan Atkins in *Royal Musical Association Proceedings*, 1957-1958.

This he did by catering for the same clients with part-songs, the other secular relief from too much oratorio. These part-songs from the nature of their brevity are more concentrated and, though they have not the quality of the later male-voice songs from the Greek Anthology, they have not suffered the eclipse of the cantata with the decline of Longfellow. "The Snow" and "Fly Singing Bird" for female voices, both with accompaniment for two violins and piano, have colour and charm. The words are Lady Elgar's, very slight verses but sufficiently fanciful to fire that same element in her husband's imagination. The set of six part-songs *From the Bavarian Highlands*, products of a holiday, have, like "Stars of the Summer Night", an orchestral accompaniment. Here, too, the verses, described as imitated from Bavarian folk-songs, and warmed with a breath of German romanticism, are by Lady Elgar, delightful in their way though not very distinctively Elgarian.

Elgar returned to part-song writing now and again up till 1914. Of these the *Five Songs from the Greek Anthology* (Op. 45) for male voices written in 1903 are the best. The vocal writing skilfully suggests descriptive orchestration and in a medium which has very little first-class music they won enthusiastic acceptance, three of them especially, "After many a dusty mile", "Feasting I watch" and "It's oh to be a wild wind", having an enormous vogue, which has never waned, as test-pieces for the most advanced choral competitions. "Go song of mine" (Op. 57) and "Death on the Hills" (Op. 72) for mixed voices indeed smack too much of the competition festival.

At the time of the production of *The Black Knight* (1893) he was thirty-six years old, but his fame was still only local. He had the consciousness that genius usually has of his own potentialities, but attempts to make an impression on the world at large had failed. His early compositions, small things such as anthems, voluntaries, part-songs and *morceaux de salon* (complete with French titles), though what were wanted of a local composer, were not the best introduction to London concert promoters and publishers. His marriage to Caroline Alice, daughter of Major-General Sir Henry Gee Roberts, in 1889 was probably the most decisive factor in his musical development—for here is another psychological enigma: she was, as far as musical creation was concerned, the male element which inseminated his productive capacity, for when she died his copious fertility dried up. It says much for his personal distinction that in provincial and Victorian England, where differences in social class were fairly rigorously observed, he, the son of a town shopkeeper—his father kept a music shop in Worcester—married, against what opposition we are not told but can easily imagine, a member of a "county" family, the daughter of a professional soldier and Knight of the Bath. He met his wife at the meetings of a choral society with which he had connections. She had literary interests and abilities, as her verses for his music testify, and she was possessed of a critical ear for music. The match turned Elgar from a local into a national composer, from a Midland musician into a great master.

After *The Black Knight* came *King Olaf* in the same year (1896) as his first oratorio *The Light of Life* at the Three Choirs Festival itself. *The Light of Life* (originally called *Lux Christi*) deals with the healing of the man blind from birth on the lines traditional for a festival oratorio. Both the secular cantata, which suffers from a clumsy libretto adapted from Longfellow in his jog-trot ballad style, and the oratorio are in fact products of their time and of their English circumstance. The composer, who on the Continent would have thought in terms of the symphony or the opera house, in England had to think in terms of the choral society and the provincial festival. Elgar at this stage of his career was treading the only obvious path open to him and was serving a prolonged apprenticeship. But in the music of both works could be discerned a new and more personal note. In *King Olaf* the new wine is being poured into the old bottles of the Victorian cantata. The music is ardent, picturesque, youthful. The short introduction in which the book of sagas is described is wonderfully evocative of the far away and long ago, but at the other end the chorus "As Torrents in Summer" goes back to the rather flat-footed, part-song style of Barnby and Sullivan which was soon to lose its superficial appeal even to Elgar's own generation. The Norse subject evidently appealed to Elgar, who claimed to be of remote Scandinavian descent on the strength of his name,* and it is worthy of remark

* Which, however, is pure Anglo-Saxon. See Grove, *Dictionary*, 4th ed., Supp. (1940), p. 1966.

that all four of these early cantatas are drawn from north European legend and all deal with fighting. But all suffer from defective libretti: *The Black Knight* and *The Banner of St. George* are prosy, *King Olaf* and *Caractacus* are badly constructed. In *King Olaf* the narrative and direct drama are mixed and distributed among chorus and soloists on no plan of characterization—thus the tenor soloist describes Olaf's return in the third person and afterwards impersonates him in the first. Elgar was careless of literary values, though when he came to write *Falstaff* he dipped into literary criticism. Indeed, literary carelessness was the bane of nineteenth-century choral music (Mackenzie provides a conspicuous instance of the damage it could do in *The Rose of Sharon*), against which Parry and his school protested by their example in rejecting it. Elgar was sufficiently aware of the clumsiness of the libretto as it stood to offer a note of explanation of its character as an imaginary gathering of bards and to join its episodes with symphonic interludes, which were, however, taken out at the instigation of the publishers. The work was a success when it was first performed by the North Staffordshire Festival Choir, then at the height of its fame, and gave to the composer the encouragement he needed.

The Banner of St. George, a patriotic ballad made out of verses no better than such things, compounds of clichés and inversions, usually are, is superficial stuff, but its epilogue, "It comes from the misty ages", has a forthright eloquence that corresponded to Elgar's love of pageantry, which, like Kipling's verses, to which it offers an oft-remarked parallel, was part of the spirit of the time, afterwards dubbed jingoism. Elgar wrote a number of things, the *Imperial March*, the *Coronation Ode*, the *Pomp and Circumstance* marches, in which the visible splendours of pomp and power are celebrated in music of a corresponding brilliance and swagger.

The same spirit mellowed and distilled to a finer essence can be detected in the symphonies and is one strain at least in his frequently used expression mark *nobilmente*. It was the expression of one part of Elgar's personality and was at the same time an exhalation from the mental atmosphere of the age before it was chastened by the Boer War and extinguished by a greater war still.

Caractacus pursues the same patriotic theme, but it is frankly dramatic in structure, and is altogether a more considerable and significant work. It deals with the subjection of the Britons to the Romans but finishes with a choral peroration in which Britain's future glories are hymned. This epilogue is something of an embarrassment to a work which would otherwise go on to the stage. It is comparable to Purcell's *King Arthur*, which also presents difficulties of presentation. The choral element commended it to the Leeds Festival of 1898 for which it was written and at any rate one attempt has been made to stage it as an opera. As a choral cantata it is handicapped by a text fitted up from the Saxon department of a Wardour Street store. The basis of it is certainly historical and its appeal to Elgar was natural since the scene of the action is the Malvern hills near his home. There is a good deal of nature music in the orchestral writing, wherein the camp on the Beacon, a forest near the Severn (painted by an independent prelude to the third scene), and the river itself are depicted as the scene of the choral action. The final scene takes place in Rome and opens with a triumphal march in Elgar's military and ceremonial vein. His music had by now acquired that free, almost wayward, flexibility which is the mark of the works of his maturity, yet it is held together by leading themes of marked character and attractive quality. There is in fact the mastery hitherto lacking, and its success at the chief of the English choral festivals was the culmination of his first period, of his attempt to tread the conventional path of choralism. He had found his distinctive voice, had obtained the ear of the nation beyond Worcestershire and was ready for a more glorious adventure, whereby he was to open a new chapter in the history of English music.

1899 marks the transition from the long, and to the composer himself painful, apprenticeship to a shorter period of great achievement. Of his seventy-five years the first fifteen were spent in growing and schooling, twenty-five were expended in his efforts to realize his genius and win recognition for it, twenty contained all the great masterpieces, and fifteen after his wife's death were spent in contemplating his life's work, the contemplation including the active direction and performance of his works up and down the country and especially at the Three Choirs

Festivals, and in the recording studios. In 1899 the *Enigma Variations* declared clearly that in this Malvern composer, as he had been called, Britain had at long last found an instrumental genius of the first order. His earlier works had never shown any indication of the imaginative intensity which was now revealed, and opinions were immediately revised. The rather petulant note that runs through Elgar literature about non-recognition, opposition even, is a true expression of the composer's own natural but not very reasonable feelings, but it has no justification in historical fact. There was a momentary jolt to the new attitude of recognition when the notorious first performance of *The Dream of Gerontius* fell flat, but it was almost immediately put right by the no less famous Düsseldorf performance. With the production of two such blazing masterpieces as *Enigma* and *Gerontius* Elgar's place in contemporary esteem and in English history was assured.

Elgar as the local musician had written music for local orchestras, just as he had written for local choral societies. The two strands are interwoven in the first stage of his career, and his thought, unlike that of most English musicians, is more instrumental than vocal in character, but his progress was in the first instance along the choral road. From part-songs and anthems he had proceeded to cantatas, and now at the turn of the century he was to complete this stage with oratorio. *The Dream of Gerontius* made such an impression that it seemed to revive the very form of religious oratorio itself from the moribund condition into which it was falling from an overdraught of Old Testament history and too much festival-going. Oratorio had tended to follow the example of Mendelssohn and become eventful, dramatic and extravert. *Gerontius* recalled its true artistic purpose as one of contemplation of eternal truth, as the form had been used by Bach in the cantatas, Handel in *Messiah* and Brahms in the *Requiem*. The movement against Mendelssohnian oratorio led by Parry and attempted since by many serious-minded composers was in the direction of philosophical oratorio. There is an element of non-religious philosophy behind the religious phraseology of Brahms's *Requiem* and Brahms's mind in this realm of experience was philosophically inclined to stoicism. Parry failed for the reasons already examined, and no one since has had Parry's qualifications to write philosophical oratorio, not even Vaughan

Williams—the subsequent tendency, due in part perhaps to the difficulty of finding a suitable text, has been to embody philosophical reflections in symphonic writing. Philosophical oratorio has yet to come—Tippett's *A Child of our Time*, if also a product of his time and the experience of world war, is an essay in this direction. *Gerontius*, with its whole-hearted absorption in religion, was therefore in a fair way to revive true oratorio, but it had no successor, at any rate till Bliss's *The Beatitudes* and Britten's *War Requiem*. Even Elgar's own two oratorios, *The Apostles* (1903) and *The Kingdom* (1906), do not succeed, because they have neither the unity nor the intensity nor the spontaneity of *Gerontius*.

The Dream of Gerontius was commissioned for the Birmingham Festival of 1900 and produced on that occasion under Richter, with Marie Brema, Edward Lloyd and H. Plunket Greene in the solo parts. The performance somehow missed fire. Many explanations have been given, some circumstantial, some musical, some even theological. There is probably some truth in all of them. The central point of the criticism of that now notorious performance was a failure on the part of the choir to realize that here they had something different from the Handel-cum-Mendelssohn tradition to assimilate and master. They failed to assimilate, let alone master, and the circumstantial reason for their failure is to be found in the death of the chorus master, Dr. C. Swinnerton Heap (1847-1900). Heap was the mainspring of all choral music in the Midlands during the last two decades of the nineteenth century and he had been the recipient of two of Elgar's dedications, the organ sonata in G and *The Light of Life*. He had taken over the office of festival chorus-master from Stockley, the Birmingham musician who had already figured in Elgar's early life, but he died in the June before the October of the festival. In despair of what else to do, the Festival authorities recalled from his retirement old Stockley, who among his other activities had been organist of a Congregational church. An elderly nonconformist was hardly the person to grasp at short notice a new music anointed by Roman Catholicism. There must also have been some failure on Richter's part to appreciate the new intimate relationship of choral and orchestral parts in the oratorio, or he could surely have done something to retrieve it. The audience, brought up on the popular tradition of Protestant oratorio, did not like the subject*—one of them said "It stinks of incense", as though that were condemnation instead of the commendation it involuntarily and unconsciously was. For the one thing clear above all else is the burning sincerity which makes it a masterpiece. Elgar was a Roman Catholic in early life and he died in that faith, though through the years of maturity it meant less to him. Someone gave him J. H. Newman's poem as a wedding present and he had pondered it for ten years before its musical transfiguration came to birth, as it happened for a particular festival, but in the nature of things from a compelling urge that would have found fulfilment somehow in any circumstances. The incense, therefore, of which it stank was a true emanation of the composer's deepest convictions about the fundamental issue of life and death. It may be admitted, however, that the poem contains some very odd metaphysics and that its poetry does not always digest completely some of its theological assertions, but it has been accepted by some critics as "the best attempt to present the unseen world since Dante". It is certainly bold in its imaginative sweep and forceful in its address to the mind. It makes a perfect text for that vein in Elgar which does not often openly declare itself in his music but which underlies all his intensely personal amalgam of thought and feeling, such as also appears reflected in the various mirrors of his friends as portrayed in the *Enigma Variations*. Elgar was not against the expression of emotion—indeed his lack of reticence has already been noted as an offence to one school of critics. But they are public emotions in which he lets himself go. When he is elusive and whimsical, as he is from *The Wand of Youth* suite right through to the violoncello concerto, he is still behaving in company, almost ostentatiously concealing his inner feelings behind the banter. But there is no note of self-consciousness in *Gerontius*, the poem has been wholly absorbed into the composer's consciousness and the orchestra is used with a new mastery for the expression of subtleties. *The Dream of Gerontius* is the most completely unified of all Elgar's major works. The big instrumental works were composed

* Some of the musicians among them had more discernment. Vaughan Williams told me that he came out of the hall with the Stanfords. Lady Stanford said "Isn't that a fine work?" The words were Lady Stanford's but Vaughan Williams had no doubt whose opinion they embodied.

in bits—the process has been described by W. H. Reed. But there
are no bits in *Gerontius*. The leitmotifs, which he uses in a manner
sometimes compared with that of *Parsifal*, are a source of unity
but only because, as he himself put it in a letter,* they were used
intuitively. He employed a more elaborate system in *The Apostles*
and *The Kingdom* but it does not save those two oratorios from
the effect of scrappiness. No, the source of the power, strength
and unity of *Gerontius* is the intensity of the imagination, the
heat of the crucible in which it was fashioned. The method of
testing by samples might not be allowed to be conclusive in the
case of a work for which integrity and unity are claimed as the
supreme merits. Yet nothing sounds more right and inevitable
than the early morning freshness of the soul's awakening into
the life beyond death in the Prelude to the second part

or the sense of fulfilment in the Angel's Farewell

There is not a harmony here that could not have been used at any
time in the nineteenth century, yet the music is quite new, quite
original, because it is the complete and perfect expression of
those two stages in the experience of the soul of Gerontius. Such
fusion of form and content is the purpose of art, yet it is rarely
achieved, so rarely as to put any major work in which it is accomplished into the category of masterpieces.

His next venture, now that his step was assured, was upon a
vast design almost comparable to Wagner's *Ring* in its magnitude
and intellectual range. He proposed a trilogy of oratorios upon

* Basil Maine, *Edward Elgar: His Life and Works*, Vol. 1, p. 105.

the foundation of Christianity, beginning with Jesus's call to his disciples, proceeding with the first days of the early church in Jerusalem and concluding with the mission to the Gentiles. The presentation of the Church Universal was never completed, the third oratorio of the trilogy, *The Last Judgment*, never composed. The method he employed in the two parts which were completed, *The Apostles* of 1903 and *The Kingdom* of 1906, was episodic, the composer putting their texts together himself. The root weakness of the two oratorios is just that lack of organic unity which *Gerontius* conspicuously possesses. The leitmotif principle is not enough in itself to make a unity of an episodic text set to a musical mosaic. Elgar may have felt that an oratorio so constructed was not wholly satisfactory; maybe the religious impulse behind it faltered; maybe he had come to a stage of his musical pilgrimage beyond oratorio. But though both works have their admirers, *The Kingdom* especially, they show as many of Elgar's defects as his merits.

Of these the chief is his uncertain grasp of form. The symphonies and the violin concerto are legitimately criticized for their undue overall length and for some disproportion in the lengths of the various sections (as for instance in the architectural lay-out of the first symphony), and for a rather haphazard key scheme. The chamber music also employs orthodox sonata form somewhat stiffly, and the departures from orthodoxy do not lead to any satisfactory new solution of the architectural problem. In a choral work formal defects matter less because there are the words and the drama to preserve unity of subject, however episodic the plot or however discursive the text. But in *The Apostles* and *The Kingdom* the text itself is both discursive and episodic and, worse still, does not always make sense. For the first of the pair the composer chose salient episodes in Jesus's life, the calling of the Apostles, the Beatitudes, the Betrayal, Golgotha and the Ascension, but the texts chosen do not always clearly carry the idea forward and in the event the oratorio rambles, and an interpretation worthy of the conception is difficult to bring off. Even when allowance for that is made it has to be admitted that there is a good deal of second-rate Elgar mingled with the fine gold. The concluding chorus of Part I with the enigmatic summons "Turn you to the stronghold, ye prisoners of hope"* is set to a tune that

* This nonsensical text from Zachariah is corrupt.

has the requisite breadth for a climax but just topples over on the
wrong side of the line dividing breadth from banality.

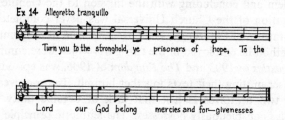

Ex 14 Allegretto tranquillo

Turn you to the stronghold, ye   prisoners of   hope, To the

Lord   our God belong   mercies and for—givenesses

The solo of Mary Magdalene's repentance contains the bold
and unusual stroke of having projected upon it a fantasy of
revelry from chorus and orchestra suggestive of the life which she
has renounced. It is an imaginative idea, but again the fact that it
is one more piece of mosaic puts further strain upon the unity of
the work. The corresponding air of Judas in the second part, also
expressive of repentance though of a different kind, is somewhat
similarly treated. These two arias are the chief dramatic moments
of the oratorio. But drama is neither Elgar's purpose nor his
method, and the music achieves its most complete absorption of
the idea in the last two episodes, At the Sepulchre and the Ascension. Their higher concentration prepares the way for *The Kingdom* to open with the temperature already raised—its Prelude
is a movement of great nobility in which the themes common
to the two occasions are restated—and although some of the
concentration is dissipated by the episodic nature of the text,
the vision of the whole in the composer's mind is more completely realized in practice. The design is pictorial rather than
dramatic or contemplative. The episodes are tapestries crowded
with figures and significant detail, illustrated with almost too
great fidelity in the symphonic texture of the orchestra. A vivid
performance will secure animation and present the various
scenes, most conspicuously that of Pentecost, as living realities.
True, the characters suggest members of an English committee
formed to direct the affairs of a new society more than Orientals
filled with a spirit that makes them speak with tongues. But that
transformation is no unfamiliar feature in oratorio and though
anachronistic is not false to life.

With *The Kingdom* English biblical oratorio lapsed, not merely

Elgar's contribution to the form. The element of edification which is proper to it lost its attractions for a public whose tastes changed at the death of Queen Victoria and the beginning of a new century —this was no doubt a contributory cause of Parry's failure to establish the ethical cantata as a substitute for the old style of English oratorio. Great Britain had been throughout the nineteenth century a land of sermon tasters with a nice discrimination in edification. In the twentieth century it refused to be preached to and composers therefore moved on to something different, to something apocalyptic as in Holst's *Hymn of Jesus* and Vaughan Williams's *Sancta Civitas*, to secular scenes like Dyson's genial pictures of English life in *The Canterbury Pilgrims* or to non-Christian themes like Walton's essay in savage nationalism in *Belshazzar's Feast*.

Elgar, however, did not abandon choral music altogether, though his mind had moved on to symphonic forms. In 1912 he produced *The Music Makers*, again for a Birmingham Festival, and in 1917 during the war the trilogy of short cantatas which together are called *The Spirit of England*. O'Shaughnessy's ode is respectable poetry and Laurence Binyon's three poems are better than occasional verse. The music is not therefore bedevilled by faulty texts, though the self-consciousness of *The Music Makers* is redoubled by the self-consciousness of the composer in sprinkling the score with self-quotations from *Gerontius* and the violin concerto, as well as the Enigma and Nimrod themes. The latter stand for the vision which is the artist's distinguishing mark from his fellow men. There is a certain biographical interest in these quotations, since they reveal Elgar's idea of himself as a seer of visions and a dreamer of dreams. They show the main Enigma theme as a self-portrait, or at any rate as the personality which is going to reflect the images of his "friends pictured within". But they are distracting occurrences in the course of a cantata on another topic and they cause a disturbance in the setting of the words, in which respect Elgar's touch is rarely felicitous.

Of the three war poems "The Fourth of August", "To Women" and "For the Fallen", the last struck a responsive note in the public's heart and was much used as the most apt music for the commemoration of the 1918 Armistice. The three pieces were not occasional music in that they were not written expressly for particular occasions or commemorative ceremonies, but like *Carillon* they were direct products of the war. "The Fourth of August" is no better than good journalism and the four-square music would suit Kipling better than Binyon. It was the last to be composed, the completed trilogy being sung by the Royal Choral Society in November 1917. The other two had been written in 1915 and already performed in 1916. They, too, are march-like in rhythm: "For the Fallen" indeed is a processional, in which the sombre and the splendid vision, public and private emotions, are intermingled in a manner true to life and somehow focused so that their immediacy has been made permanent—a rare achievement in occasional art which allows no time for that absorption which Wordsworth called "emotion recollected in tranquillity". Elgar's curious mixture of intensely personal feeling and natural grandiloquence has found the right occasion for their simultaneous utterance.

At the time of the Festival of Britain in 1951 *The Dream of Gerontius* was what most choral societies wanted to sing as their contribution to it. In half a century it had displaced *Elijah* as second favourite to *Messiah*. It has placed Elgar firmly in the English choral tradition and is in itself a work of seemingly imperishable value. But it was the instrumental works which followed it, and led the composer away from the English preoccupation with voices, that make Elgar important in the English renaissance.

The production of the "Variations on an Original Theme for Orchestra" by Hans Richter at St. James's Hall on June 19, 1899, marked a stage forward in Elgar's personal reputation, revealed another side of his personality and, much more significantly, declared to the world the historical fact that English music was no longer a purely vocal affair. The *Enigma Variations* are a landmark in English music.

The title has been a help to the work, as all good titles are to works which have in them the intrinsic qualities for a wide appeal. The title, however, would not weigh with Jaeger (of Novello's), with Parry, to whom the score was shown,* or with Richter, who, receiving it from Parry with his enthusiastic commendation, put

* See H. P. Greene, *op. cit.*, p. 157.

it into the programme of one of his own concerts. The work is a frank and unequivocal masterpiece and in that respect if in no other is not enigmatic. The Enigma is Elgar himself. All his biographers are agreed on that. Basil Maine, writing officially, says: "When all the contradictions and complexities have been accounted for Elgar still remains a deliberate enigma." Dr. W. H. Reed says: "He was himself the Enigma and remained so to the end of his life."* The word Enigma appears in the score over the original theme corresponding in position to the initials signifying "my friends pictured within" which stand above each variation. The theme is Elgar himself as the mirror in which the portraits are reflected, while the last variation [E.D.U.] is at once a musical restatement and a fuller portrait of the same person, the composer himself. Elgar liked puzzles and mystifications. To help assuage his passion for them he solved crosswords every morning; to fellow musicians he pretended that he was not interested in music but only in heraldry, chemistry, horse-racing or whatever the fad of the moment happened to be. The *Variations* arose out of a riddle addressed to his wife and were deliberately wrapped in further mysteries. Elgar played the theme to his wife on the piano and then asked her to guess who the variations which he extemporized on it were like. Musical portraiture was nothing new, and characterization, such as an opera composer must have, was not a particularly strong point with Elgar—places more than people were his speciality—but these variations were a new form of composition in that they were first thought of as what the various friends would themselves have made of the theme if they had written it, "if they were asses enough to compose". They thus impart to the music their own salient characteristics: the bluster with which W.M.B. goes out of the room (Var. 4), W.N.'s laughter (Var. 8), Dorabella's fluttering speech (Var. 10). The initials and pseudonyms naturally aroused curiosity—here was a set of enigmas for audiences which they could not possibly solve without a

* Dr. Percy Young in his semi-official biography which reflects Lady Elgar's point of view does not say so in the one word, but devotes a chapter to unravelling his complexity, internal tensions and paradoxes. Miss Diana McVeagh explains him as the victim of his own temperament and circumstances: "caustic yet considerate, suspicious yet warm-hearted, reserved yet impulsive, intolerant yet sympathetic, rude yet gallant, boisterous yet sensitive". These antitheses she summarizes in the word "provocative".

knowledge of Elgar's private life, and subsequently the composer tried to allay it by saying that "there is nothing to be gained in an artistic or musical sense by solving the enigma of any of the personalities".

The next enigma was about the theme which was said by the composer to be a counterpoint to "another and larger theme", which "goes through and over the whole set". But he refused to explain what it was and died without revealing it either to his official biographer, Basil Maine, or to his close and musically most intimate friend, W. H. Reed. "Auld lang syne" was suggested by Mr. R. Powell, husband of Dorabella, since the programme of the work is friendship, and by doing some violence to that tune, changing its first strain into the minor and either extending it or leaving it too short to serve as a complete counterpoint, it can be made to fit. The idea has been generally scouted, sometimes as unworthy or ridiculous, sometimes as merely improbable.

Attempts to pierce the mystery and to elucidate the composer's own cryptic hints designed to deepen it still further have constantly been made, but to no purpose. As late as 1960 Sir Jack Westrup made a new survey of all the evidence and all the suggested solutions in a paper read to the Royal Musical Association.* He scouted the idea of a counterpoint to the original theme and equally the idea of a literary origin. He came no nearer to a solution and, baffled of his objective, posed again the other puzzle: how came a composer, at the age of forty-two, to produce a masterpiece of which he had previously given no prophetic sign? The identity of the friends pictured in the several variations took some time to be publicly established, but that enigma at any rate was eventually solved and their biographies made publicly available. The other one never will be, nor does it matter if natural curiosity about it remains unsatisfied, for the work lives in its own right and has been played all over the world in countries where the circumstances of its origin would have little interest.

It was something new in English music in its sheer orchestral mastery. The brilliance and the delicacy of the scoring handled with such certainty of touch could not fail to be noticed and the individuality of the new voice recognized, though it spoke the current romantic language of Richard Strauss, i.e. post-Liszt and

* *Proceedings*, No. 86.

post-Wagner. It was not only a turning point in English music but in the composer's own life, in that it released a flood of inspiration and a spate of great works in which instruments steadily submerged voices.

The *Cockaigne Overture*, another bit of portraiture, was written in 1901, along with the first two *Pomp and Circumstance* marches. The oratorio, *The Apostles*, Op. 49 (1902-1903) was separated from its sequel, *The Kingdom*, Op. 59 (1905), by the *Introduction and Allegro for Strings* (1904) though it bears an earlier opus number (47), and by another concert overture, *In the South*, which belongs to the end of 1903 and is Op. 50. Then came the first symphony (1908, Op. 55), the violin concerto (1910, Op. 61), the second symphony (1911, Op. 63) and the symphonic poem *Falstaff* (1913, Op. 68). *The Music Makers* (1912) reverted to choralism but is a half-hearted work. This is a tremendous output, for the symphonic works are big in sheer size and there were in addition a number of small things, music for the Coronation and other incidental music. There only remained the chamber music, which was a war-time refuge and the cello concerto, which was to come after the war.

The first symphony was immensely successful, and after its first performance at Manchester under Hans Richter, to whom it is dedicated, perhaps as a token of gratitude for his sponsoring of *Enigma*, it went the rounds in as many as a hundred performances during its first year. Some of these were given by Thomas Beecham, then at the beginning of his career of advocate–impresario–conductor. He could hardly ignore anything so new, so modern and so successful, and he therefore put it into his 1909 tour, but he treated it so shamefully by making unauthorized cuts of increasing severity that protests appeared in *The Musical Times*. The story is narrated by Eric Coates, then a member of Beecham's orchestra*, and repeated by Charles Reid with further comment.†
Since Beecham is, besides many other things, a historical fact—he was probably the greatest performer of genius ever to emerge in this country after John Bull and John Dowland—his attitude to Elgar is of some importance, especially in view of those distressing stories of the personal estrangement of Elgar from his fellow musicians, which have been discussed, disproved and dismissed

---

* In *Suite in Four Movements* (Heinemann, 1953), pp. 123-4.
† In *Thomas Beecham* (Gollancz, 1961), pp. 75-6.

scores of times, but refuse to remain decently buried. Elgar, according to Mr. Reid, admired Beecham's work, though Lady Elgar, who from P. M. Young's biography emerges as the chief source of Elgar's touchiness and disgruntlement, did not find him "at all appealing".* Reid suggests plausibly that Beecham's underestimate of Elgar may be attributed to his overrating of Delius. What Beecham himself says, in his most serious and judicious vein, which cannot, however, always be taken at its face value, is this:

"Most of what Elgar wrote between 1895 and 1914 showed an undeniable advance over anything produced by his English predecessors or contemporaries in the more orthodox forms such as the symphony and the concerto. The writing itself is clearer and more varied in style, the grasp of the subject closer and keener, and the use of the orchestra is often, but not always, admirable. The better side of him is to be found in miniature movements, where he is generally fanciful and occasionally exquisite. His big periods and tuttis are less happy; bombast and rhetoric supplant too frequently real weight and poetic depth, and he strays with a dangerous ease to the borderline of military rodomontade that is hardly distinguishable from the commonplace and the vulgar. Here and there are cadences of a charm that is quite his own, unlike anything else in music, evoking memories without being in themselves reminiscent, and breathing a sentiment to be found in much English literature written between 1830 and 1880, notably Tennyson. But whatever the quality of the invention, his is the work of a truly serious and honest craftsman."†

This is curious criticism in some respects—writing clearer? grasp closer? when the texture is opulent and the material effusive—indeed it was the length of the A flat symphony that was too much for the writer. But the rodomontade is noted and the affinity, no more, with things English is also remarked. The preference for movements of smaller scale is noteworthy, since the breadth, impetus and size of the main movements of both symphonies and both concertos were the features that were new in English music and are the ground for the most weighty criticism. Beecham's personal taste was mostly meridional, though he got on well enough with Sibelius: he preferred Mozart

* *Elgar*, O.M. (1955), p. 179.   † *A Mingled Chime* (1944), pp. 110-11.

to Beethoven, Berlioz to Wagner, so that though he was not himself without grandiloquence, he mitigated it with wit and probably found the Elgar of the grand manner uncongenial. He once said to me, when to a general denunciation of English music for failing to capture European and American audiences I offered interrogatively *Enigma* as a suggestion, "Ballet music, my dear sir, ballet music", in the characteristic drawl. But if Beecham did less for Elgar than he did for some of his own favourites, other conductors were his advocates, Henry Wood of course, and Landon Ronald, followed by Adrian Boult and Malcolm Sargent. Toscanini and Stokowski both played *Enigma*, and the concertos have been played by soloists of the highest international standing.

The first symphony plays for nearly an hour, professes allegiance to the key of A flat but pulls constantly towards D, has a motto theme, is scored for triple wind and harps, uses the same theme for scherzo and slow movement (at very different speeds), and has no professed programme, though it is difficult not to hear in it a passionate debate between thematic personifications of moral ideas: thus the opening motto which is a march tune, solemn and marked *nobilmente*, is a majestic exordium of Beethovenian intensity. In its recurrences and the allusions to it throughout the four movements it serves as more than a structural aid to coherence; it is the dominant idea embodying the dominant emotion of the symphony. The first trio of the scherzo provided the occasion for his famous remark at a rehearsal, "Play it like something you hear down by the river", which illumines more that this single passage; there are many of these open-air passages, the "Monmouth" tune in the *Introduction and Allegro*, the orchard scene in *Falstaff*, to instance only two which have the evocative character noted by Beecham. The criticism which the symphony encountered was for its architectonics: its key scheme, though queer with its tension between A flat major and D minor from the initial wrench in the first movement to the reversal of direction in the finale, might pass and might indeed help to give to the symphony its feeling of magnitude; but the profusion of material and Elgar's way of composing it as tesserae to be set in a mosaic make it seem long and loose. The motto theme is of course in intention and in fact a source of coherence, and still more the feature of Elgar's method of composing, first pointed out by Miss McVeagh, namely the insinuation of counterpoints or strands of melody which do not at once disclose their relationship to each other or to the main themes.

This was the way Elgar composed: he took his material from the air, as he once said, as it might be in handfuls of still inchoate stuff, and then condensed it into motifs, phrases and melodies. Their interrelationship was not at once apparent to the composer, for he wrote them out on separate bits of paper, which in the case of the violin concerto, as described by W. H. Reed,* were pinned up all round the room for him to try out on his violin. The work of com-posing, i.e. putting together, had still to be done. When it was done the effect was one of profusion rather than of tight organization or organic growth like that of the German symphonists, (rhapsody in fact,—$\rho\alpha\psi\omega\delta\iota\alpha$ is the stitching together of songs), as Dr. Mosco Carner,† approaching Elgar's symphonies from a foreigner's point of view, pointed out, if we had not already noticed it for ourselves. Carner considers it a formal weakness, due not to technical deficiency in thematic treatment, since the oratorios, *Falstaff*, and even the employment of the motto theme in this very symphony prove his mastery of it, but to the "particular cast of his musical mind". He was in fact a rhapsodist.

But his rhapsodies could cohere into symphonies with the right kind of performance to ride them with a tight enough rein. No. 2 in E flat, though lacking the structural bracing of a motto, coheres from sheer intensity of its emotional outpouring. Through four long movements in which the phrases are mostly of three-, two- or only one-bar length, the torrent pours without check, its eloquence sustained through all the variations of mood, tempi and dynamics. What is the composer saying with such power and passion? The motto (verbal in this symphony, not musical) "Rarely, rarely comest thou, Spirit of Delight" seems less relevant than the dedication, which is to the memory of King Edward VII. Here indeed the Elgar of soldierly bearing, the very English Elgar, the full-living Edwardian, the patriotic artist, says without reserve what his country and his generation mean

* *Elgar as I Knew Him* (Gollancz, 1936), p. 23; *Elgar* (Dent, 1939), p. 101.
† *Of Men and Music* (John Williams, 1944), pp. 156-8.

to him. The symphony has always been read as a document of time and place, but there is evidence* in Canon Temple Gairdner's correspondence with Elgar of something more closely personal. Symphonic movements do not necessarily describe human emotions but more normally register their intensities, pressures and temperatures—abstract music is *le dynamomètre de la vie sentimentale*. But if we may not attribute specific emotions to the contents of the music, it is hard not to attach to it emotional labels by way of description. The first movement is passionate, stormy even—perhaps the motto is applicable here—the second is elegiac, the third almost hectic, the fourth reassured, triumphant and content. There was nothing more to be said after this. It summarized the age, paid respect to the monarch who gave his name to it, presented the most sublimated expression of those chivalric enthusiasms of the early cantatas; and it contains a hint of presage that this grand pageantry of English life could not continue for ever. The mood of high summer in Elgar's middle life could not be prolonged past its natural term, and most of us have seen in the cello concerto the contraction of autumn, the rich but quieter beauty of the fall of the year.

The E flat symphony bursts into full flood of eloquence with the energy that Strauss gets out of his wide-leaping themes, though Elgar's first subject is more wayward. The energy is maintained by an added impetus from the orchestration, swirling scale-passages on woodwind, frequent recourse to the trumpet used melodically, the stabs of tone from the brass chorus, splashes of colour flung upon the main texture of the music. This type of scoring Elgar derived from Berlioz who in the *Symphonie fantastique* adds dabs of colour in little motifs of no thematic significance. What was even more personal to his orchestration was elucidated by Miss McVeagh, who first pointed out that its secret was his highly idiosyncratic way of doubling: he did not simply reproduce his tune at the octave, above or below, Puccini-fashion, but underlined the constituent notes, one or two at a time or even singly, with different instruments, a kind of *Klangfarbenmelodie*, so that the tune became iridescent. This was most effective in quiet passages, in which he also had a way of often using trombone chords pianissimo. In exuberant passages he

* Diana McVeagh, *Edward Elgar* (Dent, 1955), pp. 56, 166.

switched on the lights with harp glissandi, sweeping runs up on violins for anacruses and great flourishes like a take-off into the air by the woodwind, as at the end of the first movement of the second symphony.

A third symphony was commissioned by the B.B.C. in 1932 and Elgar began to get together some of the ideas he had already had in mind for a simpler, lighter symphony* and had committed to paper. But with no Lady Elgar to keep up the pressure needed to fuse his scraps into a continuum, the symphony never materialized. Nor did the opera based on Ben Jonson's *The Devil is an Ass*, which he was simultaneously revolving in his mind. The material of the symphony was examined and sorted by W. H. Reed, who found that no one, even if he disregarded the composer's wish expressed on his death-bed that it should not be "tinkered with", could possibly complete it.

Length and structure, the debatable features of the symphonies, are also the problematical features of the violin concerto, which plays for three-quarters of an hour, i.e. longer by at least five minutes than Brahms's violin concerto. The comparison is just, for it is the only violin concerto of the twentieth century of similar magnitude, nobility and saturation—it is a better work than Tchaikovsky's, Sibelius's or even Bartók's more concise and pungent concerto. It has been played by the world's international virtuosi, Kreisler, Menuhin and Heifetz—its chief English exponent was Albert Sammons—who can hold its discursive argument together. Furthermore the composer has taken pains to remove any effect of scrappiness that Reed's description of its parturition in Elgar's studio might predispose one to expect, by casting the work in traditional form, with a full orchestral exposition before the entry of the soloist in the first movement, and in the finale sanctioning a cut from 77 to 84 or 91 in the score— either is possible.† This finale contains an innovation in his accompanied cadenza which recalls the themes of the first movement. This cadenza has a thrummed accompaniment by the strings of the orchestra played pizzicato. The effect is bewitching and is described by Tovey as "one of the most original dialogues between a solo instrument and an orchestra that have ever been imagined".

The concerto is like the second symphony in its sustained

* Reed, *Elgar as I Knew Him.*   † Letter to me from Mrs. Powell.

passionate eloquence and in having at the back of it, far back, a personal inspiration. If the second symphony was the account of the "passionate pilgrimage of a soul",* the violin concerto is inscribed with a Spanish motto almost like that of *Enigma*, "Herein is enshrined the soul of . . .". Whose soul? It has been suggested with great plausibility (and with Lady Elgar as the source of it), that the suppressed name was that of a close American friend, Mrs. Julia Worthington. Reed has described how he shared in the evolution of the solo part by giving Elgar technical advice, but Kreisler, to whom the concerto is dedicated and who was its first performer, had a hand in it too, as was confirmed by Professor Sanford Terry, the great Bach scholar who held the chair of history at Aberdeen, in a letter to *The Times*.† Terry had as a gift from Elgar a proof copy of the full score which was heavily annotated with corrections in ink and pencil. Terry showed the score to Kreisler who identified the alterations made at his suggestion. The story of Menuhin's performance of the concerto with the composer as conductor in 1932, when Menuhin was a boy of sixteen and Elgar was seventy-five, and the friendship that developed from it, has an idyllic quality, that adds further fragrance to something which is rooted in intimacies and personal associations, yet stands up as a public work of art.

The cello concerto is even more intimate in manner—the composer's exuberance has begun to ebb and he plans more concisely. Yet it, too, is public and international in its objective worth. French cellists in particular have followed that other Latin artist, Pablo Casals, in making it their own, in spite of the fact that on the whole Elgar is not to French taste, as proved by more than one failure to capture Paris with concerts of his music. In the cello concerto Elgar reverts to the device of a recurrent motto which resembles that of the first symphony in being slightly formal. It is succeeded by a first subject that is its antithesis, being in a wayward twelve-eight time which sounds wistful and resolute by turns, recognizably like the composer himself in its moodiness ranging from withdrawal and self-communion to forthright assertion when supported by trombones. The second movement is a butterfly scherzo, the third a slow movement consisting of a single long-drawn organically spun melody, like "Nimrod"

* McVeagh, *op. cit.*, p. 56.   † January 9, 1935.

or the opening of the slow movement of the first symphony in its depth of feeling. The finale is more extravert, but before the end, in place of the usual cadenza at that point, is a slow chromatic episode like an epilogue except that it is followed by recurrence of the motto and a coda in quick *tempo primo*. The concerto is thus more taut in construction and has less weight of sheer length to sustain. If the slow movement of the second symphony is compared to a summer's day from a dewy dawn to a golden sunset, the light that emanates from this concerto is still golden but the gold is that of September.

If then its construction is beyond the criticism that can be levied against the great works of the first decade, it shares the immunity with the *Introduction and Allegro for Strings* which has also the right to call itself a concerto, since it is a modern equivalent of the concerto grosso of Corelli and Handel. Its single movement would also entitle it to be classified as a phantasy, though it is more than chamber music, being scored for string quartet as concertino and a full orchestra of strings often in as many as nine parts. Its introduction in G minor sets forward three ideas; the first is a vigorous gesture, the second a tune suggested by a snatch of song overheard on the Welsh border, and the third is to become, when changed into the major, the first subject of the allegro. Instead of a development section there is an animated fugato. The whole is beautifully proportioned and brilliant, crossing the frontiers of nations, of periods and of fashions.

Falstaff, the last of the big symphonic works except the cello concerto, is the largest and most detailed piece of programme music in Elgar's output, or indeed in the orchestral music of any English composer—Delius's *Paris* being the only comparable symphonic poem. Elgar accepted the implication of this form of composition by publishing a detailed analysis in *The Musical Times* a month before its first performance at the Leeds Festival of 1913, which he conducted himself. He emphasized its basis in literary criticism, mentioning Dowden in particular, insisting that it was a "study", in the literary sense of that word, and so gave it for full title "Symphonic Study in C minor with two episodes in A minor".

This studious basis of *Falstaff* is responsible for the ambivalence with which it is regarded. It is rarely effective in the concert-hall,

as Strauss's similar character studies of *Don Juan, Don Quixote*
and *Till Eulenspiegel* are immediately effective. The comparison
is legitimate since Strauss must have been Elgar's model in
entering upon episodic and characteristic programme music. In
spite of Tovey's recognition of the episodes and characters—he
got them all right in his independent analysis except that of Prince
Henry—they are less clear to the unschooled listener than are
their equivalents in Strauss. Then again, in spite of the care with
which Elgar assembled his paragraphs and sections, the work, if
the details of its programme are not recognized, easily sounds
scrappy and even bewildering. Against this has to be set the fact
that Elgar's not very acute sense of form is less strained than in
the symphonies and concertos. The "study" is by nature episodic,
and sometimes in performance, if attention is not too closely
focused on recognizing the specific programme except the two
exquisite interludes for small orchestra, Falstaff's dream in Elgar's
wistful vein and the pastorale in Mr. Justice Shallow's orchard
with pipe and tabor effects, then a portrait will emerge, though not
its details. In short it is difficult to see in this fine work at one and
the same time both the trees and the wood. It is too copious to
to be taken in as it goes by, but to the score-reader or student its
subtleties and felicities are an unending revelation and it is consequently the scholar's, if not the concert-goer's, favourite among
Elgar's works.

The main themes, Falstaff's five and Prince Henry's, are
adequate to their task of characterization and of sustaining the
structure, though not in themselves so striking or so obviously
apt as one might have expected from the composer of the *Enigma*
portraits. Thus in one of them, the most attractive of them all,
there is some ambiguity.

Ex 15

This refers to the midnight episode at Gadshill and sounds
stealthy and purposive, but is in fact no more than a "cheerful

out-of-door ambling theme"—like the down-by-the-river theme of the first symphony and in the cut of its dotted-note figures like the first subject of the finale of the second symphony. There are numerous particular beauties, the sevenths in contrary motion of strings, for instance, when Falstaff sleeps, and there are robust swirls and skirmishes of brass in Elgar's clattering manner at the various commotions in the decayed gentleman's career. There has been nothing like it since in English music, partly no doubt because the vogue for the symphonic poem did not survive the eclipse of the romantic movement by the war of 1914. That war served, however, to divert Elgar's instrumental propensities to chamber music, and the fine violin sonata, the string quartet and the curious, eerie evocation of the wooded hill near his house in Sussex that is the piano quintet were the products of the war years.

Though the great works are concentrated into twenty years, there are plenty of smaller things to enlarge the credit balance of his remarkable career. The suites in which he enters the minds of children, *The Wand of Youth*, incidental music to a play, and the *Nursery Suite* written for the young Princesses during his tenure of the office of Master of the King's Musick, are the chief of the orchestral parerga. The early *Serenade for Strings* approaches his popular style. The popular style itself, excluding the *Pomp and Circumstance* marches which are food and drink for everyone, evoked some salon music which, as in the parallel case of Sibelius, is by many accountants put on the debit side. The early (1897) *Sea Pictures* for contralto and orchestra contain some gems, though not of the purest lustre. *Carillon*, the melodrama evoked by the invasion of Belgium in 1914, was a thrilling piece of occasional music, though it did not survive a resurrection in 1940. The transcriptions for full modern orchestra of Bach's C minor Fantasy and Fugue and of Handel's Overture to the Chandos Anthem in D minor, not to mention the National Anthem, which belong to the early twenties, were splendid lessons in orchestration and a pleasure to audiences that can be enjoyed, while the purists' backs are turned, as a "kick" or an outburst of high spirits. Here is sturdy music that nothing can damage, which is made to serve as the framework of a superb display of orchestral fireworks. Transcription is a highly technical process in which musicians take professional pleasure, and at that time in the century, before scholastic puritanism in doing its salutary work inevitably caused some incidental frowns at such libidinous conduct, it was practised by many composers—Ravel for instance on Mussorgsky, Schoenberg on Bach, Respighi on Bach, not to mention the treatment dealt to Chopin, Schumann, Rossini for the ballet. The ethics of transcription makes a good essay subject for students, but the discussion usually leads back in the end to the necessity of taking each case on its merits. Elgar's transcriptions are uninhibited, which is to be counted a merit, and were at any rate new to English music, anticipated only by Harty's transcription of Handel's *Water Music* in 1920.

All musicians used to serve their day and generation and be content that that should be their work in life. But under the influence of the romantic movement, with Beethoven glowering at them from immortal masterpieces, they, their critics and even their public began to demand nothing but masterpieces. The dichotomy of serious and light music became equated with the struggle between good and evil. English musicians, while not exempt from the requirements of the code of perpetual sublimity, were still required by institutions, festivals, coronations and public occasions to produce music of temporary validity. Elgar began as a musician serving local needs and present times and, as already related, only entered the serious category in middle life and in the changed ethos of the new century. He did not make any such hard-and-fast distinction—is it likely that he could have done?—but it may perhaps be granted that his self-critical sense was no more highly developed than that of most composers, who regularly think their latest work their best but still do not like their past achievements belittled; perhaps he was less self-critical than some. In a word there are two strains that are not always in harmony in his work even if they are not analysed exactly according to Beecham's discrimination. But a composer is entitled to be judged by posterity for his best work. On that computation Elgar is historically important for giving to English music a sense of the orchestra, for expressing what it felt like to be alive in the Edwardian age, for conferring on the world at least four unqualified masterpieces, and for thereby restoring England to the comity of musical nations.

X

Tributaries from Frankfurt, Birmingham and Elsewhere

JUST BEFORE the renaissance had got under way and while it was still customary for promising English musicians to go abroad for their serious studies a little band of English students found themselves pupils of Ivan Knorr at the Frankfurt conservatoire. They were Norman O'Neill (1875-1934), Cyril Scott (b. 1879), Roger Quilter (1877-1953), Henry Balfour Gardiner (1877-1950) and Percy Grainger, an Australian (1882-1961). Knorr was a teacher of unconventional attitude and wide sympathies. His German outlook was modified by life in Russia during his impressionable years and he believed in fostering the individual bent of his pupils' talents. His success can be seen without looking further afield than to his English pupils, all of whom made their mark and preserved their individuality. What is common to them, however, is their basic adherence to the European idiom of the day (which after all they share with Parry and Stanford) and their freedom —except Grainger maybe—from anything like conscious nationalism in which they differ from Parry and Sanford and still more from Holst and Vaughan Williams, who sought precisely independence from the general European idiom). Of the five, Cyril Scott showed himself the most revolutionary, since he for a time gave up the use of key signatures and regular bar lines, used discordant harmonies as though they were concords and handled the orchestra (e.g. in his piano concerto) in a highly individual manner. Before 1914 he was regarded as a sort of English equivalent of Debussy, that is a composer who was opening new, stimulating, slightly perplexing but undeniably fascinating paths, along which in songs and short piano pieces even the amateur could proceed. Certainly Edmund Rubbra, who

PLATE 1. A group of conductors at the Bournemouth centenary, 1910:
(left to right) Sir Edward Elgar, Sir Edward German, Sir Dan Godfrey,
Sir Alexander Mackenzie, Sir Hubert Parry, Sir Charles Stanford

PLATE 2. A page of the manuscript of Parry's *Prometheus Unbound*, in the possession of the Royal College of Music

PLATE 3. (*above, left*) Sir Hubert Parry, from a drawing by Sidney Kent. (*above, right*) Dame Ethel Smyth. (*below*) Sir Arthur Sullivan, a cartoon by "Spy"

PLATE 4. William Chappell

(*left*) Sir George Grove. (*right*) J. A. Fuller-Maitland, from a portrait by
William Strang

PLATE 5. (*above, left*) Cecil Sharp, from a drawing by Sir William Rothenstein. (*above, right*) The Rev. E. H. Fellowes. (*below, left*) Sir Richard Terry. (*below, right*) Arnold Dolmetsch

PLATE 6. (*above*, *left*) Sir Charles Stanford: the portrait by Sir William Orpen in the Great Hall of Trinity College, Cambridge. (*above*, *right*) Charles Wood. (*below*, *left*) Sir Arthur Somervell. (*below*, *right*) Frank Bridge

PLATE 7. Sir Edward Elgar and Yehudi Menuhin. (*below*) Sir Granville Bantock, from a portrait by Bernard Munns

PLATE 8. (*above*, *left*) Frederick Delius, from a portrait by James Gunn in the possession of Sir Thomas Armstrong. (*above*, *right*) Roger Quilter, from a portrait by W. G. de Glehn in the National Portrait Gallery. (*below*, *left*) Sir Arnold Bax, from a drawing by Powys Evans in the National Portrait Gallery. (*below*, *right*) John Ireland, from a drawing by Juliet Pannett.

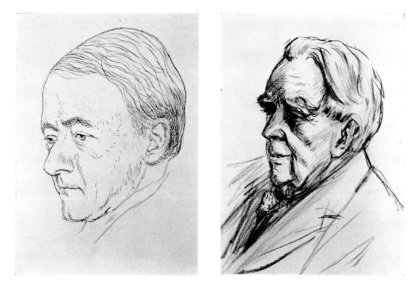

PLATE 9. Ralph Vaughan Williams, from a portrait by Sir Gerald Kelly.
(*below*) Gustav Holst, from a portrait by Millicent Woodforde in the
National Portrait Gallery

PLATE 10. (*above, left*) George Butterworth. (*above, right*) E. J. Moeran.
(*below, left*) Edmund Rubbra. (*below, right*) Gerald Finzi

PLATE 11. (*above*) Sir Arthur Bliss. (*below, left*) Gordon Jacob, from a drawing by Juliet Pannett. (*below, right*) Sir William Walton

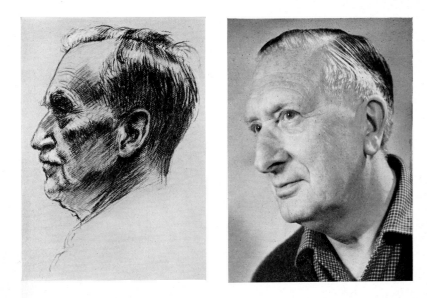

PLATE 12. (*left*) Lennox Berkeley. (*right*) Constant Lambert.

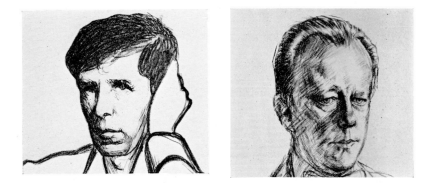

(*above, left*) Michael Tippett, from a crayon drawing by Guy Worsdell.
(*above, right*) Alan Rawsthorne, from a drawing by Juliet Pannett (*below, left*) William Wordsworth. (*below, right*) Herbert Howells

PLATE 13. Sir Henry Wood conducting a Promenade Concert, 1934, at the old Queen's Hall, destroyed during the War

PLATE 14. Benjamin Britten. (*below*) *Peter Grimes:* the Sadler's Wells
production of June 1945

PLATE 15. (*above, left*) Humphrey Searle. (*above, centre*) Ernest Newman. (*above, right*) Peter Racine Fricker. (*below*) *Etudes Symphoniques:* the Royal Ballet

PLATE 16. The Royal Festival Hall: the opening concert on May 3, 1951, with King George VI and Queen Elizabeth in the Royal Box

was Scott's pupil for both piano and composition, would testify to the beneficent stimulus he received from one then regarded as a modernist (with the usual connotation of one who used boldly dissonant harmonies) going beyond academic manners. At that time he was the best-known English composer on the Continent. But he gradually retired from prominence, and by the time he was seventy his idiom had come to sound old-fashioned and indeed ineffective.

Why? The short answer is chromatic harmony, which Scott used to excess, even to distorting old English melodies with accompaniments that at the time were enjoyed as delicious piquancies but half a century later look more like shocking solecisms. This sort of thing, for instance, in "Drink to me only with thine eyes":

Ex 16   I sent thee late a   ro—sy wreath, Not so   much honouring thee

Many of his songs are to texts by Ernest Dowson and this kind of melting harmony fitted the ninetyish mood of self-conscious heartache. When the mood was not of luxuriant misery it was quite another matter, and such a song as "And so I made a Villanelle", one of his best and best known, is at once fresh and elegant, and though almost every chord is a chord of the added sixth there are no chromatic slides. There is indeed plenty of variety of mood in Scott's large output and it would be a mistake to think of him as an ascetic oriental mystic because of his interest in the occult. He was an Edwardian, and the names of the piano pieces and the titles and authorships of his hundred songs—though he went on writing into the thirties the bulk of his work belongs to the first three decades of the century—indicate no narrow range of interest. But the ethos of Edwardian times was still romantic and favoured the rich harmony that Strauss and Debussy in their different ways and for different ends used to express its opulence. Scott remained a romantic and, like Holbrooke and Bax, navigated his craft on the ebb of the romantic movement and so missed the flood of English nationalism and the neo-classical

G

temper of the post-war world. Rubbra again is the witness* that the two tides tugged at him during his formative years, tides of taste, creed and temper, the divided ethos of the period. This, then, is the fuller explanation of the oblivion that has not exactly engulfed Scott as it engulfed Holbrooke, whose work was never well known, but has rather crept like paralysis over the performance of his work during the later years of his long life. His last big occasion was the Leeds Festival of 1934, when his cantata, *La belle dame sans merci*, had its first performance nearly twenty years after it was composed. Its chromatics were apt enough for the text, but even then it seemed to belong to another epoch. At the time I myself wrote: "Before the war his larger works were better known abroad than at home. Since the war his smaller works, songs and piano pieces, which at one time enjoyed a great vogue at home, have suffered some eclipse. Thus whereas formerly all his works pleased somebody for one reason or another in spite of their individuality, which prevented them being placed in any rigid category or assigned to any definite school, now owing to the currents having changed their courses he is left high and dry. The composer has to some extent turned aside from composition to study occult philosophy, of which the fruit has been a stimulating book, *Music: its Secret Influence throughout the Ages*." Thirty years later that judgment is confirmed by the longer perspective.

Of the other members of the group O'Neill, the eldest, devoted himself to theatre music, Quilter to song-writing; Balfour Gardiner gave up composition and was content to dispense some useful patronage. Grainger made a mark as a pianist and attached himself to the folk-song movement.

Quilter died in 1953, many years after he had given up composition. His was a small talent, but not to be despised on account of its limitations, for within them it was quite distinctive and on that very account possessed hostages against oblivion. His native fount of melody had a charm which won him a wide public among amateurs for his songs, and his workmanship was that of a jeweller who could cut and polish, embellish and refine, to perfection. His poets were Shakespeare, Herrick and Tennyson, of whom Herrick was nearest akin to him in spirit. He first made

* *Music and Letters*, Vol. 44, No. 3, p. 283.

his mark with three Shakespeare songs published in 1905. Their harmonic idiom belonged to the previous century and contained too many sevenths and ninths to commend itself to the more austere taste of the twentieth century. But such as it was it matched the words, for Shakespeare is all things to all men in all centuries. His melodic and harmonic idiom never developed, and a setting of "Orpheus with his Lute" published in 1939 did not differ in style, treatment or idiom from "O Mistress Mine" in the first set. He went on from his first Shakespeare settings to *Seven Elizabethan Lyrics* and then to Herrick for his *To Julia* cycle and for "To Daisies", which with "Now sleeps the crimson petal" (Tennyson) show his delicate talent at its happiest. Herrick's Julia seemed indeed to bring out the essence of his circumscribed musical personality and to Julia he returned for the name of his light opera which was produced at Covent Garden in the winter of 1936. This was a pretty enough comedy about a countess and a composer and the music was pretty to match. The epithet "pretty" is applicable to all he wrote without derogatory implication beyond the fact that it goes with "little". Quilter was in fact a miniaturist—across the centuries he is saluted by Giles Farnaby. Even when he wrote his incidental music to the children's play *Where the Rainbow Ends* and his *Children's Overture*, based on Crane's book of nursery rhymes, the manner and the scale is the same in an orchestral guise, and the music is attractive in the same ingenuous sort of way. In all he wrote more than fifty songs, most of them composed in nine sets, of which one was taken from Dowson's *Songs of Sorrow*, another from Blake and another from Jacobean lyrists. They are English enough certainly, but fragrant not so much with the scent of the English hedgerow as with a whiff of German sweetness and a very faint aroma of French perfume. He did not touch the folk-song revival as Grainger did nor emulate the more robust rusticity of Balfour Gardiner.

Gardiner gave up writing before the bloom had rubbed off his fresh open-air inspiration, which can be seen at its typical, best and most popular in his *Shepherd Fennel's Dance*, a short piece for orchestra based on an episode in one of Hardy's *Wessex Tales* and dedicated to Henry Wood in 1911 and for many years a favourite with Prom audiences. It may be that he realized that his was a vein that would quickly be worked out, and as a man of means he was not urged on by considerations of money or ambition. Indeed he devoted his money to giving (in 1912 and 1913) series of orchestral concerts to bring the works of his contemporaries before the public. Maybe like Elgar he felt that after the war the climate was no longer favourable to his sort of music—as indeed proved to be the case with the romantic composers to be discussed in the next chapter. At any rate he pinpoints, in a handful of delightful piano pieces, the vigorous choral ballad *News from Whydah*, a few orchestral pieces such as the one mentioned, the *Overture to a Comedy* and *A Berkshire Idyll*, and some short choral pieces, the golden noon of Edwardian England as known to a sane, cultivated and generous mind. Musically it was the beginning of a trend in English music which came to nothing.

Percy Aldridge Grainger was the youngest of the "Frankfurt Gang", being still a boy when he came from Melbourne to work at the piano with another of the Conservatoire teachers, James Kwast. (He subsequently worked with Busoni.) He made his career as a pianist and his compositions were all in the smaller forms, but he was a man of marked individuality, and after he came to England he plunged into the folk-song movement. What he did with the folk-songs he collected in Lincolnshire was to harmonize them for small ensembles or drawing-room use, either as piano pieces or as songs with accompaniment. This was done in all good faith, and cannot be reprobated even now, although the harmony is of the added-note kind that is found in Scott, Quilter and Gardiner (though freer from chromatics), since as collector and editor he was most scrupulous—his versions were meticulously faithful to what he actually heard, even to noting graces and the singer's idiosyncrasies of pronunciation. Moreover, his accompaniment to the most remarkable song in his collection, "Six Dukes went a-fishing", is impervious to changes of taste. The other bright particular star of his collection is "Brigg Fair", which he gave to Delius, with the result which all the world knows, though Delius distorted its character in the process of variation writing. The harmonization of folk-tunes is a debated question of aesthetic propriety, but all the collectors did it and approved of doing it for the sake of getting their discoveries known among the musical public, whose life was at that time founded on the domestic piano.

Grainger's interest had been engaged by a lecture from Lucy Broadwood at a competition festival at Brigg, the home of Gervase Elwes, the singer. He thereafter scoured the district, first without a phonograph and soon after with one of these primitive recording machines. A tithe of his harvest he published in *The Folk-Song Journal* of 1908, together with an essay on the use of mechanical recording, in which he was a pioneer. Composition was a secondary activity with him, but the contact with folk-song stimulated it and gave it a new direction, for in addition to making settings for various strange instrumental combinations he wrote a few original pieces for various media in a style that sounds distinctly English for the good but then novel reason that it was founded on folk-song. *Mock Morris, Molly on the Shore, Country Gardens, Green Bushes* (passacaglia) were examples of an attractive new species of composition that achieved enormous popularity, whether the material was folk or original. After he settled in America (1914) he produced some choral music, which has not crossed the ocean. He was a "character", albeit an amiable one, whose oddness was direct simplicity carried to the length of eccentricity, of which one manifestation was his use of homely English instead of the usual Italian nomenclature. Thus he described *Mock Morris* as a "room-music tit-bit" which he "dished up" for piano. His great personal beauty must have been a physical embodiment of some Nordic strain in him which led him to friendship with Grieg, to collecting Danish folk-songs and to marrying a Swedish poetess. He was certainly all of a piece and he made a distinctive if small contribution to the musical life of his time.

Besides the Frankfurt group, the academics and later the nationalist school which sought at the turn of the century to put new and more vigorous life into English composition, there was yet another group, centred on Birmingham and focused for a few years in the short-lived Musical League, embracing also some other adherents whose artistic creed could be summed up in the one word "orchestra". Elgar was of course the brightest star of this school, but after his abortive attempts to animate the Musical League he relinquished his aspirations to lead a school. Because he happened to be a Midlander and because Birmingham was at the relevant time a centre from which energy and enthusiasm spread to the West Country, the Potteries and the North, it seemed for a moment that the progressive movement active there, first under Swinnerton Heap and then under Bantock, might lead English music forward in step with continental developments. The composers of this orchestral school of thought did not repudiate the choral tradition, but their liveliest interests were engaged by the orchestra. Whereas Stanford and Ethel Smyth were descendants and disciples of Schumann and Mendelssohn through Brahms, Elgar and Bantock and their associates were in the line from Liszt and Wagner through Richard Strauss.

Elgar, who, it may be recalled, was the first Peyton Professor of Music in the University of Birmingham, deserted the choral tradition for the orchestra and became the first English composer really to think orchestrally and to swim in that medium as naturally as Berlioz had in France and as Strauss was contemporaneously doing in Germany. In the first decade of the twentieth century the rage was for tone-poems. Bantock wrote *Fifine at the Fair* even before Elgar wrote *Falstaff*. Havergal Brian, whose copious stream has somehow dissipated itself in sand,* wrote a Comedy Overture, *Dr. Merryheart*, which got as far as a Promenade concert, and subsequently a gigantic Mahleresque symphony, *The Gothic*, which had to wait more than forty years for a first performance. Julius Harrison, a pupil of the Midland Institute while Bantock was at its head, became an orchestral conductor but wrote little save a slight but agreeable suite of Worcestershire pieces (1920)—his *Mass in C* (1948) belongs to another context and was written after his retirement from the concert platform. Paul Beard and Clarence Raybould, who figured prominently in the B.B.C. Symphony Orchestra respectively as leader and conductor, were both educated at Birmingham institutions and may be regarded as products of the orchestral ferment in that city. The foundation of the City of Birmingham Symphony Orchestra in 1920, which came at the end of a long struggle waged by J. G. Halford in the nineteenth century and Appleby Matthews in the first years of the twentieth, was finally brought about through the advocacy of Neville Chamberlain in his City Council days. It

* Mr. Reginald Nettel has described the process in *Ordeal by Music* (1945).

represents one bit of the municipal socialism for which Birmingham pioneered and the eventual outcome of the city's interest in the establishment of an orchestral tradition. The appointment in 1924 of Adrian Boult to be its conductor, which marked the first major stage in his personal career, set the seal of quality and permanence upon a project in which Elgar himself and Ernest Newman in his time as critic of *The Birmingham Post* had taken a hand.

In this Midland episode of modern history Granville Bantock is the central figure. For more than thirty years his was the chief personality in the Midlands and he was Elgar's successor in certain specific offices, notably in the professorial chair of Birmingham University, which had been created through the efforts of Richard Peyton and Hermann Fiedler* for Elgar in 1905. He was eleven years Elgar's junior, having been born in 1868 in London. He came to Birmingham in 1900 to take up the post of Principal of the Music School attached to the Midland Institute and he succeeded to the professorship in 1908. Elgar continued to have a home in the West Midlands with a few intervals till the end of his life, but his withdrawal from specifically Midland activities was one result of his international fame and the consequent pull of London. Bantock, though unlike Elgar in outlook on social, political and religious matters, belonged to the same orchestral school of thought which had been nourished from the Continent, the final offshoot of Liszt. Bantock's biographer, H. Orsmond Anderton, writing in 1915 contrasted the two men: Elgar ceremonious, religious, nervous, Bantock informal (indeed rebellious), pagan and companionable but they were alike in their musical outlook, their mastery of the orchestra and their connection with Birmingham.

Bantock was the son of a surgeon of sufficient eminence to hold his own in a controversy about antiseptics with Lister, but there was no trace of music in his heredity and he had, like many others, to overcome parental opposition to a musical career. However, he got to the Royal Academy of Music, won the Macfarren scholarship in his first term—characteristically sending in a setting of Satan's monologue from *Paradise Lost*—and studied

* Later Professor of German at Oxford, brother of Max Fiedler, conductor, at Essen.

under Frederick Corder from 1889 to 1893. Corder was a Wagnerian at the time when it was a matter of partisanship, and Bantock's own impulses were to go farther in the same direction. He put his hand to piano, violin and clarinet and dabbled with other instruments, desultory studies which probably helped him to acquire his mastery of instrumentation, for it is his handling of the media of music, unaccompanied chorus as well as orchestra, rather than the matter, which constitutes the chief excellence of his music. Indeed, the poverty of his ideas, concealed so long as they were fashionable, which is to say up to the war of 1914-1918, had even before he died proved noxious, if not fatal, to the survival and currency of his music. Thus *Omar Khayyam*, which is generally recognized as his greatest work, was not performed again in Birmingham, where it was first heard in 1909, till 1951 when it was specially revived for the Festival of Britain, an interval of forty-two years. It had remained unperformed anywhere for more than twenty years.

His output was large and in all forms, though not a great deal of it is in the abstract or the operatic forms, but whether concentration and self-criticism—never characteristic of Corder's pupils, as seen also in Bax and Holbrooke—would have ensured a more solid achievement and a greater vitality is a matter of some doubt, for Bantock had a diffuse mind, intellectually curious, temperamentally sociable, imaginatively susceptible. He had a chameleon's skin for local colour, and his wanderings, spiritual no less than physical, were wide—he went round the world twice, once as a youth conducting musical comedies for George Edwardes and once in age as an examiner for Trinity College of Music. The range of his style, too, was so wide that he never developed a personal, distinguishable idiom. The exotic always lured him, but he was equally capable of an enthusiasm for old English music, which he edited and imitated. His biographer comments on his delight in "discovering" the well known for himself, so, though no scholar, he edited pieces from *The Fitzwilliam Virginal Book* for piano and wrote an *Old English Suite* for small orchestra. This side of his talent found most profitable employment in the incidental music he wrote for specific productions of plays. The Greek classics offered him in one way or another *Hippolytus, The Bacchae, Electra, The Frogs, The Birds* and

Thesmophoriazusae, Shakespeare *Macbeth*, and Arnold Bennett *Judith*. He wrote music for Maud Allan's Salome dances and for a children's play, *Fairy Gold*. Here his susceptibility to atmosphere and his eagerness to explore were of value, and the stage could supply what was lacking of substance in his musical ideas. It has been said that he would have done better as a French composer than an English—he comes somewhere near to changing his nationality in his *Pierrot of the Minute* overture—since French opera and even French concert and salon music are less exacting: elegance and aptitude are more important than durability and depth. In fact he resembled Saint-Saëns in more than physical appearance: there was the same fertility and facility and the same uncritical acceptance of the second-rate. Indeed the remark at the end of the article on Saint-Saëns in Grove's *Dictionary* could be transferred to Bantock without the change of a single word: "His imagination asserts itself far more in the treatment of his materials than in his actual invention."

Of Bantock's many sources of inspiration the chief is the Orient, which manifests itself in the titles of his compositions to the extent of nearly one fifth, not counting biblical works and the names of individual part-songs, of which he wrote over one hundred and fifty. The Orient is a large place, but Bantock took it all in his ample embrace—Egypt, Persia, India, China. It would be unkind to call these Eastern pictures, poems and evocations Brummagem goods, since they were not for export: they reflect the effect of the East on a sympathetic Western mind. His excursions into the Celtic twilight yield less sounding brass and tinkling cymbal: the *Hebridean Symphony* and the opera, *The Seal Woman*, are both satisfying pieces of work, though *The Seal Woman* is so misty as to dissolve dramatically. There is also a *Celtic Symphony* for strings and six harps, and two *Heroic Ballads* for orchestra. Greece exerted an attraction that produced, besides the various dramatic overtures, *The Great God Pan* (choral ballet), *Sappho* (nine fragments for solo voice) and a *Pagan Symphony*—and more besides—but the romantic idiom is not well suited to depict the clear outlines of the Mediterranean world. Bantock indeed wandered too far.

On one of his excursions in his own country he encountered the competition festival movement and was prompted to write much choral music outside the tradition of the main triennial festivals that survived the Victorian age. Many of his part-songs were used as test-pieces for the crack choirs of the North, but the chief outcome of his interest in choirs was a series of large-scale works for unaccompanied voices. Of these the chief was the choral symphony *Atalanta in Calydon*, which is a setting of four of Swinburne's odes in as many as twenty voice-parts to make the four movements of a symphony. *Vanity of Vanities* was another essay in the same form. But though they excited the interest of the northern choirs to whom they were dedicated they did not satisfy the public, and extended choral composition for unaccompanied voices was not even tried by his fellow composers until Thomas Wood, with the Fleet Street Choir of T. B. Lawrence in mind, attempted a similar feat, though with incomplete success, in *Chanticleer* from Chaucer and *Over the Hills and Far Away*.

Omar Khayyam was a good subject for Bantock to take, not only because of his passion for the Orient and his sympathy with the philosophy of *Carpe diem* and *Vanitas vanitatum*, but also for the paradoxical reason that in the form which FitzGerald imposed upon the oriental poet's quatrains (*rubaiyat*) what are really disconnected epigrams are made to cohere into a poem of large span. Bantock needed a grandiose form, for it was the fashion of the time, and his interest in large-scale choralism drove him towards something of oratorio dimensions, though his actual gift was for detailed illustration—even Ernest Newman criticized the elaboration of detail as a dislocation of its architectural proportions. FitzGerald's forcible organization of the poem and the prodigality of its imagery, wine, roses and the wilderness, gave Bantock just what he wanted, a big design and wealth of detail. But the structure sags even in Part I—there are three parts in all—and the musical ideas are too superficial, that is, too taken up with illustrative points of detail to get to the heart of the poem. And the same criticism can be made of the orchestral tone-poem *Fifine at the Fair*, which is described as a defence of inconstancy but hardly does Browning justice. There is, nevertheless, a good deal of charm in the incidents of *Omar*. Charm, however, is too thin a diet to keep large organisms alive.

XI

The Late Romantics

THERE IS a group of composers who have contributed a considerable body of valuable music, which is not important for any historical influence on the developing style of modern English music but which is rather a survival of the great romantic movement of the nineteenth century. Its idiom often reflects the development of Wagnerian harmony but it is, most of it, firmly based on key and there is no deliberate experiment or iconoclasm in the outlook of these late romantics. They naturally vary among themselves in the amount of modern idiom they incorporate into their highly idiosyncratic work. But they were not crusaders for independence like Parry and Stanford, and though their work is less clearly aligned to the contemporary cosmopolitan idiom of the Frankfurt group they were not concerned any more than those German-trained Britons to secure emancipation. They found the romantic temper of nineteenth-century music congenial to them, being themselves romantic at heart, and proceeded to write that sort of music which, apart from the individual personality, was the current coin of composition when they were growing up.

The chief figures in this group were Frederick Delius (1862-1934), Joseph Holbrooke (1878-1958), Hamilton Harty (1879-1941), John Ireland (1879-1962), and Arnold Bax (1883-1953). Of these Delius is at once the oldest and the most considerable figure, although Ireland, who worked in the smaller forms, may suffer less from the vagaries of taste in which we began to flounder after the turn of the mid-century than either Delius or Bax, who worked on a larger scale and were more prolific. The case of Bax is indeed striking in that his works fell into an almost total eclipse immediately after his death. It is not uncommon, of course, though it is neither very creditable or explicable, for the reputation of a respected figure to decline when he dies—the cases of John

Galsworthy and Lytton Strachey in the sister art of letters were conspicuous—but there would seem to be more hope of a future life for Delius than for Bax, so steep was his decline.

Delius is a strange figure. Sir Thomas Beecham, who knew him better than any other Englishman and was his incomparable interpreter, declared that he fitted into no tradition and was in biological terminology a musical "sport", rather like Berlioz, who similarly divides and always has divided critical opinion about his status in the hierarchy of the great. His music is admittedly limited in range, both emotionally and stylistically, yet it has marked individuality and is copious. It is far from fool-proof in performance, so that Beecham's death in 1961 robbed him of his most eloquent advocate and immediately produced the situation long foreseen, that his claim to recognition might easily be forfeited in the very year of his centenary. Holbrooke has been the least successful in catching the ear of the generations which have passed on to non-romantic interests. Partly it is because he followed the Wagnerian principle of operatic composition and found in Britain no home for his large-scale mythological trilogy of music-dramas, and partly because the general character of his music is expansive, exuberant and prolix. Harty's life was occupied more with performance than composition. He was a first-rate piano accompanist who subsequently became a conductor of high rank. But a symphony (the "Irish"), three choral cantatas, a piano concerto, an overture, a tone-poem and some songs give him a niche in this particular shrine, though his name more often appeared in concert programmes as an arranger of Handel's *Water Music*, until a growing purism took exception to romantic orchestration of classical music, than as a composer in his own right.

Ireland might dispute the label romantic more easily than the others, since his work has been influenced a little by the folk-song revival and by modern procedures. He is one of the few composers of our renaissance to write with natural sympathy and ability for the piano. His line is for chamber music and songs rather than for orchestra and chorus, though he has written in big forms as well as small. His romanticism is less pronounced than that of either Delius or Bax, his contemporary, but he is a romantic at heart and the general character of his music is in the romantic tradition. Bax on the other hand was a full-blooded, unrepentant romantic, who never flirted with modernism nor with a modern outlook. He confessed that his music was an expression of emotional states and that he had no interest whatever in sound for its own sake or in modernist schools and factions. His music is copious and lush, and though it can deal with grim ideas, as in the first symphony and the motet *This Worlde's Joie*, the approach is that of the Celtic revival. Born in London, he died in Ireland; he spent many of his post-student years in Dublin and Donegal; he was associated with the literary movement that revolved round Yeats, 'Æ', James Stephens and Padraic Colum, and himself wrote under the pen-name of Dermot O'Byrne. The result was that all his music was bathed in a Celtic haze if not always a twilight. He had no drop of Irish blood in him, but his music was the equivalent of Yeats's poetry. With developments after 1918 he had no sympathy, and, very wisely, made no attempt to make his music up to date (as Frank Bridge did). He accepted a knighthood and the office of Master of the King's Musick, but he ought to have done neither, for he was a bohemian as well as a romantic, as many a story in his autobiography *Farewell my Youth* reveals, and fitted into no official or academic capacity. Though he appeared tight-lipped in later life he came much nearer to the conventional idea of the Byronic poet or the Lisztian-Wagnerian composer than any of his contemporaries.

Delius was a cosmopolitan, so that an historian's claim to enrol him among English composers may be questionable, for he was of Dutch extraction, German ancestry, American and German training, British by birth at Bradford in Yorkshire, French by domicile for most of his adult life, Scandinavian by early associations, marriage and song setting. Germany has the best claim to him if he is not regarded as English, for he secured a good many first performances there—his piano concerto and *Norwegian Suite* at Elberfeld in 1904, *Paris* (1899) and *Appalachia* (1912) also at Elberfeld, a tone poem *Life's Dance* (1901) at Düsseldorf, *Sea Drift* (1906) at Essen, the opera *A Village Romeo and Juliet* (1907) at Berlin, the opera *Fennimore and Gerda* (1919) at Frankfurt-am-Main. But in the first decade of the twentieth century English conductors such as Beecham, Wood and Coates became aware of him, and England reasserted her claim in two Delius festivals organized by Beecham in 1929, at which the composer, though stricken in health, was present, and again after the Second World War in 1946. Born in England but living there only intermittently, he wished to be buried there, and though an atheist he was interred in the churchyard of Limpsfield in Surrey. If anyone questions the suitability of his choice—and it was questioned at the time—let him go on a pilgrimage to the grave and think of *On Hearing the First Cuckoo in Spring* or *In a Summer Garden*, and his doubts may be stilled, though Eric Fenby, his amanuensis and companion in his last years remains, doubtful.*

Delius was a nature-poet and an atheist. He was conscious of the fragility and mortality of all beauty but, a strong individualist, he was even to the end a yea-sayer to life. A famous portrait by James Gunn, after his illness (the recrudescence of a venereal infection) had paralysed him, led to a misapprehension of his character. Pitiable though his condition was it did not affect the steel fibre which had been tempered by the vicissitudes of his young manhood, as related by Beecham in his biography (1959). He became "aloof, exclusive and egotistical" and Fenby's testimony, while exciting pity contrary to his intention, confirms the judgment. Beecham curiously accepts the idea, derived in this context from a letter which Grieg wrote to Percy Grainger, that man and artist "are indissolubly wedded one to the other", yet doubts whether "the spirit of Delius was ever seriously troubled by any philosophic influence". The philosophy of Nietzsche, which prompted the composition of *A Mass of Life*, one of the peaks among his achievements—and it must be the philosophy since Delius showed small sensibility to words as such—was his substitute for Christianity, which for a millennium and a half had been the mainstay, axiom and direct inspiration of the art of music. *The Origin of Species*, a changing cosmology, and the doubts of Victorian thinkers and men of letters, so undermined the axiomatic acceptance of Christianity as ultimate truth and led to the rationalist philosophy, as well as to milder expressions of agnosticism, that they opened a gulf in front of the artist who wished to make affirmations about life. Stoicism was a common substitute

* *Delius as I Knew Him* (Bell, 1936), p. 234. But Miss May Harrison explained (*R.C.M. Magazine*, Vol. 53, No. 2) that he wished to be among friends (meaning Mrs. Harrison) and not strangers.

as foundation for large choral works in the oratorio tradition—such were all Brahms's cantatas and the *Requiem*. For Delius it was the desire to become one with Nature, our mother, our environment, our nourishment, and the source of our deep biological urge to live. Schopenhauer and Nietzsche proffered their creeds of love and life, of beauty and decay, of detachment and participation, and Delius found in *Also sprach Zarathustra* the text for his Mass. For his pagan *Requiem* no author is named—perhaps he compiled it himself, but its effect is a hymn to negation—the last thing that can be said of *A Mass of Life*. Neither Beecham nor Heseltine has anything good to say of the *Requiem* and on its single performance at Queen's Hall at a Philharmonic Concert in 1922 under Albert Coates it dropped dead. A section called "A la grande amoureuse" remains (at least in my memory) as the only positive music in the whole large work, though Heseltine commends the opening funeral march and the concluding elegy.*

A Mass of Life takes pride of place in a consideration of Delius's contribution to modern music on the ground of size and subject, though if one reflects on what is most characteristic it will be either the two great sets of variations *Appalachia* and *Brigg Fair* or the exquisite nature pieces *In a Summer Garden, The First Cuckoo, Summer Night on the River, Song before Sunrise* that come to mind. There are a dozen of these orchestral tone-poems, of which *Paris* is the biggest. But *A Mass of Life* has to be put in the balance against the works, of various kinds, in which the predominant emotion seems to be nostalgia, regret for the transitoriness of all mortal things (*Sunt lacrimae rerum et mentem mortalia tangunt*), the sheer poignancy of an acute sensibility, the almost unbearable pathos of *Sea Drift* and *A Village Romeo and Juliet* or the bitter-sweet tang of *Songs of Sunset* to poems of Ernest Dowson. *A Mass of Life* is "an ecstatic dithyramb in praise of life".† Whatever else it is—and it is certainly a welter of contradictions—*Also sprach Zarathustra* is positive and *A Mass of Life* is a triumphant hymn to the greatness of our present life,

---

* It may be that the single performance gave a wrong impression of the work, since Delius's texture requires an acute sense of orchestral balance, which was not one of Coates's prominent characteristics as a conductor.

† Heseltine.

not a future life, from its first crashing challenge to the final
exaltation of the hymn to Eternity, a paean to its variety expressed
in the dances, the noon-tide songs, the nocturnes, the chants of love
and sorrow. That Christ too came that we might have life more
abundantly is only one more of the contradictions in Nietzsche's
philosophy. But these contradictions are only repeated in Delius's
music in some passages of typical Delian wistfulness. Since
Delius's way of setting music to words is not to follow their
detailed significance, still less to engage in word painting, but to
distil the essence out of a paragraph or a poem and present it
whole in a complete movement or section, he can make clear to
the hearer what patient attention to the words would only make
so much the more unintelligible. For while the teaching of
Zarathustra is clear, the text is obscure; while its theme, the glory
of life, is consistent, its coherence from one number to the next is
hardly to be traced.

Delius designed his Mass on a large scale to a text contrived for
him by his friend Fritz Cassirer, a young conductor who was
responsible for several first performances of Delius's works,
including *A Village Romeo and Juliet*. The two men according to
Beecham's biography* fixed it up on a bicycling tour in Brittany,
for Cassirer saw that what Delius wanted was the overall significance of the prose-poem from which to evoke a musical counterpart
of its moods. Of the imagery Delius only gave to the midnight bell
and its associated thoughts a leitmotif, a four-note figure:

Ex 17

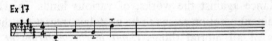

though his texture contains a few themes of some significance by
association, even if there is no Wagnerian consistency in their
appearance and use. Cassirer said "As *Zarathustra* is not composed thematically an analysis in this case would be nonsense."
It is composed, as all Delius's work is, harmonically, though
there is a double fugue in the third number. Delius once declared
that harmony was an instinct, which will not satisfy a psychologist's definition, but is a true enough account of the nature of
Delius's own innate musicality. He did not think thematically as
Beethoven did, nor contrapuntally as Bach did, nor even in tonal

* *Frederick Delius* (Hutchinson, 1959), p. 132.

imagery as Wagner did, but much more as Debussy did in terms of chords and colours. One consequence of this harmonic way of thinking is rhythmic inertia, although of course we speak of harmonic *progression*, but harmonic progression is largely a matter of dissonance and resolution. Now Delius used dissonant and chromatic chords, not indeed in the way described by Schoenberg as the freedom of the dissonance, which means that all dissonances are equal (and so unprogressive), but half-way to that state, in that the milder dissonances become consonant—thus every one of the *Songs of Farewell* ends on a tonic chord with an added sixth—and the sharper ones lose much of their asperity by the way they are disposed with their intervals widely spread across the orchestra. The first and fourth beats of almost every bar of *The First Cuckoo* provide instances of these soft discords, these highly flavoured concords which float motionless in a timeless atmosphere. There is therefore a natural languor about much of Delius's music apart from that appropriate to the nocturnal and static subjects which he liked to depict. Another stylistic feature conducive to the same end is that since his basic ideas were not thematic he is not naturally at ease with the classical procedures of thematic development. He wrote no symphony, but he did write four concertos (for piano, for violin and cello, for violin and for cello), and if they seem less than completely satisfying—the piano concerto is early, uncharacteristic and Lisztian—it is that they are rhapsodic rather than symphonic. Thematic development, like dissonance and counterpoint, is a way in which the feeling of progression is induced in music independently of injection of rhythm by stress accents. It follows that Delius is happier with variation form—though to be sure variation is a kind of development, but it need not lead anywhere—and with miniature organizations than with extended forms. So here again a deceptive notion can easily take root in the listener's mind that there is less variety of mood, less overall animation, less musical invention, than is in fact the case in Delius's very considerable output.

This is not to claim that he is a great universal artist. Indeed such a claim would be perverse, for his range of feeling is limited and with it his range of musical utterance. But within its limits, which embrace an element of the fantastic and fairytale—e.g. the "twilight fancies" of the opera *Irmelin*, the once-upon-a-time quality of *Eventyr*, the ninety-ish morbid sensibility of *Arabesque* and Dowson's *Songs of Sunset*, some aspects of nature other than the gentle ones of the small orchestral idylls, e.g. *North Country Sketches*, and the vigour of *A Mass of Life* and of some of the four dozen songs—within its limits there is a wholly distinctive vision expressed in an idiom entirely the composer's own. Yet is has to be admitted that in *Brigg Fair* what is distinctively Delian is at variance with the spirit of the English folk-song, which is a cheerful ditty, tinged with poetry, about a pair of rural lovers. And even the Cuckoo heralding the Spring is rather a melancholy bird. English folk-songs will sustain a fair variety of harmonizations—Vaughan Williams said that every generation wanted a new one of its own—and the sort of harmony that Delius used in *Brigg Fair* and *Appalachia* was used also for folk-song setting by Percy Grainger and E. J. Moeran, but in their hands it is less dream-laden, less sicklied over with too introverted a vision, than came naturally to Delius. This slightly too rich harmonic flavour is also to be found in Quilter's songs, and as Quilter, Grainger and Delius were all students in Germany in the eighties the source of this slightly un-English Englishry may be sought there. Another element from the same source in Delius's music is the large orchestra which he demanded, for this was the post-Wagnerian time, when extra wind, brighter percussion, and harp were demanded by composers to increase and variegate sonority. *Paris* for instance requires quadruple woodwind (three flutes only) and six horns and glockenspiel, *Brigg Fair* the same with tubular bells instead of glockenspiel. The *First Dance Rhapsody* asks for a bass oboe, as does *A Mass of Life*.

Delius wrote six operas: *Irmelin* (1892), first performed at Oxford in 1953; *The Magic Fountain* (1895), inspired by Florida; *Koanga* (1897), produced at Elberfeld in 1904 and in London at Covent Garden in 1935; *A Village Romeo and Juliet* (1901), his masterpiece in the dramatic medium, first produced (with German text) in Berlin in 1907, performed in London by Beecham in 1910, revived by him in 1920 and again under his direction at the Royal College of Music in 1934, and chosen by Sadler's Wells for the celebration of his centenary in Bradford and London; *Margot la Rouge* (1902), a one-act shocker composed for a prize competition, which it failed to win, and subsequently recast with Fenby's aid into the *Idyll* for soprano and baritone, which was first performed at a Promenade Concert in 1933; and last, *Fennimore and Gerda* (1910) produced at Frankfurt-am-Main in 1919 but nowhere since. Delius was his own librettist for the first two and the last two. Though a man of wide reading in several languages he had little regard for words in relation to music; as long as the vocal line carrying them could float on a sea of orchestral sound, as the line of the violin floats in the concerto, he was content to reproduce the idea and the associated feelings. Furthermore he described his scenes as pictures and there is very little drama, which is to say action and development of character. *Irmelin* should be called an idyll, *Margot la Rouge* actually became one. *Koanga* is presented in oblique narration, the answer to a request in the prologue to be told the story. In *A Village Romeo and Juliet* and in *Fennimore and Gerda* the dialogue is in plain prose injected upon the flow of the music which is organized as a series of self-contained pictures, though occasionally a poetic line is crucial to the music it prompts. (Such is the barge-man's "Ho! Travellers we a-passing by" in *A Village Romeo and Juliet* and Whitman's "Once I passed through a populous city" which transformed the harlot Margot into the rapt lover of the *Idyll*.) In consequence the operas constantly approximate to orchestral tone-poems. Indeed Cecil Gray once described *A Village Romeo and Juliet* perfectly as "a symphonic poem with the implicit programme made explicit upon the stage". There is just enough conflict, contrast and episodic action to make the opera stageworthy. The conflict is between the parents of the two lovers, as in Shakespeare; there is an enigmatic figure of the Dark Fiddler who precipitates the turns and twists of the plot (which Delius took from a story by Gottfried Keller), there is a scene at the fair and at the inn called Paradise Garden, and there are the two lovers who go from childhood to voluntary death. From these ingredients Delius distils his web of magic. In *Fennimore and Gerda*, which came eight years later, the characters are less types and symbols, more flesh and blood. This opera, too, Delius took from a novel, the Danish Jens Peter Jacobsen's *Niels Lyhne*, and he gave it a happy ending. Again the scenes are pictures in which the action and the dialogue are realistic. Natural speech is projected upon the surface of what is being told by the orchestra. Always the same way with words, even in the songs, though not quite to the same degree of mutual disregard between voice and instrument.

Of the songs one or two achieved wide popularity, especially among amateurs. "Twilight Fancies", from an early set to Norwegian words, is an excellent example of the atmospheric song cultivated in the wake of Hugo Wolf at the end of the century, that has caught the public taste. As in *Irmelin*, both song and opera, the mood is one of gentle disquiet, "to know not what" set to music. "Love's Philosophy" (Shelley) on the other hand is a good concert song and "Klein Venevil" a neatly turned trifle in the manner of Grieg. Some of the piano writing in these early songs, triplets in the right hand for instance, sounds old-fashioned, as indeed it is since they belong to the eighties and nineties, and the songs as a whole are more conventional, for good and ill, i.e. they are less distinctive but more easily accessible than the rest of his output. Between 1885 and 1919 Delius set poems written in Norwegian, Danish, English (Tennyson, Shelley, Henley and Old English lyrics), French (Verlaine) and German (Nietzsche). So that they can hardly be said to belong to the English song tradition but are like the offshoots of the *Lieder* tradition represented by the songs of Grieg, Sibelius, and Dvořák, except of course that they are cosmopolitan in flavour, not national. (The fact that Germany provided the facilities for education and publication exerted considerable influence on European song-writing in the last part of the nineteenth century.) Their general sentiment is that of the sunset of the romantic period with its chromatic harmony, which Delius grafted on to the English song tradition through his admirers and successors, Peter Warlock and E. J. Moeran, so that chromatics are fully acclimatized by the time of Walton and Britten, alike in vocal line and in accompaniment swaying beneath the line. For all their nearer conformity to the conventions of the period they still remain true manifestations of Delius's personality.

If the songs are a by-product of his genius his chamber music is in the nature of a *tour-de-force*, a going against its grain. Though that is a wrong description of Delius's way of working. He told May Harrison that even in the matter of playing the piano lessons inhibited him, so that he could play no more, and *a fortiori* structural principles and "rules of composition" had been alien to him in his student days. "He had to do it his own way or not at all" and his way was that of the rhapsodists of old, stitchers together of tunes. The string quartet, however, is a more successful work than any of the sonatas, because the four string instruments exact some amount of counterpoint, whereas the piano is a constant temptation to move in block harmony or arpeggios with a diffuse melody running over it. Moreover, the quartet has a real liveliness and vigour rare in most of his work.

The third violin sonata, which was completed with Fenby's aid in 1930 and played to Delius by May Harrison and Fenby, has shape, a concise allegro, a simple dance-like measure in his lilting compound time, and the slow movement, which is the longest, at the end. But fundamentally it is arabesque over chords which varies its speed but hardly at all its mood. There is no reason why it should stop or go on, but it woos the ear in its characteristically pensive fashion. It marks the limitations of the composer's style and idiom. The violin concerto, in spite of what has been said by admirers and detractors alike of Delius's allergy to set forms and thematic development of the kind which has made the symphonic literature of two centuries possible, is susceptible of both formal and thematic analysis, but the key to the analytical method properly applicable to Delius is organic, not architectural. Someone once likened organic growth in drama—the same applies to music—to the mode of a caterpillar's locomotion, *b* arises out of *a*, *c* out of *b*, *d* out of *c* and so on. Homogeneity of theme is more important than contrast, as in the Elizabethan fantasia, in Beethoven's late quartets to some extent, and most plainly to be perceived in our own English folk-song "The Seeds of Love" (Sharp's first catch in Somerset*), of which the formula is precisely *abcde*. The violin concerto has in point of fact a perfectly sound structural plan and its thematic organization is organic, the rhapsodic outpouring (in the derivative sense of the word "rhapsody") in fact, as Mr. Deryck Cooke showed in detail,† closely organized from within.

Only in *A Village Romeo and Juliet* does he have recourse to the method of Wagnerian leitmotif—after all Wagner's purpose in creating his type of leitmotif was to enable him to achieve *unendliche Melodie*, the rhapsodic flow which is yet coherent,

* See p. 80.   † *Musical Times*, July 1962.

unlike the rhapsody we hum to ourselves on a country walk (or as formerly in the bathroom) in which the connection is solely that of subjective association. Wagner manipulated his leitmotifs conceptually, but for Delius it is that less conscious welling-up from below of a musical idea (be it interval, rhythm, motif or harmonic progression) which immediately proceeds like the caterpillar or, to vary the metaphor, grows like a Japanese paper flower in water. His limitations are less of technique than of range of idea, extent of feeling. The only technical flaws that can be ascribed to him are that in this concerto he rewrote the solo part twice under Albert Sammons's guidance since his original draft was unplayable, and in general he left his scores without adequate phrase marks or indications of internal balance—without, in fact, practical guides to the performer. It was the chief of Beecham's many services to him that he interpreted his intentions for the realization of the notes he had put on paper. Not all conductors have the sympathetic insight or requisite flair for realizing them. A pier-head band-master cannot kill Bach but he could not even begin to recreate Delius for an audience. Delius is aloof, is an aristocrat, is not for the market place. Since he is like no other composer that ever was—though some similarities to Debussy have been observed—his contribution to our musical experience is, if limited, unique.

Bax's great natural talent was recognized early and was trained at the Royal Academy of Music by Frederick Corder, who was a Wagnerian and steeped in the romantic tradition. Corder was also the teacher of Bantock and Holbrooke, both of whom learned from him expansiveness, rich texture and full orchestral sonority. In view of Bax's early diffuseness and life-long addiction to saturated colour it was once said with much truth that Bax was the one composer of his generation who was not a pupil of Stanford and who would most have benefited from Stanford's inculcation of economy, air-holes in the texture in the shape of rests, and discipline: he could not curb prolixity, nor concentrate his invention into the memorable or distinctive theme. He says of his own student days that he was quick-brained but slow to develop, had to labour to acquire a balanced technique—balance is the rub—and made his mark chiefly as a sight-reader—his abilities to read the most complex orchestral scores at the piano at sight became legendary. All this helps to account for the impression which a survey of his large output makes clearer and clearer the more the music and its reception are regarded, that his great talent was never sufficiently disciplined, and that its all-pervading romanticism corresponded to the romantic and bohemian way in which he conducted his life, as his pungently written autobiography *Farewell my Youth* reveals candidly and attractively.

Viewed as a contribution to English music of the twentieth century Bax's output is important in that it corresponds to the Anglo-Irish literary movement of Yeats, Synge and the Abbey Theatre, though it is less important to music than their work was to literature and drama. It is disappointing to contemplate so many beauties that gleam for a moment and then are smothered in their own luxuriance, so much refinement and sensibility that for lack of concentration waste themselves. Much of his work in all the forms he essayed (which excluded opera and oratorio) failed to secure a lodgment in the repertory even during his lifetime. What seem most likely to survive are the orchestral tone poems. He was one of the few English composers of his generation to write with sympathy for the piano and some of what he wrote for one and two pianos, *Moy Mell* for instance, a short Irish tone-poem for two pianos, which is characteristic of his writing for the instruments and of his sources of inspiration but not of his diffuseness, may also take a place in representative English music of the period.

Besides the luxuriance and the romance there is to be discerned in Bax's music, especially that composed in his early maturity, an element of severe struggle. Something seems to have happened to him to tear him in half and sear his soul, and the conflict can be read at the high level of his symphonies. Almost all his music composed up to the age of fifty gives the impression of being the product of a mind at war with itself. Psychological conflict is no bar to the exercise of the creative imagination—indeed, one theory of art propounds that art is a morbid excrescence of the emotional life like the grain of sand which irritates the oyster into making a pearl. But Bax rarely becomes fully articulate: he takes too long to get what he wants to say said, and even then does not always succeed in saying it. The richness of the imaginative content of his music is patent and undeniable, yet between it and its

audience there is usually a thick undergrowth of inhibitions. It
follows almost as a logical deduction that his best works are his
shortest.

The explanation of this curious phenomenon of inhibitions
producing prolixity must be sought if anywhere in his psychological make-up, on which his autobiography throws a good
deal of light. It was not widely known during his lifetime that
for some years he pursued a second career as an author, writing
verse and stories which were published in Dublin under the
pseudonym of Dermot O'Byrne. The Irish name embodies the
whole philosophy of the Celtic twilight, the Celtic fringe and
the Celtic humour which he found in Ireland, and with which
he identified himself. This Celtic world into which he projected
himself was revealed to him by W. B. Yeats, and he makes (in
the autobiography) the astonishing confession that Yeats's
poetry, beginning in 1902 with "The Wanderings of Usheen",
meant more to him than "all the music of the centuries". It became his aim to translate into his own art all that the "Celtic
wonderland" revealed to him. Perhaps, then, we have here a case
of the jealousy of the Muses. The art of music seems to demand
with ever-increasing strictness a completely wholehearted devotion. Fewer composers seem to be able to continue their
careers now as executants than in the eighteenth and early
nineteenth centuries—Brahms gave it up, though to be sure
Britten continues it, so that it is not yet an absolute rule—but the
tendency to concentrate on one facet of the art, composition,
while eschewing conducting, playing, criticism and scholarship,
gets gradually stronger. The case of Ethel Smyth is a warning to
composers against the dissipation of energy in activities outside
music, however much they might be expected to enrich their art.
Literary work in no way diminished Bax's output nor blunted his
technique, but the divided aims of his extraordinary life may be
in the last resort the cause of this lack of stamina. Then again, the
luxuriant, bohemian exuberance of the Irish Bax conflicts with the
Londoner with the very sharp tongue—*Farewell my Youth* is
entertaining reading but is often spiteful. This witty side of him
puts its head up in a few compositions, the *Overture to a Picar-
esque Comedy* and *The Truth about the Russian Dancers* for instance,
but only rarely. Everything that matters, except the few choral

pieces, is a musical expression of the peculiar Gaelic type of romance originally exploited by "Ossian" but revived in stronger and more genuine form in Ireland at the turn of our century.

His output falls into five classes, the symphonies and concertos, the shorter orchestral pieces, the choral music, the chamber music, and the small forms for piano and vocal solo.

There are seven symphonies composed between 1921 and 1939. The first in E flat is a stern work, quite other than the romantic rhapsodizings of the tone-poems. Its spiritual conflicts may have been precipitated by the war, or they may have been personal, but whatever they were there is no concealing their existence— the symphony opens with a furious phrase in E flat minor marked *feroce*. The issues are not resolved—are indeed hardly more than forcibly stated. They are still being argued though rather less grimly in the second symphony, which is cyclic in form and professes two key centres, E minor and C. In the third symphony there is some psychological relief to all this tension. No key is named and some of the themes have a liturgical and folky-pentatonic flavour; it is easier of acceptance and has in fact proved the most popular and lasting of all. No. 4 marks a turning out from states of mind to external nature; although there is no explicit programme the opening was inspired by a rough sea on a sunny day and the symphony was written in the north of Scotland. No. 5 reverts to questioning and turbulence, but they are externalized into legend and have a resolution in an epilogue, of which the tune

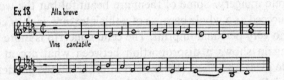

not only shows the solution of the psychological issues but is found to be blood relation of all the main themes and so unifies the symphony. The sixth symphony employs the same sort of form, but by now the question begins to be asked whether the form is after all right for the content. The seventh symphony like-wise seems to rely overmuch on rhapsodical episodes and to be traversing the same kind of experience all over again. The symphonies in fact are too much alike: they are heavily scored and sound thick when they are angry, luxuriant when they are content. When the form is satisfactory there is still lack of a logical nexus or it is concealed beneath too much protestation. One reason for their heaviness is their lack of scherzo—Bax writes his symphonies in three movements. They seem to have been born of some inner compulsion but they do not convince the listener of their inevitability. Though their construction bears inspection they still seem discursive to the ear.

Besides the symphonies there are six works in the nature of concertos, three so called, namely the cello, violin and piano (left-hand) concertos, and three less ambitiously styled. The Symphonic Variations for piano and orchestra is the first orchestral work on a large scale, dating from 1917, the Phantasy for viola and orchestra (1920) is in the condensed three-in-one form that was familiar at the date of composition (1920) in chamber music bearing that name, Phantasy,* so spelt. A Concertante for three solo instruments for a Henry Wood commemoration in 1949 uses a novel form of concertizing with orchestra: the rhapsodical first movement is given to the cor anglais, the scherzo to the clarinet, in a short intermezzo the horn plays an Irish tune, and in the rondo finale the exclusive soloists consent to meet each other in a convivial finale.

The Symphonic Variations mark the transition between the symphonic poems and the more austere form of the symphonies. The variations bear the titles of moods but not of any more concrete imagery. Some of them are beautiful but the work does not succeed as a whole because of a thick texture, lack of economy and no very personal imprint. The cello concerto is more concise, but again shows a disproportion between what are at bottom simple ideas and their elaboration into one of the greater forms. The violin concerto is the best of this group of works, since the singing of the solo instrument finds lyrical embodiment in a form of better proportions. The concerto for the left hand was written for Harriet Cohen after an accident to her right wrist, and it was played by her at the Cheltenham Festival of 1950. The special problem to be solved induced clarity both of texture and design; by now the old temptation to diffuseness and elaboration

* See p. 336.

had been conquered, though the ideas and the idiom remained
what they had always been with Bax, romantic and legendary.

There are over a dozen shorter works for orchestra, of which
three early tone-poems near together in date (1916-1917)—*The
Garden of Fand*, a successful translation of visual into auditory
imagery, *Tintagel* in a more dramatic vein, which with the help of
the title easily conjures up the thunderous Atlantic, King Arthur,
Tristan and Merlin, and *November Woods* professing to be more
"feeling than painting" but diffuse—proclaimed him of the company of Tchaikovsky and Sibelius in cultivating tone-poem and
symphony as distinct forms of orchestral composition. *Mediterranean*, a short and gay evocation, appeared in 1921, and then the
symphonies began. However, a tone-poem or two, always inspired
by some aspect of nature or fancy, was interspersed in the series
—*The Happy Forest*, an affair of colour and movement (1922),
The Tale the Pine Trees Knew, a kind of Celtic ballad from farther
north, and two pieces specifically entitled *Northern Ballad*. This
vein, also worked by Delius, had by the thirties been worked out,
though it suited Bax's type of imagination and his predilections
for sonority. *Tintagel* was well received when played in Berlin and
is probably the one most likely to survive as representative of his
peculiar talent, born just too late to catch the ebb of the romantic
tide.

His choral pieces are all short by cantata standards. *Mater ora
filium* is described as a carol, *This Worlde's Joie* and *I sing of a
Maiden* as motets; all are for unaccompanied choir and all draw
on the mediaeval simplicity of faith in the Nativity that has evoked
in so extraordinary a way the sympathy of an agnostic generation.
These and the cantatas for chorus with orchestra, *St. Patrick's
Breastplate* and *Walsinghame*, belong to the twenties. *The Morning
Watch* came in the next decade and some quite unknown settings
of the canticles with organ in the forties. All are difficult to sing
because of their chromaticism, but both the motets are good:
This Worlde's Joie with its *memento mori* refrain brings out the
dark streak, *Mater ora filium* the warmth, of the composer's two-
sided personality. *St. Patrick's Breastplate*, to a text from the Irish
Gaelic, evokes the Celtic strain in him, and being more diatonic
and more chordal is more successful than the cantata *Walsinghame*
(with tenor soloist), which is too tortuous for the setting of a

traditional ballad: the idea of its chromatic opening depicting the love that withers as against the diatonic love that endures at the end is poetical, but not poetical enough to redeem the tortured choral writing and far-fetched chromaticism, which are alien to balladry.

Of the large corpus of chamber music the best works are probably the least pretentious, the sonata for viola and harp and the oboe quintet, both of which are short, and the nonet in two movements only. The tone-colour of the sonata for viola and harp, compared with which that for viola and piano is prolix, is such as to suit a rhapsodic kind of utterance, Celtic-tinged melody and Bax's rich harmonic texture which is saved from turgidity by the nature of the harp. Irish, too, in general character is the oboe quintet in G (1923), which consists of a substantial slow movement of meditative character sandwiched between two quick movements, of which the last might represent a fair scene complete with jig. Bax was adept at writing tunes that sounded like Irish folk-songs and folk-dances. Such occur for instance in the rondo of the first string quartet (a work in which the direction *semplice* is, unusually, not out of place), in the concerto for flute, oboe, clarinet, horn and string quartet (which in spite of its title is a chamber work arranged from a flute sonata and more than usually contrapuntal), and in the Phantasy for viola and orchestra, to look no farther. The nonet resembles the concerto in its appeal through tone-colour to sensibility.

Bax was himself an accomplished pianist though he never played in public. Since most of the other leading English composers of the period were primarily violinists (Mackenzie, Elgar and Vaughan Williams) or did not seriously play the piano at all (Holst, who played the trombone, and Walton) it was only Bax and Ireland who wrote naturally and *con amore* for the piano. Indeed it looks as though their most enduring contribution to the renaissance is in the media of solo piano and song, where the piano is integral and important. Bax wrote four piano sonatas, of which the first was begun in 1910 and the last written in 1932, and one sonata for two pianos, but most of his piano writing went into characteristic pieces with poetic or descriptive titles like *In a Vodka Shop* or *What the Minstrel Told Us*. In them all he writes a rich harmony which aims at colour effects only realizable on the orchestra. In fact two of his tone poems, *Mediterranean* and *Paean*, began life as piano solos. It is not because the writing is unpianistic that these rich chromatic fistfuls of notes in chordal formations have been called the bane of late romantic writing for the piano—Bax knows how to exploit the extremes of the instrument, use of repeated notes and all the usual apparatus of arpeggios and cantilena melody derived from Chopin—it is rather that the music becomes opaque, the formal outlines are obscured by so much colour and decoration, so the texture becomes turgid. No. 2 in G is the best known of the sonatas (it has been recorded); cast in a single movement and evolving its ideas from an obsession with a single note it evokes images of old heroic tales, i.e. it is romantic in the way that mediaeval minstrelsy seems romantic. The others are similar in material and manner, i.e. orchestrally harmonic though organized into separate movements. Matter and manner are, however, better matched in the shorter tone-poems (for that is what these characteristic pieces are, rather than Songs without Words), the early ones inspired by Bax's Russian visit, which is vividly described in *Farewell my Youth*. There is no piano music after Bax turned fifty.

Like every English composer until the more instrumentally minded Elgar, Walton and Rawsthorne came along, Bax wrote songs—there are about fifty, many of them designated Irish or Celtic—but none of them achieved the currency that Stanford's or Ireland's did in their days, and Bax gave up song writing after 1926. The least officially inclined of musicians, he received the usual honours accorded to musicians of his reputation in his day, the gold medal of the Royal Philharmonic Society, honorary doctorates (Oxford and Durham), a knighthood; and on Walford Davies's death he was made Master of the King's Musick. But while he deserved the recognition he shrank from public life, and the court appointment, sinecure though it was, was incongruous with his outlook. As taste moved farther away from the romantic heyday of his youth he refused, quite rightly, to compromise his sincerity in going after alien ideals, and his last years were almost silent. His kind of music was no longer wanted and what he wrote lacked for the reasons already discussed, the stuff of permanence. At his death in 1953 he went into eclipse, but he had contributed to English music the kind of thing, the accomplished product of the *Zeitgeist*, with which in Germany composers below the first rank had always sustained their musical life, but which had been sparingly produced in Victorian England.

The perspective of history puts John Ireland into the same category of English romantics as Delius and Bax, though when he first became known to the general public around the time of the First World War he seemed more modern in that his harmony was modally favoured and garnished with added notes, and indeed he seemed later to be an English Debussy, though that description had earlier been applied to Cyril Scott. But Ireland shares with Delius and Bax a tendency to seek inspiration in a sort of pantheistic nature mysticism. Place names abound among his titles, which implies a feeling for the *genius loci*, and there is a strong streak of sympathy with primitive man and his communions with nature. *The Forgotten Rite* and *Mai-Dun*, both orchestral tone-poems, are the conspicuous though not the only instances in Ireland's music of the fertilization of music by archaeology. In this respect Ireland was a pioneer, for in the first two decades of the present century archaeology was still busily engaged in invading classical studies and had not reached the wide popularity it enjoyed in the sixth and seventh decades. It may well be that the literary background of his early home life did something to foster interest in a domain shared by topography, history and poetry. But wherever it came from—and one source has been named, the literary work of Arthur Machen—it was a constant source of inspiration. From among the piano pieces, *The Holy Boy* and *Fire of Spring* from the Preludes of 1913-1915, and *Sarnia* of 1941, testify to this attitude of reverence for the past that is characteristic of the twentieth century.

The likeness to Debussy is not so much in actual sound or reliance on pure sensibility as in the use of small forms for the piano to convey visual imagery, suggestions of place and of character without subjective emotion (i.e. without the feelings that permeate Schumann's characteristic pieces). It was Debussy's special gift to music to translate such impressions into short "preludes" for piano—hence the constant and inevitable use of "impressionist" to describe his art, apart from his association with the impressionist painters. Ireland's *London Pieces*, *The Towing Path*, *Amberley Wild Brooks*, and his Channel Island pieces are all impressions. There is more heart and less nerve-end sensation in Ireland than in Debussy, but there is a similarity in the exploitation of piano figuration (swaying duplet and triplet figures, swift scales and arpeggios, handfuls of chords) for visually and descriptively expressive ends. Even when he is writing the Sonata of 1920 or the Sonatina of 1927 this is the kind of piano writing he employs and the kind of subject-matter he deals with—it is romantic but cooler than the intra-subjective emotions of nineteenth-century composers. It withstands changes of taste, perhaps because pianists enjoy playing it, better than Bax's, and it has more substance than what so eminently pianistic a writer as York Bowen turned out in profusion. Indeed Ireland's main contribution to the renaissance was that he produced distinctive piano music, including a concerto. Furthermore, his own best music is involved with the piano, since he is in the great line of English song writers, having over eighty songs with piano to his credit; and in the field of chamber music, to which also he made a distinctive contribution, there are no string quartets but three meritorious pianoforte trios and two striking sonatas for violin and piano as well as similar duet sonatas for cello and clarinet. The piano is his natural mode of thought.

It is not entirely true, though it was said at the time of its first performance in 1932, that the piano concerto in E flat is the first English piano concerto of any merit since Field's, for Cowen, Parry, Stanford and Mackenzie all wrote concertos, of which Stanford's second made some impression in America, and Mackenzie's Scottish, written in 1897, was still to be heard occasionally more than forty years later.* Ireland's concerto certainly made a favourable first impression (though it has since been thought to have been over-praised), and matter and manner are congruent in it, i.e. it does not protest too much and is well constructed to avoid the impression that the material is over-inflated, for actually both the preceding movements are shorter than the finale; and all the material is attractive. Ireland's other orchestral works are concert overtures, an *Epic March* and a *Concertino Pastorale* for strings—there is no symphony or anything of symphonic dimensions. In *A London Overture* and the *Satyricon Overture* he shows a more robust humour than elsewhere, though there is no lack of energy and even high spirits in his quick movements or in such

* As already related in Chapter III.

a song as "I have twelve oxen". The *Concertino Pastorale* was written in 1939 for the Boyd Neel Orchestra at the time when by a quirk of taste there was a fruitful cult of the string band. Its three constituent movements have titles, Eclogue, Threnody and Toccata, but, though the feeling of nature is still there, this is almost a neo-classical work. Still, Ireland's music is very much all of a piece and at the end of his life he confessed that he only wrote what he wanted to write. *These Things Shall Be*, a choral cantata to J. A. Symonds's poem, is negative proof that his professed lack of ambition was genuine, being as hollow a work as the aspirations of the poem are shallow—Symonds was a Victorian without experience of war and, though Ireland was not, his choral writing does not transcend the glib optimism of the verse—i.e. the cantata lacks fundamental sincerity (artistic not intellectual sincerity). Such a judgment would be too harsh to apply to the church music which Ireland wrote for his own use as an organist or to the part-songs and educational pieces that were of service to the competition festival movement; these were routine work in a good tradition but not more personal than that.

The chamber music on the other hand is both distinctive and outstanding. Indeed the second violin sonata (in A minor, 1917), which irresistibly suggested the sublimation of war emotions, had an immediate and spectacular success. The earlier violin sonata (in D minor, 1908) was also a good work—it won the Cobbett prize out of an entry of 134—which declared even among some discernible influences the presence of a new individuality. The intensification of personal conviction in the A minor sonata which was responsible for the impact it made on the public was also felt in the second piano trio (in E minor in one movement, 1917), which similarly reflected the heart-searchings of war. Besides the violin sonatas there are duet sonatas, separated by twenty years, for cello and clarinet with piano, both of which were in favour with instrumentalists. Ireland was a self-critical composer and the predecessors of these works were suppressed, so that a sextet for clarinet, horn and string quartet, composed in his student days and criticized by Stanford for weakness in the finale, had to wait sixty-two years for its first performance in 1960, which showed that while Stanford was right about the discursiveness of the finale he was wrong to ignore the freshness of invention of the rest of it. Ireland's chamber music shows a progressive tendency to compression, and while it would be an overstatement to declare him a miniaturist he was certainly happiest in compact forms, and in his orchestral music was wise enough not to use extended forms —even the piano concerto, as we have seen, avoided inflation.

But if he excelled in the short forms of piano solos and songs he was not short of invention, for he was copious in their output and by no means restricted in mood. For his songs he drew on a wide variety of poets. The Rossettis are recurrent through forty years of song writing. An early success, "Hope the Hornblower", was to a text by Henry Newbolt, and the even greater success, "Sea Fever", was from Masefield. These more vigorous songs were followed by settings of A. E. Housman and Thomas Hardy, both fatalists. The more gracious kind of lyrics, by Arthur Symons, Ernest Dowson, Alice Meynell, alternated with the sterner moods. One of his numerous song sequences, *We'll to the woods no more*, consists of a pair of Housman poems set for voice, followed by a third for piano solo with the opening couplet of "Spring will not wait" for motto, which shows how (by 1927) it had become second nature to him to translate moods, as well as places and auras, into piano lyrics, with or without voice for their further articulation. His romanticism is thus of an almost classical containment, but the emotions expressed, the visions displayed, are too specific and too immediate to be more slowly distilled into the forms of absolute music. He was a romantic, but not of the heady sort who is carried away by every gust of sense or feeling. In real life he appeared to be bottled up, as though he was accustomed to discipline his feelings. This discipline of control was just enough to give the right psychological "distance" for their conversion into works of art. It was a source of strength and has given him staying power.

The strange figure of Joseph or Josef Holbrooke, though it can hardly be said to fit anywhere, since he was one of life's professional misfits, belongs to the short late romantic era of English music that flourished in the reign of Edward VII. The rather stuffy atmosphere of Victorian music-making, vigorous as it was, was freshened by the two currents of the internal renaissance and the external influence of post-Wagnerian Europe, but it was nipped off by the events of 1914. Holbrooke's fate

H

suggests that the movement would have died in any case—a diet of Wagner and an infusion of Strauss intended to cure our provincialism was no way to promote a healthier growth of English music. When he died at the age of eighty in 1958 Holbrooke was an unknown composer though he had been prolific in every branch of composition.* Understandably he was bitter about his neglect and, being himself a writer, carried on polemics against the public, the critics and the impresarios for the favours they bestowed on foreigners at the expense of the native. But it is pretty clear that his music lacked the essential qualities for survival: he had neither on the one hand a distinctive originality, such as Berlioz to whose temptestuous life his is sometimes compared, nor the sense of form which would have given shape and stability to his wild romantic posturings. He fed his imagination on Edgar Allan Poe. His first success was with *The Raven*, a tone-poem which Manns conducted at the Crystal Palace in 1900. He set *The Bells* as a choral cantata and wrote a choral symphony, *Homage to E. A. Poe, Ulalume* and *The Masque of the Red Death* were other orchestral works inspired by Poe. Five chamber works are subtitled "After Poe" and altogether there are over twenty such homages. When he came to writing operas he turned the poem by T. E. Ellis (Lord Howard de Walden), *The Cauldron of Anwyn*, into a Wagnerian trilogy, substituting Celtic for Nordic mythology. The first opera of the trilogy *The Children of Don* was given at the London Opera House (subsequently the Stoll Theatre) during Hammerstein's rash experiment in 1911 at augmenting London's supply of operas, and Nikisch was engaged to conduct it, though he fled after two performances and left the composer to direct the third and last. Somehow or other it was taken up after the war by Weingartner and given five performances at the Vienna Volksoper in 1923 followed by three more at Salzburg: *Dylan*, the second opera of the trilogy, was produced by Beecham in his Drury Lane season of 1914. Beecham says he put it in for the sake of variety in his Russian season, but there was a touch of quixotry in many of

---

* My own personal experience is significant. As a boy I used to play his variations on "Three Blind Mice" as my party piece. My *Times* cutting books from 1923 to 1960 have only five entries indexed and in those thirty-seven years I have few recollections of hearing performances of his works.

Beecham's actions which he concealed, and others failed to perceive, behind the ironic persiflage with which he covered his more gallant adventures. He also says of *Dylan** that "Holbrooke was a musician of natural ability handicapped by a poor aesthetic endowment and a total want of critical faculty. No one with the united talents of Mozart, Wagner and Verdi could have made an opera out of *Dylan*." Why then did he undertake it if not from kindness and as one action in his campaign for opera in England? The third opera *Bronwen* had to wait till 1929 for performance, when it was staged by the Carl Rosa Company.

Beecham's interest in Holbrooke had been roused by his participation in 1908 in a fantastic affair at Queen's Hall, which Beecham describes with the dry detachment and airy factuality he applies to his most improbable adventures. This was the performance by magic lantern and orchestra of *Apollo and the Seaman*, a poem by Herbert Trench, of which the stanzas were projected on a screen by William Wallace, scientist and composer—with, one gathers, faulty synchronization. Holbrooke demanded an immense orchestra which included a sarrusophone (a double-reed wind instrument of saxophone type and part of the fun of Beecham's story is the search for one of these monsters and a player for it). Holbrooke incidentally was fond of such tonal experiments, for he prescribed three English concertinas in his first opera *Pierrot and Pierrette* and wrote a serenade for harp, five saxophones, cornet and other wind.

Indeed his only originality seems to have been in sonority rather than in thematic or harmonic invention. The overture to *Bronwen* and the symphonic poem *The Viking* when played by the B.B.C. under Granville Bantock in 1943, when Holbrooke's music was totally unfamiliar to anyone of a later generation, revealed this personal and distinctive sound-texture but otherwise seemed shapeless and repetitive. Beecham describes his musical talent as "eclectic and absorptive" and names Liszt and Strauss as his models. The epithet "derivative" has in the twentieth century become damning to all hopes of independent life, whereas in the eighteenth century all composers used a lingua franca and were not required to coin an individual vocabulary as their successors are. Holbrooke has therefore suffered, in spite of his fertility,

* *A Mingled Chime* (Hutchinson, 1944), p. 129.

unconventional outlook and assiduity, simple extinction. Yet Ernest Newman in 1900 asked "how any competent observer could fail to see how significant Mr. Holbrooke's works are, both in themselves and as a landmark in our English Renaissance".

The chamber music, for which his particular talents would seem to be unsuited, was extensive, comprising as it did several suites based on national airs, piano trios and quartets, a clarinet quintet and miscellaneous sextets. Although not involved in the folk-song revival he did, nevertheless, write numerous sets of variations on traditional tunes—"Three Blind Mice" for orchestra, additional to the pianoforte set, came near to popularity at the Proms. R. H. Walthew, who was active in London from the nineties on to the twenties in various spheres of professional activity but most prominently as a composer of, and authority on, chamber music, discussed Holbrooke's chamber compositions discerningly in an article in *The Sackbut* (a periodical published by Curwen that ran from 1920 to 1934), but concluded with a melancholy diatribe about the disabilities under which English composers laboured. "The position of music, in the big sense, today in Great Britain is hopeless for our composers." This of course was simply not true, since neither Elgar nor Vaughan Williams lacked for performances of their works, nor indeed did Stanford or Edward German, at that time, but it was true of Holbrooke, who in spite of his talents was always an odd man out. He had been a pupil of Frederick Corder at the Royal Academy of Music and had acquired from him the Wagnerian technique that had become fashionable, and the technique determined the style, which was destined to be rejected as outworn after the 1914 war—late romanticism had indeed had a good run and there was not a lot more ore to be worked from that vein. Even if Celtic mythology was substituted for Nordic, it was still Wagnerian mythological music-drama just the same—Nicholas Gatty tried a shorter essay in the same style, an opera called *Greysteel*, and justified the use of Wagnerian method "for a subject of that sort", having employed other styles for his other operas, notably the delightful light-hearted totally un-Wagnerian *Prince Ferelon*. But Holbrooke's mind was utterly permeated by romantic ideas, as his addiction to Poe proves, and his personal eccentricity was part of the same picture. His failure thus constitutes his historical importance. For good or ill the twentieth century would not accept, as the eighteenth did, the competent, fluent, practitioner who followed the fashion of his times, but had not a distinctive language in which to express his individual vision of the world. Bantock was another composer who ultimately failed, though he had greater success than Holbrooke at the time, from lack of a personal idiom at a juncture of English history when, though it could not be foreseen, the cat was going to jump in a different and unexpected direction. Neo-classicism and nationalism were the forces that became dominant in English composition after 1918 and romanticism was out. Holbrooke was not, it would seem, really a good composer, but he certainly appeared to be in the first decade of the century, although even then there was needed a certain amount of special pleading.* He is remarkable for the stir he made and the completeness of his subsequent disappearance.

* Some critics never shared Newman's view, expressed in the article in *The Speaker* in 1902, or they did so for a time but later gave it up, as Newman himself probably did. I recall that when H. C. Colles died in 1943 I received at *The Times* a spiteful letter from a partisan expressing satisfaction that one of Holbrooke's detractors was now out of the way.

XII

Holst and Vaughan Williams: Emancipation

THE ACTUAL emancipation of our national music from bondage to the continent, the potential foundation of an English national school of composition, was the work of two composers, Ralph Vaughan Williams (1872-1958) and Gustav Holst (1874-1934), both men of radical temper who happened also to be close friends. They further had in common a Gloucestershire origin and education at the Royal College of Music (which was where they first met). They differed from Parry and Stanford, whom both, but especially Vaughan Williams, admired, in that they consciously realized that progressive outlook and higher standards were not enough, that they must have freedom, and, as the nature of their entanglement gradually became clear to them, escape from romanticism as embodied in Wagner and Tchaikovsky and even Brahms who dogged Stanford. Miss Holst's two books about her father,* penetrating and almost too impartial in their criticism, describe in detail his struggle to get away from the prevalent atmosphere, ideals and techniques of his youth. Indeed she overweights her criticism by a kind of axiomatic assumption that there was something unclean about the nineteenth century and that the tradition could contaminate its heirs. Certainly the romantic phase was nearing exhaustion and other harmonies besides the chord of the diminished seventh had been overworked, but even a cliché can be used if its real and not its metaphorical meaning is fully intended, so that her strictures sometimes sound too severe, though again her austerity was learned from her father, upon whom the habit of paring down his language grew until it reached the starkness of *Egdon Heath*. This austerity was fundamental and essential, but it was overdone. Historically speaking the revolt against luxury was necessary in 1895, and Holst's

* *Gustav Holst* (1938) and *The Music of Gustav Holst* (1951). Both O.U.P.

historical function was, at cost to himself and his music, to secure freedom by revolt against the whole romantic ethos and apparatus. Vaughan Williams was his partner but he had no need to go so far—his function was to graft the new on to the displaced tradition. For this he was as well fitted as was Holst for the other part of the emancipation, which was more a revolt than a revolution, for he was that curious English phenomenon the radical conservative, the forward-looking traditionalist. The book of letters which the friends exchanged, issued after their deaths by Miss Holst and Mrs. Vaughan Williams, was aptly entitled *Heirs and Rebels*.*

If this change in English music, which was part of the larger nationalist trend in Europe, was an event in ancient history which needed to be established by documentary evidence, there would be, apart from the internal evidence of the music, ample testimony that the chief instrument of revolt was folk-song. Vaughan Williams says of it himself that his first encounters with folk-song were "The Cherry Tree Carol" in Bramley and Stainer, and "Dives and Lazarus" in *English County Songs*, before he met Cecil Sharp or started collecting himself. He says in the autobiographical chapter he contributed to Foss's book†: "My intercourse with Sharp crystallized and confirmed what I already vaguely felt about folk-song and its relationship to the composer's art. With Sharp it was a case of 'Under which king, Bezonian? Speak or die.' You had to be either pro-folk-song or anti-folk-song, and I came down heavily on the folk-song side." Years later in 1963 Mr. Alan Dickinson, in the most comprehensive survey of the music to be published before the appearance of the official life by Ursula Vaughan Williams and Michael Kennedy, says flatly "Folk-song is the best clue to Vaughan Williams's renunciation of the later nineteenth century," though Dickinson if not anti-folk-song is not a committed folk-song believer.‡ For Holst, his

* O.U.P., 1959.

† *Ralph Vaughan Williams*, by Hubert Foss (Harrap, 1950). Also reprinted in the collection of essays published under the title *Some Thoughts on Beethoven's Choral Symphony* (1953).

‡ Ernest Walker once said to me, with those vocal peculiarities that his friends loved and affectionately mocked, à propos of his own views on folk-song expressed in *A History of Music in England:* "Cecil Shaap wegaads me as if not a block sheep, certainly as a vewy, vewy gway one."

daughter declares*, "The other important event [of 1905] was the revival of folk-song. . . . He had already begun to dream of a renaissance in English music; here to his delight he found English music at its very best. Folk-songs finally brushed all trace of Wagner from his work. . . . He had the deepest admiration for Cecil Sharp . . . and felt that when the time came for the English musical history of the twentieth century to be written, Cecil Sharp's name would stand out above all others." In the other book† she writes that having made the beauty of the folk-song a part of his own life he was able to "persuade his nineteenth-century harmonies to shed layer after layer of protective chromaticism until they were left standing on the chill and unfamiliar brink of a Phrygian austerity".

If internal evidence is sought of the effect of the Dorian mode on Holst's post-Wagnerian ear it can be found in *Hecuba's Lament* of 1911, a setting from Gilbert Murray's translation of *The Trojan Women* of Euripides for alto solo and female chorus and orchestra, which is fully authentic Holst but no longer chromatic (though still too prone to sequence in his daughter's view), with a time signature that allows declamation as free as a folk-singer's.

Other influences beside folk-song of course operated in the formation of both men's respective styles. In the case of Vaughan Williams one was the hymn tunes he examined for his edition of the *English Hymnal*. In Holst it was Weelkes and Purcell which he made his various choirs sing. Both were touched by the new interest in plainsong, which the monks of Solesmes and the Pope's *Motu proprio* were stimulating in the first decade of the century. Both found in Bach a classical antidote to too much Beethoven and Wagner. In fact all the general influences already described, down to a whole-hearted willingness to write for brass bands, were part of their creed and their spiritual environment. Their careers were indeed the practical embodiment of these liberating tendencies from acceptance of the German hegemony then still unchallenged.

While their principal works constitute part of the harvest and will be discussed according to their categories in Book III, the rest of their output is transitional between the pioneering of their seniors and the autonomy of their juniors (from Walton to Britten)

---

* *Gustav Holst*, pp. 22, 28.   † *The Music of Gustav Holst*, p. 16.

and needs some critical discussion, though both composers have been supplied with analytical comment by several writers, especially Vaughan Williams, who lived twenty-four years longer than his contemporary and was more prolific. Performances have been still common in the sixties, though fashion has swung back towards the German domination of what has been called the second Viennese school. Furthermore both men were of strong character and marked individuality, possessed of a social as well as an artistic conscience, so that they made an impact on our musical life at many points, amateur music and education prominent among them. Vaughan Williams had Parry's cultured radicalism, Holst Stanford's regard for good workmanship.

Their home backgrounds were very different. Vaughan Williams came of a legal family but was the son of a parson, related to the Wedgwoods and comfortably off. He had a Cambridge education and took a second class in history. His various posts as organist (South Lambeth), teacher (R.C.M.) and conductor (Bach Choir), like his lecturing and journalism, were financially irrelevant. He married a Fisher (of banking and New College, Oxford, connections). He was made an honorary fellow of his college, Trinity, Cambridge, and after refusing a knighthood accepted an O.M. from the King. He was in much the same sort of social position as Parry, though a little lower in the social scale, as such things went at the turn of the century. He lived long enough to become the Grand Old Man of English music and was buried in Westminster Abbey, but his mind was never conformist and he was always liable to explode against the government (as when he protested against the exclusion of pacifists and a Communist from radio programmes during the war). Thus the two sides of him, the radical and the conservative, were in him from the start; yet he was never in danger, with his robust physical frame and sturdy individuality, of becoming schizophrenic. It was the same with his music: the *Serenade to Music* and the F minor symphony were written within the decade of the thirties, the one traditional if a little Delius-like in harmony, the other modernistically and harshly dissonant. Indeed in the symphony the rebel and the heir are reconciled when the clash and the wide-ranging themes of the early movements are succeeded in the finale by a fugal epilogue on the terse four-note theme which is the germ of the symphony.

Similarly *Flos Campi* begins radically with a passage of unaccompanied unmeasured bitonal counterpoint and ends conservatively, academically if you like, with a diatonic canonical tune in D major. Folk-song was traditional but in Vaughan Williams's student days it was novel and its modality almost as rebellious as Debussy's whole-tone scale. The *Sea Symphony* followed the English choral tradition and it accepted the formal procedures of the symphony, but to coalesce the two conventions was itself an unconventional procedure. It was unconventional to write concertos for tuba and harmonica and it was unconventional to quote folk-tunes in a *Te Deum* for a Coronation, though coronations are nothing if not traditional. In the various choreographic works, of which *Job* is the chief, the type of dancing envisaged by the composer was of folk-dance steps and figures, not classical ballet, for which he seems to have entertained a puritan dislike.

Job is perhaps his most representative work since the more influences it absorbed the more personal it became. The immediate inspiration was William Blake's *Illustrations to the Book of Job*, which in its turn was the product of long preoccupation with the problem of evil presented in the English of the Authorized Version of the Old Testament. The music was cast in the form of a suite which included the dances common at the time when the English masque flourished—the composer insisted on calling the work a masque for dancing—sarabande, pavane, galliard and minuet. Thus the origins are in English language, English theatre, English pictorial art, English music and English dancing. There was some delay about the first choreographic presentation of the work, so that *Job* has an independent existence as a suite for full orchestra and as such had its first performance at the Norwich Festival of 1930, but its full stature is best revealed as an accompaniment, even with a smaller orchestra, to a stage presentation in which the décor is based on Blake's engravings. It therefore stands high both among the dramatic and the symphonic works of Vaughan Williams.

It also stands in the middle of his creative life, a representative token of the emancipation that had been achieved. It was a happy omen at once symbolical and prophetic, that a quarter of a century earlier his first big work to attract attention to the new voice in English music bore the title *Toward the Unknown Region*, for the rest of his life was one long exploration. Though his idiom seemed to be limited by his partiality for certain features, like consecutive fifths in his harmony, gapped mode melody and striding basses, yet he never repeated himself and could conjure endless variety from play with a few notes of the scale. *Toward the Unknown Region*, written for the Leeds Festival of 1907, sounded new at the time; though in retrospect the influences of Parry and romantic chromaticism in the orchestra seem to place it comfortably in the English choral tradition, yet its opening tonality is that of the Lydian mode and the text, which it fits perfectly, is by Walt Whitman, the iconoclast, the blunt poet of the open air. Vaughan Williams came to Whitman from Dante Gabriel Rossetti. The song "Silent Noon", from the cycle *House of Life*, is a great song but it reflects the mood of the nineties, which later became difficult to associate with the personality of Vaughan Williams. Whitman steered him into the twentieth century. He used Whitman for the *Sea Symphony* which was produced at the next Leeds Festival in 1910, and, when in 1936 he came to write *Dona nobis pacem* as a tract for the times, he incorporated *A Dirge for Two Veterans* originally conceived in 1911 and other poems from *Drum Taps*. His next poet was R. L. Stevenson on whom he drew for his *Songs of Travel*, more open-air music that first made the composer's name a household word, since copies were to be found on the piano of every self-respecting amateur singer. This taste for the robust coinciding with Vaughan Williams's discovery of folk-song found full expression in the incidental music to *The Wasps* at Cambridge in 1909, and the idiom that served to identify any dozen bars of Vaughan Williams's music for the rest of his life was therein clearly heard. In the next year the *Fantasia on a Theme of Thomas Tallis* proclaimed at the Gloucester Festival the characteristic thought as well as the new modal idiom of the composer, who was plainly not following the path trodden by Elgar. Elgar was English to be sure—the English note is to be heard in most of what he wrote, but his is not the idiom of a nationalist composer. Vaughan Williams's was, and with it the chains that bound English music to Germany were severed.

To the period of robust assertion belong not only *The Wasps*, which for all its Aristophanic origin is wholly English in feeling, but two folk-dance ballets *Old King Cole* and *On Christmas Night*, and the opera *Hugh the Drover*, which was completed by 1914 and first performed in 1924. In spite of some awkward dramatic corners which several revisions did not negotiate to complete satisfaction, this is a viable opera frequently revived which quotes folk-songs, including traditional street-cries (just as did the contemporary *London Symphony*) and "The Bonny Blue Bell" from Sharp's collection, as well as songs in the folk style, and it stages a boxing match. There are similar allusions and quotations in *Sir John in Love*, which was first staged in 1929, but thereafter the use of folk-song, except deliberately in occasional works such as the *Folk Songs of the Four Seasons* composed for the National Federation of Women's Institutes in 1950, becomes less frequent; though to be sure in 1939 he wrote *Five Variants on Dives and Lazarus*, a small set of variations scored only for strings and harp, on what was one of his favourite tunes, to serve the British Council as an English representation at the New York World Fair. He had found what he wanted for the fertilization of his own personal language in "Bushes and Briars" which he had collected in Essex in 1903, and though his devotion never wavered and he provided piano settings for his own and other people's songs, he had less need to nourish his own compositions on them since he had absorbed their essence and found the kind of modal harmony in arranging them to serve him for his personal needs without quotation or allusion. The influence of folk-song had been direct; it became pervasive and no longer detachable. It led him to formulate his belief in nationalism as a creative and indeed a liberating force, a credo which he stated in lectures given for the Folk Song Society (founded in 1898) and the English Folk Dance Society (founded by Cecil Sharp in 1911) and finally published in book form as *National Music* (1934).

His was a talent that developed slowly and late, as was Elgar's, but unlike Elgar he grew more prolific as he grew older, lived to the age of 85, composed up to the end and in his time attempted every form. Beginning as the majority of English composers do with song, he enriched the long national tradition with some single songs that attained a wide currency, of which "Linden Lea" is possibly the only English example of what the Germans call *volkstümliches Lied*, in which the words (by the Dorset poet

William Barnes) are in the folk-song style and the melody is similarly folky but not folk. But most of the best known come from sets beginning with the two books of *Songs of Travel*; there are *Five Mystical Songs* with words by George Herbert, *Three Poems* of Walt Whitman, *Four Poems* by Fredegond Shove, of which "The Water Mill", though narrative rather than lyrical, is a favourite with singers—all these with piano. In addition *Four Hymns* for tenor have a viola obbligato and *On Wenlock Edge* (Housman), which can legitimately be called a song-cycle, has an accompaniment for string quartet and piano. *Merciless Beauty* (three Chaucer songs) has alternative accompaniments for string trio or piano. At the very end of his life he published *Along the Field* (eight Housman songs) for voice and violin and *Ten Blake Songs* for voice and oboe. Besides countless English folk-song settings for voice and piano he set a couple for voice and violin and also set (for piano) several French songs, of which "L'amour de moy" found favour, and a couple of German folk-songs. This list suffices to show that though he was happy enough in the ordinary *Lied* type of song he liked to experiment with various forms of obbligato, and that like Britten and Finzi he preferred songs to be available, even if they need not necessarily be so sung, in sets. In song-writing there was no need felt for emancipation and most of these idiosyncrasies have precedents—thus even royalty ballads sometimes included an *obbligato ad libitum* (despite the contradiction in terms!); some of the early songs were published in the format of the royalty ballad. Nevertheless "The Vagabond" and "The Roadside Fire" from *Songs of Travel* sounded a new note in English song and the unmistakable Vaughan Williams idiom, which was developing in the choral and orchestral works, was heard in the medium of the song.

The choral music, discussed in Book III, followed a similar chronological pattern to the solo vocal music in that it began in the early years of the century and with increasing gaps came to a pause in 1929 with *Sancta Civitas*, the only work formally called an oratorio, and the three cantatas he wrote in that year for the Leith Hill Festival, of which he was founder, conductor and leading spirit. Then came a twenty-year gap and two more cantatas appeared, occasional works for limited resources, and finally in 1954 *Hodie*, entitled "A Christmas Cantata" but entitled (in the other sense) to be called an oratorio, which is a summary of all his vocal styles.

The dramatic works are spread throughout the composer's career, but the dates of composition and first performance have little connection; furthermore they are various in kind and comprise five ballets, five operas, incidental music and film music. The incidental music, to *The Wasps* and to five plays of Shakespeare at Stratford, which Alan Dickinson unearthed and examined after Vaughan Williams's death, is pre-war, and the first opera *Hugh the Drover* was also completed before 1914. The film music is all late, i.e. after 1940. To the twenties belong the folk-dance ballets and *Sir John in Love*, *Riders to the Sea* and *The Poisoned Kiss*. This was certainly the dramatic decade, and probably the success of *Hugh the Drover* in 1924 turned the composer's thoughts to the stage. *Job* was finished in 1930. Thereafter there was only *The Pilgrim's Progress*, composed in 1948-1949 and produced at Covent Garden in 1951. At least one of the episodes in this "morality", for it is rather a series of tableaux than a music-drama, had been composed in 1922, *The Shepherds of the Delectable Mountains*, and some of its music had appeared in another guise in the fifth symphony. There was one more ballet, or as the composer insisted "masque for dancing", *The Bridal Day*, composed by 1939, given a show on television in 1953 and first produced at Eastbourne in 1955. *The Pilgrim's Progress* was therefore last of all.

All the ballets are certainly derivatives of the masque and all are dramatically viable, but all except *Job* are modest works, such as amateurs could perform successfully. *Job* is an impregnable masterpiece and is the only one of the stage works about which there can be no doubts or reservations. The operas are none of them absolutely fool-proof or accident-immune in the theatre. The corners in the plot of *Hugh the Drover* have been mentioned; *Sir John in Love* follows *The Merry Wives of Windsor* verbally, just as *Riders to the Sea* follows Synge's play, but the dramatic pace is changed by the music so that as opera *Sir John in Love* sometimes fails to find its true operatic pace—there seems to be no other way of accounting for its occasional failure in performance, for otherwise it has all the virtues of plot, text, and music in which the farce is sweetened with imported lyrics to make it ravishing—the bridal song "See the chariot at hand" is the most conspicuously beautiful of these embellishments. In *Riders to the Sea* no discrepancy between dramatic and musical pace is found; the only problem is to adjust the singers' continuous arioso to the volume of the sea-swell of orchestral sound. The libretto of *The Poisoned Kiss* is funny and the music is meltingly sensuous, again salt wit and sweet music in combination for all the world as in Mozart, but the wit can and sometimes does misfire. *The Pilgrim's Progress* raises special problems of atmosphere, which would seem to demand a cathedral or the grounds of a ruined abbey rather than an opera house for its presentation. It is conceived for the theatre but has not had a sufficient number of performances to determine whether the alleged incompatibility is inherent or merely the superficial accident of first impressions.*

The range of subject in these stage pieces is wide and the music ranges widely and richly to accommodate its varied humanity, yet apart from *Job*, these dramatic works have some hidden dramatic weakness which endangers performance incalculably, though not invariably.

The symphonic works, that is the symphonies and the various fantasias, rhapsodies, overtures, span the whole fifty years from the early *Norfolk Rhapsodies* to the last symphony in E minor. They, too, cover a wide range of human experience and best show the actual development of Vaughan Williams's thought and idiom. They are utterly original and idiosyncratic; they are big music dealing with big things in life; they have as distinctively national a flavour as has the comparable and nearly contemporary output of Sibelius, who was faced with the same problem of nationalism. They explore various forms besides his various modifications of sonata form: No. 5 ends with a passacaglia, No. 6 with its ghostly fugue, No. 8 with a toccata; No. 2 contains a nocturne, No. 5 a preludio and a romanza, No. 4 an epilogue. The concertos are works of smaller dimensions for violin (*Accademico*), piano (rearranged for two pianos), viola (in suite form), oboe, harmonica and bass tuba—the range of sympathy is wide. Wide

* It seemed more at home, even dramatically, in the Guildhall at Cambridge than in the Royal Opera House. But see the correspondence with Edward Dent in Michael Kennedy's *The Works of Ralph Vaughan Williams* (O.U.P., 1964), pp. 596 *et seq.*

range has been mentioned twice in a single paragraph and this feature of his music belonged to the character of the man. He could be called an agnostic Christian, a man of liberal views and civic sense, quick temper as counterpart to quick sympathies, big in mind as in body, his imagination balanced but not impeded by a good intellect. His was indeed an integrated personality and the music is an expression of the personality, not a compensation or a wish-fulfilment or a bubbling fount of musical talent. This is the stuff of which great music is made. It is for posterity to decide whether his sheer musical achievement so matches the magnitude of his personality as to make him a great composer. His talent was the reverse of precocious. He had the fecundity of invention, the large output, the originality and the power of a great composer to speak direct to the heart, but his music is not to everyone's liking and it may therefore lack the element of universal sympathy or at any rate of the cogency to subdue the unsympathetic that is required of the truly great whose appeal is universal. When in 1935 the British Council invited the leading European music critics to sample a week of English music-making they used the name of Richard Strauss by which to convey to their readers the kind of music that Elgar's was; of Vaughan Williams they simply said "Here is the authentic voice of England."

Holst's personality was less catholic and more intense, but in him, too, the musician and the man were of one piece. The element in his mental life that most sharply distinguishes him from his friend and fellow composer was his attraction to Oriental thought. What Vaughan Williams found in English soil, Holst, who was of Swedish origin, sought in Oriental mysticism, though he too found nourishment in the folk-songs revealed to him by Cecil Sharp. If that dangerous word "mysticism" is to be applied to these two downright Englishmen it must be narrowly defined. Strictly it means revelation about ultimate reality obtained directly without the mediation of the intellect or the exercise of ratiocination, intuitively in short. Some people have minds which can manage this sort of short cut to truth. Vaughan Williams's vision was of the prophetic kind which sees the essence of a situation in the same sort of way as an Old Testament prophet saw through to essentials and was so able to prophesy, in the literal sense of foretell, because he knew the essence. Vaughan Williams himself described the function of art* as the attempt "to obtain a partial revelation of that which is beyond human senses and human faculties", and the symbols which are its instruments are "symbols not of other visible and audible things but of what lies beyond sense and knowledge". And elsewhere in the same essay he speaks of reaching out to what is beyond sense by means of the senses as the very thing art exists to enable us to do. Intellectually he was not agile or clever but he had a strong intelligence to put at the service of what the more intuitive side of his mind threw up. Holst's was a more speculative mind, in which contemplation was balanced by a conscientious practicality.

Practical music-making was indeed the core of his musical life. It began early with posts of organist and choir conductor in Cotswold villages, and his first job after the completion of his education at the Royal College was as *répétiteur* of the Carl Rosa Opera Company and trombonist in its orchestra. In 1903 he began his teaching career and for the rest of his life he was an assiduous teacher. He was director of music at Morley College and at St. Paul's Girls' School for almost thirty years, thus dealing with children and adults; he founded his Whitsuntide Singers for the inspiration of his amateur friends and his professional pupils and some who can only be described as disciples (Edwin Evans's correctly chosen word) in week-ends of concentrated music-making. He taught composition at the Royal College of Music but not for long, 1919 to 1923. All this experience gave him courage and ultimately certainty of touch in choral writing and in orchestration, and his unworldly attitude to outward success led him to bold originality in both those fields. The distinctive character of his handling of voices appears not only in the problematical *Choral Symphony* but in the part-songs he wrote for female voices. Here is an early example from the third group of *Choral Hymns from the Rig Veda* for female voices with harp or piano, the "Hymn to the Dawn", in which the firmament is traversed by simple, singable, ingenious, sequential modulations, and the ethos of the Orient conveyed in occidental terms:

* The Letter and the Spirit" in *Some Thoughts on Beethoven's Choral Symphony* (O.U.P., 1953).

Ex 19 Andante

As far as the orchestra was concerned he performed a similar trick of revealing the East to the West with a conscious use of oriental elements, augmented seconds, an actual pipe tune of four notes picked up in Algeria, and drum taps, in the *Beni Mora* suite (1910). Miss Holst calls it a skilful experiment and a first attempt at the music of entertainment; so indeed it is, attractive and unpretentious, and, as she further points out, a rehearsal for *The Planets*. The East exercised its influence not only in the specifically Sanskrit works (which include a full-size opera *Sita*, never published or performed, a substantial cantata, *The Cloud Messenger*, introduced at one of Balfour Gardiner's pioneering concerts in 1913 but not a success, the *Rig Veda Hymns* and the chamber opera *Savitri*, which is a masterpiece), but also in what one might call the Near Eastern elements of the *Hymn of Jesus* and the astrological basis of *The Planets*.

The counterpoise to these exotic propensities—and he went so far as to learn some Sanskrit, not to mention some small Greek for *The Hymn of Jesus*—was the English element revealed to him in folk-song and in the mediaeval carols and lyrics on which he drew for many of his short choral pieces, as also for the austerely beautiful *Four Songs for Voice and Violin*. Interest in the Middle

Ages led him via Helen Waddell's books to the theme of his last opera, *The Tale of the Wandering Scholar*. The folk-song influence was embodied after the custom of the time in *A Somerset Rhapsody*, based on four of Cecil Sharp's tunes and dedicated to him in 1907, and in quotations in *The Boar's Head* (1924); it was explicit in the *St. Paul's Suite* for strings and in arrangements for choral singing, and it is just audible in the big tune in "Jupiter". This mixture of the East, the English folk and the mediaeval seems a strangely concocted nourishment for a man's mind; to it has to be added the William Morris brand of Socialism of his young manhood in Hammersmith and the High Church brand of Social- ism of Thaxted when he went to live there in 1914. He was, however, never an ardent politician nor committed to conventional religion. Indeed there was nothing conventional about him at all, and as a person he was almost disconcertingly himself, paying little attention to worldly success or failure, hard to place in English social life, a man of exceptional integrity with a belief in companionship. He was an unselfconscious radical. His daughter's account of his works reveals many failures and a great struggle to free himself from the Wagnerian influence of his youth; he had a sure touch in the purely technical but not so sure in the imaginative elements of composition, and not a great many of his larger works seem likely to survive. But some are certainly important, most obviously the orchestral suite *The Planets* but also *Savitri* because it is unique in kind and perfect within its small scope, and *The Hymn of Jesus* of which the same can be said *mutatis mutandis*. The choral music in small forms will serve singers for many a long day and was indeed a surprisingly potent implement in the revolt which was Holst's life function, for they are quite unlike their Victorian counterparts, strong, often astringent and devoid of sentimentality.

The operas are similar compounds of sheer oddity, technical skill and touches of genius. *Savitri*, which belongs to his Sanskrit period, is wholly successful, though the text was his own—in this matter his target was often doubtful and his aim insecure—and the subject, a colloquy with Death, not *prima facie* operatic. He designed it to be played in the open air or in a small building, where a curtain is not required. It has three characters, and is scored for two string quartets, a contra-bass, two flutes and a cor anglais, with the addition of a wordless chorus of female voices. Holst took his story from an episode in the Sanskrit epic *Mahabharata*. Death comes to claim Satyavan and announces himself and his intention to the wife, Savitri. Savitri, overcoming her fear, welcomes him as a release from Maya, illusion, and Death grants her a boon in recompense, though she must not ask for Satyavan. She asks for life for herself and sings a long rapt aria on the meaning of life. But the fulfilment of her life implies the life of Satyavan, and Death is sent empty away in accordance with his promise. She has won because she is free from Maya. This esoteric wisdom is hardly externalized, the voices sing rhythmically free melodic arioso, often unaccompanied, and the varied inflection of the intervals yields the atmosphere of mystery through which project here and there well-placed lightly scored triads. The invisible chorus creates a veil of sound which by a paradox seems to us occidentals the very stuff of illusion, yet transmits the wise oriental message that we must recognize the difference between illusion and reality. This is neither comedy nor tragedy, but perhaps a morality, and it is conceived and executed in one penetrating act of apprehension.

The Perfect Fool (1921) and *At the Boar's Head* (1924) are more substantial operas of very different character but both are in one act. The first is satirical—at least that was the general impression of what Holst was about in his very odd text which few could make head or tail of, opera perhaps parodying itself, which is a risky thing to do. Some splendid ballet music with which it opens is all that survives. *At the Boar's Head*, modestly styled an interlude, is a setting of Shakespeare's tavern scenes from *Henry IV* to traditional tunes, a masterpiece of dexterity but no opera. *The Tale of the Wandering Scholar*, also broad to the point of farce, is another matter. He wisely persuaded Clifford Bax to shape a libretto for him from an episode in Helen Waddell's study of the Middle Ages, *The Wandering Scholars*, and so there are no *faux pas* either textual or dramatic. There are four characters, a lusty young wife, her not unpoetical but not too simpleton husband, a greedy parish priest, and a young *vagus* who comes to beg a meal. Holst's powers of characterization had improved in sharpness and in depth by the time he came to compose this one-act farce in 1929. He had refined his texture so that his spare orchestration was apt and its impediment to the delivery of the words, an important consideration in comedy, reduced to vanishing point. Furthermore he managed to solve the crucial dilemma of all music's attempts to make us laugh, as a change from crying or loving, namely the brevity of wit and the propensity of all music to expand and delay. This was done by the ingenuity of his rhythms. He had long before learned to handle fives and sevens and mixed time signatures and in all the operas, successes or failures, the rhythm is the most original and the most vital element. This opera is crisp and has a sudden final curtain like the click of a spring on suspended hilarity. From its brevity it can only find a place in that much mistrusted (by opera-goers) form of music drama, the triple bill—to which *Savitri* might also contribute. *The Tale of the Wandering Scholar* is good characteristic Holst, good stagecraft and good fun.

It will be apparent that Holst's contribution to English opera added hardly anything to the effort to establish a tradition of English opera as part of the renaissance, any more than did Vaughan Williams's very partial successes. Their combined output drew attention to the matter of setting of words for the stage, which the experience of wedding voice and verse in song, church music and oratorio had not advanced very much, and though in retrospect it looks rather like wasted effort since there are only these few smallish stage pieces out of a round dozen that have any life in them, yet they felt under some necessity, obligation perhaps, to make the attempt, since no European country that called itself musical was as devoid of opera as England. And arguments were not lacking* that we should never really make ourselves truly musical—i.e. able to write our own music as well as import the best from abroad—until we made opera a going concern here.

*See for instance Colles: *Voice and Verse* (O.U.P., 1928), Chapter X.

XIII

The Nationalists

IT LOOKED about the time of the First World War as if the political situation in its revulsion from all things German would reinforce the trend towards nationalism in English music which had emerged in the careers of Holst and Vaughan Williams. Vaughan Williams was preaching nationalism as well as practising it: the famous *R.C.M. Magazine* article of 1912* advocated a closer attention to specifically English sources of inspiration which the other school of modernism, what may be called the Birmingham school of thought, did not hesitate to stigmatize as parochialism. He lectured on folk-song, and Holst resuscitated Purcell. Holst in refining his own music from every alien influence really declared England to be at last independent of the Continent, and Vaughan Williams looked like becoming the founder of a nationalist school. Butterworth, who would have been his chief lieutenant in any such movement, was cut off at the age of thirty in 1916 with only a handful of compositions to his credit, but if one compares *The Shropshire Lad* and *The Banks of Green Willow* idylls with the music of his elder contemporaries Donald Tovey (1875-1940) and F. S. Kelly (1881-1916),† who also was killed in France, one sees the divergence of the streams clearly enough. The influences in the two Balliol men, Tovey and Kelly, are those of the German tradition, as represented for instance by Joachim, whereas in Butterworth the new English note is to be heard clear and ringing. There were other men killed in the war, W. Denis Browne, a Cambridge man, and Ernest Bristow Farrer, a student at the R.C.M., who have only left behind one or two songs of promise that are a measure of their loss. No one can say whether an

* "Who wants the English Composer?"

† Kelly won the Diamond Sculls at Henley in 1905 and his record for the event stood until 1938.

English school comparable in the homogeneity of its national colour and character to the Russian Kuchka would ever have emerged. But in fact it never did, and in the event it has proved to be unnecessary, for the work of making English music sound English instead of cosmopolitanly colourless, which is alas! all that the products of so distinguished a mind as Tovey's achieved, was accomplished so decisively by Vaughan Williams that when a new generation, headed by William Walton (b. 1902), came on the scene there was no need for any patriotic assertion of national independence, and the tendency was reversed, because English composers no longer risked being submerged if they bathed in the general European stream.

Nevertheless there was a group of composers between these two generations who were followers at varying distances of Holst and Vaughan Williams, or who went to the same sources, the folk-song or the Elizabethan traditions, or who picked up a certain harmonic astringency that is to be heard in Weelkes, Purcell and Holst. It would be fairer to call these men traditionalists than nationalists, in the sense that they hitched their waggon not to the star of Parry and Stanford except in the matter of standards but to the newly revived English tradition. John Ireland (1879-1962) flavoured his harmony with the modal influences of folk-song; Edmund Rubbra (b. 1901), a pupil of Holst, based his whole style on madrigalian counterpoint; Gerald Finzi (1901-1956) was a miniaturist whose lyricism is a product of the influence of folk-song though he has never actively incorporated its idioms into his own; Ernest John Moeran (1894-1950), who certainly consciously adopted as nourishment for his personal style not only folk-song and the Elizabethans but also the harmony of Delius, and Peter Warlock (1894-1930), in whose music the same ingredients though differently proportioned may be discerned, are the eldest of this school and the direct heirs of Delius and Vaughan Williams.

George Butterworth, who lives by a mere handful of compositions, has already been mentioned as marking the point of divergence towards nationalism on the nineteenth-century model. The might-have-beens of history are regarded by historians as constituting bad history. But at the turn of the century there were several possible ways in which a more vigorous school of English composition might develop. Parry and Stanford were working for higher standards and an Englishness to be obtained academically; the Frankfurt group did sound an English note though German-trained; Tovey did not and did not want to, since for him the main stream was German and good enough for anyone, nationalism being irrelevant Elgar and the Midland group were eclectics and apparently successful, their eclecticism containing some measure of unconscious Englishness. At this juncture the might-have-beens are historically important, since the precipitating cause of what ultimately happened was not artistic but political, the war of 1914. After 1918 some of the threads were picked up but given a different twist. Elgar left successors in Bliss and Walton; the Stanford line faded out in composers like T. F. Dunhill and Ireland; for Tovey's Germanic line there was no future even in Germany; Corder's romantic line did last for a generation in Bax; the nationalism of Holst and Vaughan Williams was on the whole the most fertile, though it, too, made itself redundant by the middle of the century, when Britten united all the trends. But in 1910 Butterworth's choice was a decisive swerve, which gave half a century of vigour to the renaissance when our music was at the cross-roads. Had he lived— another might-have-been—he might have been another Vaughan Williams.

His mother was a professional singer, and even while he was a boy at Eton he showed a distinct talent, which was nourished by T. F. Dunhill who was a master there, so that an early *Barcarolle* for orchestra was performed at a College concert while he was still a boy. He went up to Trinity College, Oxford, in 1904 to read classics and prepare for a legal career, but his acquaintance with Hugh Allen, Adrian Boult, Cecil Sharp and Vaughan Williams, the last two ardent folk-song collectors, deflected him inevitably to music, though his attempts to earn a living by it, first in criticism for *The Times* and then in teaching at Radley College, did no more for him than convince him of the inadequacy of his technical equipment. He therefore went for a year to the Royal College of Music, where he worked at composition with Charles Wood. Meantime he had become absorbed in the folk-song movement, which was then in full swing "restoring their songs and dances to the English people" after centuries of oblivion—the phrase was applied to Cecil Sharp on the building which bears his name. Butterworth was a good morris-dancer and collected songs in Sussex, which he subsequently arranged with felicitous piano accompaniments. The date of his set of eleven songs is 1912. In the following year he published a set of five original songs from Housman's *A Shropshire Lad*, in which the influence of folk-song is discernible in the individual idiom that was emerging. From the theme of the first song in this cycle Butterworth evolved an orchestral rhapsody, originally called *Cherry Tree* but re-named *A Shropshire Lad*, the first performance of which by Nikisch at the Leeds Festival of 1913 signified recognition of the composer as a coming man. It remained in the repertory and was followed by another idyll for small orchestra, *The Banks of Green Willow*, which makes use of actual folk-tunes. Besides these songs and idylls—there were also two *English Idylls* for small orchestra composed in 1911—there are left only a few choral part-songs and arrangements. But in these few years of tentative endeavour he contributed something to the composition of Vaughan Williams's *London Symphony* in the form of discussion, manual labour of copying and writing a programme note—according to Vaughan Williams himself the initial impetus to write a symphony came from Butterworth. Before he went to France, where he was killed in the battle of the Somme, he destroyed much of his work which he regarded as unworthy of survival. This scrupulousness and the exigent standards he had striven after in his formative years ran through his life and can be recognized in the perfection of the small things he left behind him.

E. J. Moeran (1894-1950) was educated at Uppingham in the days when it alone of English public schools paid any attention to music, and at the Royal College of Music, which he entered in 1913. The First World War cut his studies short and not much of the music he wrote before 1920 survives. But from that point onwards his output, though not copious, was steady. It contains vocal music, both solo and choral; none of it is on a large scale; the Elizabethan madrigal, not the Handelian oratorio, has been the parent of the choral music, and the folk-song on the one hand and Delius on the other have been the inspiration of his songs, which include the Housman cycle *Ludlow Town* (1920), a Joyce set (1929), and a Seumas O'Sullivan set (1946), testimony, these latter, to an abiding Irish influence upon the composer, who had a strain of Irish blood in his ancestry, and a liking for Ireland and the Irish such that it led him to spend holidays in Ireland and to take an Irish wife, and so far influenced his music as to cause an echo of Irish tunes to be audible in his symphonic music—this for instance in the cello concerto:

where besides the rhythm the cadence figure of three repeated notes is a typical feature of Irish folk-song.

Moeran's work in the field of folk-song was done chiefly in East Anglia where he collected a number of notable airs, including "Down by the Riverside".* A small number from Norfolk and Suffolk he provided with piano accompaniments which incorporate features of his personal style from a number of sources—the modal harmony employed by Vaughan Williams in similar contexts, the false relations of sixteenth-century provenance and the "added note" harmony of Delius, in which he shows an affinity with Warlock. The tracing of sources and resemblances can be a tiresome trick of over-ingenious criticism, but in Moeran not only is there no attempt to disguise his indebtedness but the diverse ingredients of his style are in the end so thoroughly absorbed that the indebted man becomes the original man, and the substance of his music as it appears in the symphony and the concertos sounds the English note because it is compounded of these English traits.

In the case of his two suites of part-songs Elizabethan models have been consciously imitated, especially in *Phyllis and Corydon*, of which the constituents are madrigals, ballets, airs, canzonets and pastorals. These are not pastiche, for the harmony makes no attempt to keep within the limits of the period. There is for instance nothing Elizabethan about this from the canzonet "The treasure of my heart":

* See my *Man, Mind and Music* (Secker & Warburg, 1948), pp. 35-9.

But it is equally true that if no Elizabethan could have written these part-songs, they could not have been written without the Elizabethans as models. They constitute one of the most successful attempts ever made to pour new wine into old bottles—Prokofiev's *Classical Symphony* is perhaps the nearest parallel. The other set of part-songs, *Songs of Spring Time*, goes to the sixteenth and seventeenth centuries for its poems and inevitably catches something of their atmosphere, yet they are not conscious archaisms and if they reflect any influence it is that of Delius ("Sigh no more ladies" for instance), though they are still neo-Elizabethan with their echoes of Byrd and Dowland, their fresh open-air melodiousness, the slightly sophisticated blitheness of England when she was young and still growing up. The influence of Delius is more pervasive; *Nocturne* for baritone, chorus and orchestra is dedicated to his memory and is meditative in his rich, brooding, over-ripe way. Only in Moeran there is nothing over-ripe.

As in the vocal so in the instrumental music Moeran was mostly content to work in the smaller forms, though on turning fifty he turned his hand to a symphony and two concertos. His first orchestral works were sketches—*In the Mountain Country* (1921), two rhapsodies *Whythorne's Shadow* and *Lonely Waters*, based respectively on a madrigal and a folk-song and therefore further instances of Moeran's willingness to ally himself with his forerunners and base his own style on theirs. After the big works he turned back to a single-movement piano concerto (the Rhapsody in F sharp 1943), the Sinfonietta (1946) a light-fingered and captivating work, and a Serenade (1948).

Chamber music, too, testifies to his positive pleasure in the mastery of form, for there is no more exacting test than to write for such tenuous media as a sonata for two violins and a string trio. The former indeed calls for ingenuity, and in it the composer succeeds in combining it with delight, notably in the passacaglia movement. Like it the Trio smacks of good English earth and has a touch of astringency in the slow movement that is also an English characteristic. The thematic material in these orchestral and chamber works should not be called "folk" or "folky", for even the second Rhapsody is not a rhapsody in the old nationalist sense of a fantasia on folk-songs but a work founded on original material. It does, however, owe its distinctive beauty to the revival of the modes, and though the themes of the Trio are instrumentally conceived, the wistful overtones of many English folksongs can be heard in them and are the source of their appeal. There is also an early piano trio and a duet sonata for violin and piano in which the melodiousness of the material is noteworthy, as in all Moeran's work, including the symphony in G minor. This is a thoughtful rather than a dramatic symphony, full of ideas which repay acquaintance as he develops them; they are not by any means recondite—melodiousness here as elsewhere is a characteristic of material which while perfectly apt to the instrumental medium has its ultimate origin in English vocal melody— but they have meaning below the surface. If incident is copious none of the movements is over long, and only the finale is so elaborate as to leave some imputation of discursiveness. In the Sinfonietta this cannot happen from the nature of the case. Here everything is on a smaller scale, the musical ideas still melodious and redolent of the English countryside (the Welsh Marches perhaps in this case for a change from East Anglia and Ireland), and the form felicitously fits the matter.

Of the concertos, that for violin came first in 1942; the cello concerto Moeran wrote for his Irish wife, Peers Coetmore, in 1946. The form is congenial to a composer whose genius runs to lyrical melody, both of the formal and of the extended order, to which string instruments lend themselves, and here, as in the symphony, the desire is created to make further acquaintance with music that however attractive is not arresting to a half-attentive mind. In both the composer makes some departures from

conventional form: thus the violin concerto consists of a vivid rondo, which is a welter of Irish dance rhythms (though not consciously
quoted tunes), placed between two slow movements of a gently
reflective kind. There is none of the usual rhetoric, and the conventional cadenza of the first movement appears divided between
the exposition and the coda with the qualifying mark "quasi" in
each place. Much of the beauty of the work consists in interplay
of the solo violin with separate elements of the orchestra. In the
cello concerto the order of movements is the normal one, in
which an impassioned first movement is succeeded by a true slow
movement of a lyrical intensity and harmonic richness that
permits its comparison with the equivalent movement in Elgar's
cello concerto. In the finale Irish rhythms of the reel or the patter
song are again in evidence. The Rhapsody for piano, in form a
one-movement concerto, is so romantic in feeling as to suggest an
unavowed programme. This group of symphonic works is so
consistent in character as to mark a stage in the composer's
development. They are cast in large but not inflated forms; they
are unrhetorical, unemphatic in manner, thoughtful in nature,
lyrical in expression, yet in them the tension is sustained and their
aim is serious. In the Sinfonietta many of the same epithets,
"unemphatic", "lyrical" and "dancing" apply, but the tension is
less as the scale is less and the result is one of immediate charm
and lively interest.

His work came to a sudden full-stop—he was found dead in the
River Kenmare at the age of fifty-six—and he found no later
advocate for what is in essence a countryman's music.

Peter Warlock (1894-1930) has many points of resemblance to
Moeran. They were born in the same year, they were personal
friends and they submitted themselves to the same influences, folk-
song, the Elizabethans and Delius, although they mixed these
ingredients into their personal style in different strengths and so
achieved different results. They are nearest together in their songs,
for Warlock never launched out upon symphonic composition.
Folk-song was a direct influence on Moeran, but Warlock only
catches the English strain unconsciously and was more immediately influenced by the Elizabethan lutenists, whose songs he
edited with Philip Wilson for modern use. Delius's chordal and
chromatic harmony remained with Warlock to the end of his

short life, but Moeran in advancing to large-scale composition naturally achieved independence and a more contrapuntal style.

Warlock, which means one in league with the devil, was the pseudonym which Philip Heseltine assumed when he was writing music. For authorship and editorial work he remained Philip Heseltine. But Warlock was not merely a pseudonym but in fact the creation of Heseltine from psychological necessity, a psychological projection, as his friend and biographer Cecil Gray avers, of all that part of Heseltine's nature that was frustrated.

It was a projection into real life as well as into art. What began as Peter, who could overcome the diffidence of Philip and write music, became a separate personality which in the end dominated and killed his creator. Heseltine died by his own act and will at the age of thirty-six, and it is told of him that before he turned on the gas in his flat he put the cat out, a characteristic act of the gentle person who had found the ever-increasing recklessness of Warlock intolerable. All the spirited and the macabre songs are the obvious work of Warlock, and so, too, in the beginning are the tender songs, but the song cycle, *The Curlew*, though signed by Warlock, is the work of Heseltine. Its text of poems of frustration in the Anglo-Celtic vein of W. B. Yeats expresses the despair at the bottom of Heseltine's heart, while he was still master of its expression and before it mastered him. It is not possible to go through all the output of the dual personality and assign this to Philip and that to Peter, for the tangle of opposites was not neatly logical nor was it static; on the contrary the fissure widened and split again until, in his biographer's words, "a deadly conflict came to be waged on every psychological front". But there is no more conflict in the actual music than there is in the similar case of Schumann, and there are, in Warlock's output of nearly a hundred songs, plenty of uncomplicated ditties: settings of Shakespeare, "Pretty Ring Time" for instance —"Sigh no more ladies" is not so straightforward that it could be called a ditty—and of Anon in his sixteenth-century incarnation who gave him "Piggesnie" and "There is a lady". The roystering things like "Rutterkin" from *Peterisms*, "Captain Stratton's Fancy" and "Jillian of Berry" are naturally assignable to Peter-Florestan and the tender carols "The First Mercy" and "Balu-lalow" to Philip-Eusebius. But it is equally pertinent to classify the songs not so much on their emotional content as on their stylistic features. He is very happy in his use of a quick syllabic type of melody with a chordal accompaniment marching in step: "Piggesnie" (the word is an old-fashioned term of endearment) is a good example, and "Walking the Woods", of which a stanza may be quoted, is another with a delicious lilt and blithe but by no means shallow sentiment.

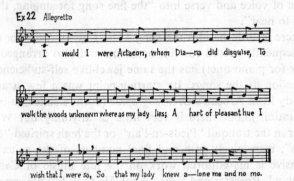

Ex 22 Allegretto

I would I were Actaeon, whom Dia—na did disguise, To walk the woods unknown where as my lady lies; A hart of pleasant hue I wish that I were so, So that my lady knew a—lone me and no mo.

Not merely the tune and depth of sentiment are different in such a song as "Sleep", but the style, which derives from the lutenists. The words are by John Fletcher, about half a century later than Anon's, but within the period in which his spirit was so obviously at home that it has been said that he was born out of time and could have found accommodation both for Philip and Peter in Elizabethan days. In "Sleep" is to be found a marriage of words and vocal line that recalls Dowland, and the accompaniment, though modern, chromatic and pianistic, can be conceived as a huge development of the primitive figuration of lute music. In general his piano accompaniments make use of chromatic harmony that derives ultimately from Delius. But he was a better song writer than Delius. His feeling for words was much more acute, and both vocal line and its accompanying harmony, however Delian, arose directly from them. Herein he was a true Elizabethan who felt words and music to be much closer together than they have subsequently become in their assertion of their independence. By far the greater part of the poems he set belonged to the sixteenth and seventeenth centuries, but there are very acceptable songs from his pen to words of Hilaire Belloc and Bruce

Blunt. One factor that makes his songs so successful is that he was a true miniaturist. None of his songs is long and few are elaborate; "Sorrow's Lullaby" is a duet with string accompaniment but is exceptional. Impulse, feeling, medium and limited range of subject combine to give his songs individuality, and he had the best quality of all, that incandescence which from its nature cannot for long be sustained and concentrated but which makes the union of voice and verse into "the fine song for singing, the rare song to hear".

There is little besides the songs. The *Capriol Suite* for strings (subsequently scored for full orchestra and also arranged effectively for piano duet) has the same jewel-like self-sufficiency and perfection as the songs. Its starting-point was a few strands of melody from Arbeau's *Orchésographie* (again a sixteenth-century inspiration!), but there is very little of anything but Warlock either in the tranquil "Pieds-en-l'air" or the high spirited "Mattachins", respectively fifth and final numbers of the suite. More extensive is his editorial work on the lute music of Campion, Dowland, Rosseter and their school. He took too conservative a view of his editorial duties in so far as he thought a direct transcription of lute tablature for piano would serve as it stood, when in fact lute figuration is not effective on the piano and some concession to the genius of the larger and later instrument is required. But he undertook the work in a crusading spirit, just as he had in his early enthusiasm for Delius made transcriptions for piano of the then unfamiliar works of that solitary genius. In controversy the crusading spirit was fortified by a vitriolic pen— a streak of Warlock coming out in Heseltine. For a short time, the decade of the twenties, his erratic career lit up London musical life with flashes here and there, but the songs continue to burn with a steady illumination, because they belong to the great tradition in which through four centuries English lyric poetry has found a true mate in English melody.

Like Moeran, Patrick Hadley (b. 1899) had a direct interest in folk-song though he was not active as a collector. Like Moeran, too, he combined associations with East Anglia and a love of Ireland. The two interests appear nakedly in the titles of two of his cantatas, *Fen and Flood* (1955) and *Connemara* (1958), both of which incorporate traditional and local melodies with their evocations of place. So the folk-song, which is a specific and recognizable influence in Hadley's music, and the positive local associations—he is a Cambridge man by birth, education and academic occupation—made him one of the few English nationalist composers after the pattern of nineteenth-century nationalists. Titles again are significant also of the influence of folk-song: his Symphonic Ballad in A (1931) and a Rhapsody for small orchestra (1942) are called respectively *The Trees So High* and *One Morning in Spring*. His output is small and not all of it is for the market place. Intimacy is a presupposition of his settings of poetry for solo voice and chamber ensembles of various constitution, for which he has a partiality. In this way he took *The Woodlanders* from Hardy, *Ephemera* from Yeats, *Mariana* from Tennyson and *The Orphan's Song* from Dobell. His vocal lines have the sort of saturated lyricism that is an inheritance from folk-song, which has itself been described* as "individual flowerings from a common stem". His textures even in the choral works for larger forces (except *La belle dame sans merci*) have a heart-easing quality to match, which is ultimately derived from Delius's added-note harmony. At the bottom of this exquisite idiom is a feeling for nature, not pantheism but man's relation to nature. What of this character is intuitively and immediately perceived in Hadley's music is made explicit in some of his chosen texts, notably of *The Trees So High* and *The Hills*. In the ballad the story (of the boy bridegroom) develops alongside the seasonally changing moods of nature so that the composer is able to exploit the pathetic fallacy of nature's sympathy with man. The music grows from the ballad and its tune, which are integral and inseparable in the composer's mind. In *The Hills* he is pursuing the same theme but deliberately avoids the dependence of his music on a text, since what he gives to his singers to sing is sometimes words without sense, the verbal equivalent of symphonic writing though always concerned with man's relation to nature, so that the cantata is really a choral symphony. So, too, in a more formal way, is *The Trees So High* a choral symphony, though more in the shape of Mendelssohn's *Lobgesang*, consisting as it does of three instrumental movements, "three independent brooks" (though thematically related in their derivation from the tune of the ballad) "which flow into one

* By Vaughan Williams.

I

stream in the last movement", where soloist and chorus sing the actual ballad, which is mainly that of Sharp's version. These uses of symphonic form in vocal composition are the most original feature of Hadley's work and by them he overcomes the well-known recalcitrance of folk-song and symphony to each other.

The title of Edmund Rubbra (b. 1901) to a place in the nationalist succession might seem questionable in that the earliest influence in his development was not folk-song but Cyril Scott, romantic and exotic rather than pastoral and native. As there was an exotic strain in Holst, who became his teacher when after a chancy education he went to Reading University and then to the Royal College of Music, the weaning and toughening process went on smoothly. But his other teacher was R. O. Morris, from whom he learned the counterpoint of the sixteenth century, and that fixed the recognizably English qualities of his music. Polyphony became second nature in his musical thinking. So much so that it distorted his first four symphonies, but equally in his two Masses (one for the Roman and one for the English rite) placed him among the greatest masters of the style. Some account of the way it works in his mind and what it means to him is to be found in the small manual, *Counterpoint* (as humane and liberal a treatise as his master's *Contrapuntal Technique in the Sixteenth Century**) in which he ranges from Hucbald to Hindemith.

There is no doubt that Rubbra's is a serious and powerful musical mind, but it does not always communicate its message either readily or fully. In the symphonies too little attention is paid to scoring, because, since they are by nature expanded madrigals, descendants of the Elizabethan fantasia, the texture does not allow much play for variegated colour. It is not that Rubbra was puritanical about orchestral colour as Parry was, but that he was so preoccupied with texture as to disregard the risk of thickness. Some alleviation of his grey scoring began in his fifth symphony (1948), and in the subsequent works of large scale he was more successful in resolving the incompatibility of his long evolving melodic lines with the inherently dramatic form of the symphony. His music in general is more meditative than dramatic, so that many of his works in all categories declare their basic allegiance to what may be called the English pastoral

* R. O. Morris (Clarendon Press, 1922).

style, a style manifested in our folk-song, in our madrigals, in our ballad operas (where it may be laced with a dash of salt water), pervasively in our song tradition and intermittently in our modern chamber music, and easily distinguishable from the French elegance and German sentiment of its counterparts abroad. At the age of fifty Rubbra took another look at the symphony, and thenceforward when he wrote a sonata movement he secured more freedom for what has been well called* his "lyrical creativity which is religious in impulse". Thus for instance the single germinative motif of the introduction to the seventh symphony expands thematically at once and arrives at two organically determined climaxes, thus securing something of the polarity required by sonata form. Here indeed he faces the same problem as Brahms did in his fourth symphony, the reconciliation of unitary and ternary forms, which had been begun by Beethoven in his third period, and he uses the same means, namely, besides the modification of sonata form, the adoption of unitary forms like fugue and passacaglia and free variation for other movements. Rubbra has indeed tried a number of formal experiments in his symphonies and concertos—and sometimes even given them strange names like Corymbus (botanical for cluster) and Collana (Greek for necklace). The attempts to shake off the impediments of his own style, one of which was an inadequate feeling of pace in scherzos, were helped by his numerous essays in concertante works, which were sometimes called *Improvisations* (violin), *Sinfonia Concertante* (piano), *Soliloquy* (cello), as well as honest Concerto (viola and piano). Herein naturally his thought found an appropriate vehicle in the cantilena of long melodic lines for string instruments, while in the Sinfonia Concertante, one of his most successful works, an exhilarating fugue in memory of Holst reconciles the claims of symphonic and polyphonic thinking.

In his vocal works these problems of reconciling a personal vision, and the personal polyphonic style which best expresses that vision, with the requirements of contrast, drama, speed and colour in large-scale instrumental works do not arise. The *Festival Gloria* (written for St. Paul's Cathedral Choir), the *Missa in honorem Sancti Dominici* and the *Missa Cantuariensis* are all striking settings in which the music interpenetrates the text, illumines,

* By W. H. Mellers in *Grove* (5th ed., 1954).

enlarges and transfigures it. The same thing happens in some of his songs, e.g. "O Lord rebuke me not" from *Three Psalms*. In this religious music he continues a vein which is deeply embedded in English music, of which the distinguishing feature is a harmonic astringency that can, like a Gothic cathedral, be both austere and grand. Its note is sounded in Tallis, in Byrd, and again in Purcell and then not for centuries till Holst.

It is strange that with this double interest in voices and the orchestra Rubbra never composed an oratorio in the English tradition. The nearest he came to it was in a late (for the purposes of this book) Cantata di camera, *Crucifixus pro nobis*, which employs a tenor solo and four-part chorus accompanied by flute, violin, harp and organ. Here there is indeed a feeling for instrumental colour in a medium that suits his contrapuntal style and encompasses in its final section a quick and joyous expression of triumph—the words are from Spenser's sonnet "Most glorious Lord of life". His other cantatas, *The Morning Watch* composed for the 1946 St. Cecilia Festival, and the ardent *Song of the Soul* (1953) are of about the same length, which is not that of a full-scale oratorio.

Perhaps because the impulse behind all the music is serious, or religious even as Mellers suggested, and there is not much that is actually light-hearted or playful, and because the style is so fundamentally polyphonic, a superficial impression of monotony may have gained currency, which is quite false. Although he has not essayed oratorio or opera Rubbra has written for many media besides the conventional ones: for harpsichord and recorder, voice with string quartet, voice and string orchestra, even bamboo pipes. In spite of the facts that there is little trace of folk-song influence, at any rate after the early piano concerto, and that his religious music does not belong to the cathedral tradition of Wesley, Harwood and Bairstow, his music is wholly English: negatively in that not a trace of foreign influence, neither French impressionism nor serialism from Central Europe, is to be found in it, positively because of its roots in Elizabethan polyphony, and generally because that is what it sounds like.

When Gerald Finzi (1901-1956) died at the early age of fifty-five there was a rush of public tributes to him which seized on the markedly English character of his music, on his identification of himself with the physical land of England and still more with its literature, in spite of his Italian name and the strain of Italian blood perceptible alike in his physique and character. His central contribution was to the long tradition of English song, for he had a fine and practised taste in English poetry and a melodic gift nourished, as he said, on folk-song but not affiliated to or fashioned by it, as the true nationalist is. His melodic idiom was derived in part from Bach and in part from Parry, who was also the formative influence in his choral writing. He left some sixty songs for voice and piano, which he arranged not in cycles but in sets. Of cantatas he left three for solo voice and strings and three for chorus and orchestra, though this reckoning leaves out of account some alternative arrangements. He recognized his own limitations, which were set by his staunchly held ideals and the essentially lyrical nature of his musical endowment, and until the last year or two of his life he worked as a miniaturist, wrote no symphony, and more often employed a string or chamber orchestra than a full band. Not only his solo cantatas but his solo concertos were thus sparingly scored, except that for cello, his last work, which showed him ready at last to embark on larger designs. These concerto-like works, apart from the clarinet concerto which is so entitled, were of less than concerto dimensions and were called *Introit* (for violin), *Eclogue* (piano), *Fantasia and Toccata* (piano). Through them all one can hear the English pastoral note, which is to say the gentle, undramatic, but strong and persistent musical equivalent of the English landscape. This is where the affinity with Parry is operative, pervasively in spirit, technically in harmony. The element from Bach appears most openly in *Farewell to Arms* and *Dies Natalis*, solo cantatas in which the accompaniment is a chorale fantasia of long flowing lines with a lighter, more English note than Bach's. His choral harmony is basically the same as Parry's—he was not Parry's pupil but E. C. Bairstow's and R. O. Morris's—as is shown in the early part-songs to words of Robert Bridges and in the non-liturgical *Magnificat* of 1952. In the *St. Cecilia Ode* of 1950 Parry's spacious handling of large choral forces is combined with a richer, more competent and fastidious mastery of the orchestra than Parry, mistakenly, ever thought necessary. His last cantata, *In terra pax*, shows his genius in integrating words and music, in this case the interweaving of the gospel story of the shepherds in the field with Bridges's "Noel: Christmas Eve, 1913"—evocative and enchanting.

But it is the songs which are most likely to survive changes of taste, fashion and idiom. There are five sets of Hardy songs, and if one would see how Finzi read Hardy's riddles one should turn to "The Sigh", where the masculine wistfulness and the poignancy of time (found also in "The Clock of the Years" and others in the set *Earth and Air and Rain*) are caught, recreated and intensified. He can also catch the air and the lilt of Hardy's unmysterious ditties, "Rollicum-Rorum" for instance and the lighter Shakespeare. But it is the irony, the questioning and fatalism of Hardy that he matches with his unique gift, which could not be claimed as great or important. Sensitive, sincere, scrupulous and ardent, he belongs to the English idealists who range from Byrd to Parry.

These composers, whom I have classified as belonging to the nationalist succession, Butterworth, Moeran, Warlock, Hadley, Rubbra and Finzi, would admit the designation, since they have escaped the German bondage of the two previous generations; they have drunk at English springs in the shape of madrigals and folk-song; they have been strengthened by the Bach revival, have been sensitive to English poetry and kept clear of foreign influences (some might say to their loss). They are unlike Elgar, Bliss, Walton and Rawsthorne, whose Englishness is of some other sort that one would not label pastoral. They share some characteristics with Britten and Tippett. But in the last resort the quality is not to be specified, demonstrated and proved, but must be perceived. As Aristotle said, the judgment is in the perception (ἐν τῇ αἰσθησει ἡ κρίσις). My judgment at least is that these men represent the only products of our nationalism apart from Holst and Vaughan Williams. They came too late to form a school as the Russians and Czechs did in the nineteenth century. But they are a product of the renaissance and are the nationalist element in that renaissance. It is significant that they are all song writers. Warlock and Finzi are half-brothers in their songs in that they have the same sort of sensibility to words. Butterworth, Moeran and Hadley are half-brothers through their folk-music affiliations. Moeran and Rubbra are alike in that they essay the larger instrumental forms from what is basically a vocal style. Moeran and Finzi both wrote good cello concertos and a little church music. All could be vaguely described as pantheists except Rubbra, whose religious music springs from more specifically Christian roots. They are thus sufficiently homogeneous as a group in spirit as well as in time to constitute the nationalist succession, such as it was, to the actual rebirth of English music.

XIV

The Post-War (1914-1918) Group

BESIDES THE group of composers who constitute the nationalist
succession, such as it was, there was another group which emerged
after 1918, whose music was marked by an athletic vigour which
was a symptom of their self-assertion against the basically
romantic axioms of the older generation of Parry, Stanford and
Elgar, and an awareness of what was going on in Europe that
Holst and Vaughan Williams ignored. They began as neo-classicists
but were subsequently seen to be crypto-romantics. They were
moderns in their day but lived to be established figures who
resisted the revival of Schœnberg's influence in the fifties—the
nationalist young men mostly died young, even before Vaughan
Williams, their founding father. This modern group, whose early
music was marked by a certain astringency, consisted of Arthur
Bliss (b. 1891), Gordon Jacob (b. 1895), William Walton (b. 1902),
Lennox Berkeley (b. 1903), Constant Lambert (1905-1951),
Michael Tippett (b. 1905), Arnold Cooke (b. 1906), Alan Rawsthorne (b. 1908) and William Wordsworth (b. 1908). Much as
they naturally differ from one another they do constitute a
generation affected by the disruption of the 1914 war, yet having
its roots in the soil prepared by the academics and the nationalists. Their Englishness was tempered by French influences,
Stravinsky being included therein and Nadia Boulanger's teaching, and by a twentieth-century outlook, whatever that may
signify. Vaughan Williams had a more radical mind than any
of these juniors, but his roots go farther back into the nineteenth
century and he had a feeling for tradition which they would not
profess. Therein lies the difference, obscured by Vaughan Williams's longevity, between the generations.

By some such rough segregation these eight composers are
seen to be the first fruits of independence, and the discussion of

their achievements is divided or duplicated between this chapter and Book III, for they are the bridge between the pre-war and post-war worlds. Individually they may be summarily compared before their corpus of works is more critically examined. Bliss, the senior of them, is an eclectic, whose imagination is fortified by a lively intellect—in this he resembles Hindemith, his contemporary. He is a resourceful musician who could have made a living as a conductor and by virtue of his intellectual distinction he was able for a period to be an administrator for the B.B.C. and to become Master of the Queen's Musick. Jacob and Rawsthorne asserted their independence of the main English traditions by concentrating on instruments to the comparative disregard of vocal and dramatic music. Jacob indeed is a specialist in instrumentation and has followed an academic career. His Englishness is in line with Holst's, derives from him back to Purcell, and is manifested in economy, clarity and, if the oxymoron be allowed, a reticent pungency. Rawsthorne's music can be described in much the same terms though he is less related to tradition and to academic associations. Walton and Lambert grew up when the Diaghilev ferment had a stimulating effect on their imaginations and cast a slightly exotic hue over their early work. Lambert did not write very much, as his short life was otherwise occupied with conducting and criticism. Walton soon consolidated his style, which in the perspective of history can be seen to be in line from Elgar. Bliss's place, too, is in the Elgar succession, though his idiom is less personal than either Elgar's or Walton's. Berkeley's development was determined and postponed by his training in Paris under Boulanger. A certain Gallic fastidiousness and elegance is no doubt native to him, and Boulanger's technical training ensured mastery of his craft, but the French pressures were too strong to be altogether good for his health and it was years before he found his feet and was able to stand securely on them. Tippett is a puzzling figure: the non-English streak in him is Celtic not Gallic, for he is a Cornishman. He was a late developer and it took him a long time to harness his speculative intellect to his creative imagination, but his work gets progressively better, more assured and less liable to miss its target. Wordsworth is a more sober personality than any of these. A descendant of the poet's brother, he was delicate as a boy and privately educated until he went to study with Donald Tovey. Tovey's ideals are a strong influence; Wordsworth did not, as Bliss, Walton, Rawsthorne did in their early days, find it necessary to flaunt his originality, but he is no longer, as Tovey still was, in German tutelage.

In Bliss's fairly copious output—he is more like Walton than like either Vaughan Williams or Britten in being only moderately fertile but is a steady and studious worker—the works which have won wide and whole-hearted admiration, as compared with the respect which is accorded to most of his output, are the *Colour Symphony* (1922, revised in 1932), the choral symphony *Morning Heroes* (1930), the clarinet quintet (1931) and *Music for Strings* (1935) the ballet *Checkmate* (1937), and the orchestral *Variations on a Theme by Blow* (1955). All of these, except the quintet, which may owe its emotional glow to the inspiration of the clarinet, are works in which the sheer skill is fortified by some stimulus, not necessarily extra-musical, but from outside the purely musical inspiration. The programme of the *Colour Symphony* is slight but it is enough to preclude the spiderwise spinning of themes and rhythms from its own entrails which limits the cogency of the string quartets and the piano concerto (1939). The quintet has the warmth of the clarinet to animate the structure. *Morning Heroes* has the unifying theme of war and explicit words, the Blow Variations a splendid tune and also an ingeniously related scheme of meaning drawn from Psalm 23, *Checkmate* a strong dramatic scenario. There is always plenty to admire in Bliss's instrumental structures but too often it is derived from the intellect rather than the imagination—intellect and imagination are obverse and reverse of the same coin of the mind. Westrup* puts it in the short form of heart and head, though that is something of a simplification. But it remains true that Bliss is less successful with lyrical than with rhythmic utterance and he has never developed a personal idiom. Idiomatically, as already remarked, he is and has remained an eclectic, and though his music is by no means derivative it does not bear an unmistakable sign manual.

He has applied his technical resource, his sheer skill and his undoubted musicality to every form of composition and his corpus of works can to some extent be classified not only by category but

* In his edition of Walker's *A History of Music in England* (1952).

by period. Thus as a young man he was stimulated, as Walton and Lambert were, by the post-Armistice feeling of break-away and adventure, so that his early chamber music assumed forms not previously exploited, and where the voice was employed it was instrumentally used. *Rout* and *Conversations* are examples. A more serious, neo-classical trend developed during the twenties, though the *Colour Symphony*, which was mistaken for the beginning of such a trend, was later seen to be romantic at heart. This latent romanticism is discernible in *Pastoral*, which was his first excursion into choralism and was succeeded immediately by *Morning Heroes* (see pp. 299-300). In the mid-thirties his attention was deflected to drama, at first via films, of which *The Shape of Things to Come* (H. G. Wells) came first, in 1935. In 1937 came *Checkmate*, the first of three ballet scores. The logical conclusion of this trend was an opera, but this was delayed by the war, and *The Olympians* to a libretto by J. B. Priestley did not appear till 1949. This was a near success which just failed to be stage-worthy—in spite of Priestley's theatrical experience—through a last act which took too long to unravel the plot. In it Bliss enlarged his rather strenuous style to take in comedy, opulence and lyrical romance, but the marriage of words and vocal line foundered, and its brilliant theatrical idea, the return of the Olympian gods to earth as a troupe of strolling players, misfired. Ten years later Bliss enrolled himself among the long line of English oratorio writers with *The Beatitudes* for the opening of Coventry Cathedral in 1961 and *Mary of Magdala* for a Three Choirs Festival. His appointment to be Master of the Queen's Musick in 1953 produced a certain amount of occasional music.

The *Colour Symphony* is a glowing work of big gestures and assured mastery, which with its affiliations to heraldry and gems in the colours, Purple, Red, Blue and Green, makes an impact upon audiences, and is frequently revived. The piano concerto, written for the New York World Fair of 1939 and played there by Solomon and Boult, is also a work of big gestures. Indeed it is the only English piano concerto composed in the continental tradition for the lions of the keyboard—Ireland's, which preceded it by seven years, is more of the magnitude of Grieg's than of Brahms's, Tchaikovsky's or Rachmaninov's concertos—and given big playing it is effective. Yet is is conventional, which is an epithet not usually applicable to Bliss's work.

There are two other concertos, one for two pianos dating from 1933 and one for violin belonging to 1955. The first is a short work in which Bliss employs a passacaglia principle borrowed from his *Introduction and Allegro*, an early work inspired by his first visit to America in 1923. The violin concerto resembles the piano concerto in being a large-scale romantic piece, in which the lack of a true slow movement—for which a slow introduction to the finale is substituted—upsets the balance between the lyrical and the energetic elements. If the piano concerto was too conventional, in the violin concerto the departure from convention is disturbing in that it makes the work as a whole sound too episodic. Structure is as a matter of fact the aspect of composition in which Bliss is most ready to adventure, and scattered throughout his complete output are many instances of ingenuity and experiment, though tonality, freely manipulated, is always retained as an element in coherence. In *Music for Strings* (1936), which is really a concerto for string orchestra like the third and sixth Brandenburgs not to mention Elgar's *Introduction and Allegro* and Vaughan Williams's *Tallis Fantasia*, the themes are fluid, and formal antithesis and recapitulation are not in evidence, but there is no doubt of an organic unity in the weaving of a complex polyphonic texture. It has the magnitude (in Aristotle's sense of substantiality) though not the size of the *Colour Symphony* and the concertos, and is a characteristic product of Bliss's neo-classicism. The correct title of the Blow Variations is *Meditations on a Theme by John Blow*, the point being that Blow's tune, which is taken from his anthem "The Lord is my Shepherd", is not stated in full till the end and the several meditations are concerned with ideas and images derived from Psalm 23, so that the work is a symphonic poem in variation form, comparable only and at a distance with Strauss's *Don Quixote* in structure, and trebly coherent because of its literary, thematic and structural unity. The individual meditations are richly inventive, the orchestral writing virtuosic; drama is not absent, being derived from "I will fear no evil"; and the originality consists in the composer having discovered a new way of writing variations. This is possibly the most completely successful work Bliss has written. Here imagination, invention, intellect and technique combine on equal terms to produce something in the grand manner which was a gift to English music from Elgar. For the grand manner is not a natural garment worn by English composers, who without being stiff-upper-lipped are conscious of a puritan as well as an imperial element in their make-up and artistically regard, if not the golden mean, at any rate a certain economy as an ideal for an Englishman to keep in mind, whatever opulence the European romantics might allow themselves. The emergence of an English grand manner in Elgar enriched the tradition and it has been saved from disappearance as a purely Elgarian fingerprint by Bliss and Walton.

Gordon Jacob, who comes next in age, does not write in the grand manner and eschews opulence. He is a functionalist artist, neo-classical and predominantly concerned with the orchestra, though he has written three string quartets, and is not a lavish colourist. Indeed his concertos, one each for viola, piano, oboe, bassoon, horn and flute, have accompaniments for string orchestra only. He wrote three symphonies, one of which is for strings only, and more important than the symphonies are the suites and sets of variations, one of which, the *Passacaglia on a Well-known Theme*, is as gay as is to be expected from its theme being the nursery tune "Oranges and Lemons". The third suite, which he wrote in 1949 for the Bournemouth Municipal Orchestra's celebration of its fifty-seventh birthday, is again a jolly work, in which there are many orchestral felicities—the sarabande is given to the brass, for instance. Ingenuity rather than sentiment is the driving force of his music—ingenuity of counterpoint; ingenuity of invention, as in the *Variations on an Original Theme*, where theme and variations were made for each other in one original conception; ingenuity of scoring, which is such that he has made orchestral arrangements for six ballets, transcribed Holst's military band pieces for orchestra, composed for military band himself and written textbooks on several aspects of orchestration. This ingenuity is not to be despised, as it is a pleasurable ingredient in craftsmanship and is specially valuable in variations, of which Jacob has written four sets; it is an ingredient in wit and in the light touches with which his works abound. The concertos and suites are modelled on the eighteenth-century type, and their inspiration, like that of their models, arises out of the nature of the instruments rather than from any external sentiment—there is no programme music in Jacob's output, though there is occasionally a title, and in the second symphony of 1943-1944 one might discern more emotional tensions than are customary with him, which might very well be the product of the war. The level of interest of all his numerous works is remarkably constant, because they are independent of romantic or external inspiration. Variety is secured by his sensibility to tone-colour—thus the viola concerto and the rhapsody for cor anglais are richer and softer in sound-quality and therefore in expression than the concertos for piano and bassoon. Sometimes there is a moment of tenderness, as at the end of the pastoral movement of the oboe concerto. But on the whole he writes an extravert and reticent music. There are some small cantatas and one large choral work for chorus and orchestra, a setting of Chaucer's *The Nun's Priest's Tale*, a secular and witty text be it noted, but *A Goodly Heritage* for female voices and strings with piano, a setting of twelve songs of the countryside, has charm, which is also to be found in the oboe quartet and the clarinet quintet. It is hard to find in English music a traditional source for this combination of qualities; the reticence is an English characteristic and belongs very much to the anti-romantic reaction of the first part of the twentieth century, the counterpoint and the feeling for instrumental texture were in the English chamber music of the seventeenth century and are present in Purcell but seem to have gone underground since. This rather dry flavour is therefore a distinctive contribution to English music, which tends overmuch towards the pastoral and ruminative, when it is not being expansive, edifying or programmatic.

Walton, next in seniority, is very much in the grand tradition, and apart from *Façade*, which lies outside all categories, writes almost entirely in the larger forms. He alone of English composers secured international attention for everything he wrote from the beginning, often before its importance was recognized at home. Thus a string quartet composed when he was twenty was played at the first Salzburg Festival of the International Society for Contemporary Music in 1923, when even his name was unknown here outside of Christ Church, Oxford, where he had been a choirboy and a very young undergraduate. His viola concerto

was introduced to London by Paul Hindemith in 1929 after Lionel
Tertis had rejected it, and more than thirty years on his second
symphony, first performed at the Edinburgh Festival of 1960,
received a cool reception from English critics only to be acclaimed
in America with an outstanding recording by the Cleveland
Orchestra and awarded two international prizes, one for the
recording by the American National Academy of Recording Arts
and Sciences, and the other, carrying even more prestige, from the
Gesellschaft der Musikfreunde of Vienna, to celebrate its 150th
birthday. Each work when it comes is a master work and there
are no failures, though the first symphony had to be completed
in two spells of work on it, and the opera *Troilus and Cressida*
was thought to be rather old-fashioned and had only a moderate
success when it was produced at La Scala. Walton, though precocious as a child, has never been a quick worker. His scores are
calculated to the last detail and they are usually heavily loaded.
For a long time he was a composer of one work per category like
César Franck, but his three concert overtures, two Coronation
marches and two symphonies spoiled the accuracy of that too
facile classification. Nevertheless part of his success is due to the
firm and clear impression made on the public by single examples
of one form at a time. Thus his four concertos are respectively
for piano, viola, violin and cello. His chamber music consists of
one piano quartet, one string quartet, one violin sonata and one
song sequence.* Oratorio is perhaps not the right designation of
Belshazzar's Feast, since it is far from edifying, but it has never
had a successor, though Walton wrote another cantata *In honour
of the City of London* for the Leeds Festival (1937), a *Te Deum* for
the Coronation of 1953, and a non-liturgical *Gloria* for the
centenary of the Huddersfield Choral Society in 1961. And (so
far) there is only one opera and one ballet (*The Quest*, 1943).

As a young composer Walton was exposed to the post-war
influences, which were anti-romantic and, through Diaghilev,
Gallic in wit and sophistication. He never had an academic
education and moved, after a year or two at a Christ Church
depleted by war, into the artistic circles that revolved round the
literary Sitwells. *Façade* for speaking voice and small chamber

---

* He wrote a second, *For the Lord Mayor's Table*, for the City of London
Festival of 1962.

ensemble, witty, evocative, smart, but too robust to be precious, really gave a wrong impression of his fundamental nature, though its constituent elements are all to be found in his make-up. But it was the viola concerto that revealed him as a romantic, as an adherent of modernity in so far as it meant a dissonant harmony but a basic adherence to tonality, as an exponent of the twentieth-century dynamism released by Stravinsky, and as an orchestrator of natural sensibility. His style, which is to say his idiom, never changed once it had been consolidated. Its chief features are protean themes that retain their identity in an extraordinary variety of shapes, a thick contrapuntal texture, an English partiality for false relation, a restless irregularity of subsidiary accents and a strict control of the larger outlines of his structures.

Walton, whose position in the post-war scene is discussed in Book III, is the least nationalist, most cosmopolitan of English composers and is the best weapon in the armoury of those who disagree with the main thesis of this book, that only by a more intensive cultivation of our own soil could we grow a healthier crop of English music. His cosmopolitanism—for he married a South American wife and lives in Ischia—is, however, founded on a cathedral training, and he at least was lucky in the time of his birth, for he emerged at the end of forty years of nationalist endeavour, when the battle for independence was won.

His friend Constant Lambert found a new outlet for an English musician's activities in the ballet, to which indeed he devoted his life as composer—his first composition while he was still a student at the Royal College of Music was a commission from Diaghilev—and as conductor. Indeed he played a vital part in the foundation by Ninette de Valois of what became the Royal Ballet. As its musical director, he was also responsible for choices of music, many arrangements, adaptations and orchestrations. In the early days of the 1939-1945 war he kept the company going without an orchestra by himself playing the piano for it on tour. Together with the exotic strain grafted on to his English training from R. O. Morris and Vaughan Williams and his connection with Diaghilev and the world of the ballet, a personal pre-dilection for coloured people enabled him to absorb jazz almost as one born to it—other indications of this trait are the dedication of his *Elegiac Blues* for small orchestra to the negro actress

Florence Mills and the setting of eight Chinese poems by Li Po. His chief and most famous work, *Rio Grande*, incorporates jazz idioms without a trace of indigestion and from them derives its sensuous sun-laden atmosphere. The work is an evocation of lotus-eating enchantment from Sacheverell Sitwell's words by means of a virtuoso piano part with choral obbligato and a percussion-bearing orchestral accompaniment. There had never been anything like it before, nor has there been since. Its dimensions are right, its seductions light and exquisite. Its success, with Hamilton Harty playing the piano part at its first performances in 1929, was instantaneous, and its temporary and popular allusions were transformed into something of permanent value, enshrining the transitory emotions of a decade.

Lambert wrote two works which could be called more serious, a symphonic piece *Music for Orchestra* (1927) and a cantata, called a masque, *Summer's Last Will and Testament* (1936). The first is a single movement evolved from an opening theme by contrapuntal and accelerating development to a simpler, louder and squarer restatement. The second is a suite in seven movements of poems from Thomas Nashe's "Pleasant Comedy" of 1593 cast in the dance and song forms of the period, Madrigal, Coranto, Saraband. Lambert had shown his neo-classical leanings—they were not more, for he deplored in his clever book, *Music Ho!*, the more extreme tendencies of his generation—in his *Romeo and Juliet*, the ballet commissioned by Diaghilev, and indeed in all four of his ballets, by the use of the old dance forms of the suite. *Summer's Last Will and Testament* is set for large orchestra (two cornets as well as three trumpets, three percussion players and two harps) and for baritone solo with chorus. Two of the movements are for orchestra only, one of them, "King Pest", being a *danse macabre*. The form is original in that while it is formally a suite, the numbers are linked, so that the poems are embedded in an orchestral texture which develops on the lines of a symphonic poem expressing in turn Nashe's passionate humanity, irony, vitality, resignation. This Elizabethan gusto released in Lambert a feeling of kinship, and his "madrigals" though modern and chromatic are in line with Tudor language, so that this is his most deeply felt work, an advance on *Rio Grande* in a certain sense if it is not foolish to talk of an advance on something which exists in its own right, form and perfection—an advance then in the sense that the composer has taken on a bigger challenge and successfully met it. He never attempted anything so big again, but his three ballets for the Sadler's Wells company (afterwards the Royal Ballet), *Pomona* (1926), *Horoscope* (1937), *Tiresias* (1950), and two substantial works for piano, a sonata and a chamber concerto (with an accompaniment of nine instruments), represent what his output might have grown to embrace had he devoted more time to composition. These piano works are anti-romantic in their percussive writing, with no arpeggios but plenty of running unisons, clattering chords, broken and syncopated rhythms, inconstant time signatures and in the concerto a great battery of exotic percussion to point the angularities of rhythm. Lambert was a product of the post-war decade and so identified himself with its ethos that had it not been for his other activities, which included editing some symphonies of Boyce, some concert conducting in which he liked to explore byways of the romantic repertory, as well as his vast and various labours for the ballet, he might, when he so prematurely died at the age of forty-six, have appeared like that slightly ludicrous figure the *avant-garde* fighting in the last ditch. But he had too much talent not limited to one field—he was a connoisseur of popular dance music —too many interests not limited to one art, too much wit, ever to have stuck in any groove or ditch.

Lennox Berkeley, though by no means one of those unclassifiable "sports" like Berlioz or Delius, stands a little apart from his generation owing to the fact that he does not belong by affiliation or training to any of the prevalent English traditions, Elizabethan, Purcellian, folk-song, academic, cathedral or choral. He has rather grown into the English traditions by the fact of being an Englishman and being domiciled in England. He did not take up music till after he had gone down from Oxford, and then he went to Paris at the age of twenty-four to work with Nadia Boulanger for six years. She taught him to write in a style based on Stravinsky flavoured with the refined piquancies of Poulenc and Roussel. All the early work, including the oratorio *Jonah* performed at the Leeds Festival of 1937, is in this brittle manner. It was not till the forties that his own style, which is by no means so desiccated or so assertive, emerged. It is on the contrary fluent, graceful and charming, and the French influences of wit, economy and clarity complete the amalgam of a distinct individuality. The fact that it is still not assertive, does not raise its voice or cultivate extravagances for their own sake, has partly concealed the extent of his work, both in quantity and range. But by the time he was sixty he had written three operas, two symphonies, five concertos, a number of song sequences, and chamber music in ample variety. This is all music on a big scale, but the composer's fastidious manners preclude the possibility of inflation. Still, the general impression left on the mind of anyone who encounters his music in the course of steady concert and festival going is that Berkeley's distinctive excellence is in works of moderate dimensions, amiable intentions and elegance rather than eloquence. The Serenade for Strings (1939), the Divertimento in B flat for small orchestra, the Sinfonietta, show this aspect of his musical personality: they have their own melodiousness, as well as the neatness and the deftness which are indeed a characteristic of all his work, large or small, but here exploited with singular felicity, and exhaling charm from the very lightness of touch. It is by virtue of these qualities that Berkeley writes well for piano and with something fresh to say for instruments like the guitar, and for harpsichord and recorder, for both of which media he has written sonatinas. When he has something more serious to say, and a vein of seriousness began to develop with the choice of religious words in the *Stabat Mater* (1946), the *Four Poems of St. Teresa of Avila* (1947) and ultimately a Mass, he still finds moderate dimensions suit his way of working best. *Stabat Mater* is set for six solo voices and chamber ensemble, the *Four Poems* for contralto and string quartet. Both are striking works which fit into no recognized category, though the composer allows a choral alternative to the last ensemble in *Stabat Mater*. This cantata has something still left of the early asperity that expresses a wry *dolor* and bitter *lacrimae*, but now assimilated to his own artistic purpose. The assimilation of matter and manner with the personal idiom, the refinement and aristocratic distinction produces in *St. Teresa* what is widely accepted as Berkeley's finest work, his most rounded achievement.

His sense of form, however, is equal to projecting larger structures, as he demonstrated notably in the first symphony (1940) and in the concertos for one piano, two pianos, flute and violin. The symphony in particular when it was played at a war-time Promenade Concert made a great impression by its abstention from any attempt to impress. The economy of the scoring and the spare texture were precisely fitted to the logic and lucidity of an argument that was not unduly pressed to a conclusion but was delightfully and stylishly expounded. Similarly the piano concertos are designed for the light-fingered pianist—one is dedicated to Colin Horsley—rather than for the bravura virtuoso. Indeed the third (1959) is laid out for accompaniment only by double string orchestra. The piano writing is always dexterous in concerto, sonata and song accompaniment alike, and Berkeley always follows the lesson he learned in France, that at any rate one of the functions of art is to give pleasure, aesthetic pleasure to the mind as well as sensual pleasure to the ear. But as he has gone on he has become both more productive and wider in range. Indeed it comes as something of a surprise on surveying the output of a composer whose manner of speech is so modest to discover what a substantial corpus of work has come from his pen since he rather belatedly found his style.

Of the three operas one is opera seria (*Nelson*), one is opera buffa (*A Dinner Engagement*), and one is in the nature of a Theocritan idyll (*Ruth*). The last would seem to accord best with the composer's genius, which is not primarily dramatic. But though he has made the right approach to what is not a dramatic story, and launches his piece successfully from the stage, the flight falters in the last scene to admit too much choral music, admirable though that is. Similarly in *Nelson* he just fails to bring off a big design through miscalculations in the presentation of the conflicts and the setting of the words so as to make the action clear. *A Dinner Engagement*, however, which is an extravaganza about the new poor in two scenes, is a success in a medium by no means easy to bring off in performance. The book by Paul Dehn is neatly turned with numerous touches of absurdity, which Berkeley has successfully projected on light-fingered recitative and air, dialogue and ensemble, over an accompaniment of one wind and one string to a part with harp and piano. Pinches of Gallic spice and dashes of parody are stirred into the soufflé with nice discrimination. The pace is right. So here is a modern *La Serva Padrona*.

Berkeley's affinity is rather with Rawsthorne than with Walton or Britten. Like Rawsthorne he has written piano concertos and much chamber music, he is less powerfully drawn to words than Britten and he eschews the size and force of Walton's instrumental music. His wit has less bite than Rawsthorne's but Rawsthorne has written nothing like *A Dinner Engagement*. There are few marks of nationality in either of their outputs, but being neither derivative nor cosmopolitan they add an invaluable element of variety, idiosyncrasy, and indeed innovation to the scene as it developed after the breakthrough by Parry and Stanford.

Two north-countrymen, Arnold Cooke and Alan Rawsthorne, follow the instrumental trail first laid by Gordon Jacob. All three composers favour chamber music, works for string orchestra and concertos. They write little vocal music. Their partiality for instruments seems to arise from the fact that they rely on the medium to suggest the ideas. Cooke, after study at Cambridge, went to work with Hindemith in Berlin and Hindemith's influence has been permanent, but Rawsthorne is curiously independent and his music shows few influences. This may have been due to the fact that he took up music rather late, got his training in Manchester, was a pupil of Petri for piano but never attempted a career as a virtuoso though he earned a living for a time by playing the piano for the Dartington School of Dance Mime. He was thirty by the time he had fashioned his idiom, which is almost atonal—he very rarely uses key signatures. He is not, however, a serialist or any other form of doctrinaire, and his harmony, which is spare and astringent, is of classical derivation, flitting in and out of keys but not aggressively dissonant or flagrantly experimental. Indeed he knows so well what he wants to say and how to say it that his music has never suffered popular incomprehension.

Basically the nature of his thought—and he is an essentially intellectual composer—is conditioned by the instruments involved, but at the same time the thought seems to have made the choice of instruments inevitable. Thus in the very first work with which he made his name as that of a man to be watched, the Theme and Variations for Two Violins (1937) he seized all the possibilities of the limited medium and in nine variations bearing names like Siciliano, Cancrizzante and Fantasia he poured his new atonal wine into these old bottles with an ingenuity that tickled the fancy and engaged the mind. Similarly with his first substantial orchestral work, the *Symphonic Studies* (1938), he used a free passacaglia on a rather abrupt theme to evolve a logically satisfying composition. The kind of themes he chooses, which sometimes have a dry humour, are often apt for variation. For in addition to the two examples already named his first string quartet (1939) was a Theme and Variations; he has also used variations for the finale of his second violin concerto, and the middle movement of his first piano concerto is a chaconne. His piano writing is naturally dexterous but he has not composed, apart from the two concertos, a great deal of piano music—a few small pieces and a sonatina—though he has written duet sonatas for violin, viola and cello with piano.

The emotional range is limited—he is not trying to say something in the most expressive medium for it but making propositions about the medium itself and arguing from that. But the rarer quality of wit, an offshoot of intellect, and rarer still irony, which thrives on understatement, is frequently to be found in his music. One might say "always" when he leaves abstract music for anything with a programme or suggestive title, such as *The Creel* for piano duet inspired by Izaak Walton, or Eliot's *Practical Cats* for speaker and orchestra, or the orchestral overtures *Street Corner* and *Cortèges*, in which various sorts of procession jostle one another.

Not only is there little vocal music up to the time he was fifty but only one dramatic essay, a score for Ashton's ballet *Madame Chrysanthème* (1955). His first extended setting of religious words, apart from the rather stiff *A Canticle of Man* for baritone and chorus (1953), did not come till 1963 in his *Mediaeval Diptych*. His chief contribution to the music of his generation is undoubtedly his concertos, one for oboe, two for violin and two for piano. Each of the last has some claim to be called the best piano concerto ever written by an English composer.

The other major figure to be born in the first decade of the present century is Michael Tippett, who is remarkable for a retarded development which accelerated in middle life to make his future (i.e. after 1960) more unpredictable than that of any of the figures of this chapter living at the time of writing it. He has great gifts of character and intellect, which were not matched initially with the sort of musical talent that "lisps in numbers". The result of a long struggle to subdue his teeming ideas and ideals to the service of his imagination by means of an adequate technique led to all of the work of his immediate post-student years—he had been a pupil of Charles Wood and R. O. Morris at the R.C.M. —being discarded. Late Beethoven was a prominent influence in it, but what emerged was an original feeling for rhythm derived from Morris and the madrigal. It was not till the Fantasy Sonata for piano of 1938 that his talent, as distinct from his individuality, plainly declared itself. This is an attractive work that has worn well. Its first movement shows the beginnings of the piano figuration which was to develop into the arabesque that became a feature of his "canticles" (Britten's term for extended song), *Boyhood's End* (1943) and *The Heart's Assurance* (1951), and later still of the opera *King Priam* (1962); the last movement has a captivating turn of rhythm for its rondo theme. An almost romantic sonata but perhaps better described in its titular "fantasy". This piano sonata had been preceded by a string quartet which the composer subsequently revised, and was followed by a work of unquestionable mastery, the *Concerto for Double String Orchestra* (see page 331). Then in 1942 came a wholly satisfying string quartet (No. 2 in F sharp) and in 1945 his first attempt at a symphony (after the discarded B flat symphony of his nonage). This symphony was important to the composer in stretching his style to encompass large-scale design, but it was in fact rather drab and provided another instance of the difficulty, experienced by Rubbra, of accommodating what is basically madrigalian counterpoint to symphonic size and processes. The second symphony, coming after the opera *A Midsummer Marriage*, showed an advance alike in mastery of complex organization and in sensitiveness to orchestral colour; the textures and rhythms of the double concerto are further exploited in the first movement and scherzo, the more nocturnal sonorities of the orchestra are explored in the slow movement, and key relationships (of tonic and supertonic) experimentally used to tie up the design. A concerto for orchestra for the Edinburgh Festival of 1963 showed his idiom and style both still changing.

It is not possible, or at least it would not be right, to consider

Tippett's evolving musical output, which has become more fluent and more copious, without reference to his personality, which is partly that of a prophet prepared to argue, partly that of an evangelist prepared to preach, and partly that of a crusader prepared to do battle for his creed. All his work is of the nature of discussion, and criticism of his work is usually in dialectical terms. Moreover, he is an intelligent and forceful, though not always a very clear, thinker. Thought with him is not inhibitive of imaginative creation: he thinks about what he composes both before and after he is composing it. In 1959 he produced a book of collected broadcasts and articles, *Moving into Aquarius*, in which every sort of antithesis is scrutinized, dream . . . blueprint, spirit . . . matter, the state . . . the individual, entertainment . . . art, outer life . . . collective unconscious; and he is concerned to reconcile them. Furthermore, as is obvious from the libretto of *A Midsummer Marriage*, which like that of *A Child of our Time* he wrote himself, he is very well aware of the use and the semantics of symbolism.

He grew up at the moment when men coming home from the war presented social issues to sensitive or enquiring minds, so that he is very much an artist with a dedicated social conscience. Both worlds, the social in which he lives and the artistic in which he functions, are equally real to him. And as Hindemith found in like case the two worlds have either to be reconciled or reduced from two to one. Hindemith in *Mathis der Maler* found that the artist's prime duty is to his art, but Tippett found that it was his duty to serve a prison sentence as a protest against war. His oratorio *A Child of our Time* was a passionate protest made articulate, and it followed an earlier cantata bearing the title *A Song of Liberty* (1937). Thus an intense struggle goes on at all mental levels, the subconscious (in his symbolism), the intellectually conscious (in his discussion of aesthetics), and the imaginative in which these ideas, these conceptual issues, have to be converted into musical images.

No wonder the task sometimes seems too big, and the compositions that emerge from it appear to lack sometimes clarity, sometimes direction. But Tippett has a spiritual resilience, outwardly manifesting itself as temperamental gaiety and intellectual sportiveness, which keeps him going, a dynamic which, as already noted, propels his work on to new courses. There are thus few perfected masterpieces in his output, and on that count a musical historian might regret that a multiplicity of gifts had detracted from his purely musical achievement. Had he perhaps developed them in a different order, so that for instance the purely musical talent had been set in motion before his intellect and emotion had sprouted so strongly, it might have been that a very great composer with a message for humanity—I mean the kind of composer Beethoven was—would have been the outcome of the intense mental struggle, as it was with Beethoven, but as so far it has only very intermittently been with Tippett. Even so his contribution to the cognitive aspects of the art has been very valuable.

Music of the serious kind is thus in mid-twentieth century no longer shallow-pated as it was apt to be in the mid-nineteenth. Light music, well made but touching no depths nor indeed intended to, shallow in sentiment, but easy on the ear, unexacting upon the attention but good entertainment, was written by Eric Coates (1896-1957), who had begun musical life as an orchestral player. This sort of thing had sometimes come as incidental music out of the theatre: thus, the *Henry VIII Dances* of Edward German (1862-1936) had an enormous vogue and as light entertainment in theatre, hotel lounge or pier head, served a useful purpose. These two names represent a whole class of confectioners. But the distinction was clear, as it hardly had been with Cowen, between confectionery and solid food, It is really a matter of mind, for if one seriously examines popular music* it is the absence of mind in it, its determined refusal to make any demands on the listener's attention, that makes it popular. Light music, in so far as it is distinguished from popular music, has more mental content and consequently wears longer. The distinction, which was first made definitive by Beethoven and the nineteenth century, has been deplored—did not Mozart write Divertimenti and is not diversion a legitimate function of music? —but it is so sharp that some epithet other than the inadequate "classical" and "serious" has been sought for what is not the music of diversion. However, if there is no word for it, we all know what it means. This "classical, serious" music is something

* As was done by Peter Stadlen in *British Journal of Aesthetics*, October, 1962.

more than diversion and craft—it is fine art. What the renaissance did was to put more mind, more aesthetic purpose, more sheer intellectual ability into what is at bottom an intuitive and imaginative activity. All the composers discussed in this chapter have been men of intellectual distinction and they represent the first fruits of the seeds sown by the pioneers. They have made English music stronger and healthier, more worthy of English culture as a whole, than it was a hundred years ago.

In Book III a kind of bird's-eye view of the situation as it has developed in the past half century will, I hope, confirm this verdict, and at the cost of some possible repetition will enable us to see in a longer perspective what in Book II has been examined in closer focus.

BOOK THREE

>>>>>>>>>>>>><<<<<<<<<<<<

Growth

XV

The Post-War Scene
in English Musical Life

THE WAR of 1914 to 1918 came down like a guillotine on the
flourishing life of Europe and ended an age. The nineteenth
century with its liberal ideas, its romantic attitudes, its expanding
economies and political developments continued, despite the
social strains and the apprehension of decadence, until the outbreak of war. When the smoke had cleared in 1920 Europe was a
different place with a new mental climate, which showed itself in
politics, social practices and the arts. The fruits of the changes
are still being gathered. It is true that in music most of the new
tendencies and techniques, especially those associated with the
names of Schoenberg and Stravinsky, had declared themselves in
the first decade of the twentieth century, but the climate was less
favourable for their spread and penetration than it became in the
anti-romantic atmosphere of post-war Europe. England, however, remained largely uninfluenced by the continental movements, an interested spectator rather than an active participant in
them. She had enough labour in her own garden to occupy her,
for the first-fruits of the English renaissance were beginning to
mature. By 1900 the harvest looked promising. After 1918 English
music resumed where it had broken off, with, however, one school
of composition, and that apparently the most flourishing since it
had Elgar at its head, failing to revive in the changed atmosphere.
Elgar virtually ceased to write, and Bantock, the next most important composer of this Midlands school, which owed its affiliations
to Richard Strauss and like him pinned its faith to over-large
orchestras, retreated into academic life. The influence of Germany
which had prevailed in Britain all through the nineteenth century
was destined to be extinguished by Holst and Vaughan Williams.

Tovey's deliberate self-dedication to German models, albeit the greatest, became an anachronism. Delius was a biological "sport" who neither changed nor developed nor exercised any influence except upon minor composers like Warlock and Moeran.

After the war England set about re-establishing the pattern of its musical life with provincial festivals, summer seasons of international opera at Covent Garden and a precarious supply of orchestral music which had been limited to London, Manchester and Bournemouth with a small something in Scotland. But the orchestral situation was radically changed by the advent of broadcasting, though it was not till 1930 that the B.B.C. Symphony Orchestra was established as a first-class orchestra of international status under the direction of Dr. (now Sir) Adrian Boult. In the nineteen-thirties London possessed three orchestras, the long-established (since 1904) London Symphony Orchestra, the London Philharmonic Orchestra (founded in 1932 by Sir Thomas Beecham), and the B.B.C. Symphony Orchestra. Outside London Birmingham, Manchester, Liverpool, Bournemouth and Glasgow possessed symphony orchestras. The provision of symphonic music on such a scale was at once the cause and the effect of a shift in public taste towards orchestral music, to some extent at the expense of the traditional enthusiasm for choral music. The strength of this new-found interest on the part of the great public, nurtured by broadcasting and the improvement in gramophone records, was demonstrated by the demand for music as the source of spiritual solace and encouragement in the Second World War.

After the end of the war in 1945 a different phenomenon manifested itself, which could not have been foreseen. Opera, which had hitherto been the cult of the few and was actually distasteful to many leaders of English musical life, suddenly established itself in public favour to such an extent that subsidy for it was provided from public funds, as in every other civilized country except Britain, which had only for one year (1932) in the Chancellorship of Philip Snowden drawn a pittance from the Treasury. The causes for this revolutionary change in public taste are to be sought in the pioneer work of Lilian Baylis at the Old Vic and Sadler's Wells and of Sir Thomas Beecham, who spent his personal fortune on it, in the scholarly advocacy of Edward Dent, Professor of Music at Cambridge, and (probably the greatest single factor) the invasion of Italy and Germany by British troops, who found opera a going concern of general acceptance such as they had never imagined at home.* This new impetus to operatic art coincided with the emergence of Benjamin Britten as a composer with a natural genius for the musical theatre. His *Peter Grimes*, produced at Sadler's Wells on June 7, 1945, is a landmark in our operatic history. Its success both at home and abroad—it was the first English opera ever to go the round of the world's great opera houses—encouraged him to continue the writing of operas and his contemporaries to take heart and try their hands at a form of art which had defeated all Stanford's efforts in the earlier years of the English renaissance.

Another new factor contributed to the new vitality of English music—the holiday festival. England boasts the oldest of all musical festivals in its Three Choirs Festival first established in 1713.† In the nineteenth century Wagner built his Festspielhaus at Bayreuth, and after 1918 many of the most beautiful cities of Europe exploited their tourist attractions by organizing summer festivals, which provided a concentration of music in superlative performances, with holiday amenities. Britain had its own tradition of festivals in provincial though not holiday centres, Leeds being the chief and the oldest of the survivors.‡ It quickly took the cue and established holiday festivals distinguished as a rule by some special feature. Of these the Edinburgh International Festival established in 1947 was on the largest scale.

A third new factor in English life was the first attempt to put musicological studies on a sound basis. The (Royal) Musical Association was founded as long ago as 1874, and was indeed something of a pioneer in the cultivation of what was called musical science, musical history and musical scholarship before the word "musicology" established itself some time round the beginning of the period under discussion—it was certainly not a nineteenth-century word, though Adler established the idea in

* "Why don't we have this sort of thing at home?" said an English tommy to me between the acts of *Rigoletto* in the Theater an der Wien in the spring of 1946.

† This is conjectural but probable. *See* Watkins Shaw: *The Three Choirs Festival* (Worcester, Baylis, 1954).

‡ Birmingham started its festival in 1768 but stopped it in 1912.

Vienna in 1885. But the papers read to the Musical Association were largely the work of amateurs in the sense that, though many reached a high standard of scholarship, their authors were clergymen such as Canon Galpin, Canon Fellowes and Dom Anslem Hughes, working musicians such as W. H. Cummings and Sir Richard Terry, dons such as W. H. Hadow and Laurence Picken, and specialists making voluntary contributions of knowledge, and it was not till Edward Dent was appointed to the chair of music in Cambridge in 1926 that such a chair was held by a musicologist. (Stainer had creditable scholarship when he held the Oxford chair, but he was primarily a practising musician.) The universities thus began to take musicology seriously, and when fully fledged faculties providing for arts degrees in music on the same level as other honour schools were formed after the 1939-1945 war, at Cambridge in 1945, at Oxford five years later and about the same time at all the younger universities, musical history at last was included on equal terms with the study of composition for all degrees, both arts graduation and the higher post-graduate degrees up to doctorates. Thus the study of musical history was quickened throughout the educational system, and the non-historical branches of musicology were stimulated in sympathy, so that ethnomusicology, the psychology of music, electrophonic production of music, musical appreciation, musico-therapy, modern acoustics, were among the subjects that were established on a basis of systematic study.

More pervasive than these specific influences were the far-reaching effects of technological advance in the sphere of acoustics. At the beginning of the century school physics was comprehensively taught from textbooks bearing the title *Sound, Light and Heat*. Research of course at the higher levels had got beyond this and the electrical discoveries upon which the broadcasting and subsequently the electrical recording of sounds are founded go back into the middle of the nineteenth century, but the tenuous and touchy relationships between the art of music and the science of physics, which began with Pythagoras, and which converged again centuries later in the discussions of temperament and tuning in Helmholz, only became active co-operation in the second decade of the twentieth century. A list of dates is as eloquent a way of writing the history of the developments from the new alliance as any other. Edison patented his first talking machine in 1878. Marconi made his first wireless transmissions in 1896. W. C. Sabine arrived at his formula for the reverberation time of buildings and applied it to the building of the Boston Concert Hall in 1898. Caruso made his first gramophone records, which were the earliest to have musical value, in 1902. Electrical recording arrived in 1925. 1920 is given as the date of the first real broadcasting with the manufacture of receiving sets in its immediate wake. The British Broadcasting Company was founded in 1922 and in 1927 became a public corporation under charter. The first director of both bodies, John Reith, had the vision to see the educational possibilities of the new medium and gave to the dissemination of music a big share of the available time. When sound broadcasting received its first serious check at the hands of television as much as 50 per cent of broadcasting time was being given to music, by no means all of it good music, though the rubbish of the B.B.C.'s Light Programme was offset by the serious intention, recondite material and minority appeal of the Third Programme, established in 1946.

The coincidence of this date with the establishment of musicology at the universities proved fruitful, for supply and demand in musical scholarship, which had hitherto been haphazard, were now brought into a profitable relationship: there was work available for the young musicologist and the B.B.C. knew where to turn for its material. At the end of ten years the balance sheet was highly satisfactory.

Apart from this specialized field of musical activity a vast change had come over the public appreciation of music; symphonic music in particular presents the most spectacular increase in public knowledge and esteem. For forty years the B.B.C. broadcast, as it still does, an enormous repertory of music in every form from mediaeval to modern, from folk-song to opera, from chamber music to public concerts. This solved at one stroke the problem that had beset the minds of our philanthropic grandparents, who, aware of the pleasure and indeed of the vaguely but certainly beneficial psychological effects of music, had provided People's Concert Societies, Sunday Leagues and, very hesitantly, subsidies of a modest character in the cause of musical evangelism. These efforts could be turned into other channels as soon as radio

K

broadcasting carried the world's classics into the poorest homes. It was feared, naturally but wrongly, that music so cheaply piped into the home would kill the demand for live music in public halls. The reverse happened: the appetite grew by what it fed on and, though financial difficulties did not disappear, orchestras and audiences multiplied and the spiritual hunger of the war years (1939-1945) still further increased both demand and consumption.

The consumption of and demand for music by gramophone is a different story, but it is intertwined both with the social story of broadcasting and with the technological advances of physics which enabled musical sounds to be recorded, transmitted and reproduced with ever increasing fidelity to the original performance. There had been in the nineteenth century in England, as in Germany, a tradition of domestic music-making which ranged from quite good performances of the easier classics of chamber music to quite bad amateur vocalism. This tradition was nearly silenced by the new accessibility of all kinds of music in good professional performances through the radio and the constantly improving gramophone. The physical weight and bulk of the commercial record, the 78 rpm disc that succeeded the primitive wax cylinder, put some limit on the size of the library a private person could collect and its fragility prevented any very great development of the lending library. But with the advent in 1950 of the long-playing $33\frac{1}{3}$ rpm record of unbreakable material the whole accumulation of centuries of music could be and was explored, much of it was recorded—more, that is, than could be heard in years of assiduous metropolitan concert-going—and apparently in spite of its cost sold in great quantities. Tape recording and stereophonic reproduction were further improvements in the decade of the fifties that did not immediately render the ordinary apparatus and its discs obsolete. The record-collector continued to acquire connoisseurship and in turn became the patron of concerts and the opera.

The creation of a new audience, extending farther down the social scale than the comfortable middle classes which had supported the various Philharmonic Societies of the big industrial cities as of London, was further encouraged by the institution of special concerts for children. A pioneer in this field was Robert Mayer, a wealthy amateur musician who at his own charges instituted in 1922 orchestral concerts for children, such as had been given in America by Damrosch. Local educational authorities all over the country approved the idea and followed the example so set by private enterprise.

Musical appreciation, a name that has stuck for want of a better, in education both juvenile and adult, was a further disseminator of knowledge. It provided an intellectual framework for the exercise of sensibility. It differed from history, to which, however, it was obviously allied, in that its approach resembled the teaching of literature. The finished work of art, not the rudiments as in the practical pursuit of music, was the object of study. Many musical persons without physical dexterity thus became students of music in a wholly serious sense. Indeed the subject, of which Percy Scholes was the persuasive advocate from 1919, when he published his little *Listener's Guide to Music*, obtained recognition in the General Certificate of Education and was seized with avidity by extra-mural departments of the universities for their extension lectures. This could hardly have happened on such a scale without the gramophone, which indeed transformed the teaching of musical history in schools, conservatoires and universities. The anthologies of musical history on records were a new instrument of learning and teaching, just as the tape recorder was a new tool in the hands of the anthropologist, the folk-lore collector and the ethnomusicologist. Nor could it have happened so quickly without broadcasting, which in addition to making the music known in performance was able to disseminate its appreciation by broadcast lessons, lectures and demonstrations. Sir Walford Davies, who had spent most of his life as a church musician, first at the Temple Church (1898-1923) and last at St. George's, Windsor (1927-1932), discovered a new career for himself and a new kind of educational work for others to develop in the illustrated wireless talk. His expositions of musical procedures were a revelation to the layman, and he recruited large new audiences by interesting them in the technical as well as the imaginative aspects of music in general and of individual masterpieces in particular. He had a genius for it, but others have found means of extending this potent form of musical enlightenment for the not particularly musical or the "ordinary listener", as he came to be hypostatized.

The laboratory work in acoustics that was involved in the development of radio and the gramophone industry provided facilities for tackling scientifically a problem hitherto treated by architects with rule of thumb, empirical observation and happy or unhappy guesswork—the sound properties of buildings. Sabine's name has already been mentioned. A good many of the Victorian concert halls had the right proportions and the right shape of roof to yield a reverberation that was neither too short and dry nor too long and resonant nor too productive of echoes. But as late as 1922 the London County Council built a circular chamber with a high domed roof in which it was quite impossible for any debate to be heard at all—it had subsequently to be conducted by internal earphones. When, however, the White Rock Pavilion was opened at Hastings in 1927 Mr. Hope Bagenal, a musical architect who had devoted himself to the study of auditoriums, had made various dispositions to secure orchestral blend, avoidance of echo and clarity of definition. His advice was also sought in connection with the building of the Royal Festival Hall which was opened in 1951. By then public taste had been conditioned to a drier acoustic than that of Victorian halls, like the Free Trade Hall in Manchester and the St. Andrew's Hall in Glasgow, by listening to radio broadcasts from studios which must of necessity have a high degree of sound absorption. Mr. Bagenal has himself amusingly described the change in aural preferences brought about by changes in architectural fashions: from the open-air Greek theatre through the lofty Gothic cathedral and the ornament-encrusted baroque palace to the Victorian hall devoted to choral singing there have been changes in the resonance preferred. The architect-acoustician can now control reflecting surfaces, reverberation periods, absorption and shape to such an extent that he guarantees something above 90 per cent of what his clients want if they will specify what they want without asking for mutually contradictory specifications. He is therefore now consulted as a matter of course in the construction of all new auditoriums; for the building of the new multi-purpose hall at Sheffield in 1932 had proved an awful warning to authorities such as those in Liverpool, who just before the war had rebuilt their Philharmonic Hall, and those at Manchester and Bristol who rebuilt theirs after bombing during the war.

A point of some social significance was the emergence of women composers who had no need of Ethel Smyth's militant feminism to win them recognition. Women singers there have always been; women pianists in the wake of Clara Schumann (notably in England Fanny Davies and Myra Hess) have made world reputations; and women violinists (Lady Hallé for instance) have played concertos; there have even been women composers who were successful song-writers (Maude Valerie White, 1855-1947, and Liza Lehmann, 1862-1918). But in 1911 at the time of the agitation for women's suffrage a Society of Women Musicians was formed in London to make the way easier for women in the musical profession. At its jubilee it was remarked that it had almost achieved its aim of making itself redundant and could crown its success with its own extinction. For at least three women, Elisabeth Lutyens (b. 1906), Elizabeth Maconchy (b. 1907), and Phyllis Tate (b. 1911), by markedly different personal styles, had established themselves, in the ranks of composers without prefix or qualification. Lutyens was one of the earliest English composers to adopt serial technique and to devote much of her energy to writing for films. She explored unconventional ensembles, both small and large: her *Quincunx* calls for twenty-six wind instruments, seven percussion players and some outsiders such as mandoline and voices. Maconchy made her mark with string quartets* and shows a disposition towards an intellectual source of inspiration rather than sensibility or emotion. If this is regarded as a masculine trait it corresponds to a robust trait in her personality which enabled her, for instance, to represent English composers in Moscow as president of the Composers' Guild. Tate's on the other hand is a more feminine talent. She began with light-fingered and light-hearted music, of which the operetta, *The Policeman's Serenade*, was a product of her student days (1932). But she developed and went on to more deeply felt works for unusual ensembles—herein resembling Lutyens—of which *Nocturne*, to words by Sidney Keyes, the aviator poet, for celesta and bass clarinet with strings, enshrines disturbing emotions of war, all the deeper because so quietly and quiveringly imagined; it is indeed a war piece with sufficient depth of focus to abide the passage of time. Her opera, *The Lodger* (1960), has real dramatic

* See pp. 336-7.

tension, with clear characterization, local colour and topical allusion.

Women had won access to symphony orchestras in the first two decades of the century—Henry Wood admitted them—but usually only as string players or harpists. Wind and percussion departments duly capitulated. Flute, oboe and clarinet were taken up by female players and produced some notable soloists. Horns, trumpets and trombones—the Salvation Army exercised some influence on the adoption of the heavier brass—found a few executants who took their places in orchestras, and a woman drummer in the Hallé Orchestra, though not the first of her sex as timpanist, accustomed the world to taking her for granted. Conducting, however, remained a male preserve, only very occasionally invaded by women.

XVI

Post-War Vocal Traditions

CHORAL

THE CHIEF tradition of music in England over the centuries has been choral. It is at once the longest and the strongest. The Tudor and Jacobean eras of English history saw the efflorescence of three schools of instrumental writing, that of the virginalists with Byrd and Bull at their head, that of the lutenists of whom John Dowland was the bright particular star both as player and composer, and that of the viol consorts among whom John Jenkins was the great name. But any hegemony in the instrumental field thus established in the seventeenth century was lost in the eighteenth, and English music was stunned by the achievements of the great Germans, not to revive till the opening years of the twentieth century. But through all fluctuations, brought about by the absence of great composers, by the dominance of foreigners like Handel and Mendelssohn, by the eclipse of instrumental music, the precarious position of opera, by puritanism, latitudinarianism and the High Church movement of the nineteenth century, by industrial revolution and agrarian depression, the practice of choral singing in church and out has been a stable feature of English musical life. The Anglican tradition, having been with surprisingly little pain evolved from the polyphonic Catholic but still English service music of Tallis and Taverner, has suffered only one break, at the Commonwealth, from the Reformation to the present day. On the other hand the position of the longer forms of choral music, the concert oratorio and the secular cantata, became critical in the first decade of the twentieth century, for the apparent promise in *The Dream of Gerontius*, that a new approach had been discovered, failed to be realized. Elgar's subsequent oratorios *The Apostles* and *The Kingdom* never attained to the universal appeal of *The Dream of Gerontius*; compared with its coherence

and unity their loose structures and less sharply focused aim con-
signed them to an equivocal place alike in critical opinion and
public affection, from which they have never emerged. Parry's
cantatas, which forsook biblical and indeed specifically religious
sources of inspiration for ethical idealism, were, as already
described in Chapter VII, "noble failures".* By the time of the
1914 war Bach had become the standby of musical festivals and
the outlook for English oratorio was obscure. New ground, however, was broken by Holst's *Hymn of Jesus*, composed in 1917 and
first produced in 1920. The text was taken from an unworked
seam of religious poetry, the apocryphal *Acts of St. John*, which
the composer had discovered during those explorations of oriental
thought that led him to Sanskrit, the opera *Savitri*, the *Rig Veda
Hymns* and to enough Greek for him to make his own version of
The Hymn of Jesus. These studies alone would have taken him
beyond the sphere of conventional oratorio and anyhow his was
one of the most radical minds that has ever operated in English
music. The only link between the mysticism of oriental Christianity and the oratorio of Protestant tradition was the ecstatic experience that he found in the *Sanctus* of the *B minor Mass*. His
daughter Imogen† even shows a tiny thematic nexus that gives the
clue to the kind of religious impulse that stirred him to the composition of this strange masterpiece—religious impulse in the
same sense as Parry's ethical idealism and Elgar's Catholicism led
them to the texts they chose for setting.

The Hymn of Jesus is, analytically regarded, a compendium of
modern devices, though its artistic aim is an electric incandescence
that is to fuse the constituent elements into a single act of worship.
The fusion is necessary because Holst was an austere composer
who preferred stark juxtapositions to bridge passages and modu-
latory transitions—*The Planets* shows many examples of this
brusque way with symphonic textures. In a good performance of
The Hymn of Jesus the joins are eliminated but they can be discovered in the score. The opening quotes "Pange lingua" on a
trumpet and the chorus begins with "Vexilla regis". Back-to-
plainsong is another instance of retroaction, like that of back-to-
folk-song and back-to-the-Elizabethans, which effected the

* R. O. Morris, *Music and Letters*, Vol. I, 1920.

† *The Music of Gustav Holst* (O.U.P., 1951), p. 62.

emancipation of English music from German tutelage and facilitated the advances into modern idiom. Modality and its new uses,
including the whole-tone scale, are cardinal elements in the style
of Holst as of Vaughan Williams and in some degree also of John
Ireland and E. J. Moeran. The chief harmonic features, however,
of *The Hymn of Jesus* are its sharp juxtaposition of tonalities,
consecutive fifths and octaves, its abrupt progressions of chords
and its chordal counterpoint. The dance rhythms in 5/4 time,
which may be compared with those in *Mars* and with the 7/4
rhythms of *The Perfect Fool*, are another radical departure, which
he did not learn from Stravinsky, from nineteenth-century
assumptions.

Holst's later choral works, the *Ode to Death* and the *Choral
Symphony*, dated respectively 1919 and 1924, have no Christian
affiliations. Holst himself was always a seeker whose search could
never be satisfied—he peered through his spectacles and wore an
expression of slightly startled surprise at what he saw. Oriental
mysticism coloured his thought for twenty years and in the oriental
wisdom he found his creed, which taught him to stick to his
appointed path and to disregard the worldly success and failure
that he encountered in following it. His later music shows increasingly the frosty exhilaration of detachment, though there was a
moment when at the first performance of his Humbert Wolfe
songs he heard Schubert in the same programme and realized
that he had paid for his austere sincerity a toll of ordinary human
warmth. In the *Ode to Death* Whitman conceives death as it
might be a marriage with the universe and he ends his "carol of
joy to thee, O death". with the invocation "Come". The exuberance of Whitman did not match Holst's moods by this time in his
life—he was forty-five—but the sentiment did. The mixture of
fire and ice was in his nature, as it is in his music, and as he grew
older both grew more intense, even if the fire lost some of its heat.
The *Ode to Death* is flame and icicle. It begins with another
instance of odd-number rhythm—7/4 time and an ostinato of
slowly swaying consecutive fifths. It proceeds to a basso ostinato
in 5/4 time over which the voices sing for the most part in a spare
block harmony. The cantata is pure Holst and in sheer sound is
far from anything written before 1914: it is a new world with but a
single inhabitant.

The *Choral Symphony* follows Vaughan Williams's *Sea Symphony* in design. Whereas Vaughan Williams made a selection from Whitman's poems, Holst went to Keats and made his selection from a poet whose work was, and is, generally regarded as recalcitrant to musical setting. He, like his friend and contemporary, set it out in the four movements of a symphony with due regard to symphonic form, i.e. there are two extended outside movements, a slow movement and a scherzo with trio. His slow movement is a setting of the "Ode on a Grecian Urn", which provided him with another occasion for his frozen ardour. The first movement, Song and Bacchanal, is an alternation of song and dance, a soprano soloist being the singer and the chorus representing the dancers—in a reiterated 7/8 ostinato. Folly's Song, which is the Trio of the Scherzo, pushes the ostinato of odd-numbered rhythms to a further pitch of elaboration: a nine-beat measure is compounded of alternate bars of 4/4 and 5/4 time, of which the 5/4 bar is organized on a regular 2 + 3 pattern, producing this:

The Scherzo is notable as an anticipation of one of Britten's favourite devices—the choral patter-song used to produce a vocal effect analogous to an instrumental scherzo. The composer, however, regarded it as sufficiently risky to allow it to be played without voices as an orchestral movement. In the finale Holst's austerity defeats his appeal to Apollo, for he writes strings of consecutive fourths for what in the ordinary language of music should be thirds. Thirds were too time-worn and too sensuous for Holst: he had put the romanticism in which he grew up behind him. But fourths are not a substitute for thirds for those who have to sing them, even if there is one of his fine swinging tunes to make up for the astringency, and the symphony, after a successful first performance at the Leeds Festival of 1925, never had another such, and only made rare appearances subsequently. Its finale scotched it.

Vaughan Williams's *Sea Symphony*, which dates from 1910, is a surprisingly successful application of symphonic form to vocal music involving the quite different principle of coherence through words. The first movement is orthodox in its first and second subjects, development and key relationships. The slow movement is in ternary form and the Scherzo is just what its name implies in both form and spirit. The finale is looser and accommodates two soloists. The unity of the work is further secured by the subject, "Behold the sea itself", as seen through the eyes of a single poet, Walt Whitman. But such a *tour de force* of construction could hardly in the nature of things be repeated, and the next choral symphony after Holst's, Britten's so designated *Spring Symphony* (1949), made no attempt to proceed farther on these lines beyond a division into four "movements". He adopted a method introduced by Arthur Bliss in *Pastoral* (1928) and *Morning Heroes* (1930), the method of the anthology on a single subject, which Britten himself had already used with brilliant success in his *Serenade* for tenor, string orchestra and horn (1943) and was to repeat in his *Nocturne* for tenor and small orchestra (1958).

Bliss conceived *Morning Heroes* as a symphony in five movements, which resemble in character and function the usual movements of a symphony, the additional movement being a prelude based on Hector's farewell to Andromache from *The Iliad*, but are not symphonically shaped internally. An orator is employed instead of vocal soloists, which alone would be enough to disrupt symphonic form. Unity of subject, war, is sufficiently strong to enable the composer to take his texts from widely different sources: from *The Iliad* he goes to Whitman, thence to Li Po, back to Whitman and *The Iliad* to conclude with contemporary poets of the First World War, Wilfred Owen* and Robert Nichols. This wide-ranging anthologizing became the chief method of producing cantata texts from 1930 onwards. Bliss had tried it on a smaller scale in *Pastoral* ("Lie strewn the white

* To whom Britten subsequently turned for the text of his *War Requiem*.

flocks"), a shorter cantata containing some good ideas, "Pan's
Sarabande" for instance, but suffering as a whole from too much
artifice and contrivance and too thick a texture. *Morning Heroes*
is similarly rich in imaginative conception and more nearly
matches the magnitude of the theme with worthy invention,
though some discrepant relationships between words, choral
writing and symphonic texture are never completely resolved. Yet
the method of the anthology as a source for cantata texts proved
its inspirational value and forthwith became a structural principle
adopted not only by Britten but by the neo-academics, who carried
on the old tradition of providing new works for the Three Choirs
Festivals, notably Dyson and Howells, to whom must be added in
this context Vaughan Williams, Gerald Finzi and John Gardner.

In *Quo Vadis?*, composed for the Hereford Festival of 1939 but
deferred by war till the Hereford Festivals of 1946 and 1949,
Dyson ransacks the poets from Wordsworth and Shelley to the
metaphysicals and hymns of the Church to present the theme of
man's earthly pilgrimage, and in the second part, which was completed ten years after the first, to find his destiny in "the white radi-
ance of eternity". His extravagance in pouring so much of the
finest poetic gold into the crucible of a musical mind predominantly extravert, that had achieved its greatest success in the
descriptive music of *The Canterbury Pilgrims*, is not beyond
reproach, since it would take an imagination of the highest
penetration, a very rich invention and something more ardent
than Dyson's detached contemplation to do such poetry justice.
But his aim is actually more modest: it is to contemplate with a
steady gaze the vision of the poets and by means of an impeccable
craftsmanship to make the vision his own. Oratorio's purpose is
and always has been edification through music, just as its contemporary, opera, is and always has been drama through music.
Quo Vadis?, therefore, was well suited to the occasion of its composition; it maintained Parry's tradition of inspiring choral
writing and also continued Parry's exploration of ethical idealism
as a field for musical expression. It inevitably falls short of the
splendour of its theme and could never follow *The Canterbury
Pilgrims* round the world. For this secular cantata, which is a set
of portraits chosen from Chaucer's Prologue to *The Canterbury
Tales*, matches in its music the poet's blithe freshness, his observation

of character and his humour, and here and there shows a touch of imaginative genius, notably at the end where the file of pilgrims sets forth from the Tabard Inn and the Knight begins his tale to this timeless, diatonic and utterly English strain:

which fades away as the cavalcade passes beyond earshot. The musical form is that of the suite, not the anthology.

Howells's *Hymnus Paradisi*, also a Three Choirs work (1950), is an anthology structure with the central idea of light, heavenly light, the *lux perpetua* of the Office for the Dead, as its subject. The texts are a conflation from several liturgies and a strong personal impulse that had been banking up behind it for years brought the composer, whose reputation was founded on exquisite miniatures, out into the sphere of big music. The contrapuntal texture is of a highly individual character. On paper it looks unnecessarily convoluted and it is difficult to sing in tune. It might be called impressionist counterpoint in that the part-writing has not the firm outlines, the cogent logic and the clearly determined progressions which are the usual features of a contrapuntal style, but instead fluid themes, half-hearted imitations and quasi-extemporizations for melodic lines. The effect of adding line upon line, however, is similar to that obtained by the flicks and dabs of Debussy's impressionist harmony: the outlines emerge, but suffused with light instead of sharp quasi-fugal edges. *Hymnus Paradisi* dissolves in a blaze of incandescence obtained by counterpoint that at first acquaintance seems too intricate and too full of redundant notes. The same style was used in *Missa Sabrinensis* and in *An English Mass*, which are non-liturgical settings of the text of the Roman Mass modified.

The method of the anthology was employed by Vaughan Williams only in his last choral work *Hodie*, first performed at the Worcester Festival of 1954. This is Vaughan Williams's Christmas Oratorio, set out for large orchestra including piano and organ,

and three soloists and chorus. It goes about the business of cele-
brating Christmas in the opposite way to that of his *Fantasia on
Christmas Carols* of 1912: it is not a continuous texture but a
series of set numbers, it contains no carols, but instead Narrative,
Song, Chorale, Pastoral, Lullaby, Hymn, March and Epilogue (so
specified), the Narrative being the ordinary recitative of the Gospel
story taken mostly from St. Luke and sung by boys' voices in
unison to organ accompaniment. The music is direct and decep-
tively simple until the Epilogue, where the significance of what has
preceded it is made explicit: a change is made from the synoptic to
the apocalyptic Gospel, the texture becomes more brilliant with
fanfares in triplets and a sweeping phrase symbolizing the Godhead, similar to those used for the same purpose in *Sancta Civitas*
and *Job* (see Example 26, p. 304); the culmination is a diatonic
setting of Milton's "Ring out ye crystal spheres". The composer
was over eighty when he wrote it and it is therefore the final
expression of a line of thought, of a specifically English feeling,
which had been manifested in his editorial work on *The English
Hymnal*, in the *Five Mystical Songs* and in the fifth symphony
rather than in the *Mass in G minor* and *Flos Campi*.

These last named are the two chief sacred works of Vaughan
Williams's middle period; the three shortish works, all to sacred
texts, composed for the Leith Hill Festival of 1930 (including
Psalm 100 and *Benedicite*), though frequently sung and well suited
for use as occasional music, are less substantial. The *Mass in G
minor* was composed for liturgical use under the prompting of Sir
Richard Terry, who had revived the masses of Byrd and the
motets of the English polyphonic school at Westminster
Cathedral. It was provided with English words for use in the
English rite. It shows to perfection how modal counterpoint can
be revived and enriched with the experience of three centuries of
harmony by key. Thus in the *Kyrie*, "Kyrie eleison" bearing the
signature of two flats is followed by "Christe eleison" with a
signature of one flat and a reversion to an ostensible G minor for
the second "Kyrie eleison", thus observing the well-tried modulation from tonic to dominant for a middle section, but actually
the passages are respectively in the Dorian mode on G and the
Dorian mode on D. The first "Kyrie eleison" is a short fugal
exposition with subject and answer a fifth apart; in "Christe

eleison", which is assigned to a solo quartet and so produces an effect of registration (in the organist's sense) of the voices, the counterpoint is imitational but not fugal and is brightened harmonically by sharpened thirds and sevenths and false relations (another feature of Byrd's style which persists in English music through the centuries). The limitations of modality, fugue and classical tonality are thus not observed rigidly but have a fertilizing effect on music that is at once new, modern, and grounded in tradition. The Mass is set out for singing *a cappella* by two choirs and a solo quartet and continually exhibits such features of neo-modality.

In *Flos Campi*, which is a suite for viola solo and small orchestra, founded on texts from the Song of Solomon and bearing superscriptions from the Vulgate, the chorus is wordless. It is a meditation on the sensuality of oriental imagery, and has therefore nothing in common with oratorio and is not primarily a choral work. It proceeds from a keyless, rhythmless arabesque in two-part dissonant counterpoint to a diatonic, rhythmic theme

Ex 25 Moderato tranquillo

semplice

which lends itself to contrapuntal imitation and canon in eight vocal parts. In idiom it is pure Vaughan Williams but it is like nothing else in his output—only in the *Serenade to Music* and the eighth symphony is there so marked an emphasis on the sensuous beauties of sound—and it has no counterpart in the works of any other composer.

Sancta Civitas is the only choral work by Vaughan Williams which bears the official designation oratorio. Its text is taken from the Book of Revelation and it is, therefore, an oratorio worlds away from the Old Testament history which had suffocated nineteenth-century English oratorio. The images here are symbols, not pure images as in *Flos Campi*, but the symbols do not call for elucidation by the composer. It is enough that the white horse of the Apocalypse can be set forth in one of those strong diatonic harmonies of consecutive triads and march forward in characteristic paeans, enough for the Angel to stand in the sun upon a great double pedal, and for the precious stones to glitter in dissonant harmony. The image of the vision of Godhead occurs in the form of a descending arc of melody. Its appearances are spread out over the years so that it is as constant as the concept itself and almost as precise as language. Here they are:

In the Mass (*a*) the theme is rudimentary, a mere hint of the invisible made manifest. In *Sancta Civitas* (*b*) the theme is the absence of a temple in the Holy City "for the Lord God Almighty is the temple of it". In *Job* (*c*) the Sons of the Morning dance their pavane before the throne of God, whose majesty is portrayed in this huge curve of falling and rising melody. In *Hodie* (*d*) it is the Incarnation, the vision made manifest in flesh. The value of isolating these images is perhaps more appropriate to aesthetics than to history, yet every facet of Vaughan Williams's art, which dominated a half century of English music, is important.

The most important English oratorio of the post-war period is derived from none of the new sources of verbal inspiration: *Belshazzar's Feast* by William Walton goes back to the Old Testament, but with a difference. Sir Osbert Sitwell had a hand in abridging and dramatizing the narrative of the fall of Babylon from the Book of Daniel and combining it with parts of Psalms 137 and 81, and Walton calls the work a cantata not an oratorio, since it is not in any way edifying. Its principal emotion is hate—fanatical Jewish hatred of its enemy. The music has a ferocity which unfits it for a cathedral and its sheer striking power was something new in English music when it was produced at the Leeds Festival of 1931. It was still in 1958 too strong meat for the Viennese who complained that it was noisy. It is. Its very large orchestra with extra percussion is amplified by two brass bands of trumpets and trombones set apart in the manner of Berlioz's *Requiem*. In the overture *Portsmouth Point* Walton had shown his distinctive way of writing short themes which are like an electrical discharge and change their intervals but not their shape in a state of continuous instrumental disturbance. This ordered turbulence is characteristic of the whole score of *Belshazzar's Feast*, which includes in its middle section a priestly march in honour of the Babylonian deities, scored as for a frontal assault. The intensity of the choral writing is to match, but, perhaps because he was once a choir-boy, Walton knew how far dissonance can be placed on voices without turning the texture to mud—voices cannot sing what instruments will play without disintegration of either intonation or musical effect. Two passages from the beginning show how bitterness can be conveyed in acrid modern harmony and what intensity of suffering is still expressible in the diatonic use of the minor mode as it might be by Brahms:

Between the ironical hymn of praise to heathen deities and the fanatical chorus of genuine thanksgiving there is a piece of declamatory narrative by the baritone soloist describing the writing on the wall with blood-curdling interjections of percussion ending in a choral shout on the word "slain". This bold and simple device matches in ferocity the elaborations of chorus and orchestra. It took some time before English choral societies below the level of Leeds and Huddersfield dared tackle this formidable masterpiece, but they came to it after twenty years and survived its hazards.

Belshazzar's Feast was the acknowledged model for Peter Racine Fricker's *A Vision of Judgment*, composed for the Leeds Festival of 1958, but the apocalyptic work was less original than its predecessor and did not establish its claim to stand alongside it nor to make a similar reputation for its composer, although Fricker had more behind him than Walton had when he wrote *Belshazzar's Feast*.

Tippett's *A Child of Our Time* was an oratorio composed *ad hoc* during the war under the stress of feeling at the abomination that had engulfed Europe. The composer called it an oratorio, wrote his own text, availed himself of the ready-made form of *The Messiah*, and employed Negro spirituals in the same way as Bach had used chorales. It made a great impression at the time, but like other works of art in which emotion has not been "distanced" as the psychologist, or "recollected in tranquillity" as the poet, refers to the same essential ingredient in artistic creation, its fire burnt itself out: it was of its time and, though the theme is indeed universal, not permanent in its appeal since the subject was more emotional than the music it evoked.

Britten's only oratorio in this period before his great *War Requiem* of 1962 was *St. Nicholas*, which was composed for the centenary of Lancing College in 1948, when other schools of the Woodard Foundation took part in the first performance. These facts together with the entertaining character of the libretto influenced its structure and imposed some restraint upon the composer in the matter of difficulty. Only the tenor solo part representing the saint of the legend "is no amateur matter". *St. Nicholas* contains much characteristic Britten and like some other occasional works transcends the occasion, which was a happy one. Its cheerfulness is not inconsistent with the element of edification which St. Philip Neri demanded of the form, for its two congregational hymns, a feature which Britten also used to powerful effect in his morality, *Noye's Fludd* (1958), confirm its essentially religious character. His *Spring Symphony* (1949), though not religious in the same sense, is animated by the same deliberate spirit of propagating happiness in a world gone wrong and at a time when *Angst* seemed to be the inspiration of much of the art of the post-war decade. In it he again uses boys' voices, which he likes with a raw edge rather than a cathedral hoot, and again reverts to the method of the anthology for his text.

It might have been expected that secular cantatas, whether cheerful or reflective, would have been forthcoming from composers as public-spirited acts to provide alternatives to requiems and counterblasts to solemnity. But the extravert line started by Parry in his *Pied Piper* never found many adherents. Franz Reizenstein followed Britten's example in his *Voices of Night* (1952) in setting an anthology cheerfully and skilfully: though a pupil of Hindemith and writing with similar ideals and methods he caught the English feeling of the open air and the spirit of the poems. But the choral ballad seems to be out of favour since Coleridge Taylor's *Hiawatha*. James Joyce's *Ulysses* prompted Matyas Seiber, a greatly gifted Hungarian who settled in England, to make a cantata with tenor solo which struck a new line, in that the prose presented him with overtones of assonances and rhythms to launch into music, fruitful imagery for translation into music, and some metaphysical ideas which suggested forms and contrapuntal devices including some use of twelve-note technique.

Compared then with the greatly increased interest in symphonic music, alike on the part of the public and of composers, the choral tradition has flagged and not found new sources of inspiration. But it is far from dead, hardly even sick, resting perhaps till the century decides in what direction modern music will decisively move and whether there will be any place for singing in it. Indeed the consecration of the new cathedral at Coventry in May 1962, which commissioned from Bliss his *The Beatitudes* and from Britten his *War Requiem*, served to turn the elder composer's attention to the form of the conventional oratorio, which he had hitherto neglected, and to elicit from the younger a new form of oratorio, which not only challenged English choral societies, as no work since *Belshazzar's Feast* had done, but was taken to Italy and sung elsewhere in Europe and America. The *War Requiem* caught "the pity of war", of which the poet Wilfred Owen speaks in the poems which Britten conflated with the Mass for the Dead to give him his text. To fill its grand design he employed three soloists, two choirs (one of boys) and two orchestras (one a chamber orchestra) together with organ. It was recognized as a major masterpiece such as the wars of this century had not hitherto produced. In that respect it belongs to the period surveyed in this book, though chronologically it falls outside its limits.

SONG

Besides the big stream of choral music another vocal tradition has been persistent in English musical life, that of the solo song, which has run steadily from Byrd and Dowland on through Purcell, Arne, Bishop and Parry to Ireland and his quondam pupil Britten, with many an individual contribution such as Hatton's "To Anthea" and Malcolm Davidson's "Christmas Eve at Sea" slipping into it through the centuries. Such songs have been mostly sung by amateurs, as Schubert's were at the time of their composition and still may be, though the song recital has followed the German *Liederabend* into music's public life. The pattern of amateur music-making, however, has suffered a considerable change under the influence of radio and gramophone, as already described and still to be observed in other contexts. Much bad performance of bad music, such as the royalty ballads of Victorian and Edwardian times, has disappeared, and the tribute which is levied on virtue by vice is now paid by the rubbish on broadcast and televised light programmes. But there has been some decline in the cultivation of the song (art-song, so as to make no mistake), as of the salon piece for piano solo and to some small extent of domestic chamber music, for which the rather self-conscious cult of the recorder is an inadequate recompense.* Historians do not normally assign much importance to salon music on the ground that its influence on composition is negligible, Chopin always excepted, but it has its place in the total musical life of the community and a change so far-reaching as that wrought by wireless broadcasting cannot be ignored in any field.

* See also p. 340.

John Ireland's "Sea Fever" was published in 1915 and it achieved success alike with the cognoscenti and the amateurs. It was a skilful and sensitive setting of a modern poem by a young poet named John Masefield; it observed the just note and accent preached by Parry and Stanford against Victorian repetitions; it had a curious modern, which is to say un-Mendelssohnian, non-Brahmsian, harmonic tang, the first fruits of Stanford's interest in the church modes and the recognition of them in English folk-song. It was heard on London platforms and appeared in competition festival syllabuses; it lifted the royalty ballad singer to higher things. It and a few of Ireland's other songs were pre-radio phenomena and they added his name to the honourable tradition of English song. Ireland set Housman, as every composer of the time did, and he set Hardy; he also set odd lyrics by a catholic cross-section of English poets. His harmony was more complex and chromatic than that of his contemporary, Ivor Gurney, a natural song-writer with a gift also for poetic composition, who was destroyed, though not killed, by the 1914 war. Gurney's songs published in 1938—he died in 1937— are not contemporary in idiom: they are diatonic, limpid, rarely touched by modal influence, backward- rather than forward-looking, individually exquisite, but hardly significant historically.

Of the same generation but having an affinity with the poets who were his contemporaries, Cecil Armstrong Gibbs (1889-1960) enriched the tradition with a few gems and a large number of admirable songs, in which just declamation informs the melodic line and the harmony creates atmosphere on the instant. His most notable success was in matching the thistledown fantasy of poems by Walter de la Mare, notably in "Silver", the very image of nocturnal immobility, and in "Five Eyes", deliciously comic in its deft patter. Gibbs had harmonic facility in the use of enharmonic, side-slipping and juxtaposed key changes. The facility was perhaps his undoing in his more extended works for orchestra, chorus and the stage, but in his songs the touch was very happy.

Peter Warlock also wrote exquisite songs, as already related in Chapter XIII. One or two Christmas carols have kept his name alive outside musical circles. Although the melodic appeal of the tunes which Warlock found for familiar Shakespearean lyrics is direct, his songs tend to be, like Ireland's, more recondite settings of English words, a field for the connoisseur, amateur as well as professional, to explore. They belong to the tradition, however. Among them are a few for voice with accompaniment other than piano; thus *The Curlew* is a sequence of four poems by Yeats set for tenor with flute, cor anglais and string quartet. The string quartet, contrary to expectation, hardly ever makes a good accompaniment for the solo voice. Vaughan Williams in *On Wenlock Edge* had added a piano to the quartet; Warlock adds two wind instruments by which to convey the wan atmosphere of the poems. But when Britten came to undertake song sequences with enlarged resources he used the string orchestra as base. This gives a better buoyancy to the voice.

Britten's first sequence was *Les Illuminations*, a setting for high voice and string orchestra of prose poems by Rimbaud, in which the words touched off a stream of felicitous musical imagery. This was followed four years later (1943) by *Serenade*, a sequence of six songs by various English poets about night—the anthology principle again—with string orchestra and obbligato horn, which has a prologue and epilogue of its own. This is a frank master-piece, of irresistible appeal. Not quite so much can be said of a perhaps subtler, certainly more searching *Nocturne* (1958), which consists of eight poems dealing with the manifold spiritual events of night severally delineated by obbligati of the wind, drums and harp of a chamber orchestra. These songs are even less detachable and the whole is something more than a sequence; it is almost a symphonic poem for voice.

Britten tends to produce his songs in sets, and few are easily detachable for separate performance, except his folk-song settings. With piano are *Seven Sonnets of Michelangelo* (1940), *The Holy Sonnets of John Donne* (1945), *A Charm of Lullabies* (1947), and *Winter Words*, a Hardy sequence (1953). In all these the words— at one time it almost seemed as though Britten chose difficult or intractable texts in a spirit of bravado—kindle a vocal line that fits them, though it is sometimes angular, sometimes melismatic, so that a singer's articulation will wring the full meaning from every consonant. Beneath, the accompaniment is usually based on figuration—in the coining of simple-sounding but highly organized figures Britten's imagination is inexhaustible. From the piano the composer evokes the atmosphere as well as the images of the poems. "Midnight on the Great Western" in the Hardy cycle is a striking instance, since the feeling of night and the rumble of wheels are almost palpable—the essence of it is a high appoggiatura of a pair of consecutive fifths in Scotch-snap rhythms with a quaver-motion bass for the railway. It may be that it is the operatic composer in him that prefers the longer sweep of the song-sequence to the individual song, such as miniaturists like John Ireland or Gerald Finzi achieve, and his mastery of instrumental characteristics enabled him to use the chamber orchestra with uncanny subtlety, while his own incomparable piano playing, which has been demonstrated all round the world in his recitals with Peter Pears, the tenor singer, produces from those deceptive figurations a world of imaginative suggestion.

Finzi's songs were mentioned in Chapter XIII. He liked to publish them in groups and to have them sung in their sequences, though unlike Britten's they are detachable and the groups have no organic unity. However, in *Dies Natalis*, which is possibly his finest single achievement in the medium of song, the sequence does approximate in form to a solo cantata—it has a prelude for string orchestra and the texts are all by Thomas Traherne, thus conforming to a modern tendency of English song composers to extend its dimensions and enlarge its accompaniment.

Britten's tendency to extend the trajectory and the substance—hence also the length—of the song found a further form besides the sequence. It is of course dangerous to overstrain the song, which by nature is short and concentrated and immediate in impact. But the partnership of voice and piano is so close, the collaboration so intimate and cogent, that attempts to use it for longer flights, for expressions of feeling that are other than lyrical, are tempting. Britten and Tippett both essayed something that would have been called a solo cantata in the eighteenth century but which they now designate canticle, a misnomer in so far as it is a diminutive used to denote what is in essence an enlargement of a song. Tippett was the first to explore the possibilities in *Boyhood's End* (1943), in which he does on an appropriate scale what Monteverdi first foreshadowed in his use of recitative turning into arioso and what Wagner did with his *unendliche Melodie*, which expanded and contracted, under the guidance of the words, between bare recitative, arioso and full song. The piano writing is often exuberant and the voice has passages of florid melisma in his setting of a selection from W. H. Hudson's autobiography, *Far Away and Long Ago*. *The Heart's Assurance*, which came later (1951), is in form not a canticle but a song-sequence (to words by Alun Lewis and Sidney Keyes); but its method is the same for both voice and piano and it reveals that its ancestry is neither Italian nor German but English—in Henry Purcell. Britten's first canticle to words by Francis Quarles (1947) is also elegiac. In the second, *Abraham and Isaac* (1952), he uses a different kind of text which is nearer to drama—it comes from the Chester cycle of Miracle Plays, from which he was later to take *Noye's Fludd*—for the new form, which he further enlarged to accommodate two singers, contralto and tenor—it was written with Kathleen Ferrier and Peter Pears in mind. In his third canticle, *Still Falls the Rain*, he adds a horn obbligato for linking the stanzas of Edith Sitwell's poem about the war from the air. That the form has possibilities has been demonstrated; that it has difficulties of coherence and unity is obvious. It remains to be seen whether it will attract other composers equally skilful in avoiding its snags and exploiting its potentialities.

XVII

Operatic Changes

A DIFFERENCE in the attitude of the public towards opera and an
increased audience for it after the Second World War have already
been mentioned as constituting one of the major changes in
English musical life precipitated by the upheaval of war. No voice
was to be heard in the fifties, as it was in the thirties, proclaiming
the "incompatible magnitudes" of music-drama, or that opera is
an "astonishing and phenomenal enormity". Sir Walford Davies,*
Master of the King's Musick, and so the spokesman of the profession, had the freedom of the microphone from which to
proclaim far and wide the aesthetic fallacies on which his ignorance
of opera was based, and his voice was eloquent. (Indeed the debt
owed to him by the art of music is still enormous even after his
operatic heresies are taken into account.) Nor was he alone
in holding that the mixture in opera of two good things results in
one bad one. Ignorance, especially in the provinces, which had
even less opportunity than the capital for striking up an acquaintance with the unfamiliar art-form, was deepened by the confused
aesthetic which still causes aberrations of taste and policy.
Roughly, very roughly, speaking, one can say that whereas the
Italians invented music-drama and then abandoned it in favour
of the sheer singing which is its chief, but not only, ingredient, the
French and the Germans in their different ways made all the
constituents into a *Gesamtkunstwerk*, a true drama in and through
music. English taste, especially among connoisseurs of opera, has
always leaned towards Italy—for years London's opera was called
the Royal Italian Opera—but the discovery of Wagner in the
eighties of the last century gradually eliminated the weaker Italian
operas from the repertory, except when an exceptional exponent
of the coloratura style called for a revival. The cult of Wagner

* *The Pursuit of Music* (Nelson, 1935).

recalled the dramatic ideals and potentialities of opera, so that Mozart and later Verdi began to be treated as something more than singers' stalking grounds. Without a regular and national opera to cover all the repertory in all the national styles, no regular and balanced appreciation of styles was formed, and many musical people were affronted by the "absurdities" of opera. Walford Davies's own upbringing, an inherited puritanism, and his own preoccupation with choral, church and chamber music, made him the mouthpiece of the opposition to opera as such. It is this last peculiarity of English musical life which disappeared in 1946.

Until June 1945, then, the course of English opera seemed to be running true to the form it had developed during the second half of the nineteenth century, inextinguishable effort and no certain achievement. Operatic mortality is admittedly high everywhere, even where there is no active and influential opposition to it, and the operas of Stanford, Ethel Smyth and Boughton, to name three composers who persisted with the form and with it made some impression on English music, cannot be regarded as successes in the sense that Puccini's, Strauss's and Britten's are successes, or even as so intermittently performed an opera as Debussy's *Pelléas et Mélisande* succeeds in surviving. Yet they cannot be written off as total losses. On the contrary they helped the cause.

As already related (in Chapter VIII), Stanford added his posthumous *The Travelling Companion* (1928) to his *Shamus O'Brien* and *Much Ado about Nothing*, both of which have been revived and could be again. So, too, Ethel Smyth* had her grand tragic opera *The Wreckers* (composed in 1906) revived at Covent Garden in 1931 and at Sadler's Wells in 1939, and there is still life in *The Boatswain's Mate* (1916). Rutland Boughton achieved an enormous success in his *The Immortal Hour*, an opera of the Celtic twilight, which strangely caught the post-war mood of the nineteen-twenties but did not stand up very well to subsequent revival. His Arthurian operas, which he based on a festival at Glastonbury, were a vein worth prospecting on quasi-Wagnerian lines, but they lacked the theatrical appeal of *The Immortal Hour*, which resembles *Pelléas et Mélisande* in its elusive heroine and its aetiolated atmosphere, so well represented in its most famous number, "The Faery Song", which went right into the next world

* See p. 66.

by the simple device of putting a pentatonic melody over two
oscillating common chords of A flat and B flat.

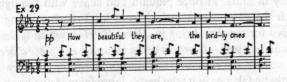

Celtic twilight was certainly popular in the post-war decade, for
Bantock produced *The Seal Woman*, founded on Hebridean folk-
melody, in 1924, Boughton his *Queen of Cornwall* in the same year,
and Vaughan Williams his word-for-word setting of Synge's
Riders to the Sea in 1927. It is a taste, however, that has palled
without certainty of recurrence, though *Riders to the Sea* remains
a small masterpiece independent of changing tastes.

Comic operas, usually with spoken dialogue, mostly serve
current theatrical needs and then fade away, or if revived seem
somewhat out of tune with the mood of later audiences. The
Playfair production of *The Beggar's Opera* in Frederick Austin's
version, which ran with some intermission for more than ten
years—it celebrated its tenth anniversary at the Lyric Theatre in
Hammersmith with its 1,685th performance—appealed to the
spirit of the twenties at the opposite pole of its preference for the
Celtic and gave some impetus to the cultivation of the form.
Other ballad operas of the eighteenth century were revived and
new ones composed, e.g. by Gerard Williams, Martin Shaw,
Alexander Brent-Smith and Alfred Reynolds, a competent man
of the theatre. The most successful of them was Thomas Dunhill's
Tantivy Towers, in which Chelsea met the Shires and a fox got
shot. Dunhill was a sober musician who edited classics for
teaching purposes, composed one beautiful song, "The Cloths of
Heaven", and wrote a book on Gilbert and Sullivan. The music
with which he clothed A. P. Herbert's libretto was tuneful, had
character and depicted representative characters except in so far
as he failed to provide jazz for his Chelsea scene—the academic
was just too strong in him to permit him that kind of unprincipled
realism. Walter Leigh, killed in the 1939-1945 war, showed a
promising talent in the field of light opera with *The Pride of the
Regiment* in 1932 and *The Jolly Roger*, which ran for six months

at the Savoy in the following year. Lennox Berkeley's *A Dinner Engagement*, twenty-one years and a whole war later, exploited absurdity in music at once piquant and suave with the lightness of touch the composer acquired from his French training. This line ended for the time being in *Albert Herring*, which is Britten's most dubious opera—*Gloriana* being regarded as a *pièce d'occasion* and in neither the romantic nor the comic tradition—because of two aesthetic falsities in it: the hero's lapse from virtue has not the sharp point of the original French *conte* from which the plot was drawn and takes three acts to mount; and, secondly, it could better, with its row of well marked characters and its village setting, have taken the form of a folk-opera in the manner of *The Bartered Bride* or *Hugh the Drover*. The wit and the humour do not mix, though there are amusing instances of both to be found in the opera.

The difficulty of getting the right sort of wit to go into music is what makes Vaughan Williams's three comedy operas insecure in performance—the quality of the music does not vary but its impact on an audience is various and unpredictable. *Hugh the Drover*, wrongly described as a ballad opera but partly justifying the designation by its quotations of folk-songs and an overall folk-melodic style of writing, is the most secure in its success, though details in the plot had to be readjusted more than once.* This is romantic comedy, say, but not comic opera. *The Poisoned Kiss* on the other hand is a romantic extravaganza in ballad-opera form and contains some ravishing separate songs; the text is both satirical and Gilbertian, yet sometimes it sounds forced, at others the whole thing comes off hilariously. *Sir John in Love* follows *The Merry Wives of Windsor* too closely and has not in consequence the speed of Verdi's *Falstaff*, so it, too, sometimes enchants and sometimes limps along. Albert Coates, Anglo-Russian by birth and education, Leipzig-trained and cosmopolitan by career as an eminent conductor, composed two English operas, *Samuel Pepys* (1929) and *Pickwick* (1936), but their Englishness did not go beyond their subject into the stuff and form of the music, which was international. Completely and unexpectedly successful in the unusual form of something between pastiche and parody was Arthur Benjamin's *Prima Donna*, composed in 1934

* Cf. above, p. 236.

but not produced till 1949. It is usually dangerous for opera to poke fun at its own conventions, as Holst did in *The Perfect Fool* (1921), but here for once wit informed the music and the composer's own amused sense of the ridiculous imparted more individuality to it than he expressed in his more ambitious operas. Yet all these never built up into a viable tradition that could have gone on from Gilbert and Sullivan in an English national style comparable to Italian *opera buffa* or German *Singspiel* and so have furnished the repertory for the English equivalent of an *Opéra comique* or a *Volksoper*.

Romantic operas also continued to be written, but their line was even more spasmodic and impermanent. George Lloyd wrote three historical operas on British subjects, of which *Iernin* (1934), written when the composer was twenty-one, promised more than its successors *The Serf* (1938) and *John Socman* (1951) actually achieved. They were all in the style of Wagnerian music-drama anglicized and so followed Boughton's lead. Tovey's *The Bride of Dionysus* to a libretto by R. C. Trevelyan, the work of a real poet, had a sort of classical nobility independent of nationality, and Bliss's *The Olympians*, which fell down in its third act, attempted to realize a brilliant idea of J. B. Priestley's about the return of the Greek gods to earth after two millennia. The third act was also the undoing of Tippett's *Midsummer Marriage*, which was more original musically than either. Its Ritual Dances survive as concert music. Benjamin's *The Tale of Two Cities* was a perfectly constructed opera but lacked the imprint of a personal idiom, which in the twentieth century, unlike the eighteenth, is demanded of a composer who is to impress himself on his contemporaries and even more on posterity. Nicholas Gatty and Lawrence Collingwood essayed Shakespearean subjects but they too lacked the intensity to raise the nineteenth-century idiom of their operas to the level of a re-creation of *The Tempest* and *Macbeth*. Alan Bush went to political ideology for his texts; his *Wat Tyler* got a performance in East Germany and his *Men of Blackmoor* (1956) was commissioned by Weimar, where it was successfully produced in 1956; its only English performance was by the amateurs of the Oxford University Opera Club in 1960. The plant thus puts forth shoots but obstinately refuses to grow. But then, too, after Strauss and Puccini the Continent has not any markedly greater fertility to show, for excluding Stravinsky's *The Rake's Progress* and Prokofiev's eight operas, no operatic composer anywhere has caused the world's telephone lines to buzz with news of a major masterpiece, though Menotti and Bernstein have brought successes of lighter weight out of America, where operatic tradition is even more tenuous than it is here.

Indeed so universal did this decline of opera appear that the opinion began to be voiced that opera was a form sick unto death and that the life of dramatic music was henceforth to be found in ballet. Diaghilev, who had put this notion about, had given it plausibility by the creations he had stimulated. He had produced from Stravinsky two major masterpieces in *Firebird* and *Petrushka* and at least two startlingly original and seminal scores in *Le sacre du printemps* and *Les noces*. The rise of a national ballet in England, fertilized by Diaghilev's magic touch, did indeed after his death elicit a remarkable series of scores of high musical value. Chief of these was Vaughan Williams's *Job*, which was furnished by Ninette de Valois with choreography unlike any other in that it was derived from Blake's engravings. In *Job* the visual, dramatic, choreographic and musical elements were fused in a *Gesamtkunstwerk*, which respected them all and achieved an imaginative unity equal to that of *Petrushka*. Bliss's chess ballet, *Checkmate*, proved that he had somewhere in him a real feeling for dramatic music, which he followed up in *Miracle in the Gorbals*. Elgar's *Nursery Suite* and Walton's *Façade* are ballet scores that possess independent musical life—indeed *Façade* is a veritable Proteus, existing in at least three forms. Lambert, Lord Berners, Malcolm Arnold and Humphrey Searle are the most prominent names in a field of composition new to the English composer, which is being cultivated in association with the Royal Ballet.

But though ballet certainly lives, equally certainly opera is not dead. Benjamin Britten (b. 1913), though a versatile composer in all forms, whose stature was recognized the world over by the time he was forty, owed his international fame primarily to his operas. Since Purcell there has been no composer for the English stage of comparable stature. Single-handed he transformed English opera.

Peter Grimes, produced within a month of the ending of the Second World War in the summer of 1945, thus marked a turning point in English operatic history. The date is symbolical of a new era; the new opera's success, the fact of its success, set up a train of operatic writing by English composers; the cause of its success was the quality and distinction of the music. Not all distinguished operas achieve immediate success, some worthy of survival certainly perish, but here the powerful dramatic quality of a well-constructed libretto conveyed in highly original music proclaimed that at last a viable opera had come out of the land without opera. It immediately went the round of all the great opera houses in the world—something that had never happened before. It encouraged Britten to write more operas instead of turning to oratorio or to symphony, of which he has only written one apiece and those, though characteristic, not important. It also fired his seniors and his juniors among English composers to try their hand at this recalcitrant medium.

Peter Grimes contains none of the familiar ingredients of successful opera, no erotic tenor, no doomed soprano heroine, no lush sentiment, no detachable arias. What are detachable are four orchestral interludes, which are structurally important in the opera as changes of scene. The tenor is the principal character but is more villain than hero; the soprano is a mother-figure. The protagonist is the community of the Borough, which is the Alde-burgh of *circa* 1830 as seen by the poet Crabbe; the second actor is the sea. The chorus is more important than the individual townsfolk who compose it, though these characters, lawyer, rector, apothecary, innkeeper, schoolmistress and retired seaman are sharply drawn. This is English *verismo* with a period flavour, not romantic opera; nor is it tragedy, and though it is concerned with a psychopath it does not, like *Wozzeck*, circle round a parcel of wastrels. It is instinct with human feeling to a degree not found in Britten's later operas. Britten's talent feeds on words, English words especially but not exclusively, and he goes far to subdue the intractability of prosaic prose to musical utterance—there are extreme instances in *The Rape of Lucretia* and *Albert Herring*. *Peter Grimes* comes to life partly from its words, which run from the colloquial to the artificial-poetic, but also from its local colour which Britten knows at first hand from living at Aldeburgh among the successors of the types he depicts, and even more from the imagery of the sea, its sight, sound and even smell. The first inter-lude depicts in twelve bars the east coast of England, and the keen air, the cry of the gulls, the surge of the shingle and the *terra firma*, in a high-lying strain for violins and flutes, an arpeggio of superimposed chords of the seventh, and the brass settling firmly on to a chord of A major.

Britten's orchestration is individual. Even so early as this opera he writes for woodwind as accompaniment to the voices. His subsequent use of a chamber ensemble in the operas composed with the limitations of the Aldeburgh Festival in mind, *The Rape of Lucretia* and *Albert Herring*, tilts the balance between wind and strings to windward, and his aversion from anything like a Wagnerian string texture cost him the success of *Gloriana*, which just failed to become airborne at the end of a splendid ensemble in the first act which cried out for the full upthrust of buoyancy that only strings can give. Sound, its quality and its texture, are no doubt part of a composer's musical thought, and Britten has a right to use what his tonal predilections determine, but he is not immune from the consequences, which are a laceration of the vocal line by the sharp edge of an oboe—or even a tap on the side-drum—another of his preferences for dry sounds. Nevertheless throughout his work for the stage, including the ballet *Prince of the Pagodas*, in which the idiom has been enlarged by conscious adaptation of the oriental orchestras of Bali, the instrumentation enhances the stuff of the music, which in turn increases the explosive power of the dramatic situation. The use of the organ and the chanting of the General Confession as the accompaniment for Ellen Orford's scene in *Peter Grimes*, with dramatic irony thrown in as the two streams of the words, in church and from Ellen's lips, cross and recross on their melodic paths, is an example on a large scale of this instrumental sense. So, too, is the similar church scene in *The Turn of the Screw*, where bells interweave their melodic pattern with associations of those deep and inarticulate emotions that emanate from a house of God, here, too, with dramatic irony. If these are gross instances there are not lacking subtleties—a celesta can sound sinister.

Britten's sense of atmosphere is not limited to the English scene, though in *Gloriana*, and the East Anglian scenes of *Peter Grimes* and *Albert Herring*, he adds a new country to operatic geography. The suffocating night in *The Rape of Lucretia*, the all-pervading restlessness of the sea in *Billy Budd*, and the air of pervasive mystery throughout *The Turn of the Screw*, envelop each opera with a single distinctive atmosphere, so that from any page of the score it is possible to identify it. *Gloriana*, written as an occasional piece—the occasion being no less than the Coronation of Queen Elizabeth II—catches in entirely modern terms the character of the times of the first Elizabeth that we know well from Shakespeare and Hakluyt, the madrigalists and the virginalists. There are specific occasions for recall in the lute songs of the Earl of Essex and the dances at Whitehall, but the strong lyrical sweetness which prevailed over the dangers, the recklessness, the intrigue of that seething cauldron of human passions and actions, is summed up succinctly by Britten in a single tune, the tune of the red rose, which may be quoted as an instance of the deceptive simplicity and the disguised complication of tunes found here, there and everywhere in Britten's output:

Ex 31

Green leaves are we, Red rose our golden Queen,

crown—èd rose a——mong the leaves so green

This is the kind of tune which the audience is taught to sing in *Let's make an Opera!*

Britten has been pretty well served by his librettists, although they have often presented him with verbal infelicities, in that they have provided serviceable dramatic frames of several different sorts. In general Britten as dramaturgist uses the interlude as an important and integral part of his music-drama. The interludes of *Peter Grimes,* depicting the seaside, the storm, Sunday morning, the obsession and conflict in Peter's mind (in passacaglia form), moonlight, and the descent of the fog, have already been mentioned as fixing the atmosphere decisively for the events of the next scene. In *The Turn of the Screw* these links, at once structural and evocative, have grown to sixteen, consisting of a Theme, which is the screw to be given fifteen turns in as many variations. The two acts are divided into eight scenes each. The theme employs the twelve notes of the chromatic scale in three groups which are used not atonally but to traverse the cycle of keys. As the libretto by Myfanwy Piper is a most skilful reconstruction of Henry James's story—it strikes only one wrong note, the materialization of the ghosts in the first scene of the second act—this opera is one of the tautest pieces of music-drama ever composed and as a piece of stagecraft is wholly successful. Its success as music depends on the degree to which it succeeds in suspending disbelief (in ghosts) in the listener. Opinions differ on this point more than they do about the success (in realizing their several intentions) of any of the other operas except *Albert Herring.*

In *The Rape of Lucretia,* the first of the chamber operas, the interludes take the form of commentaries on the action by the Male and Female Chorus (in the manner of the leader of the Chorus in Greek drama), who rather strangely view the pagan action from a Christian standpoint. In *Albert Herring,* Britten's only comic opera, if his recension of *The Beggar's Opera* and the charming children's operas *The Little Sweep* (which is the second half of *Let's make an Opera*) and *Noye's Fludd* are excluded, as they should be, from that category, interludes are also found, of which one is a fugue that amusingly depicts the hero's bewilderment at his unconscious and unwilling inebriation. In *Billy Budd* there are two interludes between the two scenes of the second and third acts, both depicting life on board ship, the first making use of a shanty and the second based on motifs already used. These interludes are structural features of an importance comparable to the formal ensembles of pre-Wagnerian operas in that they fill a space between dramatic events with extended music, which serves both of two contrary purposes, namely to relax and to sustain the interest—which is after all what the Greek chorus did long ago. There is furthermore in *Billy Budd* an instrumental passage which has a significance comparable to those passages in Greek tragedy in which the nature of our human destiny is seen through the catastrophe. It occurs at the end of the second act; it is a short passage of common chords, mostly in root position, of equal duration but diverse instrumentation which follows a soliloquy by the Captain on the mystery of good and evil. He, in upholding the social good of the law, does to death a purer good, beautiful and innocent. The stage direction reads that he enters Billy's cabin to tell him of the outcome of the clash, his doom. These chords depict what passed between the two men, and only religious terminology can describe it—atonement, reconciliation, acceptance, assent, sacrifice. It is one of those cases in which music utters the ineffable—theological terminology too often obscures what it tries to illumine, but the thing depicted is of the stuff with which theology deals. At this level the opera is pure tragedy, but the librettists, E. M. Forster and Eric Crozier, strangely shrink from so exalted an issue, perhaps because the opera would then end there. They turn from tragedy to pathos: the climax is an execution ballad, and what is fatal to its tragic character is that in the epilogue Captain Vere muses that he could have saved Billy. True, he found a vision of ultimate good for himself, but if he still felt that he might have saved the young man the conflict was still unresolved; the tragedy has lost its inevitability, even though we have been purged by pity and fear. The passage of chords remains one of the most striking pieces of dramatic music for depth or meaning and simplicity of utterance in the whole range of opera.

A Midsummer Night's Dream, which came nearly ten years later, is *tout court* a great English opera. It was first produced with chamber orchestra at the Aldeburgh Festival of 1960, but when early in the following year it was produced on the big stage of the Royal Opera House it had been rescored for full orchestra. In it

Britten successfully solved a whole tangle of operatic problems: he set the text of Shakespeare by means of a skilful abridgement and rearrangement to make an ideal libretto; he instantaneously create a spell, just as Shakespeare and Oberon do; he depicted three orders of beings, the supernaturals, the mortals and the mechanicals, and it is noteworthy that the ordinary emotions of ordinary humans are as strongly and truly conveyed as any of the abnormal emotions that are to be found up and down his operas; he produced farce, parody and even irony (as in Titania's love song to Bottom the Weaver). The actual structure of the opera is a study in itself.* The musical means employed to knit the diverse elements into a strong music-drama are as resourceful as the actual invention is pregnant and indeed simple. Such ordinary language as six conjunct notes from the scale of D moving down and up weave the fairies' spell after some string portamentos in the bass and tinkling harps in the treble have plunged the action into a fourth-dimensional wood; the key of C major is used for the sleep motif, though it is a C major arrived at by all the twelve semi-tones of the scale fashioned in four chords of varied timbre.

The motif of the lovers' predicament

permits inversions and permutations of its constituent phrases; Britten's characteristic uses of clashing semitones and consecutive fourths and such orchestral touches as his employment of recorder and percussion glint with unearthly light. Fanfares echo through the wood and the lovers resolve their imbroglio in a canonic quartet. The voices are registered: Puck uses speech; Oberon is a counter-tenor as no normal man; the fairies are boy trebles, the lovers are SATB or more accurately, soprano, mezzo, tenor and baritone; Titania is a coloratura soprano. Britten's sensitiveness

---

* One was made in *Tempo*, No. 53-54, by Professor Peter Evans, who compared the irony of the love music with Mozart's in *Cosi fan tutte*.

to words and to dramatic atmosphere finds its happiest employment here.

The other major opera to come out of post-war England was Walton's *Troilus and Cressida* (1954). Its immediate reception was mixed for the reason that it was too unambiguous. Herein was nothing to stimulate curiosity, for it was all intelligible, in the idiom Walton had fashioned for himself in *Façade*, *Belshazzar's Feast* and the overtures and concertos. Not only was it comprehensible as it came over from the stage but it was full-blooded and passionate. It was even old-fashioned in that it provided great roles for tenor and soprano in the oldest of dramatic situations, romantic love. It yielded the Italian satisfaction of vocal incandescence, the German intellectual satisfaction of music-drama and the universal appeal of one of the world's great love stories which had been converted into a firmly constructed libretto by Christopher Hassall, who took Chaucer's rather than Shakespeare's version of the tale. Moreover, it had comic relief in the role of Pandarus. It was in fact a great opera in the romantic tradition. This was thought to be untimely by those for whom the twentieth century can only be neo-classical or iconoclastic. There might be something in this view if Walton's idiom was derivative. But though his language is traditional his idiom is his own, and what he has done with it is to invest the personal tragedy of Greek and Trojan with the intensity of the deeper universal tragedy of war. In the masculine world of the Greeks it is left to the great tragic heroines, Hecuba, Cassandra and the Argive queens, to comprehend the full bitterness of war. Walton's orchestration with its sharp edges and its incisive rhythms, as well as the resignation, the ardour and the despair of Cressida's melodic lines, sound the tensions of the Trojan war as surely as they are sounded by Euripides. This deeper theme, underlying the interplay of the characters, who are clearly individualized, sweeps the opera past the inhibitions of English understatement into tragedy of true Aristotelian dimensions.

XVIII

Symphonic Music in the Twentieth Century

THERE *is* an English tradition of orchestral music. The names of Boyce, J. C. Bach, C. F. Abel, Salomon, the Philharmonic Society and Frederick Hymen Cowen (who wrote six symphonies before the end of the nineteenth century) show where the line runs. Parry and Stanford, in their efforts to rise above Victorian levels and improve the quality of English orchestral music, both wrote symphonies; Stanford and Mackenzie both wrote orchestral Rhapsodies in the current nationalist fashion. But the tradition was not as important or as vital in English musical life as the oratorio, until Elgar in the first decade of the twentieth century produced two symphonies and the violin concerto, following on the *Enigma Variations* of 1899, and so claimed for the first time for English instrumental music something like the quality and status accorded to Brahms, Dvořák and Tchaikovsky.

In this decade the London Symphony Orchestra was founded; the Promenade Concerts, inspired and conducted by Henry Wood, were at the peak of their importance as popular dispensers of orchestral music; both the Hallé and the Bournemouth orchestras were in existence and serial concerts could be heard in Glasgow, Liverpool and Leeds. But it was not till the third decade, when the influence of radio and gramophone was fully felt, that the country became orchestra-minded. The B.B.C. established its symphony orchestra in 1930 and the London Philharmonic Orchestra was founded by Sir Thomas Beecham in 1932. After the 1939-1945 war the Scottish Orchestra became a whole-time national body, and, though there were casualties, full orchestras, chamber orchestras and string orchestras had proliferated to such an extent that every region in the country had access to orchestral music, of which the consumption was enormous. A cultural revolution had been gradually accomplished in a generation, and a new eager public for music of all sorts, except chamber music, recruited.

It is not surprising, therefore, that composers turned to the writing of symphonies, concertos, symphonic suites and symphonic poems, overtures and such unclassifiable works as Elgar's *Introduction and Allegro for Strings*, Vaughan Williams's *Job*, Walton's *Façade*, Lambert's *Rio Grande*, since the opportunities of having them properly and frequently played had increased and the climate of opinion had changed from rejection to acceptance of the idea that English works were as fit for hearing alongside the classics as were those of their foreign contemporaries like Ravel, Sibelius and Prokofiev. And so the writing of symphonies as serious and as large as continental specimens began in earnest. Vaughan Williams wrote nine between 1914 and 1958, Bax wrote seven, Walton has two to his credit, Rawsthorne two,* Rubbra seven, Searle three, Malcolm Arnold five—the list is not exhaustive —and concertos have been written for piano, violin, viola, cello, oboe, clarinet, tuba and harmonica. The ballet, raised from entertainment to art, as a result of Diaghilev's invasion of 1911, and established at Sadler's Wells by 1933 and at the Royal Opera House in 1946, brought forth works either in suite form or adaptable to it for concert purposes. Such were Bliss's *Checkmate*, *Miracle in the Gorbals* and *Adam Zero*, Lambert's *Tiresias*, Malcolm Arnold's *Rinaldo and Armida* and *Homage to the Queen*, and Britten's *Prince of the Pagodas*. Denis Ap-Ivor, Richard Arnell, Arthur Oldham, John Addison and Anthony Hopkins also wrote ballet music for various companies.

A good piece of ballet music is of more value than a bad symphony. Symphonies that were not bad but showed few signs of spiritual adventure through their neo-academic technique were also written and performed and up to a point admired. Such were the first four of Rubbra's seven symphonies, William Alwyn's four, a single symphony each by Dyson, Moeran and John Gardner. Such, too, were Karl Rankl's five (Rankl, an Austrian refugee, made his home in England and was the first director of the new national opera at Covent Garden), and symphonies with an implicit war programme by Gordon Jacob and Arthur Benjamin. Two symphonies by Lennox Berkeley and three by Humphrey

* A third had its first performance at the Cheltenham Festival of 1964.

Searle, though not much more in public evidence, contain matter
of greater distinction, Berkeley's for their slightly Gallic flavour
and Searle's for their use of dodecatonic technique. But towering
over all English symphonies except Elgar's and Walton's first
(1935) are Vaughan Williams's nine, of which the violent No. 4 has
travelled farthest, though, or perhaps because, it seems to his
English admirers less characteristic of him and less English.

Vaughan Williams's first symphony was a cantata, *A Sea Symphony* written for the Leeds Festival of 1910. This is no paradox
for it is choral music in sonata form. His second turned from the
sea which surrounds Britain to London its capital—its date is
1914 though it was revised somewhat after the war. Thenceforth
his style sheds any remaining trace of Brahms and affiliations
through his master Stanford to the Continent. In the *Pastoral
Symphony* (No. 3, 1922) the method of linear counterpoint and
the modal influence of English folk-song have been absorbed to
create a highly personal but still recognizably English idiom. In
1935 came the more cosmopolitan and uncompromisingly
"modern" (i.e. dissonant) No. 4 in F minor, which bore no
ostensible programme but which to some commentators spoke
of the violence in European totalitarian politics just as clearly
as his No. 6 (1948) spoke of war. No. 8 is his only purely absolute
symphony, concerned with sonorities and orchestral scoring. All
the rest carry a programme more or less explicit, No. 7 being
specifically *Sinfonia Antarctica* and No. 9, though saying nothing
openly, betraying for the first time, when the composer was eighty-
five, something like despair. He had lived through the two most
disgraceful wars in history; he had prophesied against them in his
F minor and E minor symphonies, and now as he approached his
own end he could see nothing but atom bombs and a bedevilled
Europe. The slow movement with the sinister sound of the flügel-
horn and the familiar hobgoblins of the Scherzo speak of evil,
and though the final cadence on a soft E major chord seems to
indicate that the human spirit survives as in the deathly fugue of
No. 6 it did not, the mood is dark. Vaughan Williams nowhere
explored the subtleties of intra-subjective emotion as the great
Germans did, but the range of experience is vast—man confronting
his environment, physical in Nos. 1 and 3 and a sheer ice wall in
No. 7, social and public in No. 2, political in Nos. 4 and 6, moral

in No. 5 (for its root is in Bunyan's *Pilgrim's Progress*) and in No. 9, and musical, that of a musician exploring the world of sound in which he works, in No. 8. It may be doubted whether any symphonic composer has explored so much of life, except that Vaughan Williams preserved his reticence on the subject of romantic love.

Of English concertos it is those written for strings that have widest acceptance in that great international virtuosi have taken them up and played them in Europe and America. The piano concerto, which is the favourite form of the general public, lagged behind for the curious historical reason that the English renaissance threw up no composer to whom the piano was congenial. Parry was temperamentally averse to the element of display which is an essential ingredient. Stanford did better with his *Down among the Dead Men* Variations than with his formal concertos for piano, Elgar and Vaughan Williams were brought up to the violin and wrote uncongenially for the piano. John Ireland really broke virgin soil with his concerto in 1930 although it is in the romantic tradition both in sentiment and in technical demands. Arthur Bliss followed with one of the big bow-wow type—for Ireland's remained obstinately in the modest Englishman manner —but it was left to Alan Rawsthorne to write something distinctively his own in modern idiom and with a performer's sense of the keyboard. His first concerto (1939) contains a Chaconne remarkable for its ingenuity in transposing its bass up a semitone at each repetition and his second (1951) for its frank wit. More modest essays by Gordon Jacob and Howard Ferguson employ an accompaniment of strings only. Walton's *Sinfonia Concertante*, though scored for ordinary orchestra, with equal modesty disclaims full status. Vaughan Williams decided that his piano concerto went better with two keyboards. So that the piano hardly cuts more of a figure with the orchestra than it does as a solo instrument playing sonatas and drawing-room pieces, as far as modern English music is concerned.

With string concertos, however, it is another matter, a mere catalogue proclaims as much: Elgar, with his violin concerto introduced by Kreisler and his cello concerto, paved the way for Walton's viola concerto, introduced by Paul Hindemith in his executant days, and for the violin concerto commissioned by

Heifetz and the cello concerto by Piatigorsky—the latter flatters us by saying that the only front-rank concertos of the twentieth century for his instrument have come out of England. Rubbra and Fricker have written viola concertos, Rawsthorne, Berkeley and Britten have written violin concertos, Finzi a cello concerto. The improved status of the viola and a consequent increase in the amount of modern music written for it was a consequence of the remarkable playing of Lionel Tertis, who crowned his career as a soloist by designing an instrument that would combine the possibilities of his own huge tone, produced from a large instrument, with the agility required by players with a smaller stretch. Other instrumental virtuosi whose playing elicited concertos from composers of the present century were Leon Goossens, who obtained oboe concertos from his brother Eugene, Gordon Jacob and Vaughan Williams; and Frederick Thurston, the successor of Charles Draper, for whom Stanford wrote his clarinet concerto, and who started a similar enthusiasm for the clarinet, which, fostered by other soloists of similar calibre, Kell and de Peyer, has elicited concertos from Rawsthorne, Jacob, Alun Hoddinott, a Welshman, and Gerald Finzi (all these with string orchestra).

Peter Racine Fricker (b. 1920), who like Jacob of the previous generation thinks in instrumental terms, developed a line of concertante works (for violin, cor anglais, three pianos and drums, viola and piano), which avoided the pretensions of a symphony (of which, however, he wrote two before 1955), yet gave scope for the vigorous argument and pungent discourse, harsh counterpoint and acrid harmony, which make his music superficially sound like not very good Hindemith but which is probably an influence from Bartok exercised through Matyas Seiber, with whom he studied for a time after service in the R.A.F. In general his music is powerful and impressive but often ugly and, in the works written round 1950, full of a fashionable *Angst*. He is taking time to mellow and to find a greater lyricism.

There is thus a much more lively awareness among English composers of the last two generations of the inspirational possibilities of instruments, and a greater public appreciation of the concerto with orchestra, whether of strings only or of the normal full band, than among their predecessors. Neither inspiration nor appreciation was unknown to our Victorians, but with the multiplication of orchestras symphony and concerto occupy a new place in English musical life. In fact at the mid-century more new music was to be heard in these categories than from their contemporaries abroad. Much of it does not survive long in the crowded state of our programmes but all the individual works so far mentioned appear to have some staying power.

A different form of instrumental awareness developed partly by chance, and was favoured by the general neo-classical taste of the thirties. This concerned the small string orchestra. Here in a sense is another instance of retrospection leading to a new forward urge. The string band for which Vivaldi wrote in the eighteenth century acquired a large repertory from Italian composers. Bach, too, wrote his concertos with string accompaniments. In the nineteenth century, when the symphony orchestra was expanding and conquering by reason of its sheer variegation of tone-colour, composers would occasionally throw off a lighter work, usually in suite form, for strings only: Grieg, with the Holberg Suite, for instance, and Dvořák, Tchaikovsky and Elgar with their Serenades for strings. In the first decade of the twentieth century both Elgar and Vaughan Williams produced something for string orchestra which, without straining the medium, was music of greater moment, respectively the *Introduction and Allegro* (1905) and the *Fantasia on a Theme of Thomas Tallis* (1910). Both of these works found their way into the programmes of symphony orchestras in Europe and America. But a quarter of a century later they formed, together with Bliss's *Music for Strings* (1935) and Tippett's *Concerto for Double String Orchestra* (1939), a modern English equivalent of Handel's Concerti Grossi, also written for a concertino of strings with string orchestra, and by a lucky accident found an instrument to hand for the cultivation of their medium.

The accident was Boyd Neel, a young medical practitioner with a gift for conducting, who in 1932 had the idea of forming a small string orchestra (nineteen players became his standard size) in order to cultivate intensively what had hitherto been casual. He has related* how he came to form the orchestra which bore his name for a quarter of a century, how it developed a style of its own largely through a democratic manner of rehearsing, how

* *The Story of an Orchestra* (Vox Mundi, 1950).

his repertory grew by the unearthing of the buried treasure of the eighteenth century and how it stimulated the composition of new works for the purely string ensemble. No sooner had the public's taste for this unfamiliar fine-grained instrumental texture been confirmed by Boyd Neel's immediate and increasing success than other similar orchestras were formed. With the collaboration of wind players *ad hoc* an orchestra of Mozartian dimensions could be assembled for the performance of such works as could be designated "for chamber orchestra". The reaction against the inflated orchestra of the romantic decadence—Mahler was not much played before 1945; Scriabin, who had boomed in the early twenties, disappeared from the concert repertory; only the Strauss of the tone-poems remained popular—favoured the small orchestra, and for twenty years, even with the interruption of war, Boyd Neel's orchestra and its rivals flourished. It was used by the British Council for proclaiming the message of English music abroad; it produced from Benjamin Britten his *Variations on a Theme of Frank Bridge*, composed at short notice for the Salzburg Festival of 1937, and, as a tenth birthday present in 1943, a *Prelude and Fugue for Eighteen String Players*; it blazed a trail in the Antipodes; it made a whole library of gramophone records. It seems almost certain that it attracted the attention of other countries to the merits of the medium, for the Italians began to create highly proficient consorts of strings for the revival of their own glorious past in the history of the violin. In 1953, after twenty years as a professional conductor, with only a brief reversion to medicine during the war, Boyd Neel relinquished his orchestra for the Faculty of Music at Toronto University, but his orchestra continued in being in one transformation or another, since the corpus of string music now formed a category with which the public could not dispense.

The twelve-note method of Schoenberg's school made very little impact on composers in England, nor was there much interest outside specialist circles in the second Viennese school during the period of this survey—closer examination of it was to follow in the next decade. *Pierrot Lunaire* was fairly frequently performed, Berg's violin concerto had been performed before the 1939 war and *Wozzeck* was put on at the Royal Opera House in 1952, but no composer except Elisabeth Lutyens seemed inclined to explore this foreign and formidable territory, no matter what reports were brought back from the festivals of the International Society for Contemporary Music by the enthusiasts who attended them in search of *avant-garde* tendencies. Even after the ending of the war in 1945, when all over the world serialism exploded like a delayed-action bomb, although by then Schoenberg was in America, Berg was dead, and Webern had been killed early in the occupation of Vienna, it was some time before the new technique at last caught the attention of progressive and experimental musicians. However, Humphrey Searle emerged as a gifted composer who took it seriously and used it in all his works composed after 1946 in so far as he was prepared to take what he wanted from it and handle it in his own way. Searle (b. 1915) had an orthodox education in classics and in music, but a period of study in Vienna with Webern led him by successive stages not only to write in Webern's style for short pieces for which it is best fitted, but to embark on works of larger scale, at first with words for their skeleton but later in two symphonies* and a piano concerto. There were other influences in Searle's make-up to save him from doctrinaire or merely extreme manifestations of serialism, namely a partiality for Liszt the archromantic, about whom he wrote an excellent monograph, and an interest in ballet, which also extracted a book from him as well as the score of *Noctambules*. Weird nocturnal sounds, silence and whispers from the territory first explored by Bartok, are another element in his scores, of which *Night Music* for chamber orchestra and the *Poem for Twenty-two Strings* are also in this vein along with *Noctambules*. There may be some significance in the fact that when Searle wants to add concepts and poetic imagery to music he avoids the song and the cantata —though there is a short dialogue-opera on Gogol's *The Diary of a Madman*, in which incidentally he uses electrophonic tapes to depict the wilder hallucinations—and plunges for that most intractable of all media, the speaking voice with (or against?) music. Thus he has written three large melodramas, *Gold Coast Customs* (Edith Sitwell), *The River Run* (James Joyce), and *The Shadow of Cain* (again Sitwell), for speaker, and orchestra,

* A third followed at the Edinburgh Festival of 1960 and a fourth commissioned by the Feeney Trust for Birmingham in 1962.

with parts for male-voice chorus in the Sitwell pieces, and he had set "The Owl and the Pussy Cat" and two of T. S. Eliot's *Practical Cats* for speaker, flute, cello and guitar. So much is enough to establish that he has an ear for strange and exotic sonorities, such as study with Webern would naturally promote. But when he comes to write symphonies his orchestration is not unconventional, though in Nos. 1 and 3 there is a certain amount of additional percussion. He has, however, a partiality for brass, which he uses, conspicuously in the second symphony, to secure rhythmical propulsion by so direct a method as repeated fanfare figures. His use of serialism is therefore saved from the chief consequence of the "emancipation of the dissonance", to wit rhythmic stagnation, and in his first symphony the ordinary emotions of mystery, agitation and decision are conveyed, while in the third something like a programme* is the acknowledged starting-point and the expressive purpose of the music.

Searle's use of serialism is free in so far as he permits gravitation to a tonal centre to be felt, is not restricted by an obsession with the number twelve, and, though the textures and the counterpoint sound gritty, as the repudiation of the harmonic series in favour of an arbitrary series always does, Searle is the master of his technique and uses it now in one way, now in another of his own intuitive choice for his own ends, which are increasingly felt to be those of large-scale instrumental music, as contrasted for example with Britten's reliance on words, but at the same time linked to life's experience and not limited to experiment with musical material. He has indeed been called a romantic and a poet.

* Experiences in Italy and Greece. Thus in the slow opening movement the slabs of sound fitted in juxtaposition, rather than anything at all like development, are an aural equivalent of Mycenaean masonry.

XIX

The Domestic Revolution

THE TWENTIETH-CENTURY pattern of chamber music, of the domestic use of the piano and the cultivation of some other small forms (e.g. recorder playing) was also somewhat different from that of the nineteenth century, which largely followed German example—the German colonies in Manchester and Bradford had a considerable influence on private music-making which radiated from the North. Radio and the gramophone were again the chief instruments of change, but others were the person of Walter Wilson Cobbett and the formation of a Federation of Music Clubs.

Clubs, such as the long-established University Music Club at Oxford and the Oxford and Cambridge Musical Club in London, had been one firm pillar of support for quartet playing alongside the public concert; all the more as they preserved the intimate conditions for which Haydn and Mozart had composed the backbone of the repertory. For mutual support a National Federation of Music Societies (which was not, however, limited to chamber music) was formed in 1935. The smaller organizations outside London were assisted with expert knowledge, co-ordination of programme-making, and money. It had already become apparent that radio transmission and gramophone recordings could present chamber music with a higher degree of fidelity to the living performance than in the case of choral and orchestral music, and even had some small advantages over concert performance. So that what was lost in public attendance at chamber concerts was made up by this wider, modern form of dissemination. Concerts of chamber music grew fewer, but clubs survived and more was made public through the new mechanics.

Cobbett had started to prime the pump of composing chamber

music as far back as 1905 by instituting a series of competitions for the various kinds, duos, trios, quartets and quintets. These continued for many years and produced large entries and some fine compositions. Cobbett, who was a wealthy merchant and amateur violinist, had a passion for chamber music sustained through his long life of ninety years. His competitions produced a new form, to which the name "Phantasy" was applied as a rough modern equivalent of the Jacobean fantasia for viols, a tabloid, as Stanford described it, of elements of a complete multi-movement work compressed into a single movement, but allowing free play to the composer's fancy as to how he would do it. Cobbett's stimulus to chamber music did not end with the competitions: he commissioned works; he established prizes for performers at the conservatoires; he endowed the Worshipful Company of Musicians with money to encourage the practice of chamber music by such means as it saw fit; and in 1929 he subsidized the publication of a *Cyclopaedia of Chamber Music*.

With or without stimulants such as these most of the composers of the renaissance wrote chamber music: by the end of the First World War Elgar had produced his violin sonata, his string quartet and his piano quintet; Charles Wood, professor at Cambridge, who died in 1926, left eight string quartets beautifully fashioned in traditional style and Irish in flavour; Bax produced three quartets between 1918 and 1936, Bliss two and Vaughan Williams two separated by more than twenty years. The next generation continued to feel as their elders— that they had not really done their duty to themselves till they had written a quartet—so we find Walton with one, Britten with two, Tippett with three and Rawsthorne with two (of which the first is only a Theme and Variations). Rawsthorne also has to his credit a quartet of clarinet and lower strings, three duet sonatas, and an increasing interest in instrumental combinations. Elizabeth Maconchy had by 1950 written six string quartets, which form the core of her creative effort.

It would be difficult to make any bullet-proof generalizations about common tendencies or an English style discernible in these composers and their fellows except perhaps this: various efforts were made to loosen the architectural formula of the four-movement work based on sonata form. The one-movement phantasy has already been mentioned: Britten made his own use of it in his first chamber work written at the age of nineteen, the Phantasy quartet for oboe and violin, viola and cello. "Dialectic" was the name Alan Bush gave to his single-movement string quartet (1929) and this indicates, albeit obscurely, the form in which it is cast, which is both original and cogent. The dialectic is Socratic rather than Hegelian, for the quartet opens with a long unison passage, the definition of the subject as it were, and the sections which follow are arguments brought against it with a view to further clarification, which is achieved in a fugato. The work bears key signatures and uses recapitulation. Key signatures are discarded by Rawsthorne and Maconchy though their works are not atonal. Walton's quartet has no signature but that for the good old-fashioned reason that it is in A minor. Phyllis Tate dispenses with signatures but describes her quartet as "in F". Britten writes his first string quartet in D (with signature) but uses in his first movement a contrast, of thematic substance certainly, but much more markedly of tempi. His second quartet (in C) is distinguished by its finale, which is a Chacony, in which four groups of six variations at a time are separated by cadenzas. His first movement, like that of Rawsthorne's second quartet, employs the outlines of sonata form of the ordinary kind. Vaughan Williams in his light-weight "For Jean on her Birthday" quartet (1944) sheers right away from a sonata movement—the first is called Prelude and the last Epilogue—and gives the chief prominence to the viola instead of the violin. Tippett's solution of the problem of finding a vehicle other than sonata form for matters of moment was to adopt in his second string quartet (in F sharp) the procedures of the madrigal, i.e. imitative counterpoint and tied-over notes such as the madrigal composers used to lend rhythmic independence to the parts and to evade the metre of the bar-line. What in vocal music is a polite conversation becomes, when transferred to nimble instruments like strings, a vigorous argument. The texture, though animated, is fairly dense, and the themes are what Morley called "points", which are taken, imitated and dropped for congruent successors. A few bars from the first movement show both features—the imitation and the phrasing across the bar line. (See p. 338, Ex. 34.)

This was a notable success but hardly one to be imitated.

Rubbra is essentially a contrapuntal thinker, and his two string quartets,* which are not formally adventurous, produce a rich texture—his symphonies composed on similar principles of linear growth often sound like overgrown quartets. Rawsthorne's texture is very spare. The contrast when each composer's second quartet appeared in the same programme at the Cheltenham Festival of 1954 was enlightening, in that besides the juxtaposition of two minds alike only in a certain intellectual distinction, it called attention to the preoccupation with texture, which was part of the reaction from romanticism concerned only with expression. The interest in texture was also a powerful incentive to the composition of chamber music with wind instrument and with unusual combinations, though it was not the motive behind Howard Ferguson's octet (1933), which was designed to fill up a programme in which Schubert's octet was the main feature. The young man's ambition proved to be by no means overweening, and, judged by its untarnished freshness after twenty years of experiment and the vitality drawn from its roots in tradition, it remains one of the successes of English chamber music of the period.

The domestic piano began to be pushed out of the parlour and the drawing-room by the radio set. Changed social conventions no longer required its presence, even if unplayed, as a mark of cultural respectability. Furthermore when a piano was retained it shrank in size. No longer would second-hand grands of enormous dimensions be coaxed out of doubtful fathers by precocious sons, as described for instance by Mr. Richard Church in his

* A third was produced at the Cheltenham Festival of 1964.

autobiography *Over the Bridge.* The war changed living habits, put people into flats or small suburban houses, where minute baby grands could just be accommodated—for a few years longer it must still be a grand, though in time mini-pianos smaller than the old cottage upright were admitted. Hymn singing, song accompaniment, and the amateur's solo to oblige the company all shrank too. So that easy piano music for the pianist brought up on Mendelssohn's *Songs Without Words* and Brahms's Rhapsodies was harder to come by. Cyril Scott had written his *Lotus Land, Water Wagtail, Cherry Ripe,* modern characteristic pieces, before 1914. Percy Grainger and Roger Quilter, also members of the Frankfurt school, did the same, but the chief composers of the renaissance neglected the piano, Arnold Bax and John Ireland excepted who both wrote sonatas as well as small pieces. Piano sonatas were also written by Bliss, Lambert, Tippett, Berkeley (who writes well for the instrument and has two admirable concertos, one of them for two pianos, to his credit), Ferguson and Thea Musgrave, to name no others. Lambert's sonata represented a phase during the anti-romantic reaction after 1918 when the piano came to be regarded as an instrument of percussion and the Chopinesque ideal of a singing tone was at a discount. The toccata came back and the revived harpsichord attracted a few composers, even so unlikely a one as Delius (with his Dance of 1919 composed for Mrs. Violet Gordon Woodhouse). The revived clavichord, too, though not percussive, produced from Herbert Howells a small collection of neo-Elizabethan pieces called *Lambert's Clavichord.** They are equally well suited to the piano and the tendency towards percussive writing declined in face of the traditional if paradoxical genius of the instrument, which is obstinately for fluency.

In London concert life the piano recital predominated over every other kind of recital. Many such were official débuts of English youth and of Americans making their first assault on Europe. In the provinces piano concertos were the chief bait offered to audiences of orchestral music. But the repertory offered rarely included English piano music—none of the piano sonatas mentioned gained a place in the normal repertory and they were

* Not Constant Lambert but Herbert Lambert, the portrait photographer of Messrs. Elliott and Fry.

only spasmodically heard. But English pianists taught by English teachers began to make international reputations with Dame Myra Hess (a product of Tobias Matthay's school of pianism), and Solomon at their head. Clifford Curzon, Cyril Smith and Denis Matthews represented the next generation. British pianists also began to appear at the international competitions which sprang up all over Europe, John Ogdon's shared first prize in Russia in 1962 being the most conspicuous success ever achieved in this new kind of musical activity.

A word may be added to the tale of semi-private music, on the revival of two instruments considered obsolete, the recorder and the guitar. School music had in the main meant learning the piano, and the casualties, owing to the pressure of games and the curriculum, and to the authorities' lack of serious belief in its value, had been enormous. Consequently it took a long time for the truth to dawn that many more people were musical than could play the piano, however badly, and would like to know more about the art. The musical appreciation movement was the answer to the problem so posed.* The spread of knowledge about music thus brought about was complementary to the experience of music now available to anyone who wanted it over the radio. But still the practical side—for art means doing —was absent from the enthusiast's experience. A simple bamboo pipe, which might be home-made, was the easiest way to obtain it. From there it was a short step to a proper recorder and thence another short step to a consort of recorders in various sizes. With the example of what a skilful and artistic player like Mr. Carl Dolmetsch could do with it, the revived recorder became popular at all levels of musical society from the infant school to the fourth Brandenburg Concerto.

The guitar's vogue came a little later and at one stage, in the 1950's, coincided with a new development in folk-singing among the urban population. Andrés Segovia, the great Spanish guitarist, really began it when he came to England in 1928, reminding the English musical public that the instrument is not a banjo nor a mandoline nor merely an Iberian folk-instrument, but a relation of the lute, which along with harpsichord and recorder was in process of revival. A Philharmonic Society of Guitarists was

* See p. 291.

formed in 1929; a boy named Julian Bream less than twenty years later was astonishing the world outside the enclave of guitarists with his virtuosity; and a new if small class of compositions was being made known. The artist-guitarist, to be distinguished from the self-accompanying folk-singer, also played the lute, and so Dowland was added in full authenticity to the Elizabethan revival which had been a feature of the first two decades of the century. The popularity of the guitar as a strumming instrument, a portable companion on a hike, a fashionable accomplishment among the young, came up on one of those unaccountable waves of mass desire which produce short vogues of entertainment—this particular one was called "skiffle" and was based on the idea that the unskilled could make music. The guitar was found in practice not to be so easy that the unskilled could play it, and many instruments soon found their way into pawn-shops, but what stuck was the suitability of the guitar for accompanying folk-songs alike in sociable sing-songs and on the concert platform. The piano arrangement of folk-songs, having produced some excellent settings from Vaughan Williams, the greatest of them all, from Sharp himself, from Moeran and from Britten, slumped in esteem and common currency, and the guitar took its place. The mouth-organ was re-named harmonica to improve its status, and Vaughan Williams wrote a concerto for it and its principal exponent, Larry Adler.

Also in connection with folk-music the accordion, which had sprouted a keyboard with black and white notes like a harmonium, obtained a wide popularity. It showed a surprising capacity to provide a rhythmic lift which was valuable for folk-dancing. It was of course also cultivated as an instrument in its own right, but its coarse tone, abuse of the tremolo, and monotonous sound precluded it from serious artistic use. An international confederation was formed in London in 1951 and recognition was secured from the Federation of Competition Festivals. This was popular music finding a new channel and had some social significance. Folk-music devotees, though conceding the accordion's merits for dance accompaniment, deplored the way in which, being easier to play, it has extruded the violin from many dance teams, even in Scotland, where back in the eighteenth century the violin had ousted the still flourishing bagpipe from the dance floor.

All periods are constructions by historians, as the constellations are by astronomers, not natural phenomena. All periods of history may be called transitional, and the period 1918 to 1960 is no exception, but it had some measure of self-containment and its ethos is observably different from what went before and what came after. In composition it was notable as the *floruit* of Vaughan Williams and the emergence of Britten as a genius comparable in English history with Purcell. Elgar and Delius died in 1934, as also did Holst, who was, however, no romantic, and the date marks the end of nineteenth-century romanticism. Walton's romanticism which took its place was of a different brand. In the period the full impact of the new acoustics which made the recording and the transmission of music universal was felt, and their influence penetrated, in the various ways described in preceding pages, into every corner of our musical life. Symphonic music vied with choral music as the Englishman's main musical diet. The ballet brought a new public into the theatre, and the opera struggled into the consciousness of musicians who had previously rejected it. The musical franchise was indeed extended. This was the chief fact in the social history of music in our time; composition is an individual affair and its history is wayward. In both fields history records a consolidation of the musical life of Britain in the first part of the twentieth century amid the upheavals brought about by political, social, technological and intellectual forces.

XX

Scholarship and Criticism

HOW FAR can a deeper scholarship, a more liberal criticism and a wider appreciation of music be regarded as factors in our musical renaissance? "Factor" suggests a causal contribution towards a result, as though scholarship and criticism have helped to bring about a more vital art, whereas, as everyone knows, theory follows practice, criticism comes after creation, and knowledge *about* music is a consequence of knowledge *of* music by first-hand acquaintance.

But any form of knowledge, even discursive knowledge about music, broadens the basis of communication, and music is of its very nature a form of communication implying two parties to it, the creator and his audience. It follows that a great composer can only arise in a society that is ready for him: composers cannot write in a vacuum; they will not spin notes for themselves alone if there is no interest in music in the society in which they live—as Vaughan Williams argues in his book *National Music*. History shows that composition flourishes only in a music-loving society: Italy made opera in the seventeenth century, Austria made Mozart in the eighteenth, and England produced nobody for nearly two centuries after Purcell. The dark night of our eclipse coincided with the decay of our learning and the poverty of our taste (i.e. listeners' response). Our renaissance advanced with the revival of our learning. A renaissance of composition presupposes logically, if not chronologically, some sort of renaissance of response. A quickening of musical life in a society is only possible if listeners are in a state to respond to it. The old name for this kind of response to music was Taste. In 1831 Dr. Crotch, the only bright star that kept a pin-point of light visible in the darkness and eclipse of English music from about 1760 to about 1840, published his Oxford and Academy lectures (from which an excerpt was quoted in Chapter II) the object of which was the "improvement of taste".

Musical appreciation as now understood is a comparatively recent attempt, already described,* to carry out Dr. Crotch's ideas of improving public taste by systematic study. Its history was written by Percy Scholes in 1935,† who names as its pioneer Stewart Macpherson, whose text-book *Music and its Appreciation* came out in 1910. But Scholes also quotes a significant passage from Burney writing forty years before Crotch: "There have been many treatises published on the art of musical composition and performance but none to instruct ignorant lovers of music how to listen or to judge for themselves."

Listen or judge. There we have the connection between listening, appreciation, criticism, discrimination and taste, terms assumed by Burney and Crotch to be kinds of musical activity that can only be improved by knowledge. Anyone who listens will soon begin to discriminate, and discrimination is the beginning of criticism. Serious criticism is the application of knowledge to the business of discriminating, and the accumulation of knowledge, made by the critic to fortify himself in the exercise of his duties as a judge of music, is the beginning of scholarship. We thus reach the position that music on the receptive side involves listening, then discrimination, hence taste, thence taste fortified by knowledge which emerges as criticism, and criticism seriously pursued must result in scholarship. Did then the advances in the listening aspect of music act as a factor in bringing about our renaissance? Consider a few dates and events.

In composition I have accepted the date put forward by other historians for the renaissance as 1880, when Parry's *Prometheus Unbound* was performed at a Gloucester Festival. The preliminary ploughing of the land from which the present harvest is being gathered was done in the three revivals already discussed, folk-song, the Tudor composers and Bach, together with some more democratic movements and the academic pioneering done by Parry and Stanford. From Crotch's day till Parry's the only English music was Mendelssohn diluted, and between Burney and Crotch there was only Handel diluted. In the sphere of knowledge during the same period we have an Essay on Criticism in the

* See p. 291.   † *Music, The Child and The Masterpiece* (O.U.P.).

preface to Burney's *A General History of Music*, from which the extract just quoted was taken, published in 1776. Simultaneously Hawkins published his *A General History of the Science and Practice of Music*. These two were the first English histories and they were the last of comparable scope and quality for a century and a quarter until *The Oxford History of Music* began to appear under Hadow's editorship. As far as historical scholarship and research are concerned the nineteenth century is a blank save for Grove's *Dictionary of Music and Musicians*.* We may at least therefore draw the negative deduction that the dark period of our music coincided with the dark empty pit of our scholarship. The compilation of Grove's *Dictionary* entailed historical work and Parry himself served his apprenticeship as a historian upon the great Dictionary of 1879, which, almost contemporary with Parry's *Prometheus Unbound*, may, like it, be said to mark a revival—the renaissance of English musical scholarship.

Mention has already been made of the movement forty years before in the field of old music with the establishment of the Musical Antiquarian Society for the publication of the Elizabethans and Purcell, and of still another movement in the same direction for the study of an even more recondite subject in the foundation in 1888 of the Plainsong and Mediaeval Music Society.† Both societies were from the nature of their objects faced with the technical problems of textual criticism involved in editing ancient documents for modern publication. The work of Fellowes, Terry and their colleagues has been described at length in Chapter V.

After the great outburst of publishing the Tudor music by Fellowes, his contemporaries and collaborators there was a pause, during which the term "musicology" came into use to indicate the kind of scholarship which is required for editing old music, and the subject (which of course includes a wider range of studies in the art and science of music) began to find a place in the new degree courses at the universities. With the establishment of an honours degree in music (B.A. as distinguished from the degrees

---

* Perhaps the work of W. S. Rockstro (1823-1895), though soon superseded, ought not to be totally excluded, since it ranged from the music of antiquity to another *A General History of Music* (Sampson Low, 1886).

† See pp. 89-91 and 101.

of Bachelor and Doctor of Music which are almost wholly concerned with the techniques of composition) at Oxford and Cambridge, and the establishment of full chairs at provincial universities, it became possible to train musicians for work which had hitherto been left to amateurs. After 1946 and the establishment of the B.B.C.'s Third Programme there was not only an impetus towards a more thorough study of musical history but also a practical outlet for such knowledge. The (Royal) Musical Association had from 1874 provided a medium for the dissemination of musical *Wissenschaft*. To it came a proposal in 1948 from Professor Anthony Lewis that a scheme of systematic publication should be undertaken of old English music ("old" was roughly defined as music composed before 1800 with possible extension to non-copyright music published after that date), something in fact on the lines of the German *Denkmäler der Tonkunst*. The formidable problem of finance was unexpectedly and fortunately resolved by a grant from the Arts Council out of its special allocation for the Festival of Britain of 1951, which it was at that very moment engaged in organizing.

The project, *Musica Britannica* was soon launched. The first three volumes represented three different centuries, the *Mulliner Book* edited by Denis Stevens from the sixteenth, *Cupid and Death* edited by Edward Dent from the seventeenth, and Arne's *Comus* edited by Julian Herbage from the eighteenth. The editorial committee nominated by the Royal Musical Association included Dr. Fellowes, Professor Dent and Mr. Thurston Dart from Cambridge, and Professor Westrup from Oxford, the general editor being Professor Lewis of Birmingham University. The policy of publication necessarily remained flexible since competent editors with specialist knowledge were needed, but editorial method was determined to combine the functions of both library and performing editions, since it has been a characteristic of English musicology through its brief life to aim at practical revival as well as study. Its largest piece of work during its first fifteen years of steady publication was the issue of the *Eton Choirbook* edited by Dr. Frank Harrison, the antiphonary of the mid-sixteenth century containing polyphonic antiphons by twenty-five composers going back to the time of Henry IV.

The work of the (Royal) Musical Association kept alive interest in scholarship, which was neglected by the universities until 1945, though the initiative for its formation came from John Stainer, then fresh from Oxford, and its first president was Ouseley, then Professor at Oxford. The Association's intended function was to be similar to that of other learned societies, which meant that it was to publish its proceedings, as it still does.* Its importance was that it revealed the immense range of studies that are comprised in what in the last thirty years or so has been called musicology—not only history, which is its chief single subject, but acoustical science (now tending to be transferred to natural science), instruments, exotic music and ethnomusicology, and also critical appreciations both textual and aesthetic, education, psychology and biography. The full deductions from this ample range of studies are now beginning to be drawn, as was recorded in Chapter XV as a post-war phenomenon, at the universities, by the B.B.C. and by foreign students. Music, it is now clear, is fitted to be ranked as one of the humaner letters and suitable for a general university education. By 1880 then musicology had begun to play its part in musical enlightenment concurrently with taste and composition.

The part played by criticism is less easily assessed, but it, too, fits the pattern of the two-wave theory. For organized criticism, as distinguished from sporadic critical studies such as may be written at any time by any *littérateur*—such as Stendhal, for example—is part of journalism, and newspaper criticism, as distinguished from essays such as Addison contributed to *The Spectator* in Handel's time, did not begin till the 1840s or thereabouts. *The Morning Post* has the credit for beginning the regular reporting of concerts, but *The Times* was the first paper to appoint a professionally competent music critic. This was J. W. Davison (1813-1885), who reigned from 1846 to 1879. All through his life Davison was engaged with work for the musical press which hitherto had provided the sole vehicle for regular musical criticism. It is worth noting in passing that *The Musical Times* began publication in 1844 and that its files now constitute the best quick guide to his source material for a historian of English musical life. Davison's paper was *The Musical World* (1836-1891). His opposite number was H. F. Chorley, who wrote for the weekly *Athenaeum* (1833-1868). Both were conservatives: Chorley, who was ten years

* See Chapter XV.

senior, could not abide the violence of the young Verdi, and Davison was hostile to Schumann and Wagner. He, too, was anti-Verdi—"If Verdi continues writing successfully there will not be a voice in all Italy in ten years"—but admired Berlioz with reservations. Chorley was a connoisseur of singing and to him the doings of the Italian opera are the important things in the year. His articles do indeed reflect the feeble state of English taste and English music in mid-Victorian times, though within his limitations he was a knowledgeable and a readable critic.* Davison was more broad-minded and was willing to encourage native music, e.g. Sterndale Bennett. *The History of The Times* praises him for two things—his good reporting and his gift of exegesis. He wrote columns from the first Bayreuth Festival, in which any prejudice he may have had against Wagner is not allowed to intrude upon his mingled exposition and criticism. *The History of The Times* sums him up by saying "On the whole he began a tendency in the paper's music criticism noticeable ever since, to swim against the tide of popular favour."

Davison was succeeded on *The Times* by a German, Francis Hueffer, who held office from 1879 to 1889, and it fell to him to notice Parry's *Prometheus Unbound*. Hueffer, unlike Davison, was a convinced Wagnerian. He was a well-educated man, and as his notice of *Prometheus* shows (see Chapter VII) a very good critic.† How good may be gauged by comparing his notice with the one that appeared in *The Musical Times*, which is probably from the pen of Joseph Bennett (1831-1911) of *The Daily Telegraph* and which is pilloried by Hadow in his essay on criticism, along with Chorley for his obtuseness about *Tannhäuser*. *The Musical Times* notice of *Prometheus Unbound* is printed in full in the Appendix, *The Times* notice in Chapter VII, which deals with Parry.

Hadow's essay which he prefixed to his *Studies in Modern Music* (Vol. 1, 1892) contains this passage, in the context of misjudging Wagner:

"Time went on, but experience does not seem to have brought

---

* Sufficiently so for his *Thirty Years' Musical Recollections* to be republished in 1926, with an Introduction by Ernest Newman.

† His successor, J. A. Fuller-Maitland (1889-1911), said that he cleaned up the profession a good deal. The professional etiquette as well as the English prose of the London music critics, it seems, had become loose.

wisdom, It is a matter of recent memory that our critics found *Lohengrin* 'dull' and *Walküre* 'monotonous', that they could see no beauty in *Siegfried*, and no melody in *Tristan*. Brahms gained a hearing in this country through the generosity of a brother composer [Stanford]. The critics attacked him from the beginning and we have at the present day professional directors of public taste who are not ashamed to assail the *Deutsches Requiem* with infelicitous gibes. Even our own greatest musician had to pay the penalty for daring to be original. The account of *Prometheus* in *The Musical Times* of October 1880, and the account of *Judith* in *The Musical Standard* of December 1888 are standing examples of the way not to criticize. In the latter case the reviewer fell foul of the libretto, with what success the readers of his article will still remember. It is a little imprudent to select passages as unworthy of the book of Judith unless one has the Apocrypha at hand, so as to make sure that they are not in it."

This was no doubt the passage which led Fuller-Maitland to say in his biography of Hadow in *Grove* that the essay "broke through the prejudices created by a narrow ring of professed music critics and opened the door to a wider treatment of the subject". The references in it to gibes at Brahms's *Requiem* must be to George Bernard Shaw, who was writing his weekly criticism in *The World* from 1890 to 1894. He undoubtedly had a blind spot about Brahms, but this freebooter of criticism, who had no drop of reverence in his make-up, was pretty shrewd in his judgments, which certainly did not coincide with those of Hadow about Parry. He attacked Parry, Stanford and Mackenzie as a mutual admiration society, doing so all the more lustily, no doubt, because the first two at least were regarded with something near to reverence by the more intellectual musicians of Hadow's circle. ("However, who am I that I should be believed, to the disparagement of eminent musicians? If you doubt that *Eden* is a masterpiece, ask Dr. Parry and Dr. Mackenzie, and they will applaud it to the skies. Surely Dr. Mackenzie's opinion is conclusive; for is he not the composer of *Veni Creator*, guaranteed as excellent music by Professor Stanford and Dr. Parry? You want to know who Dr. Parry is? Why, the composer of *Blest Pair of Sirens*, as to the merits of which you have only to consult Dr. Mackenzie and Professor Stanford. Nevertheless, I remain unshaken in my opinion that these gentlemen are wasting their talent and industry. The sham classics which they are producing are worth no more than the forgotten pictures of Hilton and the epics of Hoole.")* He was anti-academic because he accepted unquestioningly the old antithesis between knowing and feeling, which asserted that knowing kills the immediacy of feeling and feeling overides knowledge. He was therefore a thorn in the flesh of the Parry–Stanford–Mackenzie group. He candidly explained why: "It must be remembered that I am violently prejudiced against the professional school of which Dr. Parry is a distinguished member. I always said, and say still, that his much admired oratorio *Judith* has absolutely no merit whatever. I allowed a certain vigour and geniality in his *L'Allegro ed Il Pensieroso* and a certain youthful inspiration in his *Prometheus*. But even these admissions I regarded as concessions to the academic faction which he leans to; and I was so afraid of being further disarmed that I lived in fear of meeting him and making his acquaintance; for I had noticed that the critics to whom this happens become hopelessly corrupt and say anything to please him without the least regard to public duty." His last observation is testimony to the force of Parry's personality, which like charm is a quality very hard for anyone who never encountered it to measure. Time has shown Shaw to be wrong about Brahms but painfully right about the pioneers of our renaissance. It is not the business of a weekly review of current music to show historical foresight, and if you had taxed Shaw with failure to appreciate what Parry and Stanford were trying to accomplish for English music, he could have answered that he was not concerned with such issues but only with the work in hand. This is, by the way, a permanent problem of journalistic criticism: do you quench the smoking flax, or do you modify the expression of your judgment of a work, artist or movement, because it is a means to some further end which you judge firmly to be desirable?† Or he could have said that however excellent were the

---

* *Music in London 1890-94* (Constable, 1932), Vol. I, p. 260.

† I cite two cases from my own experience, one each way. I adversely criticized Casals's interpretation of Elgar's cello concerto and was fiercely upbraided by the B.B.C. for jeopardizing their work in trying to project English music on to an international plane. On the other hand when after 1946

aims of Parry and Stanford to revitalize English music, they would never do it with their oratorios and other academic compositions. This would have been strong ground, but all the same it would have been proved wrong in the final event. For what in fact happened was that these academic works, though ultimately proved to be not much better than Shaw said at the time, have provided the submerged foundations on which our new edifice has been built. They were in fact historically important.

On one point Hadow and Shaw are at one—both wrote magnificent prose: Hadow supple and allusive, Shaw direct and racy. The tedious flatness of Victorian journalism as practised by Chorley and Davison (to some extent), and worse by Joseph Bennett, was banished after 1900. During the present century responsible English criticism has been written in a readable, vigorous, clear and healthy prose. Fuller-Maitland made no pretensions to stylistic elegance, but the precision of his first-hand musical knowledge gave clarity to his plain English. Colles, who succeeded him on *The Times* (1911-1943), wrote a more spacious and sinewy prose—he had come under Hadow's influence at Worcester College, Oxford, where he was organ scholar—in which under its reserved surface there was room for felicities and, when required, pungencies. Tovey following Hadow was allusive but more ebullient and undisciplined (rather as Beethoven to Mozart). Edward Dent, like Hadow, wielded a rapier, but its point had been sharpened on Cambridge wit instead of Oxford irony. Ernest Newman was vigorous and anti-academic in the Shavian way, amusing in a forensic fashion, and indeed achieved, as no other critic of music has ever done except Hanslick and Berlioz, an international reputation as writer as well as scholar, which was confirmed by his masterly biography of Wagner. Arthur Fox-Strangways, who wrote what was for many years the only authoritative book on Indian music and in 1920 founded the periodical *Music and Letters*, a quarterly of the highest literary standards, had as a journalist a pithy, epigrammatic style. Richard Capell wrote a study of Schubert's songs that has become a classic of criticism. While these men tended on the whole to look

Covent Garden was trying to secure international singers to learn their roles and sing them in English I applauded their efforts and did not grumble if one of them had a difficulty over our English "th".

at the art from a German point of view Francis Toye, who wrote monographs on Verdi and Rossini, robustly proclaimed his Italian allegiance. Eric Blom, who like Fuller-Maitland and Colles edited one of the successive editions of *Grove*, was also like them in being the master of plain statement and implied judgment.

Of a later generation of literary stylists with music for their subject there have been connoisseur critics like W. J. Turner, who was a poet, and Dyneley Hussey, versed in all the arts. Martin Cooper in some ways resembles Edward Dent, though his affiliations are not with Cambridge but Oxford, in being a fine linguist who combines wit with scholarship in his opinions; a Francophile, he has books on Gluck, *opéra comique* and French music of the last century to his credit. Desmond Shawe-Taylor and Philip Hope-Wallace, who have mostly concentrated on journalism and devotion to opera, are modern Chorleys, who exercise their discrimination with mingled enthusiasm and irony. All of these critics of the present century fortified their criticism with sound learning, each combining a special subject with a wide general knowledge; both of which are necessary in criticism, wherein it differs from musicology—a little about a lot instead of a lot about a little. The art of criticism as practised by these men comprises regular journalism (daily, weekly, monthly), lengthier contributions to learned periodicals, monographs and books, broadcasts on general musical topics and programme annotations. Programme notes go back to Grove, and even earlier,* and in Tovey one of the most unpromising forms of technical writing became a branch of literature.

A catalogue could be filled with the titles of books written by these men and some others to whom journalism was only an occasional occupation, which have done much to bring music in on equal terms with literature to cultivated, and in particular to university, circles.† It was the conspicuous absence of music from the interests of cultivated people that made Victorian

---

* To Thomson, Reid Professor in Edinburgh, in 1838 and to John Ella in London in 1845.

† A representative selection might include Professor (of history not music) Sanford Terry's several books on Bach, Percy Scholes's *The Great Dr. Burney*, Gerald Abraham's Russian biographies and Winton Dean's study of Handel's oratorios.

England so barren—as a confirmation of this strange lacuna from the opposite angle it is to be noted that it was the presence of Germans in the textile trades of the North of England which secured the foundation of the Hallé Orchestra.

In one respect criticism suffered a set-back after the Second World War, during which papers had been greatly reduced in size. Even when more space became available music received less than it had enjoyed before the war, except in *The Times*. The Sunday papers which had carried a column of notices and an article were now reduced to a single topical piece which was neither the one nor the other, and *The Daily Telegraph* which had for many years carried a music page in its Saturday issues contented itself with two short features. The new demands for criticism of radio and television may have been a factor in this regrettable curtailment.

Criticism of the music provided in profusion by the radio was an intractable problem for which no wholly satisfactory solution has been found in forty years. Sheer quantity is such that no newspaper critic could begin to "cover" it, and for the assessment of quality of performance the B.B.C. has to rely on its own staff and a panel of listeners which it recruits to work under the direction of its Audience Research Department. Another difficulty has been that the critic could not be sure what it was he was hearing: "balance and control" played tricks with the knobs so that, for instance, balance between a singer and his orchestral accompaniment was transferred from the performers to the engineers, and the quality of the tone was dependent on the recipient's receiving set; certain kinds of music, e.g. large-scale choral works, suffered inevitable distortion, while chamber music might on the other hand even gain something by its narrower focus on the listener's armchair and miniature score. The fact that such broadcast music was lacking in depth, monaural instead of binaural, was only slowly realized as a difference for which allowance must be made.

But from the beginning the B.B.C. wished its music to be criticized and had consistently welcomed outside press criticism; they even appointed a radio critic, Percy Scholes, who between 1925 and 1928 delivered spoken judgments over the air. When *The Listener* was founded in 1929 place was found in it for two kinds of criticism, a retrospective comment on recent broadcasts by an outside critic, to whom considerable latitude of judgment was

M

given, and an article of an expository nature usually on the music of some performance in prospect commissioned from outside *ad hoc*. This proved to be a valuable arrangement, and the commentator on current events learned how to allow the discounts to be made for the disabilities of transmission recounted above, since he would normally use the same machine, but could from time to time check his impressions by attendance in the studio. But for the outside journalist the problem admitted only of partial and piecemeal solution. He could select a few items from the week's *Radio Times*, as his colleagues did who were responsible for a column of comment on drama, talks, features, and limit his criticism, subject always to the drawbacks of monaural and knob-controlled listening, to that, or he could limit his evaluations of programme policy and the activities of the Symphony Orchestra to the B.B.C.'s public concerts or special occasions.* No outside criticism of individual artists was possible for sheer lack of space, time, and energy, and artists therefore could get no support from independent criticism if for any reason they fell foul of the monopoly. It is a sad fact that adequate criticism of the music put out over the air is impossible, since the vast audience of radio and television needs instruction as much as Dr. Burney's "ignorant lovers of music", and to learn to discriminate as much as Dr. Crotch's readers a century earlier.

If Parry was chiefly responsible for battering down resistance to music at Oxford and Stanford for making it a power at Cambridge, it is Hadow who is the hero of the movement for building a worthier music upon a more liberal criticism. He was himself a practising musician but was professionally a classics don. Having taken first classes in *Literae Humaniores* he went on to become a Bachelor of Music after training with C. H. Lloyd. His first excursion into the literary side of music was to lecture for Stainer, then Professor. These lectures subsequently became the manual on sonata form in Novello's series of textbooks. But it was in his *Studies in Modern Music* (1892 and 1894) that he showed how critical biography should be written. These two volumes, each

---

* The latter was my own policy in *The Times*. For special events I used to go to the studio, though this had the inverse drawback of the balance distortion in that what I heard in the studio was balanced not for the studio audience but for the microphone.

with a prefatory essay, one on Criticism and one on Form, made the older-fashioned type of biography look jejune and out of date. Hadow also edited the *Oxford History* and himself wrote the volume on the Viennese period. The latter part of his life he devoted to education, a fact which musicians are bound to regret. His influence was far-reaching: he was behind Parry, he was behind the developments at Oxford which Hugh Allen inherited and carried forward; Percy Buck and H. C. Colles, both of his college (Worcester), stood for the broad humane attitude to music and to musical education which he was the first to preach. While he thus developed an Oxford school of criticism, Dent was beginning his career of historical research at Cambridge, which is now bearing rich fruit. The logical outcome of all this ferment at the two older universities was the establishment of an arts degree in music at both and the institution of full professorial chairs at the younger universities. No longer has musicology to depend for its living on such happy accidents as Dr. Fellowes's picking up at a tennis tournament the idea of securing adequate editions of the English classics. Fears that its recognition by the universities would be to the detriment of counterpoint were very soon seen to be illusory. So far from being mutually exclusive studies, they are complementary, and the evidence of three quarters of a century is that a healthy criticism, a humane approach to the art, a well-disciplined musicology, are the concomitants of a vigorous musical life and a flourishing school of composition.

APPENDIX: *THE MUSICAL TIMES* ON
PROMETHEUS UNBOUND

The following is *The Musical Times* notice of the Gloucester Festival, October 1880 (this was C. H. Lloyd's second festival at which he put on the *Mass in D*, Henry Holmes's cantata *Christmas Day*, Leonardo Leo's *Dixit Dominus* and Palestrina's *Stabat Mater*):

"In the evening the first of the secular concerts was given in the Shire Hall, when an attractive miscellaneous programme was provided. Commencing with Beethoven's overture to *Fidelio* in E, the first part included songs by Miss Hilda Watson, Miss de Fontlongue, Miss Wakefield and Mr. F. King, all of which were fairly rendered and applauded with a warmth which is a distinguishing feature of the Shire Hall performances at a Festival. The most impressive item in the concert, however, was the composition of Mr. C. Hubert H. Parry written specially for the occasion, which, considering that it assumed the form of a cantata, appeared somewhat strangely in the programme as 'Scenes from Shelley's *Prometheus Unbound*'. It is so much the custom to praise the 'ambition' of even so young an artist as Mr. Parry that we think it is time to protest against this delusive criticism and to remind such composers that all the founders of an 'advanced' school have themselves been scholars. Trace the careers of the greatest men in creative musical art—not excepting the so-called Prophet of the Future, Richard Wagner—and it will be found that they have for years been accumulating knowledge, gaining experience and working towards a definite ideal, the perfect embodiment of which is often the culminating point of their artistic life. If then these are the musical teachers of the world, where can be the "ambition" of a composer who, merely accepting the doctrines of one of these original thinkers, sets himself to work with models already formed and boldly proclaims himself a 'disciple' of the artist who has formed them? That distinct individuality which is shadowed forth in the works of a real creator in any art is always more deeply shown in maturity;

but an inexperienced imitator can but develop into an experienced one. Mr. Parry's composition had not advanced very far before we discovered that he was an ardent admirer of the 'music of the future' and resolved to show us how he read Shelley's fine poetry by the light of his musical theory. Knowing this, we were of course not astonished to find that in the declamatory passages which form a very considerable portion of his work, the words are set with such a total disregard of the effect of the music upon the hearers as almost to make us believe that the composer had ignored the necessity of such consideration altogether. True it is that there is much power evinced in the orchestral colouring, and that in many parts we have detached phrases of real beauty; but these are very few and far between, and the dullness which gradually spread itself over the large audience was made even more apparent by these transient gleams of light. As a rule the orchestra is oppressively heavy; and in the early part of the work the choir is kept at such constant strain that the hearer almost sighs for relief. We cannot but believe that had the composer been less fettered by the school to which he has wedded himself his real poetical feeling would have been more constantly evinced, especially in the solos, some of which contain stretches of pure melody which seem to have strayed in by accident and been incautiously allowed to remain. The Song of the Earth 'I felt thy torture, son' and the quartet 'Life of life thy lips enkindle' may be cited in illustration of this fact; and we must also say that there is much dramatic feeling shown in the vigorous chorus of Furies. The solo of Prometheus chained to the rock is mere declamation, unredeemed in any part by the melodious treatment which lifts the monologues of Wagner into interest; and the address of Jupiter is sadly deficient in that contrast demanded for the due expression of the poetry. Undoubtedly the Finale contains the best writing in the work, the text being treated with much skill and dramatic effect, and some excellent contrapuntal points being noticeable throughout. For so elaborate a composition it is almost needless to say that more rehearsals than could be given to it were absolutely necessary, but all the members of the choir and orchestra worked with an evident desire to do justice to the composer, and the result was on the whole a highly creditable performance. No praise can be too great for the excellent manner in which Mr. E.

Lloyd sang the difficult music assigned to Jupiter. Miss Anna Williams and Mme. Patey were also thoroughly efficient; and Mr. Francis gave the music of Prometheus correctly, but neither his voice nor his method of delivery tended in the least to mitigate the harshness of many of the phrases which fell to his share. The marks of approbation were not very demonstrative during the performance of the work; but at its conclusion Mr. Parry who conducted, was called forward and loudly applauded.

"The second part of the concert included Mozart's symphony in E flat which was finely played; Spohr's Recit and Air 'E mi lasci cosi' and 'Tu m' abbandonui' so exquisitely rendered by Mme. Albani as to create a perfect enthusiasm; and solos by Misses Damian and de Fontlongue, Messrs. Maas and F. King, Mme. Albani also giving the Irish ballad 'The meeting of the waters', and the concert concluded with Gounod's Jupiter Festival March from *Polyeuecte* for orchestra and chorus."

Select Supplementary Bibliography

(This list contains titles of books not quoted or mentioned in the text nor referred to in the footnotes. They are grouped under the chapters to which they are particularly relevant, but some of them may also have some relevance in other contexts. The place of publication is London except where otherwise stated.)

CHAPTER I

J. A. Fuller-Maitland: *English Music in the Nineteenth Century*. Grant Richards, 1902.

H. C. Colles: *The Royal College of Music: A Jubilee Record, 1883-1933*. Macmillan, 1933.

J. F. Barnett: *Musical Reminiscences and Impressions*. Hodder & Stoughton, 1906.

CHAPTER II

J. W. Davison: *Music during the Victorian Era: From Mendelssohn to Wagner*. William Reeves, 1912.

C. V. Stanford: *Studies and Memories*. Constable, 1908.

— *Interludes, Records and Reflections*. John Murray, 1922.

Myles Birket Foster: *History of the Philharmonic Society of London: 1813-1912*. John Lane, 1912.

CHAPTER III

W. H. Hadow: *Studies in Modern Music*. Two series, Seeley, 1893-1895.

— *Collected Essays*. O.U.P., 1928.

Herbert Sullivan and Newman Flower: *Sir Arthur Sullivan: His Life, Letters and Diaries*. Cassell, 1927.

Gervase Hughes: *The Music of Arthur Sullivan*. Macmillan, 1960.

Christopher St. John: *Ethel Smyth: A Biography*. Longmans, 1959.

CHAPTER IV

Journal of the Folk Song Society (especially Vol. I).

Journal of the English Folk Dance and Song Society (especially Vol. V).

Cecil J. Sharp: *English Folk-Song: Some Conclusions.* Novello, 1907; 4th ed., Mercury Books, 1965.

A. H. Fox-Strangways and Maud Karpeles: *Cecil Sharp.* O.U.P., 1933; 2nd ed., 1955.

William Purcell: *Onward Christian Soldier: a Life of Sabine Baring-Gould.* Longman, 1957.

Erik Routley: *The English Carol.* Herbert Jenkins, 1958.

CHAPTER V

Edmund H. Fellowes: *Memoirs of an Amateur Musician.* Methuen, 1946.

— *The English Madrigal Composers.* Oxford, Clarendon Press, 1921.

Joseph Kerman: *The Elizabethan Madrigal.* Philadelphia, American Musicological Society, 1962.

Hilda Andrews: *Westminster Retrospect: A Memoir of Sir Richard Terry.* O.U.P., 1948.

Mabel Dolmetsch: *Personal Recollections of Arnold Dolmetsch.* Routledge, 1958.

CHAPTER VI

J. R. Sterndale Bennett: *The Life of William Sterndale Bennett.* Cambridge, C.U.P., 1907.

Cyril Bailey: *Hugh Percy Allen.* O.U.P., 1948.

John F. Russell and J. H. Elliot: *The Brass Band Movement.* Dent, 1936.

Leith Hill Musical Festival, 1905-55. Epsom, Pullinger, 1955.

CHAPTER VII

J. A. Fuller-Maitland: *The Music of Parry and Stanford.* Cambridge, Heffer, 1934.

Donald Francis Tovey: *Essays in Musical Analysis,* Vol. V. O.U.P., 1937.

CHAPTER VIII

Charles Villiers Stanford: *Musical Composition*. Macmillan, 1911.
Donald Francis Tovey: *Essays in Musical Analysis*, Vol. III. O.U.P., 1936.

CHAPTER IX

Mrs. Richard Powell: *Edward Elgar: Memories of a Variation*. O.U.P., 1947.
Percy M. Young: *Letters of Edward Elgar and Other Writings*. Selected, edited and annotated by Percy M. Young. Geoffrey Bles, 1956.

CHAPTER X

Derek Hudson: *Norman O'Neill: A Life of Music*. Quality Press, 1945.
J. Sutcliffe Smith: *The Story of Music in Birmingham*. Cornish Bros., 1945.
Frank Howes: *Percy Grainger* in *Recorded Sound*, No. 3, 1961.

CHAPTER XI

Clare Delius: *Frederick Delius: Memories of My Brother*. Nicholson & Watson, 1935.
Arthur Hutchings: *Delius: a Critical Biography*. Macmillan, 1948.
Robert H. Hull: *A Handbook on Arnold Bax's Symphonies*. Murdoch, 1932.

CHAPTER XII

R.C.M. Magazine, Vol. LV, No. 1 (Vaughan Williams Memorial Number), 1959.

CHAPTER XIII

Cecil Gray: *Peter Warlock*. Cape, 1934.
Mary Grierson: *Donald Francis Tovey*. O.U.P., 1952.

CHAPTER XIV

Ian Kemp: *Michael Tippett: A Symposium on his Sixtieth Birthday*. Faber, 1965.
Frank Howes: *The Music of William Walton*. O.U.P., 1965.

CHAPTER XV

Hope Bagenal in *Proceedings of the Royal Musical Association,* Session LXXVIII, 1951-1952.

CHAPTER XVII

Michael Hurd: *Immortal Hour: The Life and Period of Rutland Boughton.* Routledge, 1962.

S. L. Grigoriev: *The Diaghilev Ballet, 1909-29.* Constable, 1953.

Mary Clarke: *The Sadler's Wells Ballet.* Black, 1955.

CHAPTER XVIII

Lionel Tertis: *Cinderella No More.* Peter Nevill, 1953.

CHAPTER XX

Edgar Hunt: *The Recorder and its Music.* Herbert Jenkins, 1962.

CHAPTER XXI

Percy Scholes: *The Mirror of Music, 1844-1944: a Century of Musical Life in Britain as reflected in the pages of the Musical Times.* 2 vols. Novello and O.U.P., 1947.

Asa Briggs: *The History of Broadcasting in the United Kingdom.* Vol. I: *The Birth of Broadcasting.* Vol. II: *The Golden Age of Wireless* O.U.P., 1961-65.

Simon Nowell-Smith, ed., *Edwardian England,* O.U.P., 1964, contains an essay which I contributed on the music of the period.

Index

25